Shakespearean Illuminations

Marvin Rosenberg.

Shakespearean Illuminations

Essays in Honor of Marvin Rosenberg

Edited by
Jay L. Halio and Hugh Richmond

DELAWARE

Newark: University of Delaware Press
London: Associated University Presses

Associated University Presses
440 Forsgate Drive
Cranbury, NJ 08512

Associated University Presses
16 Barter Street
London WC1A 2AH, England

Associated University Presses
P.O. Box 338, Port Credit
Mississauga, Ontario
Canada L5G 4L8

The paper used in this publication meets the requirements of the American National Standard for Permanence of Paper for Printed Library Materials Z39.48-1984.

Library of Congress Cataloging-in-Publication Data

Shakespearean illuminations : essays in honor of Marvin Rosenberg / edited by Jay L. Halio and Hugh Richmond.
p. cm.
Includes bibliographical references and index.
ISBN 0-87413-657-1 (alk. paper)
1. Shakespeare, William, 1564–1616—Criticism and interpretation.

I. Halio, Jay L. II. Richmond, Hugh M. III. Rosenberg, Marvin.
PR2976.S33895 1998
822.3′3—dc21 98-13769
CIP

PRINTED IN THE UNITED STATES OF AMERICA

Contents

Preface

ALTHOUGH his interests are much more extensive, Marvin Rosenberg is best known and highly regarded the world over for his contributions to the study of Shakespeare's plays. Far more than a theater historian, he has brought to his work an intimate knowledge of the working theater and, as a literary scholar, a perceptive understanding of Shakespeare's texts. This combination has distinguished him from many others in Shakespeare studies; indeed, as a pioneer in the analysis of Shakespeare's plays *as plays* he has led the way for many of the rest of us who find his work eminently useful in our teaching and in our own research.

This collection of essays, written in his honor, is by way of tribute not only to Rosenberg's impressive scholarly achievements, but to his warm and endearing nature as teacher, colleague, and friend. Many of the essays focus on illuminations gained through performance, which is Rosenberg's special interest, while others treat aspects of language and text that he also recognized and dealt with in his work. Some essays, like those by Lois Potter and Dunbar H. Ogden, take a broad approach and treat a number of issues and plays. Others, like those by Sidney Homann, Philip C. McGuire, Ralph Berry, Bernice W. Kliman, and G. B. Shand, concentrate on particular plays, although the insights they provide have broader implications relevant to the study of other works.

Many of the essays overlap in approach and subject. For example, June Schlueter and James P. Lusardi discuss the character interactions of Hamlet and Laertes; they are also concerned with staging the scenes in which these characters appear together. The study of language is central to all of the essays, of course, though it is of paramount interest (in different ways) in the essays by Tom Clayton, John F. Andrews, and Michael Goldman. Political aspects of the plays appear preeminent in Günter Walch's essay, but Zdenek Stribrny also has some pertinent comments on how Eastern Europeans regard *Hamlet* and *King Lear*—not quite the same way as Westerners do, and for good reason.

While many of the essays here treat the practical aspects of interpretation and production, some like those by Ellen J. O'Brien,

Barbara Hodgdon, and Stephen Booth are more concerned with theoretical aspects and their applications. Some are historically oriented, like those by Maurice Charney, Dunbar H. Ogden, and Cary M. Mazer; others, like John Russell Brown's, direct our attention to current trends in the theater. All, we believe, have something valuable to contribute, especially to understanding Shakespeare—Shakespeare in the theater—a dimension of Shakespeare studies that has by now demonstrated its significance and importance to all those who wish to experience his plays as fully as possible.

The collection begins with Shakespearean illuminations derived from, or discernible in, performances of the major tragedies—Bradley's "Big Four" and Rosenberg's "Masks." Essays on language, politics, and historical influences follow. The volume concludes with a miscellany on actors and acting, directing and staging, and finally Ogden's study of women in the liturgical drama of the Middle Ages: in the end is our beginning.

Shakespearean Illuminations

I
The Major Tragedies

Mapping the Role: Criticism and the Construction of Shakespearean Character

ELLEN J. O'BRIEN

> Poststructuralist theory threatens to make character an altogether inappropriate category of analysis.
>
> —Alan Sinfield, "When Is a Character Not a Character?"

THE death of character criticism has been regularly reported since at least the 1930s. In his important essay, "When Is a Character Not a Character? Desdemona, Olivia, Lady Macbeth, and Subjectivity," Alan Sinfield offers a brief history of those epitaphs, with particular attention to the implications of current work on modern subjectivity (56–57). Yet he also notes that character criticism, if not altogether well (at least in theoretical terms), is very much alive—has, indeed, "remained the dominant mode."[1]

While noting that "some scholar-critics . . . rely on [character criticism]," Sinfield suggests that it survives because "it has the advantage of opening the plays, relatively, to the ways nonprofessional audiences and readers think and live" (57).[2] There is certainly truth in this. But I believe there is also a more fundamental reason—and one that is of critical importance to the "professional" reader: "character," in some form, is one of the basic elements of theatrical performance and has been acknowledged as such since Aristotle.[3] It need not, of course, be "character" in the sense of a modern subject, but when actors stand before us and perform a text, we almost inevitably perceive something for which we have no better word than "character." As G. B. Shand observed in response to an early draft of this essay:

> I suppose we perceive in most cases, a signifier that looks like a person (maybe that's the definition of character?), a sign that looks like a subject. . . . So "character," with its dual connotations of "person(a)"

> and "sign" is the perfect word for what we experience in performance and it actually contains the critical problem within its own connotations.

When we look at the playtext, character as a structural principle is as fundamental as it is in performance: if we remove the words and actions of the characters from the text, what remains?

Thus, simply to deny the legitimacy of "character" as an "appropriate category of analysis" is to make a fundamental aspect of both text and performance inaccessible to criticism. On the other hand, simply to retain Bradleyan notions of character as a category of analysis is to approach much of the text with tools inappropriate to its construction. As Catherine Belsey has demonstrated,

> . . . in the period between the precarious unity offered by the moralities and the stable, transcendent unity of the Restoration stage . . . the stage brought into conjunction and indeed into collision the emblematic mode and an emergent illusionism. (26)

As a result, the drama of 1576–1642 offers "intimations of the construction of a place which notions of personal identity were later to come to fill" (40). Seizing on these intimations, character criticism has traditionally constructed modern subjects: psychological unities. Yet in these dramatic texts, Sinfield asserts, "the presentation of the dramatis personae must be traced to a textual organization in which character is a strategy, and very likely one that will be abandoned when it interferes with other desiderata" (78). If we limit our field of vision to those elements of the Shakespearean text that come into focus when we look at character in this way, we are blinded to the other strategies of the text. As Sinfield points out, "when the individual and the universal come into focus, the social, the historical and the political become blurred or fade from view" (78).

Yet the problem with traditional character criticism lies not only in its unexamined acceptance of modern subjectivity as a definition of "character," but in a corresponding naïveté about the nature of theatrical character. The work of Belsey, Sinfield, and others has demonstrated the inadequacy of essentialist-humanist conceptions of character to the Shakespearean playtext. But if we are to find a way of dealing with the important element of those texts that the term *character* represents, we need to bring the work on subjectivity into interaction with performance theory and practice. Using the example of Gertrude, it is the project of this essay to take a step in that direction: suggesting an approach to the playtext that allows us to address the material traditionally subsumed under "character" without limiting our awareness to what is visible within the blinders of either Bradleyan or nontheatrical conceptions of character.

In his effort to recuperate *character* for criticism, Sinfield argues persuasively for redefining the term as "continuous consciousness"—an essential step forward in reforming our understanding of the term. While the essay deserves reading in full, the gist of his argument is suggested by the following excerpt:

> None of the opponents of character criticism I have been invoking disputes altogether that dramatis personae in Shakespearean plays are written, at least some of the time, in ways that suggest that they have subjectivities. The objection is to jumping from that point to a Bradleyan or essentialist-humanist conception of character. My contention is that some Shakespearean dramatis personae are written so as to suggest, not just an intermittent, gestural and problematic subjectity, [*sic*] but a continuous or developing interiority or consciousness; and that we should seek a way of talking about this that does not slide back into character criticism or essentialist humanism. This way of talking would not suppose that performances attempted an unbroken illusionistic frame; or that this continuous interiority is self-constituted and independent of the discursive practices of the culture; or that it manifests an essential unity. The key features in this redefined conception of character are two: an impression of subjectivity, interiority, or consciousness, and a sense that these maintain a sufficient continuity or development through the scenes of the play. (62)

As Sinfield ably demonstrates in the rest of the essay, such a reconception of the term *character* enables us to move beyond character criticism that simply reproduces modern subjects and excludes political concerns.

It does not, however, distinguish "character" in playtexts from "character" in novels or in other nonperformance texts. Without that distinction, it is all too easy to read in a way that distorts the nature of both the playtext and the "character." Therefore, I am proposing that we take this process of redefinition one step further, by theorizing the nature of theatrical character. As Sinfield notes, the text "*suggest*[s]" an "*impression* of subjectivity, interiority, consciousness" (emphasis mine). Clearly, the impression is not in the text but in the mind of the reader. Yet a playtext differs from a poem, a novel, or a treatise, in that it implies an intervening interpretive process between the text and its ultimate "reader." In a playtext, the elements of the text that suggest subjectivity are there for the use of the actor in creating the performance—indeed, I would say, in constructing a character. When the text is received by an audience in the mode for which it was written, the audience experiences character (however defined) through the work of the actor. When we "read" character in Shakespeare's texts, we are doing the actor's work, more or less consciously.

And that work is not simply "realization" of a character already present in the text. There is no preexisting Platonic Gertrude in the sky (or in the text) which the actor merely attempts to reproduce. As Patrice Pavis has observed:

> *Mise-en-scene* is not the staging of a supposed textual "potential." It does not consist in finding stage signifieds which would amount to no more than a repetition, inevitably superfluous, . . . of the text itself. That would entail disregarding the signifying materiality of verbal and stage signs and positing theatrical signifieds capable of setting aside their signifying matter and eliminating any difference between the verbal and the non-verbal. (26)

An important element in the creation of mise-en-scène is the construction of signifiers who look like persons: the "characters" experienced by the audience. Here, the work of the actor becomes essential. In Terry Eagleton's words:

> An actor in the theatre does not "enact"; rather, he *acts*—functions, performs, behaves. He "produces" his role, not as a conjurer produces a playing card, but as a carpenter produces a chair. The relation between text and production is a relation of *labour:* the theatrical instruments (staging, acting skills and so on) transform the "raw materials" of the text into a specific product, which cannot be mechanically extrapolated from an inspection of the text itself. (65)[4]

William B. Worthen has also pointed out the centrality of the actor's labor:

> . . . the text . . . necessarily differs from *any* discourse that represents it—reading and criticism as well as acting. Text and performance are dialectically related through the labor of enactment. . . . (452)

If "character" is the product of the actor's work, then "character" cannot reside in the playtext. Thus we need another name for the "raw materials" of the text from which the actor produces the character. *Role* seems to me an apt term for this. Although my use of the term is slightly different from Eagleton's, the adjustment seems beneficial both in maintaining a parallel with common theater terminology and in making the essential distinction between "role" and "character." To return to Eagleton's chair metaphor, then: the actor is given a "role" in the text (as a carpenter is given wood) from which he "produces" a "character" (as a carpenter produces a chair).

Role versus Character

What then, constitutes, the role? At the simplest level it is the words of the playtext to be spoken by the actor and the actions implied by those words and by the other words of the playtext. The shape of the role may depend upon which dramatic text we are considering: the First Quarto Gertrude is clearly different from the Gertrude of the commonly conflated First Folio and Second Quarto, but, as Steven Urkowitz has demonstrated, there are also subtle differences between the First Folio and Second Quarto versions of the role (1986, 1988). Editorial emendations or interpolated stage directions may create still other versions of the role, as do cuts or alterations for performance. We can only discuss the role as defined by a particular text. Within a given text, the role is shaped by the nuances of every word, metrical feature, rhetorical structure, spatial arrangement, and so on. While such elements define the boundaries within which the possible performances of that Gertrude-role exist, they do not define a single character for the role.

Character emerges as the actor decides how to use the materials of the role, making the moment-by-moment choices that create a reading of that role and using her own voice and body to perform it.[5] Character is complete only in the moment of performance and potentially different (within the constraints of a particular production) in each performance. In criticism, character is what the reader produces, *standing in the place of the actor.* Finally then, character is to be read in the performance of the actor or the critic—not in the playtext. Any performance of character is, of necessity, a "reduction" of the multiple potentialities in the role, but only in the sense that a wooden chair—however exquisitely designed and crafted—is a reduction of the potentialities of the wood from which it is produced. The reductiveness of the performance is no more to be lamented than the reductiveness of the chair. What is essential is that we recognize it by distinguishing between character and role. To do so also allows us an advantage we do not have in examining the chair: we can return to the original wood and consider its other possibilities.[6]

To speak of "role," then, is to address those elements in the playtext from which the actor works to produce a "character." Role-criticism enters the interpretive process at a point prior to the construction of character, prior to issues of consciousness, interiority, and subjectivity. It can therefore provide the foundation for many different approaches to character: it serves a focus on the discontinuities in a role as easily as it serves the search for a through-line. While it can be used to construct A. C. Bradley's psychological unities, it can also be used to construct Sinfield's continuous consciousness. In addition, it allows us to address materials that may not cohere smoothly even into a continuous consciousness, as well as those that do. Perhaps most importantly, it should enable us to consider other forms of character that may yet emerge as postmodern theater evolves.

It seems useful then, to reserve the term *character* for discussion of the performance constructed by the actor—or if by the critic, in awareness that he is constructing something that is not inherent in the text. In discussing the text, I would propose that we replace traditional character criticism with role criticism.

Mapping the Role

In undertaking role-criticism, I find it useful to think of myself as a mapmaker, a sort of textual cartographer dedicated to charting, as fully and objectively as possible, the raw materials that make up a role. I say "as objectively as possible" advisedly, recognizing that

> the map . . . constitutes the terrain rather than simply describing it. . . . For map-making is surely one of those material cultural practices by which, quite as much as with plays, novels and poems, we produce (and impose) meaning. . . . Maps are never innocent. (Hawkes 1992)

While the words of the role remain constant (within any given text), what they signify to the actor or reader (and what actions they imply) may vary wildly from age to age. Both the acting practices and the critical practices of the day will help to determine how the role is perceived in a particular time. Admittedly, I can only chart what is visible to me as a particular twentieth-century subject. As Catherine Belsey notes, "the meanings in circulation at a given moment specify the limits of what can be said and understood" (5)—and certainly of the maps that can be drawn. There can be no ultimate objectivity or completeness in mapping—or in any other form of interpretation. Like all interpretative processes, mapping makes meanings for its own time. Still, the effort to strip away the accretions of traditional "character"—both theatrical and critical—and to approach the role itself with an awareness of its potential to produce multiple characters, does offer a more open-ended and more self-conscious approach to the production of meaning than traditional character criticism.

Mapping the verbal elements of the role is the more familiar part of the task, inviting us to examine such things as uses of figurative language, verse and prose, metrical features (placement of caesura, end-stopping, rhyme, feminine endings, etc.), different kinds of speech acts, and passive versus active language. The list could go on ad infinitum and its useful elements will be specific to each role. It is therefore essential to ask as many questions as possible to avoid missing the elements of the terrain that shape the role in subtle ways. Much of this is, of course, fodder for traditional character criticism; the question is what we do with it.

Mapping the visual elements of the role—physical actions, spatial relationships, and so forth—is less familiar and more complex. Its focus is more semiotic, more external, moving us further from the center of character criticism. Yet what we see of a "character" (in the mind's eye or on the stage) functions as an important set of signifiers—along with what we hear from and about her. The most obvious indication of spatial relations and actions comes from the stage directions of the Folio and Quarto texts.[7] But most actions called for by the text are implicit in the dialogue rather than made explicit in stage directions. (When Claudius says, "Let him go, Gertrude" [4.5.123][8] we have an implied stage direction indicating that Gertrude is doing something like holding onto Laertes or attempting to do so.) Less obvious are the implications of such things as entrances and exits: who enters/exits when? with whom? under what circumstances? Dialogue within scenes may also set up implicit spatial relationships between characters that function as potent signifiers. Yet this kind of signifier is often invisible to character criticism with its focus on interiority. Role-criticism brings it into focus by working at a point that precedes interiority and by thinking in broader semiotic terms.

In short, mapping the role is a form of close reading, but one that differs from traditional close reading in two ways. First, it assumes as fundamental the distinction between role and character just discussed. Second, to steal a phrase from Stephen Booth, it is "close reading that tries to avoid resulting in readings" (43). In other words, it is primarily concerned with the multiple potentialities of role, not with the narrower selection from those potentialities that constitutes character. Though it describes the materials from which the character would be constructed, and may even speculate on various forms that character might take, it tries to resist the temptation to say, "this is what this character must be."

In contrast, the traditional character critic acts as a route-planner rather than a mapmaker, defining a psychologically "consistent" "character" by choosing a single route through the territory defined by the role, and in so doing, rendering invisible all other potential routes.[9] In its pursuit of psychological consistency, such criticism is often forced to ignore, downplay, or rationalize discontinuities. A full awareness of the role requires the work of the cartographer instead: laying out all the features of the role in as much topographical detail as possible—whether or not those features seem to lead us along a single route.

Mapping is not complete, however, with a simple charting of the textual obligations. While resisting final readings, textual cartography is very much involved in discerning and mapping patterns. Just as the cartographer might use color to define a mountain range rather than simply indicating each individual peak, the role of the critic contributes to the interpretative process by highlighting patterns that run though the role. Thus a map may bring into focus a complex of patterns in such spatial and verbal signifiers as entrance-exit configurations, stage images, figurative language, and speech acts. Some of these patterns will be consistent throughout the play—perhaps suggesting a core of continuous consciousness. Others may shift or simply disappear—perhaps suggesting either development of that consciousness or its breakdown (at the moment when, in Sinfield's terms, the character ceases to be a character). Both the patterns and the moments where they break or shift can help us to define the potential routes through the play, the various characters that can be constructed from the materials of the role.

The Example of Gertrude

The potential of role-criticism for stripping away centuries of critical and theatrical traditions that have naturalized particular psychological readings of many roles, and thus limited their signifying potential, enables mapping to open the way for new readings. The role of Gertrude in *Hamlet* provides a case in point.

Patterns and Shifts

As I have just suggested, the first step in mapping the lay of the land is to establish which Gertrude-role we are mapping. While the difference between the Second Quarto and the First Folio are subtle, the First Quarto offers a markedly different role.[10] Thus, for the purposes of this essay, I have mapped the Second Quarto and will note the major First Folio variants. Since limits of space preclude a full detailing of even one map here, I will first briefly sketch several patterns in the role that help to define the boundaries within which Second Quarto/First Folio Gertrude-characters can be constructed, and then explore the implications of the shift points and break points in those patterns—cruxes in the production of character and possible indicators of ideological concerns.

Mapping the First Folio and Second Quarto produces a series of patterns (in entrance-exit configurations, the use of names, epithets, direct address, and figurative language) all of which shift at or around the closet scene.[11] The fact that all of these patterns shift at nearly the same point strongly suggests that something changes at the closet scene, whether we perceive this as a psychological change in a unified subject, a development in a continuous consciousness, or a shift in the signifiers presented to the audience. In any terms, it is an important crux in the role, though one that is frequently ignored in both criticism and performance. Gertrude has often been seen as a "sheep in the sun" (Bradley, 135) or a woman obsessed with Claudius—in either case unchanged by Hamlet's closet scene revelations. Yet the patterning of the role suggests that something *does* happen there.

Examining the specifics of several of these patterns allows us to begin narrowing the viable interpretations of the role. Prior to the closet scene, Gertrude uses little figurative language, all associated with Hamlet, and all quite simple. Indeed, up to this point in the play, Gertrude has only one significantly figurative speech:

> Good Hamlet, cast thy nighted colour off,
> And let thine eye looke like a friend on Denmarke.
> Doe not forever with thy vailed lids
> Seeke for thy noble Father in the dust. . . .
>
> (1.2.68–71)

From the closet scene forward, there is a marked increase in both the amount and complexity of Gertrude's figurative language—and a new pattern to its apparent function. An early and striking example occurs after Hamlet's address to the Ghost prompts her "Alas, hee's mad" (3.4.105):

> Foorth at your eyes your spirits wildly peep;
> And as the sleeping souldiers in th'alarme,
> Your bedded haire, like life in excrements
> Start up and stand an end. . . .
>
> (3.4.119–22)

The personification here makes Hamlet's spirits, hair and, by extension, his madness the active agents in the scene, figuratively extending the earlier assertion of madness and building toward its reiteration in

> This is the very coynage of your braine;
> This bodilesse creation extacie is very cunning in. . . .
>
> (3.4.137–39)

Here the active agents are "extacie" and Hamlet's (presumably maddened) "braine." The responsibility for Hamlet's behavior is thus shifted to madness—to which Hamlet is specifically set in opposition:

> ô gentle sonne,
> Upon the heat and flame of thy distemper
> Sprinckle coole patience. . . .
>
> (3.4.122–24)

Such manipulations of personification recur throughout the rest of Gertrude's figurative language, and it is possible to argue that all of this language seems designed to shift responsibility in similar ways. Ophelia is thus the victim of "an envious sliver" and the "garments, heavy with theyr drinke / [which] Puld the poore wretch from her melodious lay / To muddy death" (4.7.173, 181–83). Implicitly, then, she is not a suicide, not responsible for her own death. But Hamlet is the usual beneficiary of Gertrude's responsibility-shifting figurative language. In the very next scene, personification of sea and wind sets up a speech that both obscures the fact of Polonius' death and perhaps seeks to mitigate its consequences. In response to Claudius' "What Gertrude? How does Hamlet?" she replies:

Mad as the sea and wind when both contend
Which is the mightier, in his lawlesse fit,
Behind the Arras hearing some thing stirre,
Whyps out his Rapier, cryes a Rat, a Rat
And in this brainish apprehension kills
The unseene good old man.

(4.1.7–12)

The extended figurative assertion of Hamlet's madness may function simultaneously as a denial of Hamlet's responsibility for what he has done—supported by "lawlesse fit" and "brainish apprehension"—and a delaying tactic that keeps Claudius from discovering the murder as long as possible. The grammatical structure can be interpreted in the same way. Neither "Whyps out his Rapier" nor "kills" is given a grammatical subject: Hamlet's actions are presented as though occurring without his agency.[12] In addition, the crucial verb, and hence Hamlet's guilt, is withheld until the last word of the fifth line of a six-line speech. After the closet scene, much of Gertrude's figurative language seems to function in similar ways as a buffer between Hamlet's actions and Claudius' response.

There is a suggestive intersection between this pattern of figurative language and that of the spatial relations implicit in the Gertrude-role—particularly those involving Hamlet and Claudius. As I have argued elsewhere, the visual patterning of the role establishes an initial association between Gertrude and Claudius, and then, after the closet scene, shifts to associating Gertrude with Hamlet and Claudius with Laertes (O'Brien 1993). Prior to the closet scene, Gertrude's entrances are all made with Claudius or his surrogates.[13] Similarly, her exits before the play-within-the-play are either made with Claudius or directed by him. But here, too, things change after the closet scene. What happens at the end of the scene itself is unclear in the Second Quarto stage directions: although only a singular "exit" is given, Gertrude is included in the immediately following entry (along with the King, Rosencrantz, and Guildenstern), creating a rare exception to the so-called law of reentry.[14] The Folio gives her no exit, making the succeeding dialogue with Claudius (and without Rosencrantz and Guildenstern) a continuation of the same scene. In succeeding scenes, the Second Quarto and Folio texts concur: Gertrude enters with Claudius only on large formal occasions whose public nature would seem to require a joint entrance of King and Queen. Her exits fall into two groups. In 4.1 and 4.7, the exit seems to require some urging from Claudius, who repeats "come" or "let's follow" twice within a few lines. This might well invite some hesitation or resistance on the part of the Gertrude-actor. In 4.5 and 4.7, the text offers only a mass exit ("exeunt"). But in both scenes, Claudius is focused on a volatile Laertes, not on Gertrude, and there are reasons to suspect an early or separate exit for Gertrude.[15] Even if Gertrude does exit "with" Claudius and Laertes, the verbal focus in both scenes is on the interaction of the two men. During the fifth act fencing match, Gertrude's offer to wipe Hamlet's face and the immediately following exchange between Laertes and the King combine to imply visual association of Gertrude with Hamlet while again linking Claudius with Laertes.

This association seems to be reinforced by patterns in the use of Hamlet's name. Not surprisingly, from 4.1 on, both Gertrude and Claudius use Hamlet's name with greater frequency than before, but the percentage of Gertrude's uses that are in direct address rises from 50 to 100 percent, while Claudius' use of direct address falls from two-thirds to less than half.[16] Obviously, both have Hamlet much on their minds now, but increasingly, Claudius tends to talk *about* him while Gertrude talks *to* him, a fact that strengthens the visual association of mother and son. All of this corroborates the existence of a fundamental shift in the role at the closet scene. And the specifics of this shift, like those of the other patterns we have examined, seem to invite construction of a Gertrude who responds to Hamlet's closet-scene harangue by distancing himself from her husband.

Breakpoints

At this point, it may be tempting to reach for closure and proclaim the death of the Claudius-obsessed Gertrude. Yet there are a few moments where the patterns break—and, as Sinfield has demonstrated, the breakpoints can be as revealing as the patterns. The most obvious of these occurs in 4.5, when Laertes bursts in, leaving the "rabble" to guard the door as he confronts Claudius with Polonius' death. Claudius' twice-repeated "Let him go Gertrude" strongly implies that she attempts to restrain Laertes in some way—an action that even feminist critics have taken as evidence of an obsession with Claudius that endures to the end of the play, thereby eliminating the possibility of a post-closet-scene rift. In both criticism and performance, this obsession is often treated as Gertrude's defining characteristic. A second anomalous moment—one we are less likely to notice without the map—occurs just before this action, in Gertrude's response to learning that the "rabble" are calling for Laertes to be king:

> How cheerefully on the false traile they cry.
> O this is counter you false Danish dogges.
>
> (4.5.110–11)[17]

These lines are surprising on several counts. If the "traile" these "dogges" seek is the trail leading to Polonius' murderer, then Gertrude would seem to be deriding the pack's failure to scent the true track—which would lead to Hamlet. Even more directly than her restraint of Laertes, this would be a striking discontinuity in the role, strongly at odds with her post-closet-scene association with Hamlet. Moreover, in the light of Gertrude's map, the hunt metaphor itself is unexpected, differing from the rest of her figurative language—both before and after—in several ways. This time, the burst of metaphor does not center on Hamlet—or even on Ophelia. It is her only negative epithet in the play. Indeed, for a speaker elsewhere given to effacing human responsibility, this speech is strikingly accusatory. And rather than the by-now-familiar habit of personification, we find something like its opposite: men reduced to beasts. Within the Gertrude-role, such language is peculiar to this moment.

What do we do with these anomalous elements? Unlike the changes that occur around the closet scene, these do not appear to set up new patterns that continue throughout the play. Instead, they stand as isolated elements, difficult to assimilate into essentialist character. Faced with such material, the traditional tactic of character criticism is to construct a rationale that negates the conflicting evidence and obscures the discontinuity. Indeed, at an earlier stage of my own obsession with Gertrude, I confess to having done precisely that. But if, instead of closing down options at this point, we use the map to open them up, we make accessible a much richer set of possibilities—including those that do not function primarily in terms of psychologized character. To do this, we need a detailed local map of the territory surrounding the breakpoint. The more we attend to the specific details of the role, the less likely we are to naturalize discontinuities that may mark ideological strains within the play.[18]

Let us look, then, at what immediately precedes Gertrude's action. Laertes' entrance is preceded by a messenger who describes the approaching danger:

> Save your selfe, my Lord.
> The Ocean, over-peering of his list
> Eates not the flats with more impitious hast
> Then young Laertes in a riotous head,
> Ore-beares your Officers: the rabble call him Lord,
> And as the world were now but to beginne,
> Antiquity forgot, custome not knowne,
> The ratifiers and props of every word,
> They cry choose we, Laertes shall be king,
> Caps, hands, and tongues applau'd it to the clouds,
> Laertes shall be king, Laertes king.
>
> (4.5.99–109)

Although the opening words make this a warning to the King, the focus of the speech is not on the threat to Claudius but on a vision of collapsed order, of social chaos. The image of an ocean swelling out of its bounds not only gives cosmic scope to the event, but implicitly naturalizes the social order. Thus Laertes' overbearing of the officers becomes not simply (or even primarily) a revolt against Claudius, or even against the political power structure but a violation of the (to the orthodox Elizabethan) God-given structure of the universe. As if to underscore the "unnaturalness" of the event, the focus then switches to the "rabble" (already introduced as Laertes' "riotous head") and their audacity in choosing their own monarch. In a speech of 10½ lines, half a line centers on Claudius, 3½ on Laertes (and his unruly followers), and 6½ on the activities of the "rabble." Such weighting functions to frame Laertes' action not as personal revenge (like Hamlet's), but as a rebellion that has "put the bottom rail on the top"—invoking profound hierarchical anxieties in a way that Hamlet's attempts to kill the King specifically do not. Perhaps, having made Claudius' guilt manifest in his failed prayer, the play is now teetering too close for comfort to the abyss of justified rebellion, and so must reassert the horror and unnaturalness of revolt in order to contain its own implicitly revolutionary impulse.

It is this speech that prompts Gertrude's attack on the "false Danish dogges." And anomalous though that attack may be within the patterns of the role, it is deeply connected to the messenger's language. Gertrude's beast image takes the messenger's reference to the "rabble" one step further, reinforcing the horror of rebellion with visions of power under subhuman control. Politically, the image fits Elizabethan orthodoxy better than it does the patterning of the Gertrude-role. Indeed, at this moment, the role may speak more as a mouthpiece for the famous Elizabethan fear of disorder than as a subject intent on her own personal affairs. Are these "false dogs" on a "false trail" not because they are after Claudius rather than Hamlet, but simply because they are running amok in daring to choose their own king? The driving force in this moment may well be ideology rather than subjectivity.

Only a few brief lines intervene between this politically charged language and Gertrude's restraint of Laertes. And in those lines, Laertes barely succeeds in keeping his followers from bursting into the royal presence with him: hierarchical inversion lurks just offstage. In the lines that follow Gertrude's restraint, Laertes' language seems to justify the greater concern for order invoked by Gertrude and the messenger, explicitly rejecting all the glue that holds the social structure together:

> To hell allegiance, vowes to the blackest devill,
> Conscience and grace, to the profoundest pit. . . .
> (4.5.132–33)

In this context, attributing either Gertrude's vehement metaphor or her restraint of Laertes to personal obsession seems decidedly beside the point. The map suggests that there is much more to be protected here than the object of a personal obsession. The highly charged language surrounding the moment underscores its political—not its private—implications. And with so many other patterns in the role suggesting that the closet scene instigates a rift between Gertrude and Claudius, to take this single gesture and speech as proof that Gertrude passes through the closet scene unchanged seems not only reductive but a serious distortion of the role.

Still, to assert the strength of the case for reading this sequence in political terms is not to choose a single route for Gertrude—even through this moment. The critical point is for the actor (or critic) to make a clear decision on the relation between this moment and the other elements of the role. It can be treated as a stepping aside from character—a moment when political forces rather than individual subjectivities are being embodied on the stage. Or it can be integrated into a Gertrude-character: the problematic elements can be contained by constructing Gertrude as (for instance) someone with a deep need for order who feels it crumbling around her or someone whose very identity is bound up with being Queen. What is given in the role is the physical action of restraining Laertes. It is the actor's (or critic's) work in developing a specific Gertrude-character that fills that action, endowing it with meaning as the character is embodied. To enumerate or evaluate the merits of the many possible readings of this moment is beyond the scope of this essay. Nor is it the project of role-criticism to argue for any single reading. The map does not determine the route, though its features may incline particular readers in particular directions, depending on the weight they give to different elements and their presumptions (political and personal) about the nature of human motivation.

Resisting Closure Cartographically

Mapping the role, with its fundamental distinction between character and role, enables a mode of criticism grounded in both critical and performance theory. In practice, it can broaden our sense of the semiotic possibilities of the role, by pulling into focus subtle details of speech and action that might otherwise escape our attention. In those details, we may discern patterns, which in turn provide the basis for our construction of some form of character. In the Gertrude-role, the shift point at the closet scene suggests that a Gertrude unchanged by that moment will be working against the structure of most of the role. While mapping dictates no single way to play that change, it does suggest that a satisfying construction of the Second Quarto Gertrude will take us through the shift in some way rather than ignoring it. A more detailed drawing of the map would indicate other patterns that also help to define the corridor within which the viable routes for a Gertrude built on the materials of the Second Quarto will run.

Against the coherence of such patterning, the anomalous moments of the role stand out more clearly. Both Gertrude's restraint of Laertes and her vehement hunt metaphor seem to stand aside from the patterns of the role—rather than marking a shift or development. After this scene, the patterns of the role can again be brought into persuasive coherence. Yet while it is important to include the anomalous moments in our mapping of the role, it does not follow that they should be regarded as the key to the construction of character: to replace obsession with ideology as Gertrude's driving force would still be to ignore the bulk of the role, substituting one closed reading for another.

Ultimately, mapping is perhaps most valuable as a means of discouraging closure on "character"—reminding us that theatrical character exists only in performance, whether in the mind or on the stage. Even Sinfield, in the midst of arguing for continuous consciousness, makes pronouncements that imply a single reading of any given point in the role: "On her first appearance, Desdemona is spectacularly bold, confident, and unconventional" (52); later, she is "abjectly fearful" (53). While these are perfectly viable readings, other, equally valid, constructions of this consciousness are also possible. Because we are responding to materials designed for character construction (of one sort or another) and because critical habits die hard, the temptation to see character rather than role on the page is powerful and ongoing. By entering the text with a focus on the complex of elements that make up the role rather than on the impression of subjectivity to be created from those elements, mapping serves to discourage closure. In so doing, it reminds us of the multiple potentialities of the role and of the actorly work involved in the construction of character. Keeping the map in view helps to keep our eyes—and our minds—open.

Notes

1. Porter also argues for the viability of character, though in very different terms.

2. Similarly, Burns attributes

> the current vogue for books by and about Shakespearian actors, normally centering on the Royal Shakespeare Company, to their ability to [fill] a gap for the average playgoer that academic criticism has deliberately vacated—the gap where "character" used to be. Bradleyans to a man or woman, the classical actor as celebrity sets the tone for all but the most stringently academic "discussion" of Shakespeare—which is fine as a focusing of attention on the stage, but limiting in its unanalytic repetition of received wisdom, its preservation of the traditional "Shakespeare" as a valued cultural object. (221–22)

3. See Burns, 18–28, on the translation issues involved in discussing Aristotle's treatment of "character."

4. This is the clearest articulation of the nature of theatrical character I have ever encountered. Ironically, Eagleton's discussion is not intended to illuminate the nature of theatrical production but is an extended analogy designed to illuminate the nature of nondramatic texts. Yet what seems to Eagleton so self-evident as to be useful as analogy is rarely understood by critics analyzing dramatic texts.

5. These choices of the actor are, of course, also affected by directorial and design choices.

6. Pavis makes a parallel, though not identical, distinction between (1) "the dramatic text: the verbal script which is read or heard in performance"; (2) "performance: all that is made visible or audible on stage, but not yet perceived or described as a system of meaning or as a pertinent relationship of signifying stage systems"; and (3) "*mise-en-scene:* the confrontation of all signifying systems, in particular the utterance of the dramatic text in performance. *Mise-en-scene* is not an empirical object, the haphazard assembling of materials, the ill-defined activity of the director and stage team prior to performance. It is an object of knowledge, a network of associations or relationships uniting the different stage

materials into signifying systems, created both by production (the actors, the director, the stage in general) and reception (the spectators)" (24–25). My project requires slightly different distinctions: "role" is a part of what Pavis refers to as the "dramatic text," but it is necessary for my purposes to separate the text on the page from the text heard in performance. "Character" is what the actor performs and thus part of what the audience experiences as mise-en-scène.

7. Admittedly, the status of even these is problematic. Yet while we cannot attribute them with any certainty to Shakespeare, they seem likely to be derived from performance practice of his time and are as close as we can come to an explicit Shakespearean stage direction. Considered as one piece of evidence among many rather than as definitive, they offer a reasonable starting point for visual cartography. Later texts often add stage directions, sometimes invented by editors with little sense of performance. These can be read as interesting evidence of the role created by that particular edition, or, when they recur throughout the editions of a specific period, as indicators of the preoccupations of the age. For specific examples, see O'Brien 1993.

8. References to *Hamlet* are taken from the Second Quarto as printed in Bertram and Kliman. As in that edition, act-scene-line numbers are those of the *Riverside Shakespeare.*

9. Important to remember here is that even the destination of the route to be chosen is not a clearly defined point beyond the narrow fact of Gertrude's death. In Shand's words, "Destinations are unknown territories sharing a common name" (letter to the author). As he demonstrates in "Realising Gertrude: The Suicide Option," one Gertrude-actor may be embarking on a course toward suicide, another toward accidental death.

10. See Shand, "Queen of the First Quarto," and Urkowitz.

11. These are more fully mapped in O'Brien 1986.

12. The First Folio reads, "He whips his Rapier out, and cries a Rat, a Rat," producing a hypermetrical line to no apparent purpose other than regularizing the grammatical structure. Compositorial emendation has been suspected here.

13. In the closet scene itself she enters with Polonius (strongly associated with the King by their collusion in arranging this encounter with Hamlet); in the next scene she enters with Horatio, strongly associated with Hamlet. For a more in-depth discussion of Gertrude's visual patterning, see O'Brien 1993. As I noted there,

> since the Folio and Quarto stage directions give only mass entrances, entering "with" someone does not necessarily mean more than entering at the same time. However simultaneous but separate entrances in Shakespeare can be implied by dialogue or made explicit by including a phrase like "at several doors" in the stage directions. In the absence of such evidence to the contrary, I assume a single entrance for everyone listed together. (28)

14. The law of reentry asserts that characters in Shakespeare do not normally exit at the end of one scene and immediately reenter at the beginning of the next. "As C. M. Haines has pointed out, most of the exceptions [to this law] occur in battle scenes. . . . The other exceptions are in large measure suspect" (Beckerman, 176).

15. See O'Brien 1993, 28–30.

16. To this we should add two direct addresses from Gertrude to "my son" from the closet scene forward and one earlier (2.2.36); Claudius does refer to Hamlet in acts 4 and 5 as "your [Gertrude's] son" (4.1.3, 4.5.80, and 5.1.291) and

"our son" (5.2.289) but never again addresses Hamlet as "son" or attaches "my" to "son" after 1.2.

17. The line is frequently cut in production, only making her restraint of Laertes more difficult to read.

18. On the relation between discontinuities and ideological strains, see Sinfield 73–74.

References

Beckerman, Bernard. 1962. *Shakespeare at the Globe: 1599–1609*. New York: Collier Books.

Belsey, Catherine. 1985. *The Subject of Tragedy: Identity and Difference in Renaissance Drama*. London: Routledge.

———. 1980. *Critical Practice*. London: Routledge.

Bertram, Paul, and Bernice W. Kliman, eds. 1991. *The Three-Text Hamlet: Parallel Texts of the First and Second Quartos and First Folio*. New York: AMS Press.

Booth, Stephen. 1994. "Close-reading Without Readings." In *Shakespeare Reread: The Texts in New Contexts,* edited by Russ McDonald. Ithaca: Cornell University Press.

Bradley, A. C. 1961. *Shakespearean Tragedy*. London: Macmillan.

Burns, Edward. 1990. *Character: Acting and Being on the Pre-Modern Stage*. New York: St. Martin's.

Eagleton, Terry. 1978. *Criticism and Ideology*. London: Verso.

Hawkes, Terence. 1992. *Meaning by Shakespeare*. London.

O'Brien, Ellen J. 1993. "Revision by Excision: Rewriting Gertrude." *Shakespeare Survey* 45:27–35.

———. 1986. "Unheard Is Not Unseen: Stage Images for Shakespeare's Silent Presences." Paper presented at the seminar, Stage Images in Shakespeare. Congress of the International Shakespeare Association, West Berlin, 1–6 April.

Pavis, Patrice. 1992. "From Page to Stage: A Difficult Birth." In *Theatre at the Crossroads,* trans. Loren Kruger. London: Routledge.

Porter, Joseph A. 1991. "Character and Ideology in Shakespeare." In *Shakespeare Left and Right,* edited by Ivo Kamps. New York: Routledge.

Riverside Shakespeare, The. 1972. Edited by G. Blakemore Evans.

Shand, G. B. 1991. "Queen of the First Quarto." Paper presented at the annual meeting of the Shakespeare Association of America, Vancouver.

———. 1994. "Realising Gertrude: The Suicide Option." *Elizabethan Theatre* 13:95–118.

Sinfield, Alan. 1992. "When Is a Character Not a Character? Desdemona, Olivia, Lady Macbeth, and Subjectivity." In *Faultlines: Cultural Materialism and the Politics of Dissident Reading*. Berkeley: University of California Press.

Urkowitz, Steven. 1988. "Five Women Eleven Ways: Changing Images of Shakespearean Characters in the Earliest Texts." In *Images of Shakespeare: Proceedings of the Third Congress of the International Shakespeare Association, 1986,* edited by Werner Habicht, D. J. Palmer, and Roger Pringle. Newark: University of Delaware Press.

———. 1986. "'Well-sayd olde Mole': Burying Three *Hamlets* in Modern Editions." In *Shakespeare Study Today,* edited by Georgiana Ziegler. New York: AMS Press.

Worthen, William B. 1989. "Deeper Meanings and Theatrical Technique: The Rhetoric of Performance Criticism." *Shakespeare Quarterly* 40 (winter): 441–55.

Gertred, Captive Queen of the First Quarto

G. B. SHAND

MOST playscripts reach print bearing traces of past or future production. In tracing the future, most scripts take measures (frequently unsuccessful!) to determine material and interpretive aspects of that production. This essay, an exercise in actorly reading, looks narrowly at Q1 *Hamlet* (1603) as a potential performance document.[1] It follows a single role, that of the Queen, with an eye to describing how, and how thoroughly, that role is written to be acted. In so doing, it speculates that the Q1 Queen-role is a prescriptive project to deny the Queen-actor multivalent or disruptive options, giving that actor plenty to play with, but in the end only one performable game to play.[2]

In an earlier study of the other Queen of Denmark (in Q2/F),[3] I went moment-by-moment through the usually acted conflations, sitting constantly inside the later Queen-role to determine whether the frequently performed suicidal through-line could be mapped textually, or whether it simply represents self-indulgent actorly (or directorly) resistance. I found that that Queen-role engages a sophisticated actorly intelligence in a set of moments of choice (not only about what she does or says, but about what she sees and hears, what she understands and feels, all in the context of what it means to be a woman in Shakespeare's Elsinore), moments in which more than one playable interpretive option is frequently available.[4] That role requires of its actor a final decision between unthinking accident and willed self-destruction, either of which must (and may) be the logical culmination of a succession of more or less psychologized choices made within the bounds of text and the contingencies of production. Insofar as a playtext determines its (actorly) reader, in other words, Q2/F seems willing to trust a particularly skilled and independent Queen-actor.

My parallel attempt now to sit inside the Q1 Queen-role shows that role to be strikingly more straightforward, offering moments of actorly choice that may fine-tune performances differently, but never leading the Queen-actor to so radical an interpretive intersection as that offered by the later texts. The exercise nevertheless reinforces a sense of Q1 as a script with its own clear practical intelligence, committed, for whatever reason, to a different, tighter, less interior realization of the Hamlet story than we find in the copiousness of Q2/F.[5] The script's theatricality, while infrequently tested on the stage, has nonetheless been borne out over the years by Hardin Craig's positive response to Ben Greet's 1928 production, by Gunnar Sjögren's report on a 1968 production in Sweden, by Nicholas Shrimpton's glowing review of the 1985 Orange Tree version in Richmond, by Scott McMillin's demonstration of the script's carefully controlled doubling options, as well as by its narrative efficiency and technical simplicity.[6] That theatricality, when tested in the realm of character, gives the actor plentiful textually grounded material for performance, and yet offers her (offered him) noticeably limited optionality, almost as if the script were seeking to control actorly process more strictly, less confidently, than does Q2/F; even as if it understood actorly process quite differently.

Q1's overall vision of character in action is consistently spare. Conflict is more tightly focused, more black-and-white than in Q2/F. Villainous responsibility for the final events, for example, is clustered on Claudius. Leartes [*sic*] does not provide his own mountebank's unction for an unbated sword—it, like the entire duel scheme, is here provided by the King alone.[7] Rather than Q2/F's tantalizing motivational indeterminacies, intention tends to be uniformly single and clearly announced. There can, for instance, be little doubt as to the Queen's conscience and allegiance, from the closet scene on.[8] Q1 can be mounted efficiently, I suspect, with little of the time-consuming weighing of complex actorly alternatives that characterizes rehearsal and production of Q2/F. What Hart Crane called Shakespeare's "hazards,"[9] the profound contracts of risk and challenge presented to audience and to player, are mainly absent from Q1's straight-ahead version of the revenge tale.

Though unitarily constructed, the Queen-role's accomplished theatricality is nevertheless demonstrable. For instance, it presents the actor with an unsubtle but extended set of invitations to contest with Corambis, insistently exploiting Gertred's gendered subordination in Claudius' Elsinore. Most actors, whatever their process, are highly sensitized to potential conflict with other characters. They seek it out. The skilled actorly text commonly exploits and organizes this instinct dramatically. Here, a kind of jousting with Corambis may begin in 2.2, and grow into a pattern of strikingly unequal contestation between male counselor and female monarch almost whenever they appear together, until the scene of his death.[10] Among its other effects, this contest defines and contains the Queen socially and politically: Corambis would dare no comparable set of competitive and dismissive exchanges with the King or even with Hamlet.

Near the beginning of 2.2, Corambis comes before the King and Queen, accompanied by Ofelia, and bearing news about Hamlet. In the course of his report, Q1's potential contest takes root. At the conclusion of Corambis' "I have found / The very depth of Hamlets lunacie" (744–45), the Queen responds (to the King, to Ofelia, to the audience, or to herself, but most definitely not to Corambis) "God graunt *he* hath" (746; emphasis mine). Wherever the line may be directed (and whether prayerful or no), its use of the third person excludes Corambis for a moment, an act that does not go unnoticed or unrequited by the counselor. Shortly, Corambis will begin his disquisition on Hamlet's madness, excluding the Queen as addressee by speaking strickly to the King, rather than to "My liege and madam" as in Q2/F:

> Now *my Lord,* touching the yong Prince Hamlet,
> Certaine it is that hee is madde: mad let us grant him then:
> Now to know the cause of this effect,
> Or else to say the cause of this defect,
> For this effect defective comes by cause.
>
> (776–80; emphasis mine)

At this point the Queen ups the ante, interrupting to speed him along ("Good my Lord be briefe," 781), whereupon he may merely brush her aside before returning to the masculine auditor about whom he really cares: "Madam I will: *my Lord,* I have a daughter" (782ff.; emphasis mine), and he resumes, once again focusing entirely on the King.

Nor has he quite finished with Gertred. At the conclusion of Corambis' description of his Hamlet theory, the King, as in Q2/F, turns to the Queen for her opinion, "Thinke you t'is so?" (814), but Corambis instantly forestalls her response:

> How? so my Lord, I would very faine know
> That thing that I have saide t'is so, positively,
> And it hath fallen out otherwise.
>
> (815–17)[11]

The actorly invitation to Corambis is to cut her off without a word when her royal husband has just invited her to speak, and it is surely significant not only that he does so, but that the world of

Q1 permits him to do this. Moments later, upon the approach of Hamlet, he will be the one who dismisses the Queen, politely but firmly, "Madame, will it please your grace / To leave us here?" (831–32), to which she can only respond, "With all my hart" (833), and be on her way. If the Queen-actor is noting this treatment, and letting resentment of it develop, it will even be conceivable that the Queen's later horror at Corambis' death is softened somewhat by a little tickle of satisfaction.

The script extends the potential for contest with Corambis into 3.1. As Gertred agrees to the King's invitation to see Hamlet's play, Corambis once again takes charge, making plans for her and shunting her aside in the process:

> Madame, I pray be ruled by me:
> And my good Soveraigne, give me leave to speake.
>
> (1188–89)

He then lays out his spying plan to the King alone, ending with "My Lord, how thinke you on't?" (1200). Pressed by the King, who has already preempted her voice with his own approval ("It likes us well, Gertred, what say you?" 1201), the Queen can only consent, and as the scene concludes Corambis virtually objectifies her as the unwitting stepping-stone to his own advancement:

> My selfe will be that happy messenger,
> Who hopes his griefe will be reveal'd to her.
>
> (1203–4)

Whether aside or to the King, this couplet isolates, even objectifies, the onstage Queen. Should the Queen-actor choose to have her character overhear this moment, the further potential for animus against Corambis is clear. This is part of the baggage she may bring to the closet scene, baggage provided by a script that readily accommodates interactorly contest and provides the little dynamic edges on which it may build.

Q1's skill with the Queen-role is also apparent in its placing her, as a silent figure, in an emotional pressure cooker based simply on listening and observing and storing responses. Where Q2/F, after the closet scene and 4.1, excuses the Queen from the stage, Q1 keeps her on right to the end of what the later texts mark as 4.3, Claudius' tense exchange with the apprehended Hamlet. Her journey through this extended scene is carefully prepared. Immediately after the closet scene, the beginning of a telling new fissure between

Queen and King is marked in the slightest of ways: the King enters asking for news of "our sonne" (4.1.1603); something in the Queen's tale of Corambis' murder, or possibly in her underlying new unease with him, alters the possessive pronoun, and begins to separate him from her: when she has finished, a mere thirteen lines later, he responds, "Gertred, *your* sonne shall presently to England" (1616; emphasis mine), and his recognition of a potential or actual shift in the lines of alliance is signaled to her.

Q1's Queen now must silently witness the subsequent capture, interrogation, and "protective" banishment of Hamlet, remaining onstage until the King's curt dismissal after Hamlet's departure: "Gertred, leave me, / And take your leave of *Hamlet*" (4.3.1660–61). This silent Queen, newly tuned in by the closet scene to the King's treachery, thus lives through the entire process between King and Hamlet, including the explosive culmination of a little war-by-naming (another instance of actorly contest) which is threaded through Q1, but that is absent from the other versions. Back in 1.2, the King started it, establishing a pattern of possession by naming, laying claim to Hamlet in public as "Sonne *Hamlet*" (172, 186). This continues in Q1's play scene, where the King begins "How now son *Hamlet*" (3.2.1275), and Hamlet for the first time, in the liberty of feigned distraction, responds (with plentiful potential for insult) by calling him "father." Now, in 4.3, sparring over the location of Corambis' body, they trade "sons" and "fathers" three times before Hamlet tops the King by shifting to "mother" at line 1654. His actual "farewel mother" is therefore lexically integrated, as it is not in Q2/F, part of a set that has become increasingly marked for contestation in the course of the play, and that may well, to the Queen's ears, echo Hamlet's direct criticism of her remarriage in the closet scene:

> *King*. Your loving father, *Hamlet.*
> *Hamlet.* My mother I say: you married my mother,
> My mother is your wife, man and wife is one flesh,
> And so (my mother) farewel.
>
> (1655–58)

And Hamlet goes without taking his actual leave of her.[12] It may be her evident distress at this that prompts the King to send her off after him. Keeping her onstage until this moment may therefore take the Queen further toward understanding the situation she has slid into, and toward sealing her new alliance with the Prince.[13] Certainly the King, as the moment concludes, seems to recognize her openly as Hamlet's ally, as he sends her off to bid Hamlet farewell and only then, having separated himself from her, reveals to the audience his plan for Hamlet's execution (1662–68). The relationship content of her dismissal here seems most like the much later moment in 5.1 of Q2/F, where Gertrude is sent off to "set some watch over your son" (296) while the scheming King hangs back to counsel patience in Laertes.

In these two ways, then, by exploiting actorly contest, and by building pressure on a silent but actively attentive player simply by scripting her presence as witness, Q1's Queen-role gives evidence of being simply but meticulously crafted for an actor. Another striking sign of this, allied with the script's capacity to build pressure on a silent player, is the extent to which it stages marginality in the person of the Queen, a strategy also deployed, but with more ambivalent potential, by Q2/F. In all texts there is clear opportunity for that marginal position to become a site of discontent, but Q1's treatment seems particularly single-minded. Unlike the figuratively spotlit Gertrude of 1.2 in Q2/F, for example, Q1's Queen is by contrast ignored by, perhaps even consciously excluded from, the words and acts of the first court scene. She is not even mentioned in the King's opening speech: no explicit or implicit presentation of recent bereavement and even more recent (and questionable) remarriage, no suggestion of her political status as "imperial jointress." Where the Q2/F Kings paradoxically may even empower the marginalized Gertrude to a considerable degree, both as actor (by focusing attention on her uneasily dual domestic condition), and as narrative participant (by allowing her an explicit share of the throne), Q1 begins by containing both character and actor, taking her for granted at best, ignoring her altogether at worst.

As Q1's scene proceeds, so does this apparently systematic containment in the margins. On the subject of Hamlet's continued mourning, the Queen is excluded, for the first of a number of times, from a dialogical exchange that is specifically hers in Q2/F. Instead, the King here carries the full weight for the royal/parental side. Hamlet's lines to the Queen in Q2/F, "'Tis not alone my inky cloak, good mother" (1.2.76ff.), are here exclusively and markedly to his uncle-father:

> My Lord, ti's not the sable sute I weare:
> No nor the teares that still stand in my eyes,
> Nor the distracted haviour in the visage,
> Nor all together mixt with outward semblance,

Is equall to the sorrow of my heart,
Him have I lost I must of force forgoe,
These but the ornaments and sutes of woe.

(179–85)

The Queen is only permitted to add her voice to the exchange after the King's ponderous cliché on death and everyman. Then the royal party is gone, without even the doubled (and therefore potentially supercharged) requests for her accompaniment that mark Q2/F.[14] Indeed, once again, she is not mentioned at all in the King's exit speech. He simply takes his leave, and she goes with him. Unless the Queen-actor adopts a subversive resistance to her apparent treatment as a virtual prop rather than as a living creature, she is likely to be left playing, at least on the surface, a one-note sign rather than a multivalent subject, what Steven Urkowitz has described as "only the idea or symbol of a Queen and mother, a costumed figure who stands for royalty in her regal costume."[15]

This is not to say that Q1 gives the Queen-actor no opportunity to explore a sense of alienation from the world of Claudius, which will be of use to her later in the role. Indeed, it seems to make such alienation abundantly available, but within much more restricted parameters for performance. For instance, where Q2/F's royal couple are given small moments of partnership, as at the beginning of 1.2, or even in their brief duologue in 2.2, and where Claudius is given some tenderness and solicitude toward his new wife in small details such as his use in 2.2 of "my sweet Queene" (Q2) or "my dear Gertrard" (F), or his delicacy before her on the subject of Hamlet's "transformation" (2.2), Q1 renders the Queen's marital relationship more a given symbol than a living thing, and we might even speculate, at the fictive level, that the marriage originated in political necessity rather than in love.[16] Q1 has markedly little in the way of invitations to affection on the part of the royal couple. It is crude psychology, of course, but one might go so far as to suggest that a performable reason for the swift development of the Queen's new loyalty to Hamlet in the closet scene is that the Prince in that scene is simply the first person in the entire action to show concern for her.

Certainly, her move to Hamlet's side in the closet scene is more narrowly determined by the script than is the process her counterpart may undergo in Q2/F. Nonetheless, the scene is similarly prepared, in that if the Queen-actor has paid intelligent attention to the inset play, she may bring into the closet inklings of a charge of murder against her husband. Harold Jenkins believes that her understanding is inconsistent and unprepared,[19] but the ground for its growth in the observant Queen-actor is discernible. At the playing of the Dumb Show, for example, the Queen has heard Ofelia express a persistent obsession with understanding:

> What meanes this my Lord? (1297)
> What doth this meane my lord? (1299)
> Will he tell us what this shew meanes? (1301)

One actorly by-product of Ofelia's interpretive bemusement might well be that the listening Queen, too, is alerted to seek out the significance of the presentation, particularly when, after the miming of a King's murder, her son underlines a royal wife's specific protestation against remarriage by pointedly asking her (and not the King) for her opinion of the piece, before engaging Ofelia in (rather too loud?) conversation about his mother's cheery demeanor despite his father's recent death, along with a reminder of marriage vows in Ofelia's "Still better and worse" (1375), and in Hamlet's "So you must take your husband" (1376). When the inset play resumes, the noble play-husband is murdered, and Gertred's new husband flees the scene. Despite these interpretable events, which Hamlet will underline in the closet scene with direct description of his father as murdered, and of the new King as a murderer, Jenkins observes that the Q1 Queen's knowledge is an inconsistency, for "Hamlet has given her no account of it" (34). I think that the observant Queen-actor has been given a quite substantial account, albeit more in show than in text, and that the evidence of Q1's closet scene is that she has interpreted, quite correctly, what she has seen and heard. The difference from Q2/F is that she is not given performable options as to what to do with her knowledge.

Which brings us to the closet scene proper (3.4). Not only does it move the Queen efficiently to Hamlet's side, but it does so with clear theatrical intelligence, without inviting the actor to deal with complicating alternatives. From the moment of Hamlet's entry, Q1 deploys its own plan for softening up the Queen. She is instantly made to feel more vulnerable, her danger more explicit and acute, than in the analogous moment in Q2/F. Hamlet prefaces any conversation with "first weele make all safe" (1496), a line that invites him at least to secure the door by which he has entered, thus locking her in and any help out, possibly even to check around to see that they are alone. Any such action on his part, threatening both entrapment and discovery, is likely to spark urgent apprehension in the Queen, upping the ante far more directly, even sensationally, than in Q2/F.

Next, in the exchanges with Hamlet following the death of Corambis, Q1 brings the Queen quickly and explicitly into alliance with her son. Hamlet's concern in this version is fine-tuned differently from Q2/F, and it is in part that difference that conditions her move to him. He is, to begin with, much more direct about the death of his father, and about the new King's guilt:

> and he is dead.
> Murdred, damnably murdred, . . .
> here is your husband,
> With a face like *Vulcan.*
> A looke fit for a murder and a rape, . . .
> can you looke on him
> That slew my father, and your deere husband,
> To live in the incestuous pleasure of his bed?
>
> (1522–35)

She is quick to take his meaning, and proclaim her innocence:

> But as I have a soule, I sweare by heaven,
> I never knew of this most horride murder.
>
> (1582–83)

In keeping with Q1's consistent lack of invitation to psychologized interior complexity, Hamlet here is more concerned that his mother recognize the material fact of murder than that she save her incestuous soul, and he is markedly less obsessed with the sexuality of her fault. Indeed, he seems to imply that her sexual guilt is quite narrowly circumscribed (an implication which, as with the later treatment of the poison plot, concentrates the play's evil in the King). Crucial to this implication is his use of the term *rape* (1528). That her incestuous condition stems from a rape seems to absolve her in the Prince's eyes, and conceivably in her own, at least of initiating or willing the incest, and this might in turn begin to enable the Queen (whose conscience, after all, is not that of a Christianized Lucrece—she is not even given Q2/F's later soliloquy on the subject of her sick soul) to forgive herself more readily, and to join forces against the man who has murdered her husband and violated her chastity. Such self-forgiveness is a huge simplifying step beyond Q2/F's complicating potential for deep and obscure self-condemnation.

Now her straightforward alliance with Hamlet is further eased, for the terms he offers here shift suddenly away from Q2/F's Christian perception of guilty stains on an eternal soul, toward a simplistic pagan stress on fame, shame, and revenge:

> O mother, if ever you did my deare father love,
> Forbeare the adulterous bed to night,
> And win your selfe by little as you may,
> In time it may be you wil lothe him quite:
> And mother, but assist mee in revenge,
> And in his death your infamy shall die.
>
> (1588–93)

To this she responds, out of an apparently comfortable relationship with her God, and with no apparent sense of the collision here between pagan and Christian precepts:

> *Hamlet,* I vow by that majesty,
> That knowes our thoughts, and lookes into our hearts,
> I will conceale, consent, and doe my best,
> What stratagem soe're thou shalt devise.
>
> (1594–7)[18]

This seems to me to illuminate the absence from Q1 of the developed suicide option so evident in Q2/F. While the guilt-ridden and isolated Gertrude of the usually acted conflation may be invited to a despair exacerbated by the promptings of conscience and by an expanding sense of personal responsibility, the Queen of the First Quarto seems blessed with a comfortable and constant relationship with an easier God, and with a much narrower sense of personal fault. Although her role is just over half the size of the Q2/F Gertrude, she has three times the number of references to God, heaven, her soul, and prayer, culminating in this vow to Hamlet that seems virtually to have secured her absolution. After this point in the closet scene, her God seems no longer concerned about her incest, her infidelity to her first husband, or her direct or indirect share of responsibility for Denmark's rottenness. She has only two further prayerful moments, neither of them concerned with her own spiritual state. Following the closet scene, Q1 limits her to being a willing (if strikingly inactive) accomplice in a simple old-fashioned revenge action.[19]

From this point on, Q1 narrows the path for the Queen-actor. To begin with, Q1's version of Ofelia's madness (4.5) is not so problematic for the Queen as it is in Q2/F. Where the girl's Q2/F entry is an unwanted intrusion into the Queen's physical and spiritual space, Ofelia here simply arrives before the Queen and King, and the Queen is issued no textual invitation to play reluctance. Nor is the confrontation preceded by any textual indication of guilty conscience on the part of the Queen. On the whole, it is as if enrollment in Hamlet's revenge plan, however vague at this point, has absolved her of all thoughts of guilt, thoughts that in any event seem confined to her own personal state in this play, rather than extended to her responsibility for others.

Nor is she granted the complicating Q2/F opportunities to observe the King's behavior and so puzzle out the details of his final scheme. As 4.5 moves into its last moments, the Queen, who in Q2/F may be left onstage to witness the beginning of the King-Laertes alliance against her son, seems not to have heard the King's lines to Leartes ("thinke already the revenge is done / On him that makes you such a haplesse sonne"—1800–1801). Her stage-directed reentry and her evident surprise at Horatio's revelations in the next scene suggest that she exited in 4.5 without witnessing, or certainly without comprehending, the sinister new liaison between Leartes and the King.

In 4.7 Q2/F presents options for the Queen-actor to discover Laertes and the King in midplot when she enters with the news of Ophelia's death. In Q1, however, her arrival is delayed until the scheming is done, and there is no apparent sense, as there is particularly in Q2, that she might stumble onto something furtive and notice it.[20] Even her description of Ophelia's death is relatively empty of complicating possibilities. Instead of the potential internalized and self-aware meditation of Q2/F, Q1's Queen goes directly into her considerably more sparse and conventional narrative, proceeding chronologically to the news of the drowning, and making none of Q2/F's excursions into verbalized meditation that might encourage complex internalized growth.

In holding her to its singular through-line, Q1 nevertheless offers her one more opportunity to experience the King's blatant dissimulation and the extent to which he simply dismisses her. His falseness at the close of the burial scene (5.1) is obvious, as he speaks aside with Leartes, reassuring him that "This very day shall *Hamlet* drinke his last" (2075), and then invites the Queen to exit with him (as opposed to their separate and clearly disenchanted departures in Q2/F):

> Come *Gertred,* wee'l have *Leartes,* and our sonne,
> Made friends and Lovers, as befittes them both,
> Even as they tender us, and love their countrie.
>
> (2079–81)

Given that she is now fully, if generally, aware of his nature, her response, "God grant they may" (2082), might suggest an incipient attempt to play at his game herself. But it is too little too late. For the remainder of her action, she is invited to perform nothing more subversive or self-actualizing than this small moment.

In the final scene, no complicating options are made available. This Queen has not acquired the specific information that might lead her to recognize the fencing match as the King's plot, nor has her actor been invited to consider the deep despair that is so possible a choice in Q2/F. Instead, she comes into 5.2 as a clear but secret ally of Hamlet, primitively shriven by their exchange in the closet scene, awaiting but not materially assisting his revenge against her husband. While Q2/F's Queen-actor may carry quite complex anticipations and awareness into the scene, this Queen may simply enter expecting to witness Hamlet's achievement of his revenge, an expectation that will lend a blunt irony to her own death.

To keep her unsuspectingly on course, Q1 does not even show her the mechanics of the poisoning. The King's offer of a special pearl or union, so underlined in Q2/F, is not mentioned in Q1. Instead, he has either prepared the poisoned cup in advance of the fencing, as he seems to intend when plotting with Leartes (4.7.1878–81), or his placing the pearl in the drink now is deliberately covered by the Queen's business with Hamlet and her napkin, and so hidden from her:

> *King*. Here *Hamlet,* the King doth drinke a health to thee.
> *Queene*. Here *Hamlet,* take my napkin, wipe thy face.
> (2155–56)

And she crosses to Hamlet, or he to her, just as the King would be spicing the potion before his order to "Give him the wine" (2157). Finally, at her moment of drinking, the articulated and complicating defiance so prized by commentators on Q2/F, and by Gertrude-Actors, is also denied her:

> *Queene*. Here *Hamlet,* thy mother drinkes to thee.
> *(Shee drinkes.)*
> *King*. Do not drinke *Gertred:* O t'is the poysned cup!
> (2160–62)

It is of course conceivable and playable that the stage direction is simply typeset a half line early in the interests of space, and that she does not drink until after the King has urged her not to, but even so she does not get Q2/F's wonderful line, "I will, my lord, I pray you pardon me" (5.2.291), and with it go some of her options for this moment, at least as embedded in text. The writerly instinct here may be related to that of the numerous nineteenth-century texts and promptbooks that emended toward wifely politesse at just this point, altering her Q2/F blend of defiance and apology to apology pure and simple:

> *King*. Gertrude, do not drink.
> *Queen*. I have, my lord. I pray you pardon me.[21]

In those nineteenth-century versions, as in Q1, the script tightens the focus on the struggle between the Prince and the King and in doing so simplifies drastically the range of actorly choices open to the Queen-actor. Indeed, it sees to it that the manly action of villainy and virtuous revenge is not finally tainted by any uncontrolled actorly instinct to play the disruptive accessory female right through to some inconveniently complicating conclusion of her own.

It is conceivable, of course, that all this spare Q1 treatment of the Queen really amounts to nothing more than another instance of mindless patriarchal obliviousness, in which the Queen is mainly given little performable optionality because no one has paid her any heed. But much of her scripting displays real theatrical intelligence and craft, and very often, where her options for performable choice are straitly contained, the comparable moments in Q2/F are complex, seeming to invite (and to trust?) a more open interpretive process. My sense, in other words, is that the constraining simplicity of the Q1 Queen-role results from deliberate and accomplished theatrical shaping of the role toward a single prescribed signifier, toward a Queen who, despite the performable invitations I have described, remains more a contained gesture than a negotiable subject. True subjectivity would entail granting her independent agency, clearer options for interiority: these she, and her actor, are finally denied. A reading that sought to address the issue of priority might even argue that Q1's narrative restrictedness, represented here by its systematically contained Queen, is a determined backlash against the disruptive and indeterminate actorly possibilities of Q2/F.

Notes

An earlier version of this essay was written for Janis Lull and Linda Anderson's 1991 Shakespeare Association of America seminar on "bad" quartos, at which time Thomas Clayton kindly gave me detailed information about his then forthcoming collection, *The "Hamlet" First Published.* Generous and helpful commentary, for which I am most grateful, has since been provided by Bernice Kliman, by the late Antony Hammond, and by members of the seminar on "Language in the So-Called Bad Quartos" at the 1996 International Shakespeare Conference in Stratford-upon-Avon.

1. I am mindful of Janette Dillon's stern caveat against mistaking an enthusiastic "nostalgic fantasy" (86) for hard evidence of the performative primacy of Q1. My agenda here has no direct interest in authorship or priority; it simply aims to unpack some of the performative potential in a script that, like any playtext, participates actively, if partially, in constructing performances.

2. Many observers comment on the "bad" quartos as simplifications of their "good" cousins. Kathleen O. Irace, for example, speaking of an incident in Q1 *Hamlet,* says "like other differences between the short quartos and the longer versions, this alteration speeds the plot at the expense of complexity and depth" (27). My project here is to be specific about the apparent impact of such simplification on a single role.

3. "Realising Gertrude: The Suicide Option."

4. Many of those options are recorded in Marvin Rosenberg's encyclopedic study of *The Masks of Hamlet* (1992).

5. In an intriguing recent study, Dorothea Kehler associates this simplicity with a Roman Catholic made-to-tour understanding of the role ("The First Quarto of *Hamlet:* Reforming Queen Gertred"). Janis Lull's earlier assessment, namely "that the Q1 text affirms the ethics of the post-feudal honor culture, especially the value of heroic individualism, while the F text shows Hamlet accepting the newer Protestant ethic by subordinating his individual will to divine providence," is another suggestive response to the simpler Q1 revenge tale, whether or not one accepts her linked view on priority/authenticity ("Forgetting *Hamlet,*" in Clayton, *The "Hamlet" First Published*).

6. See Craig's preface to Weiner, ed., *Hamlet: The First Quarto, 1603,* iii. And see Sjögren, "Producing the First Quarto *Hamlet,*" 35–44; Shrimpton, "Shakespeare Performances in London and Stratford-upon-Avon 1984–5," 193–97; and McMillan, "Casting the *Hamlet* Quartos: The Limit of Eleven," in Clayton, ed., *"Hamlet" First Published,* 179–94. Sjögren finds that "the play could have been produced by twelve actors: four stockholders, three boys, three older apprentices and two local talents" (37)—this represents a generous distribution of the roles and, I suspect, one that avoids doubling Ofelia or Gertred into men's parts. Shrimpton reports that the Orange Tree version was played by nine (194). Greet's production is also reported on, though not very helpfully, by Isaac, 189–209. Marvin Rosenberg has collected numerous responses to William Poel's 1881 production in "The First Modern Staging of *Hamlet* Q1," also in Clayton. See also Speaight, 51. (And note the potential similarity of the *Hamlet* situation to that proposed by Taylor for the Quarto of *Henry 5:* "We Happy Few: The 1600 Abridgement," in Wells, *Modernizing Shakespeare's Spelling.*) Irace explores the script's theatricality extensively in chapters 2, 3, and 4 of *Reforming the "Bad" Quartos.*

7. Steven Urkowitz develops this point effectively in "'Well-sayd olde Mole'," 49–55.

8. Frequently noted. See, for example, Kehler, 398.

9. "To Shakespeare," in *The Poems of Hart Crane,* 131.

10. Q1 is quoted from the parallel-texts edition by Bertram and Kliman, using their lineation supplemented by Folio's parallel act and scene numbers for ease of reference. Quotations from Q2/F are from *The Riverside Shakespeare,* ed. G. B. Evans et al.

11. Lest we think that Corambis might not be interrupting, that the King's question might be directed to his counselor, we should note that the logic of the moment, with Corambis' opinion already complete, invites second opinion rather than reiteration; and in any event, the King consistently employs the familiar *thee* and *thou* with the Lord Chamberlain, reserving the more formal and respectful *you* for his wife.

12. At least, no such leave-taking is scripted: the Hamlet-actor may, of course, make a decision to remedy that in the playing. I am imagining, for the moment, that he does not.

13. A 1991 *Hamlet* at Stratford, Ontario, partly followed this impulse, allowing the Queen (Patricia Collins) to witness Hamlet's banishment in 4.3, unseen on the upper level.

14. In fact, Q1 does not once adopt that telling Q2/F exit technique, discussed in O'Brien, "Revision by Excision," 29; and Shand, 101–2.

15. "Five Women Eleven Ways," 300. As several participants observed at the 1996 "bad" quartos seminar in Stratford-upon-Avon, the putative move from "good" to "bad" texts seems frequently to be a systematic stylistic (or streamlining) move away from interiority in the scripting of character.

16. Note Claudius' Q2/F admission to Laertes in 4.7: "My virtue or my plague, be it either which—/ She is so conjunctive to my life and soul, / That, as the star moves not but in his sphere, / I could not but by her" (13–16). While it could be a Machiavellian calculation, it could also be a quite straightforward indicator of the attitude from which he plays with her throughout. There is no such declaration (and perhaps, therefore, no such attitude) in Q1.

17. Introduction to the Arden *Hamlet,* 34.

18. The importing of the latter lines from a memory of *The Spanish Tragedy* is irrelevant to this argument. Wherever they originated, their place now is in the fabric of Q1, as a speech-act generated by the Queen in response to the immediate theatrical moment. There is no other actorly way to deal with them.

19. Despite her having been won over to Hamlet's side, the King's glozing may be so successful at the beginning of Ofelia's mad scene (4.5), that for a single moment the Queen wavers (as she need not be understood to do in Q2/F), only coming fully back onside with Hamlet in the following scene (unique to Q1), when Horatio tells her of the King's plan for Hamlet's death in England, and she comments directly on Claudius' dissembling, on the "treason in his lookes / That seem'd to sugar o're his villanie" (1818–19). Such wavering, it seems to me, is adequate to account for her protection of the King against Leartes in Q1, where it seems inadequate to the invited complexities of Q2/F. (I deal with this point in "The Suicide Option," as does Ellen J. O'Brien, in her unpublished paper from the Berlin World Congress, "Unheard Is Not Unseen: Stage Images for Shakespeare's Silent Presences.")

20. See Urkowitz, "'Well-sayd olde Mole'," 58.

21. As printed, for instance, in Simpkin, Marshall, and Company's 1839 edition, used as prompt text by Henry Betty, who later wrote the same reading into his prompt copy of the 1843 Charles Knight and Company version; the apologetic reading also appeared in the much-used nineteenth-century "French's Standard Drama" version (n.d.). Both Bernice Kliman (270) and Rosenberg (889) comment

on the implications of this emendation; Ellen J. O'Brien has a more developed contextualizing of it in her study of nineteenth-century revisions of the Queen-role ("Revision by Excision," 33–34).

References

Bertram, Paul, and Bernice W. Kliman, eds. 1991. *The Three-Text Hamlet*. New York: AMS.

Clayton, Thomas, ed. 1992. *The "Hamlet" First Published (Q1, 1603): Origins, Form, Intertextualities.* Newark: University of Delaware Press.

Crane, Hart. 1986. *The Poems of Hart Crane,* ed. Marc Simon. New York: Liveright.

Dillon, Janette. 1994. "Is There a Performance in This Text?" *Shakespeare Quarterly* 45:74–86.

Evans, G. B. et al. 1974. *The Riverside Shakespeare.* Boston: Houghton.

Irace, Kathleen O. 1994. *Reforming the "Bad" Quartos: Performance and Provenance of Six Shakespearean First Editions.* Newark: University of Delaware Press.

Isaac, Winnifred F. E. C. 1964. *Ben Greet and the Old Vic* London: Greenbank.

Kehler, Dorothea. 1995. "The First Quarto of *Hamlet:* Reforming Widow Gertred." *Shakespeare Quarterly* 46:398–413.

Kliman, Bernice. 1988. *"Hamlet": Film, Television, and Audio Performance.* London: Associated University Presses.

McMillin, Scott. 1984. "The Queen's Men in 1594: A Study of 'Good' and 'Bad' Quartos." *English Literary Renaissance* 14:55–69.

O'Brien, Ellen J. 1993. "Revision by Excision: Rewriting Gertrude." *Shakespeare Survey* 45:27–35.

———. 1986. "Unheard Is Not Unseen: Stage Images for Shakespeare's Silent Presences." Paper contributed to the Seminar on Stage Images, World Shakespeare Congress, West Berlin, 2 April.

Rosenberg, Marvin. 1992. *The Masks of Hamlet.* Newark: University of Delaware Press.

Shakespeare, William. 1982. *Hamlet,* ed. Harold Jenkins. London: Methuen.

Shand, G. B. 1994. "Realising Gertrude: The Suicide Option." In *The Elizabethan Theatre XIII,* edited by A. L. Magnusson and C. E. McGee. Toronto: Meany.

Shrimpton, Nicholas. 1987. "Shakespeare Performances in London and Stratford-upon-Avon 1984–5." *Shakespeare Survey* 39:193–97.

Sjögren, Gunnar. 1979. "Producing the First Quarto *Hamlet.*" *Hamlet Studies* 1:35–44.

Speaight, Robert. 1954. *William Poel and the Elizabethan Revival.* London: Heinemann.

Urkowitz, Steven. 1986. "'Well-sayd olde Mole': Burying Three *Hamlets* in Modern Editions." In *Shakespeare Study Today,* edited by Georgianna Ziegler. New York: AMS.

———. 1988. "Five Women Eleven Ways: Changing Images of Shakespearean Characters in the Earliest Texts." In *Images of Shakespeare,* edited by Werner Habicht et al. Newark: University of Delaware Press.

Weiner, Albert B., ed. 1962. *Hamlet: The First Quarto, 1603*. Great Neck: Barron's.

Wells, Stanley. 1979. *Modernizing Shakespeare's Spelling*. Oxford: Clarendon.

Reading *Hamlet* in Performance: The Laertes/Hamlet Connection

JUNE SCHLUETER AND JAMES P. LUSARDI

As Marvin Rosenberg remarks about Laertes in *The Masks of Hamlet,* "Not much attention has been paid to him by scholar-critics and theatre observers" (253). It is usually thought sufficient to note that he represents a foil to the protagonist and to summarize familiar differences. But, as Rosenberg adds, "there is more to Laertes than difference"; there is also identity with Hamlet that gives the role "dimension and subtext" (253–54). This identity of the two characters in the context of difference is what engages us here and what we seek to develop as it is manifested in the texts of *Hamlet* and as it may be realized in performance. While taking into account Shakespeare's deployment of Laertes in relation to Hamlet at earlier points, we shall concentrate on the two sequences in act 5 that involve their direct interaction, the encounter at Ophelia's grave (5.1.217–302) and the climactic duel that proves fatal to both (5.2.223–362). It is these sequences that deepen the design of the Laertes/Hamlet connection and offer the "subtextual resonances" (253) that the production may exploit.

In this essay, we employ an analytical model that we adopted as scholars for a book on *King Lear,* and as teachers for a course we team-taught at Lafayette College that covered several Shakespearean plays in different genres. It is essentially threefold. Like other readers, we are preoccupied with patterns and problems of meaning, but we pursue these by scrutinizing the text for the signals that may guide production. When we identify moments that represent textual and performance cruxes, we analyze those moments and the sequences of which they are a part to suggest possible ways of realizing them in performance and thus of shaping and sometimes fixing meaning. We then turn to actual productions for a close look at ways in which performance has in fact staged and interpreted text. Our purpose is not the writing of production history but rather a performance-oriented "reading" of Shakespearean plays.

From among a host of productions, we have chosen to discuss two landmark cinematic *Hamlet*s, the 1948 Laurence Olivier film version and the 1980 Derek Jacobi BBC-TV version (Rothwell and Melzer, nos. 98 and 140). We chose these because of the sustained interest they have generated over the years, because of their ready accessibility, and because of the differences in their treatment of the Hamlet/Laertes connection. In the BBC production, David Robb's mercurial Laertes is paired with Jacobi's nervously mocking, impulsive, unpredictable Hamlet. Both are potentially dangerous. In the Olivier version, Terence Morgan's Laertes finds himself matched with what Rosenberg describes as a "power" Hamlet (133). As the director, Olivier does some reshaping of the role of Laertes to meet the dramatic exigencies that he himself creates as an imposing and flamboyant presence in the leading role. In both productions, it is the handling of visual imagery and cinematic detail that illuminates the relationship between the two characters.

The Laertes/Hamlet Connection in the Texts

In 1.2 of *Hamlet,* Claudius holds court following his marriage to Gertrude. The newly crowned King attends first to matters of state, then turns to Laertes to invite his suit, leaving Hamlet unacknowledged. In at least one production, the BBC, Laertes is disturbed over Claudius' breach of protocol; as he bids the King farewell, he pauses to face Hamlet, obviously embarrassed and concerned. This scene is the last in which an audience sees Laertes and Hamlet together until act 5, when the two meet first to grapple in the graveyard and then to fight their fatal duel.

When Laertes and Hamlet meet in the graveyard, both are newly returned to Elsinore. Laertes, having come in "secret" from France to avenge his father's death, is supported in 4.5 by the cheers of the Danish "rabble," who want him for their king. Hamlet, having outwitted Rosencrantz and Guildenstern and survived the lucky chance of a pirate's raid on his way to England, has announced his return in letters he has written. He is presumably intent on carrying out his resolve of 4.4: "O from this time forth, / My thoughts be bloody, or be nothing worth." While one son has responded on the instant to the news of his father's murder, the other has returned after a long course of avoiding the retributive justice his father's Ghost has urged. Now, in the graveyard, both are distraught over the death of Ophelia, and both are intent on action. Their scuffle at the gravesite is a foretaste of their final meeting.

Enraged at Hamlet as the cause of two deaths and manipulated by Claudius in the venting of his wrath, Laertes will resort to the treachery of a poisoned sword, reinforced by a poisoned drink, to exact revenge. Hamlet, after his "tow'ring passion" in the graveyard, will moderate his own rage but strengthen his resolve; he knows the villainy of his uncle and finally understands the part of providence in all affairs.

When Hamlet and Laertes meet in the last scene of the play with the court assembled to witness their duel, Hamlet asks pardon of Laertes, blaming his madness, not himself, for his misdeeds. Accepting Hamlet's apology, Laertes yet insists on protecting his "honor." Thus reconciled and unreconciled, they choose their foils. Accomplished swordsmen, they fight with aplomb, Hamlet gaining the edge while unaware of the dishonorable plot against him. Once he and Laertes are both doomed by the envenomed sword, the two exchange forgiveness, and Laertes proclaims, "the King's to blame," cueing Hamlet to kill his uncle. In the final scene of the play, both Hamlet and Laertes achieve their revenge, and Fortinbras, the third avenging son, whose father was killed by Hamlet's father on Hamlet's birthday, arrives to claim the crown at Hamlet's death, even as silence grips Laertes and Hamlet eternally.

Clearly, at least part of the strategy of the final scenes is to counterpoint the two avenging sons and to prepare the way for the third. But further dramatic parallels and ironies are suggested in these final encounters between Laertes and Hamlet. A production sensitive to the complexities of their graveyard grapple and "brothers' wager" can provide a number of visual articulations of the Laertes/Hamlet connection, all suggested by the implied stage directions of 5.1 and 5.2.

From the moment of Laertes' return to Elsinore, the text has urged identification of the pair. A reader encountering the Danes' heralding of Laertes as Claudius' successor can hardly avoid recognizing that Laertes has assumed Hamlet's role. Endorsing the quick action of this irate son, the crowd, by the Messenger's account, "call him lord":

> They cry, "Choose we! Laertes shall be king!"
> Caps, hands, and tongues applaud it to the clouds,
> "Laertes shall be king, Laertes king!"
>
> (4.5.109–11)

Backed by "a riotous head," Laertes, not Hamlet, threatens Claudius, choosing words with an ironic ring for an audience still waiting for Hamlet to end his delay: "O thou vile King, / Give me my father!" (119–20). Even more ironic are the figures Laertes chooses to describe the drop of blood that might restrain him, for they mock the would-be avenger Hamlet, who indeed may say (and, in essence, has said) what Laertes theoretically poses:

> That drop of blood that's calm proclaims me bastard,
> Cries cuckold to my father, brands the harlot
> Even here, between the chaste unsmirchèd brow
> Of my true mother.
>
> (4.5.121–24)

Claudius' treatment of Laertes in 4.5 recalls, by contrast, his treatment of Hamlet in 1.2. In 1.2, Claudius gives Hamlet audience only reluctantly and scoffs at his grief, calling it unmanly. Reasoning with his nephew/son, the King reminds him that this father lost a father and that his father lost his; Hamlet's continuing grief is a "fault to heaven, / A fault against the dead, a fault to nature" (101–2). Claudius admonishes him to "throw to earth / This unprevailing woe" (106–7). More fatherly to Laertes than to his nephew/son, Claudius in 4.5 permits Laertes voice, inviting the furious young man to articulate his wrath so that he may neutralize it. Reasoning with Laertes even as he positions himself as accomplice, the King wins the young man's confidence, praising him as "a good child and a true gentleman" (153). Where in 1.2 he relies on Gertrude to prevail upon Hamlet to stay in Elsinore, knowing his credibility with his nephew/son slender, with Laertes he twice reprimands Gertrude for intervening, preferring a man-to-man talk. And, after Ophelia's display of madness, he endorses Laertes' revenge as a legitimate and desirable pursuit of filial grief: "Laertes, I must commune with your grief. . . . And we shall jointly labor with your soul / To give it due content" (205, 214–15).

In 4.7, the King and Laertes devise their treachery against the prince: an unbated sword, an envenomed tip, a poisoned cup. But even here, where Claudius reveals to Laertes Hamlet's dangerous demeanor—"he which hath your noble father slain / Pursued my life" (4–5)—and urges revenge, an audience is reminded of the similar circumstance in 1.5, where the Ghost reveals Claudius' treachery to Hamlet—"The serpent that did sting thy father's life / Now wears his crown" (40–41)—and urges revenge. An audience's knowledge that poison was the instrument of old Hamlet's murder in the garden and is now to be employed in Claudius and Laertes' design further encourages the connection between these two persuasion sequences, which culminate in pledges of revenge: in 1.4 by Hamlet—"Now to my word: / It is 'Adieu, adieu! Remember me.' / I have sworn 't" (111–13)—and in 4.7 by Laertes—"But my revenge will come" (30).

The Graveyard Sequence in the Texts

If the strategy of the final two scenes is further to impress upon the audience the connection between Laertes and Hamlet, then the graveyard encounter between the two young men becomes especially significant, for it is here that the audience sees the two together for the first time since 1.2. The altercation with Laertes over or in Ophelia's grave provides the best opportunity for a stage image of this connection, and we shall discuss that moment shortly. But even before the graveyard grapple, the arrangement of the verse and the repetition of language support the connection. While the mourners continue still unaware of Hamlet's presence, for example, the lines of Laertes and Hamlet are juxtaposed:

> *Laertes.* What ceremony else?
> *Hamlet.* That is Laertes, a very noble youth. Mark.
> *Laertes.* What ceremony else?
>
> (223–25)

And hereafter the two share verse lines. From Hamlet's discovery of the identity of the corpse—"What, the fair Ophelia!" (242)—through his altercation with Laertes, after which Laertes speaks no more in the scene, the first or last line of either's speech completes the pentameter line begun by the other.

But even were their lines not shared, the linguistic connection between the two would be apparent. Laertes, leaping into Ophelia's grave, calls for dust to be piled upon them, to form a mountain "T' o'ertop old Pelion or the skyish head / Of blue Olympus" (253–54). Hamlet, proclaiming a commensurate willingness to be buried alive with Ophelia, uses the same imagery:

> And if thou prate of mountains, let them throw
> Millions of acres on us, till our ground,
> Singeing his pate against the burning zone,
> Make Ossa like a wart!
>
> (283–86)

In their graveyard scuffle, Laertes' fingers find Hamlet's throat, to be met by the latter's warning that he too is dangerous and should be feared. In response to Laertes' extravagant expression of the grief occasioned by his love for Ophelia, Hamlet hyperbolically challenges that love: "I loved Ophelia. Forty thousand brothers / Could not with all their quantity of love / Make up my sum" (272–74).

Hamlet, in short, will not let Laertes "outface" him. Nor will he allow Laertes to assume his part. Upon the grieving Gertrude's lament that she had hoped Ophelia would be her Hamlet's wife—"I thought thy bride-bed to have decked, sweet maid, / And not t' have strewed thy grave" (245–46)—Laertes leaps into the grave atop his sister, pleading with those participating in her maimed rites to "pile your dust upon the quick and dead" (251). Incensed at Laertes' histrionic display of brotherly love for Ophelia, Hamlet (as he admits to Horatio in 5.2) experiences a "tow'ring passion" and makes his move.

Whether that passion prompts Hamlet to plunge into Ophelia's grave after Laertes remains problematic. The Q1 stage directions have Laertes leap into the grave and Hamlet leap in after him; the Q2 directions are silent; F directs Laertes, but not Hamlet, to leap into the grave (Bertram and Kliman, 238–41). John A. Mills, in *Hamlet on Stage: The Great Tradition,* records the behavior of distinguished actors at Ophelia's funeral: Edwin Forrest, Edwin Booth, Henry Irving, and John Barrymore did not leap into the grave after Laertes; Edmund Kean, Richard Burton, and Nicol Williamson did (84, 120 passim). Though in over three hundred years of stage tradition, Hamlet has often leapt into the grave, and in contemporary productions he often continues to do so, Harley Granville-Barker objects to the Prince's descent. Not only would two men struggling on the top of a coffin be incongruous, but Hamlet's leap into the grave upon his announcement "This is I, / Hamlet the Dane" (257–58), the only point at which it would be practical, would neutralize the "royal dignity of the phrase." Moreover, Hamlet's leap would make Hamlet, not Laertes, the aggressor, which the language suggests he is not (1 : 139n).

Whether or not the two struggle in the grave, clearly the two grapple, for Hamlet warns Laertes to "take thy fingers from my throat" (261), and Claudius commands they be plucked asunder. Their altercation, though, could take place with Hamlet outside the grave and Laertes within or with both outside. In speaking his challenge to Laertes ("What is he whose grief / Bears such an emphasis? . . ." [254–55]), Hamlet might stand at the lip of the grave, leaning or kneeling to shout, "This is I, / Hamlet the Dane," at which point Laertes could clench his fingers around Hamlet's neck. Or Laertes might leap out of the grave to confront Hamlet, beginning the scuffle with "The devil take thy soul!" (259). The stage image that results from the two joined so closely in their grapple that someone must pluck them asunder becomes proleptic of the similar image in the duel scene when Claudius must again call out, "Part them! They are incensed" (5.2.305). By the same token, the grave as the setting for their scuffle looks to their own joint deaths in 5.2, obliquely predicted by Hamlet when, at the funeral, he pledges to fight with Laertes "Until my eyelids will no longer wag" (270). Though their love for Ophelia is the cause of their graveyard altercation and the "theme" upon which Hamlet promises further fight, 5.2 reveals that Laertes and Hamlet have more in common than their professed love for the dead Ophelia.

When they meet in 5.2, an audience will not only recall their quarrel over who loves Ophelia more, but hear also Hamlet's regretful admission to Horatio: "For by the image of my cause I see / The portraiture of his" (5.2.77–78). The two young men who embrace the "brothers' wager" in 5.2 are brothers in deed and in death. Though their grappling outside the grave may be an effective visual articulation of this kinship, the stage image of the young mourners fighting in that narrow, sunken space that houses the dead till doomsday and in which Ophelia lies seals the connection between the brothers/lovers/avenging sons/dead men with staggering force.

The Graveyard Sequence in the BBC *Hamlet*

In the BBC-TV production, directed by Rodney Bennett, Derek Jacobi as Hamlet completes his graveyard musings on death by smelling his hands, which have recently held the skull of Yorick. But his lesson in mortality is incomplete. As he turns to Horatio (Robert Swann), he spies the funeral procession crossing upstage against the horizon: a Priest (Michael Poole), in white vestment and black shawl, followed by black-robed and hooded pallbearers carrying a litter that is bed for a body wrapped in white. Even before the royal party enters the frame, Hamlet recognizes the King (Patrick Stewart), the Queen (Claire Bloom), and the courtiers. He does not at once see Laertes (David Robb), who walks alongside the litter. Hamlet and Horatio move from their downstage position on the gravesite to conceal themselves stage right behind a gray sarcophagus as the camera cuts to the procession, now approaching and stopping at the newly opened grave, bordered on the remaining three sides by a low fence. The pallbearers go about their business, depositing Ophelia (Lalla Ward) above the aperture and holding onto the cloth strips with which they will lower her into the grave. Upstage, facing the camera, are the Priest and Laertes, behind them the Queen and the King. At Laertes' "What ceremony else?" the camera cuts to Hamlet and Horatio, sitting against the sarcophagus, their backs to the mourners, for Hamlet's surprised recognition of the voice belonging to the "noble youth."

Laertes and the Priest grimly discuss the "maimed rites" offered for one whose death was "doubtful," facing not each other but the grave, which rests between them and the camera. At Laertes' command, the pallbearers lower the body into the grave, the camera following the figure in the winding sheet, her face exposed, to the dirt floor. When Laertes rebukes the "churlish priest" with the innocence of "my sister," the camera cuts again to Hamlet to register the shock and pain of his recognition that it is Ophelia who is being buried. Returning to the funeral party, the camera shows Gertrude casting her "sweets" upon Ophelia and then moves into the grave to spy on the resting form, with funeral sprigs now decking the white cocoon. Laertes turns his head sharply toward Gertrude at her wistful reference to Hamlet. Provoked and resentful, folding his hands and looking once more at his dead sister, he curses the man responsible for his sister's—and his father's—death. With the cry "Hold off the earth awhile," he stays the gravedigger's ready shovel and descends into the grave, tenderly kissing his sister and pulling the white cloth over her face, then emotionally calls for the earth to be piled on the two of them. This is Hamlet's cue to advance.

Moving round the sarcophagus toward the funeral party, the shouting Prince challenges Laertes' grief, as the stunned and motionless mourners look on. Crouched in the grave, Laertes listens in amazement to this ranting voice. When Hamlet identifies himself, Laertes snarls "The devil take thy soul!" and, matching the fury of the Prince, leaps out of the grave to clutch at Hamlet's throat. Their scuffle is brief but violent, Hamlet throwing Laertes to the ground (an action he will later repeat in the dueling sequence). They are parted when Horatio grabs Hamlet and moves him upstage of the grave and two of the pallbearers seize Laertes, holding him in the right foreground. Still shouting his challenges, Hamlet, restrained now by his mother in the upstage left corner of the space, professes his love for Ophelia, even as Laertes, confined in the downstage right corner, struggles to break free. Claudius briefly enters the space between them to pronounce, "O, he is mad, Laertes," to be followed by Gertrude, who approaches Laertes as Hamlet, at last standing free, sustains his angry hyperbole. It is to a breathless and agonized Laertes that she also offers the assurance "This is mere madness." Finally, Hamlet approaches Laertes to ask, "What is the reason that you use me thus?" Upon the Prince's "I loved you ever," Laertes literally spits his defiance at the enemy who claims to be a friend. His passion spent, Hamlet responds to the gesture dismissively, "But it is no matter," and, turning away, almost casually issues his exit threat: "The cat will mew, and dog will have his day."

In this production, the visual connection between Hamlet and Laertes in the graveyard is understated. Hamlet does not leap into the gaping grave to join the grieving brother, and, when they grapple, they are quickly parted. But the strategy of the staging is nonetheless to establish the connection, first through generating stage parallels that complement those the language already suggests and, secondly, through directing the energy of the sequence toward Hamlet and Laertes' efforts at physical contact.

Hamlet does not see Laertes when the funeral procession enters; he discovers the identity of both Laertes and Ophelia by listening to Laertes' voice. Similarly, Laertes does not see Hamlet when he advances from behind the sarcophagus; the grieving brother leaps out of the grave only after Hamlet's voice proclaims himself the Dane. Just as Hamlet appears to materialize from the sarcophagus that concealed him, so Laertes materializes from Ophelia's grave. The brief scuffle between the two is tremendously animated, but the stage image of the two being parted and restrained prevails over the quick, almost blurred, struggle that momentarily joins them.

From the point of their parting, the intention of each of the two actors is to get at the other, the obstacle being one or more characters restraining them. The stage image of Hamlet in the upstage left corner and Laertes in the downstage right suggests a boxing or wrestling ring, in which the refereeing forces unfairly keep the two from coming together. Both strain toward the arena between them, where the two meet only in expectations. Finally, with Hamlet unharnessed and Laertes still in tow, Laertes can only spit at Hamlet over the distance that separates them, unable otherwise to establish contact with the opponent for whom circumstances, intention, and fate insist on the connection.

At the end of the sequence, when Hamlet walks off, Claudius immediately turns to the now unleashed Laertes first to scold him and then, having dismissed Gertrude, to stand face-to-face with his confederate, his arms in a reassuring gesture resting on the young man's shoulders. The stage image of this conspiring pair, who in the aftermath of the graveyard altercation remind themselves of their plot against Hamlet's life, becomes the one consummated physical connection in the sequence. But the other image, of the straining and restrained angry brothers in grief, is also telling. If the two could not connect in 5.1, surely the fencing match of 5.2 will provide satisfaction.

The Graveyard Sequence in the Olivier *Hamlet*

In the graveyard sequence in the Laurence Olivier film, with Olivier directing and playing the central role, Hamlet and Horatio (Norman Wooland) crouch at the newly dug grave that yielded Yorick's skull. As Hamlet completes his musing on this relic of the court jester, with significant reference to "my lady's chamber" (the Alexander passage is cut), a tolling bell alerts him to the advancing procession. Tossing the skull into the grave, he joins Horatio in mounting a rise in the foreground where they conceal themselves alongside a tomb. Upstage, the figure of the Priest (Russell Thorndike) moves steadily toward the grave, followed by soldiers carrying the unenclosed body of Ophelia (Jean Simmons) atop a litter. From their position by the tomb, their backs now to the camera, Hamlet notices the King (Basil Sydney), the Queen (Eileen Herlie), and the courtiers and wonders who is being buried with such "meager" rites. (In this production, it is Horatio who explains that the diminished ceremony betokens a suicide.) Where in the BBC version Hamlet had no view of the funeral from his hiding place, here he watches every movement, pointing and excitedly repeating "Mark," both before and after he recognizes Laertes (Terence Morgan) on the latter's question "What ceremony else?" Only distance prevents him from identifying the body. After the exchange with the Priest, an overhead shot shows Laertes, Gertrude, and Claudius standing by the grave while soldiers lower the white-clad body into it. As the body disappears, Laertes raises his voice to rebuke the Priest, and the camera cuts to Hamlet and Horatio clutching each other in recognition.

Laertes' leap into the grave is more histrionic in the Olivier production than in the BBC. When Gertrude has strewn her flowers, and after the grieving brother, gazing intently into the grave, has pronounced his curse, a spade suddenly passes before the camera from which the Priest in the right foreground plucks and casts a handful of dirt. Laertes abruptly halts the burial, flinging up his arm, and drops from the frame. In a long shot, he is seen descending into the earth and then lifting Ophelia in his arms, so that the heads of the two are visible above ground level. First scattering at the gesture, the funeral party then gathers and stoops at the head of the grave. All are startled by the dominating voice of Hamlet, which sounds before he appears. The King bolts upright, and all eyes turn upward from the brother's embrace to the materializing Dane.

If Laertes' gesture in leaping into the grave was flamboyant, Hamlet's appearance is equally so. Striding into and almost filling the frame, his back to the camera, Hamlet stands among the tombstones with his arms outstretched, yards away from the funeral party, which appears above the line formed by his arms. Laertes and Ophelia appear in the angle formed by Hamlet's right arm and side. It is from this position that Laertes, dropping his sister and scrambling from the grave, charges up the rise toward Hamlet. In the struggle that ensues, Laertes wraps his fingers around Hamlet's neck and drives him downhill. But the camera leaves the grappling pair for a tracking shot of the King commanding "Pluck them asunder" and Gertrude rushing to Hamlet. He is now by the grave, where others are holding the young men apart. Hamlet pauses in his fury only long enough to tell his mother, "I loved Ophelia." As in the BBC production, he breaks free before Laertes, in time to show he "can rant as well as thou." He then turns away while Gertrude intervenes with Laertes but returns with the question, sincerely put, "What is the reason that you use me thus?" When a silent Laertes offers him no satisfaction, he turns away again, this time for good, speaking his exit lines with his back to everyone as he leaves the cemetery. The others follow, leaving Laertes crouched at Ophelia's grave, weeping, and Claudius standing above him, ready for the plotting of Hamlet's death.

As in the BBC production, Hamlet does not leap into the grave with Laertes, but there are complementary movements that otherwise establish the connection between the two young men. Just as Hamlet drops Yorick's skull back into the open grave after caressing it, so Laertes drops the body of Ophelia, whom he held in an embrace. The grave had indeed become "my lady's chamber." In the embrace between brother and sister, Laertes plays not only loving brother but lover as well—the image of the bridal bed union of Hamlet and Ophelia that Gertrude wished in her epitaph. The two men do, of course, come together in the struggle, though the camera chooses not to linger upon them. And, as in the BBC version of the graveyard sequence, they strain to reach one another when others pluck them asunder.

Perhaps the most significant difference in Olivier's treatment of the Laertes/Hamlet connection is a consequence of his cuts and transposition of scenes. Thus he makes the plotting of Hamlet's death, 4.7 in Shakespeare's scripts, the immediate sequel to the graveyard scene. The change strongly colors the interpretation of Laertes. While Shakespeare shows Laertes to be a willing confederate of Claudius, with an independent taste for treachery, even before he learns of his sister's death, Olivier turns Laertes into an avenging conspirator as a direct result of Ophelia's death and of his confrontation with Hamlet at her funeral. The design is pointedly realized as Laertes and Claudius in the aftermath mount the steps to the castle and Laertes pauses at the arched entryway to look back on the gravesite. Framed by the arch, he reflects, in lines lifted from the beginning of 4.7, "And so I have a noble father lost, / A sister driven into desperate terms. . . ." At this point, the camera reverses angles to show Laertes from the back in the doorway and over his shoulder the gravedigger covering Ophelia with earth, as the young man continues to celebrate "her perfections." On these words, he turns to enter the castle, vowing "But my revenge will come." In short, Olivier shapes a Laertes that is powerfully motivated to engage in the treacherous enterprise of the dueling sequence.

The Dueling Sequence in the Texts

From the brief but passionate struggle in the graveyard, Hamlet and Laertes move in the final scene to the dishonorable duel of honor that will bring vengeance, forgiveness, and death to them both.

The dueling sequence in this final scene contains several opportunities for the visual articulation of the connection between the two young men. Opening the sequence with an invitation to Hamlet—"Come, Hamlet, come and take this hand from me" (5.2.223)—Claudius puts Laertes' hand into Hamlet's. (In Q1, Hamlet offers his hand himself—Bertram and Kliman, 256.) Though modern editions often provide the gratuitous stage direction *"The King puts Laertes' hand into Hamlet's,"* none speculates as to when the two part. They may, in fact, retain the posture throughout the verbal exchange—Hamlet's apology and Laertes' acceptance—that ensues. An audience, knowing Laertes' plot, may find the image of the two young men hand in hand in a gesture of trust an ironic comment on Laertes' dishonor and on Hamlet's naïveté or his disingenuous apology. Laertes may drop Hamlet's hand when Hamlet lamely blames his offense on his distraction, registering skepticism and distrust. He may drop the hand before his own reply—"I am satisfied in nature" (242)—unable to retain the gesture through his lying. The two may part as quickly as Claudius joins them, or they may continue to touch flesh through Hamlet's endorsement of this "brothers' wager." Once Hamlet calls for the foils (Claudius does so in Q1—Bertram and Kliman, 258), it seems that they would, in anticipation of the weapons, drop hands; yet when Hamlet praises Laertes' swordsmanship and Laertes thinks he is being mocked, Hamlet affirms his sincerity by referring to their clasp—"No, by this hand" (256)—or, perhaps, by offering his hand again. Clearly, the hand-joining is an opportunity for both of the characters to express the emotional complexity of the moment, but so also is it a visual reminder to an audience of the connection between the two.

All eyes in the state chamber and in the offstage audience are fixed on this agile pair for the minutes that sustain the duel. However the fight is orchestrated, with Hamlet scoring two hits and a draw, the climactic third hit—Laertes' wounding of Hamlet—and Hamlet's increased riposte provide an animated image of the two fiercely fighting for their honor, their revenge, and their lives. Though modern editions often suggest that Laertes' "Have at you now!" (305) signals his touching of Hamlet with the poisoned sword, the exact moments of Laertes' hit, of the exchange of swords and of Hamlet's retaliation are undefined in Q2 or F. Q1 is more specific: it eliminates the tie bout and provides a stage direction after the abbreviated interaction between Hamlet and Laertes that follows Gertrude's drinking of the poisoned cup: *"They catch one anothers Rapiers, and both are wounded, Leartes falles downe, the Queene falles downe and dies"* (Bertram and Kliman, 262). Presumably, as soon as Hamlet is hit, he knows that Laertes' rapier is unbated and therefore forces the exchange of weapons in the "scuffling" that is called for in the F stage direction (ibid., 263). Laertes' touch and Hamlet's are usually played as two distinct hits, accomplished somewhere within the four half-lines that separate Osric's "Nothing neither way" (304) and Horatio's "They bleed on both sides" (307) (both absent from Q1). The second of those half-lines is the King's "Part them! They are incensed" (also absent from Q1), which may punctuate both of the fatal blows, sustained in the grappling that recalls the graveyard scuffle. In production, this portion of the duel may last several minutes, with each touch separately profiled. But staging the twin touches with the poisoned weapon as the consequences of their grappling lends force to the hapless connection between the young men.

Having both sustained fatal hits, Hamlet and Laertes bleed. Laertes informs Hamlet they are dead, tells him the "King's to blame," endorses Hamlet's slaying of Claudius—"He is justly served. / It is a poison tempered by himself" (329–30)—and exchanges forgiveness with the Prince. His last lines provide yet another opportunity for the joining of him and Hamlet. He may reach out his hand to connect with Hamlet's, as Q1 indicates: "Hamlet, before I die, here take my hand" (Bertram and Kliman, 264). Or Hamlet, after killing the King, may make his way back to Laertes for his "I follow thee" (334)—into the grave in the graveyard scene, into death in earnest now.

The Dueling Sequence in the BBC *Hamlet*

The dueling sequence in the BBC production opens with a somewhat formal tableau: Claudius, who first has the camera's attention in a close-up, stands behind the clasped hands of Laertes and Hamlet, whom he has just joined. The camera backs up to reveal the young men and, assembled upstage behind them in the spacious chamber, Gertrude and a full panoply of courtiers and attendants symmetrically arranged to observe the central action. Though the camera tarries on the extended arms and clasped hands of Hamlet and Laertes, who both wear under their dueling vests white shirts with abundant folds of material in the sleeves, even before Hamlet has completed his first line, "Give me your pardon, sir. I have done you wrong," the hands drop to the men's sides. The two stand facing each other a few feet apart, Hamlet on the right and Laertes on the left, framing the King, as Hamlet proceeds with his apology. Just after his proclamation of madness, Hamlet moves upstage left to continue his lines while holding his mother's hand, which he lightly kisses, as though apologizing to her as well. Returning to his original position, he glances at Claudius as he passes him on the phrase "Hamlet's enemy" and ends his speech facing Laertes again. The camera moves in on Laertes for his response. While Laertes delivers his lines coolly and emphatically on the issue of "no reconcilement," he then becomes more conciliatory and distinctly uncomfortable as he promises not to wrong Hamlet, virtually swallowing the words. To signal the "good faith" among them before this public competition, Claudius approvingly places his left hand on Laertes' right shoulder, while Hamlet extends his hand once again to Laertes. As they break, it is apparent that Claudius' right hand has been touching Hamlet. For an instant, the frame contains the image of hands touching in a three-way connection of villainous camaraderie and unsuspecting trust. This early orchestration of hands will characterize the strategy of this final sequence in establishing the connection between Laertes and Hamlet—and their broken connections with the King.

The duel itself develops a tension between the participants that gives a special, if unintended, force to Hamlet's remark "I'll be your foil, Laertes." The difference in demeanor is at once apparent. While Hamlet's approach to the match is high-spirited, almost lighthearted, Laertes' is deadly serious. Through the first three bouts, Hamlet's composure and flexible skill are met by Laertes' murderous daring and reckless agility. Thus, in the brief first bout, Hamlet takes Laertes by surprise, striking his dagger from his hand and, as he retrieves it, touching him on the arm. During the protracted second bout, Hamlet avoids the thrusts of his lunging opponent, knocks him down, and, when he rises, feints and stings him in the derriere. In the short but rough third bout, Hamlet again disables and disarms Laertes, bringing him to the ground, only to have Osric (Peter Gale) intervene with "Nothing neither way." Through these bouts, as the action of the combatants fills the playing space, there are several moments of body contact. But the real opportunity for connecting the two visually comes in the incensed scuffle that prompts Claudius to command their parting, a struggle that culminates in bleeding "on both sides."

In this production, Laertes' "Have at you now," nearly whispered in bitter satisfaction, does not anticipate or coincide with his wounding of Hamlet but rather marks the fatal blow already delivered. Having disarmed his opponent in the third bout, Hamlet lifts the rapier by the blade and extends it to him hilt forward; Laertes accepts it with open hand but only long enough to jab the point into the palm of Hamlet's hand. The astonished Hamlet cries out, still holding the weapon by the blade. Seeing and feeling that the blade has no protective tip, a grim Prince deliberately seizes it by the hilt with his good right hand, slowly advances on his rival, and flips his own rapier with the bated tip to Laertes.

There is at once violent play. The two are no longer fencing but fighting in earnest. This is a wild, two-man melee, with Hamlet whipping and slamming his sword at the terrified Laertes, who is clearly on the defensive. Claudius' "Part them! They are incensed" is an impotent command in this setting, for anyone attempting to come between these raging fires could well give up his life. The one minute that ensues between Osric's "Nothing neither way," after which Laertes twists his sword in Hamlet's hand, and Horatio's "They bleed on both sides," spoken seconds after Hamlet's weapon touches Laertes' shoulder, is thus filled with exciting but deadly combat. But it is Laertes' touching of the poisoned rapier to Hamlet's hand and Hamlet's touching of that same weapon to Laertes' shoulder, not the physical embrace of combat, that reunites the pair. Earlier, the two had stood facing each other, the one to apologize, the other to express his satisfaction in nature. Now, their bleeding wounds suggest a perverse replay of that preliminary ceremony, where hands and shoulders were center stage, an ostensible token of trust. As Laertes stands unsteadily, informing Hamlet that they are both dead, that the "treacherous instrument is in thy hand," the camera frames Laertes and the rapier, extended by Hamlet from outside the frame. Like Hamlet, who earlier received the envenomed tip into his hand, Laertes now reaches for it, but he is unable to complete the gesture. As Hamlet recoils, Laertes sinks under the effect of the poison.

The eyes of the assembled courtiers are on Laertes as they form a corridor along the arena in which the dead body of Gertrude lies upstage left, the dying Laertes lies downstage right, and Hamlet and Claudius stand between. Summoning what strength he still possesses, Laertes implicates the King, and Hamlet, hearing the accusation, self-mockingly acknowledges the doubly—trebly—deadly plan. Strangely hopeful that he might still make amends, Claudius approaches Hamlet, his arms outstretched, about to come to rest on Hamlet's shoulders. But this final stage image of the connection between Claudius and his surrogate son is aborted, not only by an audience's recollection of the same embracing posture between Claudius and Laertes in the graveyard—which Laertes has now abjured—but also by Hamlet's response to Claudius' villainy. Smiling ironically, Hamlet turns to the advancing Claudius and drives into his midsection the envenomed sword that has slain both him and Laertes. Then, pursuing the stricken King to a table stage right, the Prince flings him backward across the tabletop and pours the poisoned drink into his mouth, before he contemptuously pushes his body to the floor.

The camera is now low so that it may accommodate the prone Laertes in the foreground, the fallen Claudius, and, upstage of both, a weakened Hamlet leaning on the table. As Laertes calls for Hamlet to exchange forgiveness with him, once again, the hand-joining becomes a visual image of their kinship. Laertes in death spasms raises his left hand, and Hamlet staggers forward to seize it and pull the struggling man to his knees. Laertes holds on desperately, barely able to speak, and presses his lips to Hamlet's hand as he dies. The two young men, both of whom have lost their fathers and their beloved Ophelia, and have now accomplished their revenge and exchanged forgiveness, die within minutes of each other, victims of the same envenomed rapier that mocks the handshakes and shoulder clasps that the treacherous King insisted begin their fatal duel.

As a postlude to the carnage of so many princes in Elsinore's court, this production offers a stage image that both continues the touching of hands and shoulders and redeems the gesture as one of trust and love. Horatio, holding the dead Hamlet on his shoulder, caresses his friend's head with his hand, uniting the man whose story has so intrigued this audience and the man equipped to tell the story to those who are yet ignorant

> Of carnal, bloody and unnatural acts,
> Of accidental judgments, casual slaughters,
> Of deaths put on by cunning and forced cause,
> And, in this upshot, purposes mistook
> Fall'n on th' inventors' heads.
>
> (5.2.383–87)

The Dueling Sequence in the Olivier *Hamlet*

The Olivier dueling sequence begins with the same trumpet fanfare that sounded in 1.2 to herald the royal processional. In the vast court setting, Hamlet and Horatio stand on a downstage platform watching the six trumpeters ranged along the gallery opposite with its sweeping staircase to the main level. They begin their descent as the royal party upstage makes its progress down the staircase to triumphal music. As the more elaborate of the two processionals approaches the central space where it will meet Hamlet, it becomes apparent that the King is holding not the Queen's hand but Laertes'. As he and Hamlet approach one another in what will become the playing space for the duel, Claudius transfers Laertes' hand to Hamlet, standing between them as the two stand face-to-face, both of them costumed in tunics and shirtsleeves. (In the graveyard sequence, they were distinguished in appearance, Hamlet in sailor's garb and Laertes in courtier's apparel.) Hamlet holds

Laertes' hand throughout his humble apology, while the court, intent on Hamlet's words, gathers to listen. Laertes' response is cut in this production, replaced by the intrusion of Gertrude, who, taking her son's hand and kissing him, pairs off with him even as the King pairs off with Laertes.

In this production it is Laertes who calls for the foils, while Hamlet deposits his mother on her throne. As the young men remove their tunics and prepare for their encounter, a subtle Laertes secures the unbaited foil from Osric (Peter Cushing) and glances significantly downstage at the enthroned Claudius. The camera continues to focus attention on the two foils, bated and unbaited, throughout the sequence, underscoring the treachery to which Laertes has maliciously lent himself. Only its fatal exposure will provoke in him the recognition and remorse that make reconciliation with Hamlet possible.

Claudius' toast to Hamlet is ceremonious here, the kettledrums and trumpets responding to his call. A zooming camera finally holds the entire court within its frame, the toasting King on the throne, center stage, Hamlet and Laertes standing downstage on either side. Hamlet and Laertes go through the initiatory moments of the march, after saluting the King and flourishing their rapiers, standing for some time with blades pointed at each other as the drum rolls. The camera moves to Hamlet and his bated point, next to Laertes in the comparable position opposite him, and then focuses on the nearly touching tips of the blades before the duel begins.

This is an animated duel. The first bout is shown in full, and when Hamlet scores his "palpable hit," the King again makes a ceremonious display of drinking to Hamlet, this time dropping the poisoned "union" into the cup. The second bout, however, is heard rather than seen; the camera fixes on the troubled Gertrude and on her preoccupation with the cup of poisoned wine, until the off-camera clashing of swords ceases with Hamlet's announcing of another hit. The Queen's fatal toast, the King's sudden horror, and a grim Laertes' twinge of conscience initiate the third bout. This inconclusive exchange, again shown in full, ends with Hamlet and Laertes chest to chest, their rapiers and daggers locked. As the familiar court music sounds through the interval, the camera focuses first on Claudius staring with chagrin at Laertes and next on Laertes contemplating the dishonorable touch he is about to administer. With a look over his right shoulder at the conspiratorial Osric, he moves slowly to his left and then flashes his sword at the unsuspecting Hamlet on "Have at you now." Hamlet immediately turns, clutching his right shoulder, and, while the camera cuts from one to the other, the music dies.

Seeing that the tip of Laertes' sword is unbated, the tight-lipped Prince deliberately takes his waiting weapons from Horatio and advances on Laertes. With a sweeping blow, he quickly disarms his assailant, the rapier spinning upward and falling at his feet. Stepping on it to prevent Laertes from retrieving it, Hamlet offers Laertes his own sword, then claims the unbated weapon himself. Together with Horatio he examines the naked point and gazes at Laertes. Again advancing, he brushes aside Osric's feeble attempt to "part them" and violently engages his wronger. Finally, backing Laertes up to a column and then onto the steps of the riser leading to the throne, Hamlet delivers the point to Laertes' left wrist. The flow of blood brings gasps from the court audience, which has been responsive with applause, with cheers, and with expressions of excitement throughout. Horatio's "They bleed on both sides" is cut from this production. In its place are parallel questions: Osric to the bleeding Laertes, "How is 't, Laertes?" Horatio to the bleeding Hamlet, "how is it, my lord?"

From the floor of the throne room, caught in the arms of Osric, the dying Laertes confesses and judges himself to a Hamlet now mounted on the gallery above. The camera stays with Hamlet, replicating his perspective on Laertes below or studying his face as he hears the full extent of the treachery. It is, of course, Laertes' revelations that motivate his spectacular revenge upon the King: the electrifying leap from the gallery to destroy his antagonist below. In its aftermath, Laertes pleads with Hamlet that they exchange forgiveness. Foregrounded in his downstage right position, Laertes, lying Pietà-like in Osric's arms, reaches out his arm to Hamlet, who stands with Horatio in the upstage left corner of the frame. Though the two do not touch, the angle of the camera is such that Laertes' outstretched hand is profiled against Hamlet's white shirt. The Prince turns toward him and reaches out his hand in exoneration. The camera holds the dead Laertes in the foreground as Hamlet walks slowly upstage to the throne. Whereas the court had earlier surrounded the dying Claudius, pointing their swords at the villainous King, now they surround Hamlet, kneeling in obeisance and respect as he speaks his final words, dying in the throne.

Like the scene in which the royal family first appears (1.2) and like the play-within-the-play scene (3.2), the Olivier duel scene collects the entire court into its arena, making the reaction shots of the King and Queen, Horatio, and the courtiers as central as the Laertes/Hamlet duel. Yet despite the frequent shift in focus, it is the duel that commands attention, the duel that secures the connection between the ill-fated sons.

References

Bertram, Paul, and Bernice W. Kliman. 1991. *The Three-Text Hamlet: Parallel Texts of the First and Second Quartos and First Folio.* New York: AMS Press.

Bevington, David, ed. 1992. *The Complete Works of Shakespeare.* 4th ed. New York: Harper.

Granville-Barker, Harley. 1946–47. *Prefaces to Shakespeare.* 2 vols. Princeton: Princeton University Press.

Lusardi, James P., and June Schlueter. 1991. *Reading Shakespeare in Performance: King Lear.* Madison, N.J.: Fairleigh Dickinson University Press.

Mills, John A. 1985. *Hamlet on Stage: The Great Tradition.* Westport, Conn.: Greenwood Press.

Rosenberg, Marvin. 1992. *The Masks of Hamlet.* Newark: University of Delaware Press.

Rothwell, Kenneth S., and Annabelle Henkin Melzer. 1990. *Shakespeare on Screen: An International Filmography and Videography.* New York: Neal-Schuman.

Whose Work Is This? Loading the Bed in *Othello*

PHILIP C. MCGUIRE

LONG acclaimed as one of the four "great" Shakespearean tragedies, *Othello* has gained during this decade the additional distinction, perhaps dubious, of being the Shakespearean play most vividly invoked during the U.S. Senate's Anita Hill-Clarence Thomas hearings in October of 1991. At one point during those proceedings, Sen. Alan Simpson of Wyoming, dramatically interrupting himself to admonish, "Remember this scene," quoted with some flair Iago's lines to Othello about the value of reputation:

> Good name in man and woman, dear my lord,
> Is the immediate jewel of their souls.
> Who steals my purse steals trash; 'tis something, nothing.
> 'Twas mine, 'tis his, and has been slave to thousands.
> But he that filches from me my good name
> Robs me of that which not enriches him
> And makes me poor indeed.
>
> (3.3.168–74)[1]

"What a tragedy," Senator Simpson concluded, referring at least as much to what was unfolding in the Senate hearing room as to *Othello,* "what a disgusting tragedy!"

By thus appropriating Shakespearean words, Senator Simpson not only succeeded in casting now Justice Thomas as the victim, but he also framed the knotty, perplexing, deeply disturbing issues that those hearings brought searingly into public view in terms that the American people found familiar—as opposed to accurate—and thus reassuring. Invoking Shakespearean lines fostered the comforting sense that the Bard, at least, knew what to make of such contradictory, refractory, ineradicably messy material even if neither we the people nor our senators did. Such reassurance was all the more effective given the flagrant inadequacy of the Senate's processes and institutions—and of the senators themselves—in dealing with those issues.

Senator Simpson's use of the lines from *Othello* is a particularly striking instance of the role that Shakespeare—less imprecisely, that culturally fashioned entity that goes by the name "Shakespeare"—plays, and has long played, in the always ongoing process of cultural formation by which, in Clifford Geertz's words, "this people or that, this period or that, makes sense to itself" (167) and, I would add with emphasis, *of* itself and *for* itself. The operative word is "make." The process is one of constructing, of fashioning, at least as much as it is one of finding or discovering what is already somehow "there." *Othello* participates in that process, shaping and being shaped in ways that become clear if we look at how its final moments have been performed and edited.

As *Othello* closes, Lodovico, in his capacity as the emissary to Cyprus of the Duke and Senators of Venice, calls upon Iago to "Look on the-tragic loading of this bed" (5.2.374).[2] "This is thy work," he tells him, then adds: "The object poisons sight; / Let it be hid" (11.375–76). What is it that audiences see, and have seen, when, responsive to Lodovico's words (even if Iago is not) they look upon the bed? What is the "object" to be hidden from their sight? They see Desdemona's body—with "whiter skin . . . than snow / And smooth as monumental alabaster" (5.2.4–5)—but is hers the only corpse tragically loading the bed? The question arises principally because of Othello's dying words: "I kissed thee ere I killed thee. No way but this, / Killing myself, to die upon a kiss" (5.2.370–71). Does Othello in fact die as his words indicate he wants to, as or after he kisses Desdemona, and does his corpse lie on the bed with, or even on, hers?

Neither the Quarto (1622) nor the Folio (1623) version of *Othello*—those closest in time to when the play was conceived and first performed—enables us to answer either of those questions. The stage direction in the Quarto is simply *"He dies"*:

> *Othello.* I kist thee ere I kild thee, no way but this.
> Killing myselfe, to die upon a kisse. *(He dies.)*

In the Folio, the corresponding stage direction is, even more simply, *"Dyes"*:

> *Othello.* I kist thee, ere I kill'd thee: No way but this,
> Killing my selfe to dye upon a kisse. *(Dyes.)*

The imprecision of the stage directions generates a spectrum, a field, a range, of possibilities in reference to which those who perform and those who edit *Othello* across the centuries can choose. The absence of specific guidance in Quarto and Folio means that the choices made regarding where and how Othello dies are all the more likely to be indicative of, and responsive to, the cultural values and assumptions prevailing (or emerging) during a given era, particularly those that are ideological in the sense of being least easily available to analysis and critique.

From the late eighteenth through the midnineteenth centuries, James R. Siemon has shown, productions consistently denied Othello the death "upon a kiss" that he desires. Siemon tells of

> stage Othellos [from that era] in their death throes struggling [but failing] to reach Desdemona: Macready dragging himself, supported by furniture, from the footlights toward the distant bed; Kean falling backwards dead just before he can kiss his Desdemona; Phelps, Wallack, and Edwin Booth dying in similar attempts; Gustavus Brooke pulling down the bed curtain over himself and revealing in the process the unkissed Desdemona; Salvini staggering backward while keeping "his full front to the audience" and dying just before he can reach the bed. (49)

Those productions established a gap between the death Othello envisions for himself and what actually occurs. The kiss he wishes to die upon is never given, and thus in them what Roderigo says of Iago proves true of Othello in his final moments: "your words and your performances are no kin together" (4.2.190–91).

Toward the end of the nineteenth century, the situation changed. Then, as Siemon explains,

> . . . actors finally do reach the bed for a kiss in the late nineteenth century, [but] they are condemned to slide or roll back off. So Edwin Forrest kisses Desdemona "while upon one knee" and then falls to the floor, and in an 1895 Henry Jewett promptbook, Othello "kisses Desdemona falls from bed and rolls down steps onto stage." (49)

When audiences at such productions—as well as those of the previous era—looked upon "the tragic loading of this bed," they saw Desdemona's corpse on the bed in what Siemon calls "lovely, lonely isolation" (50), separated from Othello's body on the floor.

The distance between the corpses visually confirmed the sense of eternal separation from his beloved that Othello, consigning himself to hell, calls down upon himself:

> Whip me, you devils,
> From the possession of this heavenly sight,

> Blow me about in winds, roast me in sulphur,
> Wash me in steep-down gulfs of liquid fire!
>
> (5.2.286–89)

Keeping Othello's corpse and Desdemona's apart establishes the possibility that "the tragic loading of this bed" and the "object [that] poisons sight" are not one and the same. In such circumstances, covering or concealing Othello's corpse because it "poisons sight" means that Desdemona's body remains visible to survivors and audiences. Looking on it, they possess "this heavenly sight" denied to the dead and now hidden Othello. Alternatively, if Desdemona's corpse is covered, both Othello, whose corpse remains visible, and the audiences are denied that "heavenly sight."

Since at least World War II, however, audiences looking on the bed on which Desdemona lies have regularly seen a radically different sight: Desdemona and Othello loading the bed together after he has died upon a kiss. They are not, as in the nineteenth century, separated in death. Instead, they are coupled in death, and thus paired they jointly constitute both "the tragic loading of this bed" and "this object [that] poisons sight." Consider as an example what is arguably one of the most widely seen productions of *Othello* in history: Stuart Burge's 1965 film, starring Laurence Olivier and based upon John Dexter's stage production for the National Theatre. Othello, who was kneeling on the bed and holding Desdemona's body upright in his arms as he spoke the speech ("Speak of me as I am") that concludes with his act of fatally stabbing himself, kisses Desdemona and dies with his arms around her. As the room empties, their corpses lie side-by-side and face-to-face, and, as the camera slowly pulls back across a room that is now empty, it remains focused, in the words of Jack J. Jorgens, "on the darkening image of the two bodies embracing on the bed" (296).

The sight offered to audiences of the Burge-Olivier movie is also the sight that six editions of *Othello* (see appendix 1) now widely used as the basis for teaching and criticism as well as performance encourage their readers to envision. They provide additional and, to my mind, even more compelling proof of how, responsive to the imprecision of Quarto and Folio stage directions, editors across a span of the three most recent decades have constructed endings for *Othello* starkly different from those available to nineteenth-century audiences. Two of the most recent of those editions—the Stanley Wells-Gary Taylor edition in the New Oxford *Complete Works* (1986) and David Bevington's in his fourth edition of *The*

Complete Works of Shakespeare (1992)—give their readers the stage direction *"He kisses Desdemona and dies."* It answers in the affirmative a question that Quarto and Folio simply pose and which prior to the late nineteenth century, productions of *Othello* answered in the negative.

Four other currently used editions provide stage directions that directly contradict the eighteenth- and nineteenth-century performance tradition that kept Othello off the bed. M. L. Ridley's Arden edition (1962, revised) specifies that Othello *"Falls on the bed, and dies."* So does G. Blakemore Evans in the Riverside edition (1974). The same stage direction, with "He" added at the beginning, is found in Normal Sanders' New Cambridge edition of *Othello* as well as Gerald Eades Bentley's Pelican edition (1969, revised). Each of these six current editions amplifies the stage directions *"He dies"* and *"Dyes"* found in Quarto and Folio *Othello,* respectively. Responsive to, serving, and shaping preferences and assumptions that are as much cultural as personal, each strives to make precise what the two earliest versions of *Othello* left imprecise, to provide answers to questions they left unanswered. In doing that, our current editions of *Othello* reduce a range of possibilities to (what will be accepted as) a single, ostensibly definitive certainty.

Two productions of *Othello* prepared for television viewing during the 1980s illustrate, in different fashions, the cultural force associated with the sight of Othello and Desdemona together in death on the bed. In a manner reminiscent of the Burge-Oliver film, Janet Suzman's 1988 production—based upon her stage production at the Market Theatre in Johannesberg, South Africa—ends with an overhead shot of the bodies of Othello and Desdemona on the bed, but the image is not a darkening one. The bodies remain fully visible, and the final credits are superimposed upon that sight, in effect compelling audiences to read the credits with reference to, and in terms of, those paired corpses. To a degree that the Burge-Olivier film with its darkening image does not, Suzman's television production exempts the audience from the playtexts' injunction—voiced by Lodovico in both Quarto and Folio—"Let it be hid." Audiences are instead given the opportunity to continue looking upon the "object [that] poisons sight" well after the play's events have ended.

Conversely, the "object" that Suzman insists on showing is one that Jonathan Miller in his 1981 production for BBC-TV keeps out of sight in a way that goes beyond "Let it be hid." In Miller's production, which has a claim along with the Burge-Olivier film to being the most widely seen in history, Othello stabs himself while sitting on the bed on which Desdemona's corpse rests, but the camera shows him from an angle that does not allow any sight of her body. Dying, he bends down after speaking of the kiss he wants to give her. As he does, however, he passes out of view of the camera and thus of the audience, who never actually see the kiss and never see Desdemona and him together in death on the bed. Lodovico forces Iago to look upon the "object [that] poisons sight," but Miller pointedly prevents his viewers from ever seeing it. It is kept from their view, kept out of their sight. Instead, the camera offers viewers the sight of those—all men and all white—who are looking on the "tragic loading of this bed" with stunned horror or, in Iago's case, smiling, sometimes giggling satisfaction. Miller can focus on the act of seeing and reacting rather than on the "object" being even because, as stage practice since 1945 and current editorial practice demonstrate, a firm consensus about what that "object" is exists. His blocking need only suggest that "object," and, given their expectations, which are both culturally determined and culturally determinative, audiences will envision what they do not actually see. In *Macbeth,* placing Duncan's murder offstage and thus out of sight forces audiences to imagine the killing, and that act of imagining involves and implicates them in the assassination. In similar fashion, Miller's production of *Othello* implicates his audiences. The camera work requires that they complete "the tragic loading of this bed" by envisioning the "object" that never poisons their sight.

Trevor Nunn's 1990 television production of *Othello*—based upon his earlier stage production for the Royal Shakespeare Company—demonstrates the persistence of the "object" poisoning "sight" that Miller's audiences are called upon to imagine rather than see. Nunn's audiences see Othello stabbing himself while standing near the bottom of the bed. He moves up along the right side of the bed, kisses Desdemona, then dies on his stomach beside her, next to hers with his left arm across her body and his face toward her as she lies on her back, her face turned upward. Audiences then watch as Iago and the other onlookers stare at the bed. Iago moves to the foot of the bed, gazing impassively, arms folded across his chest, as Lodovico orders him to "look on" his "work." As he continues to look, the camera shows audiences—as if through Iago's eyes—the two corpses lying on the bed, then returns to a shot of Iago, gradually tightening the focus onto his face so that the others standing by pass out of view. The camera then redirects the audience's gaze back to the bodies on the bed—again seen as if through Iago's eyes—after which it centers a last time on Iago's face in a very tight shot that lasts until the screen goes black. Lodovico tells Iago, "this is thy work," but Nunn's production challenges that "thy" more directly than Miller's production did. By compelling audiences to see through Iago's eyes as they "Look on the tragic loading of this bed," Nunn's production implicates them in what has happened and thus makes Iago's "work" their work as well.

Taken up as a group, the four productions I have just considered strongly suggest that, in clear contrast to our predecessors in the eighteenth and nineteenth centuries, we want at the end of the play to see—on the stage or in our mind's eyes—Othello, mortally wounded by his own hand, kiss Desdemona's corpse. We also want to see—or, if reading the playtext, to envision—Othello and Desdemona not apart but, like Romeo and Juliet, together in death. Perhaps we want that because we seek as the play closes a final glimpse of the sight, vividly invoked by what we today hear as Iago's racist talk of "an old black ram" "tupping" Brabantio's "white ewe," which we were denied at the start of the play. Perhaps we want Desdemona and Othello together, tragically loading the bed, to be the "object [that] poisons [our] sight" because attitudes toward miscegenation have shifted enough that we choose to see what earlier generations kept out of sight. Perhaps we have a craving for potent combinations of eroticism and violence that actors, audiences, editors, and readers of earlier times either lacked or were unwilling to indulge. Perhaps we want that sight because, even as it offers evidence of enduring differences (male/female, black/white, older/younger), it also affirms the power of the desire, hideously frustrated in this instance, to escape, elude, overcome, and transcend those differences—if not in this life, then in death, or even, in the case of Suzman's production, in a future South Africa free of apartheid if not in the South Africa of 1988.[3] Whatever the reasons for wanting that sight, those who perform and edit *Othello* for us, as opposed to earlier generations, ensure that we get it or, in the case of Miller's production, all that we need to envision it for ourselves.[4]

Any account of who is lying where and with whom at the end of *Othello*—including mine to this point—is incomplete if it does not address the issue of where Emilia's body lies. Mortally wounded by Iago, she asks, "O, lay me by my mistress' side" (5.2.245). What does that request mean? Is Emilia asking to be placed so that she can die beside Desdemona? If so, does she mean on the bed where Desdemona's corpse rests or *alongside* it? In either case, do audiences see her request carried out? What about the possibility that Emilia is asking to be *buried* beside Desdemona? If so, how does a production establish whether or not that request is honored?

The Quarto and Folio versions of *Othello* offer even less guidance with respect to Emilia's dying request, whatever it may mean, than they did with respect to Othello's desire to die upon a kiss. The Folio has no stage direction whatsoever:

> *Gratiano.* The woman falls:
> Sure he hath kill'd his Wife.
> *Emilia.*I, I: oh lay me by my Mistris side.
> *Gratiano.* Hee's gone, but his wife's kill'd.

The Quarto does provide a stage direction:

> *Gratiano.* The woman falls, sure he has kild his wife.
> *Emilia.* I, O lay me by my mistresse side. (*Exit* Iago.)
> *Gratiano.* Hee's gone, but his wife's kild.

Unfortunately, "*Exit* Iago" says nothing about Emilia. Later, after what prove to be Emilia's last words, the Quarto (but not the Folio) provides another stage direction:

> Moore, she was chast, she lov'd thee cruell Moore,
> So come my soule to blisse, as I speake true;
> So speaking as I thinke, I die, I die. *(She dies.)*

"She dies" corresponds to the stage directions at the moment of Othello's death: *"He dies"* (Quarto) and *"Dyes"* (Folio). In all six of the current editions considered earlier, the editors routinely add information—found in neither Quarto nor Folio—specifying how (with a kiss) and where (on the bed) Othello dies. The same editors' treatment of Emilia is markedly and revealingly different. As appendix 2 demonstrates, all but one of them follow Quarto and Folio in indicating nothing whatsoever about the response to Emilia's dying request and in providing no additional information about how and where this woman, who is neither the daughter of a (Venetian) senator nor the wife of a general, dies. David Bevington alone breaks with the long and still dominant editorial practice of following Quarto and Folio in passing over Emilia's request in silence. He chooses to make specific what Quarto, Folio, and his fellow editors leave vague. Expanding the *"Exit"* that Folio gives[5] following Montano's "I'll after that same villain, / For 'tis a damnéd

slave" (250–51), Bevington provides the following stage direction: "*Exit* [*with all but Othello and Emilia, who has been laid by Desdemona's side*]." In breaking sharply with prevailing editorial practice, including Bevington's own earlier editorial work,[6] that stage direction is evidence not only of his astuteness but also of the current concern, in Shakespearean scholarship and in the culture-at-large, with matters of gender.

Increasingly intense over the past two decades, that concern predisposes one to attend to women characters in general and, in this case, Emilia specifically. It also allows one to see how, collectively and cumulatively sustained over the centuries, the editorial silence regarding where Emilia lies arises out of and reinforces long-standing cultural values and assumptions so deeply embedded that they have been hidden from sight. The silence that has long been Emilia's editorial fate is revealingly congruent with why and how she is slain. She dies at the hands of Iago, her husband, because, determined to testify on Desdemona's behalf, she refuses to be silent. She defies his repeated commands as her husband that she stop talking: "Go to, charm your tongue. . . . I charge you get you home. . . . "Zounds, hold your peace. . . . "Be wise, and get you home" (190, 201, 226, 230). "Let heaven and men and devils," she declares, "let them all, / All, all, cry shame against me, yet I'll speak" (228–29). The silence that editors overwhelmingly observe with respect to where Emilia's body lies is, effectively if not intentionally, an extension of the "work" Iago does when, responding to her defiance, he mortally stabs her. As editors, they wrap her in a silence equivalent to what he must impose on her with sword or dagger. By treating the wife who speaks in defiance of her husband's command as a character unworthy of attention or comment, editorial authority aligns itself with the husbandly authority that Iago murderously asserts.

Bevington's stage direction is not only a break with long-established editorial practice; it is also at odds with the stage history of *Othello*. It signals and accelerates a shift, an adjustment, now (as always) underway in the cultural field of vision—in the ensemble of values, beliefs, practices, and proscriptions that both arise from and determine what "this people or that, this period or that" will allow themselves to choose to see. I have not done my own study of that history, but the evidence now available to me suggests that rarely, if ever, is Emilia's request honored in performance, whether that request is taken to mean "let me die at Desdemona's side" (on or alongside the bed) or "bury me beside Desdemona."[7] James R. Siemon observes that in the fifty-eight promptbooks of eighteenth- and nineteenth-century productions he analyzed, "Emilia is never granted her wish to be laid by Desdemona although some productions provide a 'couch' for her repose" (49). She as well as Othello are kept from Desdemona, whose "lovely, lonely isolation" is thus preserved. In *The Masks of "Othello,"* an exhaustive study of the play's stage history that includes productions in this century, Marvin Rosenberg makes no mention of one in which Emilia is laid by her mistress's side.[8]

In the Burge-Olivier, Suzman, Miller, and Nunn productions, no one lays Emilia beside Desdemona, but those productions do not (mis?)treat her request with the theatrical equivalent of the editorial silence to which, Bevington excepted, appendix 2 attests. In the Burge-Olivier production, Emilia, stabbed from behind by Iago as she stands at the foot of the bed stroking Desdemona's hair, sinks to the floor, leaning against the bed. Gratiano, Desdemona's uncle, moves to her and crouches beside her, but on hearing her ask to be placed by "my mistress' side," he stands erect, perhaps shocked or startled, and neither he nor anyone else acts upon her request. Emilia speaks her final lines with her head close to Desdemona's—a configuration that briefly privileges the two women—and she then dies, falling backward to the floor. The camera denies audiences any subsequent view of her. Thus, she is, in effect, hidden from sight.

Both the Miller and the Suzman productions show Emilia struggling, unassisted, to reach Desdemona's side. In Miller's production, no one on stage—and they are all men—responds in any way to her request or even acknowledges it. Viewers see everyone but Othello exit, reacting not to Emilia's words but to Iago's attempt to escape, and Othello, who remains in the room, provides no help. Emilia is left to make her way unaided and in pain from the foot of the bed, where she fell when Iago stabbed her, past Othello, who does not move to assist her, to a point almost level with Desdemona's shoulder. There she dies, not on the bed but in a quasi-kneeling position beside it, her head coming to rest near her lady's side. When Othello, moving to get the other "weapon in this chamber" (5.2.261), walks out of the picture, the camera briefly remains on the two dead women, registering them together and thus momentarily privileging them. That, however, is the last audiences see of them. Swinging away from them, the camera then follows Othello across the room as he looks for another sword, and the rest of the scene—including, as discussed before, his dying kiss—is choreographed and shot in a way that keeps out of sight not only Desdemona's corpse but also Emilia's, kneeling in death at her side.

The Emilia in Suzman's production specifically addressed "Lay me by my mistress' side" to Othello. He does not help her, but as if clearing a space for her, he reacts by backing away from the head of the bed where he has been crouching. Struggling unassisted like her counterpart in Miller's production, this Emilia manages to climb partly onto the bed and dies there holding Desdemona's left hand. With a gesture that has no equivalent in Miller's production, Othello acknowledges her devotion to Desdemona by closing her sightless eyes. As in the Miller production, she then passes out of view as he searches for a weapon, but the Suzman production, in contrast to Miller's, gives its viewers another sight of her. A tightly focused head shot ensures that Suzman's viewers, unlike Miller's, see the dying Othello kiss Desdemona then, resting his head on her bosom, expire. The camera then follows the line of Desdemona's left arm and moves slowly across Emilia's body, directing attention to her a last time. However, the production's final shot, over which the credits run, keeps Emilia's corpse out of sight as it shows Othello and Desdemona together in death on the bed.

In Nunn's production, Emilia specifically addresses her request to be placed at Desdemona's side to Gratiano, but, as in the other three productions, neither he nor anyone else acts upon it. Unaided, the mortally wounded Emilia reaches for and takes Desdemona's left hand in hers, and while their hands are together, the camera allows audiences to see the wedding ring each woman wears. Pulling herself to a nearly erect position besides the bed, Emilia, singing "Willow, willow, willow" (5.2.257), smooths Desdemona's hair and tidies the sheets of the bed in which she has been strangled. That final act of service to her mistress done, Emilia moves away from the bed and sits in a chair, from which she speaks her final lines:

> Moor, she was chaste. She loved thee, cruel Moor
> So come my soul to bliss as I speak true.
> So speaking as I think, alas, I die.
>
> (5.2.258–60)

Looking for a weapon, Othello passes between the camera and her as, dying, she slips to the floor and out of sight of the audience, who do not see her again.

By acknowledging and, in different ways and to different degrees, briefly privileging Emilia's dying, Burge, Miller, Suzman, and Nunn go beyond the prevailing editorial silence. Each, however, then proceeds to marginalize Emilia, hiding her corpse from sight, subordinating it to the vision—actual or imagined—of Desdemona and Othello together in death on the bed. Bevington's stage direction specifying that Emilia *"has been laid by Desdemona's side"* presumes that one or more of the watching men assist her, in contrast to the four productions considered to this point, each of which conspicuously establishes that no one responds to her request to "lay me by my mistress' side." The stage direction is ambiguous in the same way that her request is. What does *"by Desdemona's side"* mean? If it is taken to mean beside Desdemona on the bed (rather than alongside the bed), Bevington's stage direction provides a basis for privileging Emilia's death and her relationship to Desdemona more fully and centrally than any of the four productions does.

Thanks in part to Bevington's stage direction and to feminist concerns, it is now easier to envision yet another, different loading of that bed, a loading that pairs Desdemona and Emilia in death rather than Desdemona and Othello. The now-conventional sight of Desdemona and Othello together in death on the bed emphasizes the fact of miscegenation, thereby fostering the impression that the problem is a function of this particular marriage (including the race and personalities of these two spouses) and of society's racist response to it. The sight of Desdemona with Emilia (rather than Othello) is compatible with and thus authorized by the words of Folio and Quarto *Othello,* yet it has long been hidden from view—absent from productions and ignored by editors and critics alike.

Were audiences presented with—and readers encouraged to envision—such a sight, they would find themselves challenged to face a gruesome truth about *Othello* that is too rarely acknowledged and too consistently hidden from view: what today's culture allows and prompts us to see as sexism is at least as virulent as the racism we can see there. What happens to *every* wife in this play is at least as bad as, if not worse than, what happens to the only black person in it. Othello is horribly, wickedly misled, but his death is self-inflicted, a choice that he makes and carries out. No woman in the play gets a similar chance to give her own life its closing definition by bringing it to an end herself. "I'll kill myself for grief" (5.2.199), Emilia laments, but she dies at Iago's hand, not her own. When she asks Desdemona, "O, who hath done this deed," Desdemona claims responsibility: "Nobody; I myself" (11.127–128). Patently at odds with the facts, her claim, with its equation of "nobody" and "I myself," registers just how little control she has had over her own dying. In fact, every woman in the play who is a wife is slain, and those who kill them are their husbands. Only one of the three women who appears on stage and speaks during *Othello* does not have a husband, and she is the only one whom audiences do not see killed. That one woman is Bianca, and she—perhaps (again) not coincidentally—is what Othello takes Desdemona to be: a whore.

Were one to see (or, if reading, to envision) Desdemona and Emilia paired to death—the "tragic loading" of a bed on which Othello's corpse did not also lie—that sight, fashioned from among the diverse possibilities that Quarto and Folio versions of *Othello* present, would accentuate their common fate as women murdered by their husbands, thus focusing attention upon the institution of marriage rather than upon the particulars of a specific marriage that is miscegenous. Emilia dies not only because of Iago's malevolence but also because her refusal to stop speaking at his command violates the ideal of wifely obedience, of which, ironically, Desdemona herself is the paragon. When, in the presence of the Duke and Senators of Venice, Desdemona's father Brabantio asks her, "Do you perceive in all this noble company / Where most you owe obedience," she eloquently insists that her duties as a wife have displaced those of a daughter:

> You are the lord of duty,
> I am hitherto your daughter. But here's my husband;
> And so much duty as my mother showed
> To you, preferring you before her father,
> So much I challenge that I may profess
> Due to the Moor my lord.
>
> (1.3.184–91)

Desdemona later demonstrates her dutiful obedience to the Moor she has taken as her husband and lord. In the presence of Lodovico and of those who have accompanied him to Cyprus in his capacity as the representative of the Duke and Senate, Othello strikes her, then orders her to leave: "out of my sight" (4.1.250). "I will not stay to offend you," she responds and begins to depart, prompting Lodovico to comment: "Truly, an obedient lady" (252). When Lodovico asks Othello to "call her back," Othello obliges, then, with sexually drenched sarcasm, declares, "And she's obedient, as you say, obedient, / Very obedient" (260–61).

Emilia, in contrast, refuses to obey her husband's commands during the final moments of *Othello.* When Iago orders, "get you home," she refuses: "I will not" (5.2.230). "Tis proper I obey him," she says as he tries to silence her, "but not now" (202). Earlier, Emilia had valued her husband's desires more than her duties to her mistress; she took and gave to him the handkerchief Desdemona dropped and then, despite her dismay, did not tell her what had become of it. Now, when "My mistress here lies murdered in her bed" (192), she reverses those priorities, subordinating her duties as wife to her obligations as Desdemona's serving lady. "I am bound to speak" (191), she declares and, at the cost of her life, proceeds to "speak true" (259). In so doing she proves herself to be true to, faithful to, Desdemona, even though such truth requires violating, being false to, her duties as Iago's wife.

Desdemona's dying words also illustrate the limits and contradictions of marital fidelity. When Emilia asks, "O, who has done this deed," Desdemona answers: "Nobody, I myself, farewell: / Commend me to my kind lord, O, farewell!" (128–29). Those words are her final expression of her love for Othello, but they are also a distortion of what audiences have seen happen. In contrast to Emilia, who persists in speaking "true" no matter what the consequences for her husband, Desdemona dies conforming to the ideal of the wife faithful to the point of subordinating all to the welfare of her lord and husband. What she declares before the Senate when asking to accompany Othello to Cyprus remains true even now: "My heart's subdued / Even to the very quality of my lord" (1.3.253–54).[9] More true to her "kind lord" than to the facts of her own murder, she is, even with her last breath, an exemplar of wifely fidelity. In an irony that makes excruciatingly clear the limits and contradictions of such fidelity, Othello takes Desdemona's last words protecting him as proof that she is the false wife he has killed her for being. He insists on telling (what he thinks is) the truth: "She's like a liar gone to burning hell, / 'Twas I that killed her" (5.2.137–38).

In *Othello* both the murder of Desdemona and its full disclosure require violating the marital bond. On one level, that is proof of the havoc Iago has wrought in perverting relationships. On another, it is an indictment of the ideas of wifely fidelity and obedience as well as the conception and practice of marriage those ideals buttress. Seeing Desdemona and Emilia paired in death would foreground the conflict during the final moments of *Othello* between two kinds of truth, two kinds of fidelity: to one's husband and to the facts as one knows them. Desdemona is true to the former, and Emilia, ultimately, to the latter. Perhaps the most telling critique of the institution of marriage that it is now possible to see the play offering is that both Desdemona, the wife who is true to her husband, and Emilia, the wife who insists on speaking "true" even if that means being false to her husband, die murdered by their spouses. Neither form of truth enables either wife to survive.

By having Emilia in her final moments subordinate her marriage to Iago to her relationship with the lady she serves, the play both repeats and varies the realignment of priorities Othello carries out at the conclusion of act 3, scene 3, when he subordinates his marriage to Desdemona to his relationship with Iago, who, in what is tantamount to a perversion of the marriage vow, pledges to serve him with exclusive and total loyalty: "I am your own forever" (3.3.495). In each instance, the bond between two persons of the same sex overrides the bond between husband and wife. Othello comes to value his lieutenant more than his wife, Emilia her mistress more than her husband. What Emilia does in her final moments is also a variation of what Iago pledges when he vows absolute loyalty to Othello: she gives herself totally to "wrong'd" Desdemona's "service" (3.3.483). The sight of Emilia (rather than Othello) lying in death on the bed with Desdemona would accentuate the challenge that her final allegiance to Desdemona poses to the notion—deeply embedded in English-speaking cultures over the centuries *Othello* has been performed and powerfully affirmed by the pairing of Desdemona and Othello on the bed—that marriage has primacy among the relationships humans form.

Oliver Parker's 1995 film of *Othello* places Emilia by her mistress's side on the bed, and in so doing it breaks with centuries of performance and editorial practice. Wounded by Iago, Emilia falls toward the floor, and the man, possibly Gratiano, who catches her finds her blood on his hand as she asks, "Lay me by my mistress' side." Audiences do not see his response. Instead, the film shifts out of the room as it follows Iago's flight and the pursuit, which ends with him knocked to the floor and kicked in the room where Roderigo, the other person in the play whom Iago kills with his own hands, lies dying. The film then cuts to a shot of Desdemona's lifeless face as audiences hear Emilia speaking the beginning of what will be her final lines: "What did thy song bode, lady?" (5.2.255). As Emilia continues speaking the camera shows her to be lying by her mistress's (right) side. Her request—in contrast to that of countless other Emilias—has been heeded. On "I die," her eyes close, and the camera holds, briefly, on her face. Gazing on that sight, audiences hear Lodovico's voice beginning to ask, "Where is this rash and most unfortunate man" (5.2.291), then see him enter. As Othello, sitting on a chest near the foot of the bed, answers—"That's he that was Othello. Here I am" (5.2.292)—visible behind him are the bodies of Emilia and Desdemona. Thus, Parker's *Othello* makes visible a sight—consistent with Quarto and Folio—that had been hidden from previous audiences across more than two centuries: the two murdered wives paired in death on the bed and thus part of what Lodovico will shortly call its "tragic loading."

However, as the Parker film moves to its conclusion it discloses the difficulty—in the current cultural situation—of actually confronting that sight, of looking steadily, directly upon it and its implications. Once glimpsed, the sight of the two murdered wives together on the bed is subsequently hidden, or at least displaced, in a manner that is itself revealing. Parker's audiences never again see the two women paired together on the bed. Instead, they are subsequently seen only when one (or both) of the men who were their husbands is also visible. Othello delivers the speech that concludes with his self-inflicted death wound standing at the foot of the bed, with his back to it, facing those to whom he is speaking and the camera, which is positioned so that audiences cannot see the corpses of Desdemona and Emilia. After stabbing himself with a dagger that Cassio secretly passes to him as an act of loving service to the man whose lieutenant he still considers himself to be, Othello sits back onto the bed, then pulls himself slowly, in severe pain, along the bed until—in accord with current performance and editorial practice—he can kiss Desdemona's lips. The camera's focus remains tight on Othello's face, and as he bends down to kiss Desdemona, her face and, beyond her, Emilia's face come briefly into view. The shot associates the dying Othello with the dead wives. Then, as Othello's lips touch Desdemona's, Emilia's face disappears from view—eclipsed, so to speak, by the reunion in that kiss of husband and wife. After that kiss, Othello expires, falling to Desdemona's left, on his front with his face turned toward hers. The camera's focus is on the back of Othello's head, and neither Desdemona nor Emilia is visible. Thus audiences are strongly prompted to envision the bed tragically loaded with the bodies of Desdemona, of her black husband, and of the white woman (also a wife) who was her attendant, but they are never permitted actually to see that sight. In fact, the film denies them that sight even when Lodovico roughly forces Iago to his knees at the foot of the bed, demanding that he "look on the tragic loading of this bed." Parker's audiences see Iago looking on his "work"—much as Miller's audiences do—but they do not see the "work" itself, do not see the bodies of Desdemona, Emilia, *and* Othello, which are (kept) out of sight, hidden.

Were audiences compelled not just to envision but actually to "look upon" those three bodies, they would be confronting an aspect of *Othello* to which recent critics such as Karen Newman[11] have directed attention. In *Othello* (white) women are not simply juxtaposed to blackness but also linked to it as elements of that which the prevailing social order, masculine as well as white, posits as the Other. *Othello* is, after all, the only Shakespearean tragedy in which the protagonist is a black man, and it is also, perhaps not coincidentally, the only one with a villain, a white man, whose death is not mandated by the Shakespearean playtext(s). In fact, the only characters whom audiences across the centuries have seen die during the final scene are the play's only black man and the only women in it who are wives.

Although Parker's film elects not to show its audiences the bed tragically loaded with the bodies of Desdemona, Emilia, and Othello, it does compel them to look upon a sight that is an even more extraordinary departure from performance and editorial practices. As Lodovico departs for Venice, the room empties except for Cassio and Iago, who has been kneeling at the foot of the bed. Iago, clearly in great pain from the wound inflicted by Othello, pulls himself onto the bed. Lying on his left side, he curls himself near the bottom of the bed, then lies there, looking directly into the camera. The next shot is of Cassio opening the window shutters and letting sunlight into the room. As he turns to look back on the bed, the camera follows his gaze, which rests upon the sight of the bed tragically loaded with three corpses and upon Iago, who, breathing slowly, lies with his head resting on Othello's knee, amid what Lodovico has said is his "work." Iago is looking not at that "work" but unflinchingly into the camera and thus at the audience(s), at us. What Parker's audiences look upon is a sight that is as far, perhaps, as one could reasonably envision from the sight, presented to audiences of the eighteenth and nineteenth centuries, of Desdemona's corpse in "lovely, lonely isolation" on the bed.

That final shot of the loaded bed gives way to a one of a sunset over the sea and to a sequence showing a burial at sea. When two wrapped bodies (Othello and Desdemona? Desdemona and Emilia?) are dropped from the longboat, the camera follows them as they plummet into the depths, into a darkness that fills the screen and hides them from sight.

The question of where Emilia and Othello lie as or after each of them dies is not unlike a question that the play, in both its Quarto and Folio versions, has Desdemona ask at a crucial juncture—directly after the scene in which Othello judges Desdemona false.

That scene ends with Othello telling Iago, "Now art thou my lieutenant," and with Iago responding, "I am your own forever" (3.3.494–95). The dialogue of the next scene begins with Desdemona asking the Clown, "Do you know, sirrah, where Lieutenant Cassio lies," and he replies, "I dare not say he lies anywhere" (3.4.1–3). Their exchange plays upon at least three different meanings of "lie": to rest or recline, to dwell or reside, and to tell untruths. Later, Othello's increasingly disoriented, almost feverish musings before losing consciousness charge "lie" with sexual resonances as well:

> Lie with her? Lie on her? We say "lie on her" when they belie her. Lie with her? Zounds, that's fulsome. . . . It is not words that shakes me thus. Pish! Noses, ears, and lips.—Is't possible?—Confess—handkerchief!—O devil!
>
> *(Falls in a trance.)*
>
> (4.1.35–43)[12]

It is not too much of an exaggeration to say that *Othello* is a play about lying—about who lies where, to whom, and with whom.

"This is thy work," Lodovico tells Iago, but, as I hope this brief overview of technical and editorial practices has shown, the fact of the matter is that the process of loading the bed in *Othello*—of deciding who lies where and with whom—is not simply Iago's work. Nor, given the imprecision of Folio and Quarto stage directions, is it (as many would assert) Shakespeare's. Nor, I want to stress, is it simply the work of editors, actors, and directors. It never has been, and it is not now. It is our work too as audiences and as readers. It is "ours" in the sense that the performance choices and editorial decisions with which we are most familiar and with reference to which we constitute our *Othello*s are cultural in character, "the consequence," as Nathaniel Mackey puts it, "of actions and assumptions that are socially—rather than naturally or genetically—instituted and reinforced" (51) and, in the case of Parker's film, challenged. Those choices and decisions contribute in two ways to the ongoing process by which we today, like others before us, make sense of ourselves to ourselves, and for ourselves. They give us, as we "look on the tragic loading of this bed," an "object" that arises from, is responsive to, and shapes the consensus prevailing or developing at any given moment in history. At the same time, those choices conceal other alternatives that are equally compatible with the words of the original playtexts of *Othello*. Those alternatives—hidden from gaze as if they were objects that would poison sight—would challenge us to make different, often troubling sense to ourselves, of ourselves, and—as Senator Simpson has helped us to see—for ourselves.

Appendix 1

Ridley's Arden Edition (1962, revised)

I kiss'd thee ere I kill'd thee, no way but this,
Killing myself, to die upon a kiss.
(Falls on the bed, and dies.)

Bentley's Pelican Edition (1969, revised)

I kissed thee ere I killed thee. No way but this,
Killing myself, to die upon a kiss.
(He [falls upon the bed and] dies.)

Evans's Riverside Edition (1974)

I kiss'd thee ere I kill'd thee. No way but this,
Killing myself, to die upon a kiss.
([Falls on the bed and] dies.)

Sanders's New Cambridge Edition (1984)

I kissed thee: ere I killed thee. no way but this,
Killing myself, to die upon a kiss.
(He [falls on the bed and] dies.)

Wells and Taylor's New Oxford: *Complete Works* (1986)

I kissed thee ere I killed thee. No way but this:
Killing myself, to die upon a kiss.
(He kisses Desdemona and dies.)

Bevington's *Complete Works* (1992, 4th ed.)

I kissed thee ere I killed thee. No way but this,
Killing myself, to die upon a kiss.
([*He kisses Desdemona and*] dies.)

Appendix 2

Ridley's Arden Edition (1962, revised)

Gratiano. The woman falls, sure he has kill'd his wife
Emilia. Ay, ay, O lay me by my mistress's side. *(Exit Iago.)*

Montano.
I'll after that same villain,
For 'tis a damned slave.
(Exeunt Montano and Gratiano.)

Emilia. Moor, she was chaste, she lov'd thee, cruel Moor,
So come my soul to bliss, as I speak true;
So speaking as I think, I die, I die. *(She dies.)*

Bentley's Pelican Edition (1969, revised)

Gratiano. The woman falls. Sure he hath killed his wife.
Emilia. Ay, ay. O, lay me by my mistress' side. *(Exit Iago.)*

Montano.
I'll after that same villain,
For 'tis a damned slave.
(Exit [*Montano, with all but Othello and Emilia*]*.)*

Emilia. Moor, she was chaste. She loved thee, cruel Moor:
So come my soul to bliss as I speak true;
So speaking as I think, alas, I die. *(She dies.)*

Evans's Riverside Edition (1974)

Gratiano. The woman falls; sure he hath kill'd his wife,
Emilia. Ay, ay! O, lay me by my mistress' side. *(Exit Iago.)*
Montano.
I'll after that same villain,
For 'tis a damned slave.
(Exit [*with all but Othello and Emilia*]*.)*

Emilia. Moor, she was chaste; she lov'd thee, cruel Moor;
So come my soul to bliss, as I speak true.
So speaking as I think, alas, I die. *(Dies.)*

Sanders's New Cambridge Edition (1984)

Gratiano. The woman falls; sure he hath killed his wife.

Emilia. Ay, ay; O, lay me by my mistress' side.

Montano.
I'll after the same villain
For 'tis a damnèd slave.
(Exeunt Montano and Gratiano.)

Emilia. Moor, she was chaste; she loved thee, cruel Moor;
So come my soul to bliss, as I speak true;
So speaking as I think, I die, I die. *(She dies.)*

Wells and Taylor's New Oxford: *Complete Works* (1986)

Gratiano. The woman falls. Sure he, hath killed his wife.
Emilia. Ay, ay. O, lay me by my mistress' side. *(Exit Iago.)*

Montano.
I'll after that same villain,
For 'tis a damnèd slave.

Emilia. Moor, she was chaste. She loved thee, cruel Moor.
So come my soul to bliss, as I speak true.
So, speaking as I think, alas, I die.
(She dies.)

Bevington's *Complete Works* (1992, 4th ed.)

Gratiano. The woman falls! Sure he hath killed his wife.
Emilia. Ay, ay. O, lay me by my mistress' side.
(Exit Iago.)

Montano.
I'll after that same villain,
For 'tis a damnèd slave.
(Exit [with all but Othello and Emilia who has been laid by Desdemona's side].)

Emilia. Moor, she was chaste. She loved thee, cruel Moor.
So come my soul to bliss as I speak true.
So speaking as I think, alas, I die. *(She dies.)*

Notes

1. Quotations and line numberings follow David Bevington's *Complete Works of Shakespeare,* 4th ed. (New York: Harper, 1992). For a witty account of this moment and others like it during the hearing, see Barry G. Edelstein, "Macbluff," *The New Republic* (11 November 1991): 13.

This essay is an expanded version of a lecture—also entitled "Whose Work Is This? Loading the Bed in *Othello*"—delivered at MIT on 5 March 1992 and subsequently published as no. 33 in the MIT Working Papers in Cultural Studies series, edited by David Thorburn and, in a condensed version, in *Civitas: Cultural Studies at MIT* 2 (1993): 1–8. This version extends the original discussion in several ways, most conspicuously by taking into account two productions of *Othello* not available to me in 1992: Trevor Nunn's 1990 production for television and Oliver Parker's 1995 film. This essay does not discuss Orson Welles's 1952 film of *Othello,* restored and rereleased in late 1991, primarily because it omits the lines (and associated actions) with which I am most concerned—Emilia's request "O, lay me by my mistress' side" (5.2.245) and Othello's final words: "I kissed thee ere I killed thee. No way but this, / Killing myself, to die upon a kiss" (5.2.369–70).

2. The Quarto version of *Othello* has "tragic lodging of this bed."

3. See Orkin's essay for a discussion of the ramifications of *Othello* within South African culture. Miller's production, like the others in BBC-TV's "The Shakespeare Plays" series, was intended for worldwide distribution. By ensuring that its audiences never actually see Othello and Desdemona paired on the bed, the production reduced the possibility that it would compromise the commercial success of the series by offending broadcasting authorities and/or audiences in countries where miscegenation remains a volatile issue.

4. In doing that they are being neither more nor less true to what many like to call "Shakespeare's intentions" or "the play itself" than was Senator Simpson—or the staff member who provided him with the quotation about "good name." The senator, after all, chose not to refer to the fact that the character from whose mouth the words come is the villain of the play. Nor did he mention that Iago speaks them as part of a successful scheme to destroy the black general he ostensibly serves by convincing him that his white wife has been unfaithful. Senator Simpson also did not note that the same character who so eloquently extols the value of reputation had earlier responded to the distraught Cassio's lamentation—"I have lost my reputation. I have lost the immortal part of myself"—by dismissing "reputation as "an idle and most false imposition; oft got without merit and lost without deserving" (2.3.257–58, 262–64).

5. Quarto has "Exit Montano and Gratiano."

6. In his 1973 revision of Hardin Craig's *Complete Works of Shakespeare,* the corresponding stage direction is *"Exit* [*with all but Othello and Emilia*]*."*

7. None of the current editions with which I have worked, including Bevington's, offers a note or gloss indicating that Emilia's request may have had this meaning in the early seventeenth century. If Emilia's words did originally mean "bury me beside Desdemona," the problem arises of how in performance to convey whether or not that a request would be honored. To convey to today's audiences the sense that Emilia is asking to be buried with Desdemona, it would likely be necessary to change Emilia's words to "O, bury me by me mistress' side"—thereby subordinating textual accuracy to historical accuracy.

8. Rosenberg does note (116) that Salvini allowed Emilia to live, which is one way to sidestep the problems that her dying request poses. Another would be to cut the request. The edition of *Othello* in the Wells-Taylor New Oxford *Complete Works* adds the phrase "with Emilia body" to the final, stage-clearing *"Exeunt,"* thereby ensuring that as the play concludes her corpse is *not* lying beside Desdemona's.

9. The corresponding lines in Quarto are "My heart's subdued, / Even to the utmost pleasure of my lord." "Utmost pleasure" has sexual resonances that "very quality" does not.

10. One element of which is Bevington's stage direction that Othello "[. . . *kisses Desdemona and*] *dies.*"

11. See her "'And wash the Ethiop white': Femininity and the monstrous in *Othello.*" Another essay that draws attention to the conflation of racial and sexual differences in *Othello* is Emily C. Bartels, "Making More of the Moor: Aaron, Othello, and Renaissance Refashionings of Race."

12. The corresponding lines in Quarto are:

> Lie with her, lie on her? We say lay on her, when they bely
> her; lye with her, Zouns, that's fulsome, handkerchers, Confession,
> handkerchers. *(He fals downe.)*

References

Bartels, Emily C. 1990. "Making More of the Moor: Aaron, Othello, and Renaissance Refashionings of Race." *Shakespeare Quarterly* 41:433–54.

Bentley, Gerald Eades, ed. 1969. *Othello. The Complete Works.* Pelican edition revised. Edited by Alfred Harbage. New York: Viking.

Bevington, David, ed. 1992. *The Complete Works of Shakespeare.* 4th ed. New York: Harper.

Craig, Hardin, and David Bevington, eds. 1973. *The Complete Works of Shakespeare.* Revised edition. Glenview, Ill.: Scott, Foresman.

Edelstein, Barry G. 1991. "Macbluff." *The New Republic* (11 November): 13.

Evans, G. Blakemore, ed. 1974. *The Riverside Shakespeare.* Boston: Houghton.

Geertz, Clifford. 1980. "Blurred Genres: The Refiguration of Social Thought." *The American Scholar* 49:165–79.

Jorgens, Jack J. 1977. *Shakespeare on Film.* Bloomington and London: Indiana University Press.

Mackey, Nathaniel. 1992. "Other: From Noun to Verb." *Representations,* 39:51–70.

Newman, Karen. 1987. "And Wash the Ethiop White': Feminity and the Monstrous in *Othello.*" In *Shakespeare Reproduced: The Text in History and Ideology,* edited by Jean E. Howard and Marion F. O'Connor. New York and London: Methuen.

Orkin, Martin. 1987. "*Othello* and the 'Plain face' of Racism." *Shakespeare Quarterly* 38:166–88.

Ridley, M. R. 1958; reprint, 1962. *Othello.* New Arden edition. Cambridge: Harvard University Press.

Rosenberg, Marvin. 1961. *The Masks of "Othello."* Berkeley: University of California Press.

Sanders, Norman, ed. 1984. *Othello.* New Cambridge edition. Cambridge: Cambridge University Press.

Siemon, James R. 1986. "'Nay, that's not next': *Othello* V. ii in Performance, 1760–1900." *Shakespeare Quarterly* 37:38–51.

Wells, Stanley, and Gary Taylor, eds. 1986. The *Complete Works.* The Oxford Shakespeare. Oxford: Clarendon Press.

King Lear versus *Hamlet* in Eastern Europe

ZDENEK STRIBRNY

BEFORE tackling the theme indicated in the title, I should try and answer one specific question: how far did the new textual debate about *King Lear,* beginning in the early 1980s, influence theoretical and theatrical interpretation of the play in Eastern Europe?[1] Judging from the instance of the Czech Republic, the new sharpened awareness of substantial differences between the Quarto and Folio versions was grasped, at least by specialists, fairly soon and developed in their own way.

In 1985, Charles University Press published a monograph by Milan Lukeš, professor of dramatic art and a translator of Shakespeare and of other English and American playwrights.[2] Although he finished his manuscript evidently before the publication of *The Division of the Kingdoms: Shakespeare's Two Versions of "King Lear,"*[3] he was able to make use, as his bibliography shows, of Gary Taylor's two essays[4] and of Stephen Urkowitz's book *Shakespeare's Revision of King Lear* (Princeton 1980). Backed by his own experience in translating *King Lear* into Czech, Lukeš concluded that "the difference between Q1 and F1 is that between two equally valuable versions," and he summarized his views as follows: "Although Q1 is closer to the author's text and F1 to the stage text, this does not exhaust the differences between the two. Comparative analysis of the two versions . . . shows a protracted time of development of the text, in which the author, the actors, and also censors played a part, and so, indirectly, did the political situation, which underwent stormy changes during that same period. . . . Both the Quarto and the Folio texts show lacunae, so that the modern synthetic text is justified."[5]

I agree with Lukeš's conclusion because in a small country we can hardly afford the luxury of separate Czech editions of the first and second Quartos and the first Folio, however valuable they are for theoretical discussion. I greatly admire such multiple texts editions as Michael Warren's *Complete King Lear 1608–1623* or René Weis's *King Lear: A Parallel Text Edition* or the two editions by

Jay Halio of F1 and Q1 *Lear* in the New Cambridge Shakespeare,[6] but I think that we should concede that they are geared to the special interest of scholars, teachers, and students whose differential readings have been cultivated by the recent concepts of plurality, otherness, or Derridean difference/*différance.*[7] On the other hand, general readers both in the English-speaking and non-English-speaking countries will probably continue to read Shakespeare primarily for pleasure so that they will tend to prefer texts that will not complicate Shakespeare's own ambiguities, pluralities, differentiations, and deferments (like the ending in *King Lear*) by textual problems. Of course, it will hardly be possible for future editors and translators to believe that they are giving their readers "a true text" envisaged by George K. Hunter in his fine eclectic New Penguin *King Lear.*[8] A clear-cut binary opposition between "true" and "false" cannot be maintained in view of the enormous variety and complexity of texts accumulated throughout almost four centuries and now presented by means of the most advanced copying techniques.

In the case of *Hamlet,* it is obvious that even in non-English-speaking countries we shall need separate translations and editions of the basically different Q1 and F1. I can support this view by an example from my own country where the first Czech translation of Q1 *Hamlet* (by Lukeš, 1978) has been a remarkable success on our stages both before and after the Revolution of 1989 because it has presented a provocative alternative to the traditional versions. Perhaps a Czech translation of *The Tragedy of King Lear,* even though it is less radically different from the alternative Q version, might also prove to be attractive, especially for experimental companies.

This brings me to the problem of texts for staging Shakespeare. Dramaturges, directors, and actors not only in non-English-speaking but also in English-speaking countries need a text that is more or less settled when they start playing it, although some alterations can be introduced during rehearsals or even in between performances. Before their playing text is settled, however, they may be very much interested in both the Folio and Quarto versions as well as in the emendations and commentaries of eighteenth-, nineteenth-, and twentieth-century editors, offering them stimulating choice of readings that may support their specific artistic visions and aims. Moreover, they will feel free to cut their text to comply with the time limits imposed on them by the theater traffic and to strengthen their own interpretations of the play. Let me give one striking, and by now classical, example. In his production of *King Lear* in the 1960s, Peter Brook left out the final lines of the two servants in 3.7 who comment critically on Cornwall's blinding of Gloucester and are ready to apply some flax and whites of eggs to Gloucester's bleeding face and to get Tom of Bedlam to be his guide. Some critics reproached Brook for his cut without realizing that he did nothing else than follow the text of F1, which suited him in stressing the unalleviated cruelty of the scene. It is of course true that Brook also left out the Fool's prophecy at the end of 3.2 that is found only in the Folio and that he retained some conspicuous Q passages.[9] It is probable that he did all this without pondering whether this or that passage came from Q or F. Such textual inconsistencies have to be expected and accepted when serving the individual directorial vision of the play. It would be pedantic to take the strict position of textual puritans and to blame directors and translators for being textually promiscuous or licentious in their cuts.

The opposite tendency of modern directors is to enlarge upon the text by keeping a character on stage after his textual exit. A well-known example is Grigori Kozintsev's treatment of the Fool in the film version of *King Lear.* In his book *King Lear: The Space of Tragedy* Kozintsev confessed:

> I couldn't bear to lose the Fool half-way through the play. Oleg Dal [the actor] helped me to grow even fonder of his character. A tortured boy, taken from among the servants, clever, talented—the voice of truth, the voice of the poor; art driven into dog's kennel with a dog's collar round his neck. Let one of the soldiers carrying the bodies [of Lear and all three daughters] finally aim a kick at his neck with his boot, to get him out of the way! But his voice, the voice of the home-made Pipe, begins and ends this story; the sad, human voice of art.

For his cyclic vision of *King Lear,* in which the end echoes the beginning, Kozintsev needed the Fool from the start to the very end, when he turned out to be "both the last man to stay by him and the only one to mourn him."[10]

Kozintsev's screen image of the Fool, whose skinny body, closely shaved skull, and sorrowful face was reminiscent of a boy from Auschwitz, exerted a strong influence on later stage productions of the tragedy in Eastern Europe. In the Slovak production directed by Pavol Haspra in Bratislava in 1975, a more aggressive Fool attacked the spectators with his rough words and gestures even before they were able to take their seats and he refused to "go to bed at noon," sticking to his guns to the very end. His speeches, except for the opening impromptu, were not noticeably enlarged by extratextual additions; rather they echoed, underlined, or satirized the most revealing pronouncements of other characters. As in Kozintsev's film, the Slovak Fool embodied the voice of both the poor naked wretches of Lear's kingdom and of contemporary art made tongue-tied by authority.

* * *

I will now turn to my specific theme of *Lear* versus *Hamlet* in Eastern Europe. Although my previous remarks have pointed out some original features in the interpretation of *King Lear* on Eastern European stages and screens, and although I am convinced by R. A. Foakes's argument about the general shift of interest from *Hamlet* to *Lear* in the second part of our century, I believe that the shift has not gone so far in the East as it did in the West. Probably the main reason is the extremely strong position held by *Hamlet* for a long time in Eastern cultures. (It would be interesting to explore what the situation is in countries even farther east and south, as India; it is certainly noteworthy that the only journal devoted to a single play anywhere in the world, as far as I know, appears in New Delhi and is entitled *Hamlet Studies,* edited by R. W. Desai.)

Trying to establish the total number of all Czech editions of the two plays so far, I have arrived at the following data: *Hamlet* 23, *King Lear* 13. Not only quantitatively, however, but also qualitatively Czech translations and productions of *Hamlet* have tended to surpass those of *King Lear.* In the collection of reviews of Shakespeare productions in the first three decades of this century by a representative Czech critic, Jindřich Vodák, 12 items are devoted to *Hamlet* as against only three concerned with *King Lear.*[11] Although Vodák considered *King Lear* to be "Shakespeare's greatest achievement," he was not really bowled over by any of the three productions he reviewed, as he was by Eduard Vojan's Hamlet in 1905 and again as late as 1920, or by V. I. Kachalov and the whole *Hamlet* of the emigrant group of the Moscow Arts Theatre visiting Prague in 1921.

In my lifetime, I remember two outstanding Czech *Hamlet*s (one at the National Theatre in the years 1959–65 and the other one, based on Q1, at the Prague experimental theater, On the Balustrade, in 1978) but not one memorable *King Lear.* The only fully successful Slavonic *Lear*s I have seen on stage was the Slovak *Lear* (1975) just mentioned and a Polish *Lear* directed by Jerzy Jarocki with Gustaw Holoubek in the title role, presented as a guest performance at the Shakespeare Conference in Weimar in 1979. (I should add that we have seen three distinctive British *Lear*s in Prague: Peter Brook's Royal Shakespeare Company production with Paul Scofield in 1964, Michael Elliott's TV version of 1983 with Laurence Olivier in the title role, and Deborah Warner's Royal National Theatre production with Brian Cox in 1991.)

The last *King Lear* I saw in Prague in 1991 was sadly disappointing, although it was produced at the prestigious National Theatre and directed by Barry Kyle of the Royal Shakespeare Company who had brought with him the Rumanian-born American designer Marina Draghici for both setting and costumes and David Finn for lighting. The eclectic text (translated by Lukeš) was matched by eclectic costumes, absorbing unmistakable allusions to totalitarian paramilitary uniforms down to black boots, and eclectic music, ranging from tons of heavy metal and rock to violin tones from Beethoven's symphonies. The postmodern setting, too, presented an eclectic mixture of up-to-date electronic and bureaucratic devices (a video with a large screen, telephones, and piled-up registration files) with an ultrarealistic kitsch panorama of the White Cliffs of Dover, parodying the worst products of socialist realism. Large portraits of the King and a big statue without a head were reminiscent of the time when portraits of Communist leaders were omnipresent and the largest Stalin monument in the whole Soviet bloc was dynamited in Prague after Khruschev's speech at the Twentieth Party Congress. The trouble with Barry Kyle's Prague *Lear* was most likely its unfortunate timing. Kyle's original idea, conceived during his visit to Prague in 1988, was to produce a play about the consequences of totalitarian rule and to do it equally poetically as politically. The actual production, however, started only in 1991, after the Velvet Revolution of November 1989, during which some theaters were turned into arenas of public political discussions and most of the drama moved into the streets and squares of Prague and, later on, into the first freely elected Parliament whose sessions were watched on TV by millions of viewers. Evidently, Kyle tried hard to adapt his production to the new situation, introducing motives of expiation for the arrogant abuses of power by the old rulers and stressing the dangers of new abuses by postrevolutionary arrivistes. All this, however, seemed too contrived, too crudely spelled out for Czech audiences who had been used to subtle political allusions and evasive hints that could be explained away when pinned down by totalitarian surveillance. To be sure, there were some brilliant moments in the production (e.g., in the storm, when Lear and the Fool were wrapped into a huge torn red banner of revolution, or in the breathtaking duel scene) and some superb acting, especially by the Fool, who was presented as an elderly wise man ironically playing Beethoven's "Ode to Joy" on his violin (instead of Kozintsev's young boy warbling his native wood-notes wild on his pipe). Despite all the sound and fury, contrasted with moments of pensive calm, the production as a whole did not seem to reach a tragic grandeur, so that it was called by one of the jibing critics "The Tragedy of Errors."[12] Although I do not subscribe to such a flippant rejection, I must regret that a great opportunity could not be embraced fully.

In Russia, the reception of *King Lear* received a shock by the beginning of the twentieth century when the aging Leo V. Tolstoy published his essay *On Shakespeare and on the Drama* (1906), the most violent attack ever made on Shakespeare in any country.[13] Before writing his essay, Tolstoy conscientiously reread not only Shakespeare (in Russian, English, and German) but also some Shakespearean criticism and some of the sources of his plays.[14] Of all Shakespeare's dramas he selected *King Lear* for a close analysis to prove that Shakespeare was immoral, lacking in art and sense of beauty and measure, and that his plays were deficient in plots, in appropriate and unmotivated in characterization, exuberant or vulgar in language, and full of anachronisms. He even went so far as to argue that the old anonymous *True Chronicle of King Leir* was "incomparably and in every respect superior to Shakespeare's adaptation." Evidently, he judged Shakespeare's poetic dramas by the standards of his own realistic novels, unwilling to accept the conventions of Elizabethan drama or the richness of Shakespeare's imagery. (I leave aside such psychological explanations as Tolstoy's professional jealousy or his subconscious identification with Lear's fate.)

Tolstoy's violent denunciation called forth many responses both in the West (G. B. Shaw, G. Wilson Knight, George Orwell, René Wellek, etc.) and in Russia where many scholars and directors have felt it their duty to explain the reasons for Tolstoy's opposition to Shakespeare (Viktor Shklovsky, A. A. Smirnov, Leonid Pinsky, Alexander Anikst, Grigori Kozintsev, etc.). In the long run, Tolstoy's extreme views have been absorbed as a kind of shock therapy against the uncritical adulation of the Bard or as a challenge to understand and interpret him better and deeper.[15]

Nevertheless, *King Lear* has never surpassed *Hamlet* in popularity anywhere in Eastern or East Central Europe. To support my personal experience by more objective data, I have consulted each issue of the World Shakespeare Bibliography in the *Shakespeare Quarterly* since 1961, when R. W. Dent introduced a special section devoted to "Current Productions." The total number of items concerning the productions of *Hamlet* and *King Lear* respectively in the individual Eastern European countries is shown in the table.[16]

	Hamlet	*King Lear*
Bulgaria	13	10
Czechoslovakia	63	28
Hungary	35	19
Poland	59	10
Rumania	29	8
the former Soviet Union	178	64
Yugoslavia	26	8

It is evident that the only country where the numbers of productions of the two plays come near to each other is Bulgaria. It must be added, however, that in Bulgaria the most popular Shakespeare tragedy has been, since the nineteenth century, *Romeo and Juliet.*[17]

Free adaptations and offshoots of *Hamlet* are also much more frequent in Eastern Europe, as far as I know, than those of *Lear.* Still, I do not doubt that *King Lear* with its torturous complexities has become a great challenge, probably a growing challenge, for Eastern European theaters, scholars, critics, and also playwrights. I can support this view by my last piece of information. Václav Havel, whose absurd plays contain several allusions to *Hamlet,*[18] plans to finish his discontinued offshoot of *King Lear* as soon as he concludes his political career.[19] His experience as the president of the Czechoslovak Republic who abdicated when he felt that he was no longer supported by the majority of the Slovaks, and then, after the peaceful division of the kingdom, was reelected president of the Czech Republic, may stand him in good stead.

Notes

1. This essay was originally prepared for the seminar "Renewing *King Lear,*" chaired by R. A. Foakes, and cochaired by Dieter Mehl, at the Sixth World Shakespeare Congress in Los Angeles, 7–14 April 1996.

2. Milan Lukeš, *Základy shakespearovské dramaturgie* (Foundations of Shakespearean Dramaturgy) (Prague: Acta Universitatis Carolinae, 1985).

3. *The Division of the Kingdoms: Shakespeare's Two Versions of "King Lear,"* eds. Gary Taylor and Michael Warren (Oxford: Clarendon Press, 1983).

4. "Three Studies in the Text of *Henry V,*" in Stanley Wells and Gary Taylor *Modernizing Shakespeare's Spelling* (Oxford: 1979); and "Copy Text and Colla-

tion," in *The Library,* 6th ser. vol. 3, 1981. Taylor's paper "The War in *King Lear,*" *Shakespeare Survey* 33 (1980), is missing in Lukes's bibliography.

5. Lukeš, *Zaklady shakespearovské dramaturgie,* 172.

6. *The Complete King Lear 1608–1623,* ed. Michael Warren (Berkeley and Los Angeles: University of California Press, 1989); *King Lear: A Parallel Text Edition,* ed. René Weis (London and New York: Longman Annotated Texts, 1993); *The Tragedy of King Lear,* ed. Jay Halio (Cambridge University Press: New Cambridge Shakespeare, 1992); *The First Quarto of King Lear,* ed. Jay Halio (Cambridge University Press: 1994).

7. Cf. Margreta de Grazia, "The Questions of the One and the Many: The Globe Shakespeare, *The Complete King Lear,* and the New Folger Library Shakespeare," *Shakespeare Quarterly* 46 (Summer 1995): 245–51.

8. *King Lear,* ed. Geroge K. Hunter (Harmondsworth: New Penguin Shakespeare, 1972); see esp. his "Account of the Text," 313.

9. I owe this information to R. A. Foakes who has studied Brook's promptbook.

10. Grigori Kozintsev, *King Lear: The Space of Tragedy* (Berkeley and Los Angeles: University of California Press, 1977), 238; original version *Prostranstvo tragedii* (Moscow: 1973). Cf. Kozintsev, "King Lear," in *Shakespeare in the Soviet Union,* eds. R. Samarin and A. Nikolyukin (Moscow: Progress Publishers, 1966), 204–63; original version in *Shekspirovski sbornik,* eds. A. Anikst and A. Stein (Moscow: Vserossiyskoe teatralnoe obschchestvo, 1958). See also Kozintsev, "*Hamlet* and *King Lear:* Stage and Film," in *Shakespeare 1971,* Proceedings of the World Shakespeare Congress, Vancouver, August 1971, eds. C. Leech and J. M. R. Margeson (Toronto and Buffalo: University of Toronto Press, 1972), 190–99.

11. Jindřich Vodák, *Shakespeare—Kritikuv breviár* (Prague: Melantrich, 1950).

12. Jana Paterová, "Tragedie plná omylů," *Práce,* Prague: 6 March 1991.

13. Leo N. Tolstoy, "O Shekspire i o drame," Kriticheskij ocherk, in Sbornik statej *Chto takoe iskusstvo* (Moskva: Sovremennik, 1985). First published in Russian in Moscow in 1906 and in English translation in London and New York in the same year.

14. See George Gibian, *Tolstoi* [*sic*] *and Shakespeare* ('S-Gravenhage: Mouton, 1957).

15. See Leonid Pinsky, *Shekspir.* Osnovnye nachala dramaturgii (Moskva: Khudozhestvenaya literatura: 1971), 316–17; Grigori Kozintsev, "Korol Lir," in *Shekspirovski sbornik 1958,* eds. Alexander Anikst and A. Stein (Moskva: Vserossiyskoe teatralnoe obshchestvo, 1959), 202–3.

16. I thank my wife Mariana for sparing me the drudgery of plodding through the increasingly thicker volumes of the Annual World Shakespeare Bibliography in *Shakespeare Quarterly* 13 (summer 1962)—45 (no. 5, 1994). In January 1996, I made an additional quick check at the current Prague exhibition of settings for Shakespeare's plays in Central Europe between the two wars. Although the selection is clearly far from being fully representative, the following numbers of exhibits of *Hamlet* and *Lear* settings may be of interest: Croatia H-6, L-0, Czech Republic H-10, L-0, Germany (only Mannheim) H-3, L-2, Hungary H-2, L-0, Slovakia H-2, L-2, Slovenia H-4, L-0, Switzerland H-5, L-3.

17. Special reasons for the popularity of *Romeo and Juliet* in Bulgaria are elucidated by Alexander Shurbanov and Boika Sokolova in their essay "From the Unlove of *Romeo and Juliet* to *Hamlet* Without the Prince: A Shakespearean Mirror Held Up to the Fortunes of New Bulgaria," in *Shakespeare in the New*

Europe, eds. Michael Hattaway, Boika Sokolova, and Derek Roper (Sheffield Academic Press, 1994).

18. Vāclav Havel's allusions to *Hamlet* are discussed by Lois Potter in her essay "Fire in the Theater: A Cross-cultural Code," in *Shakespeare and Cultural Traditions,* eds. Tetsuo Kishi, Roger Pringle, and Stanley Wells (Newark: University of Delaware Press, 1994).

19. See Michael Simmons, "The Tracts of His Tears," in *The Guardian,* 22 July 1992. According to Simmons, Havel has been intrigued with the problem "How far does a man with worldly power collapse when he finishes his office."

Staging *King Lear* 1.1 and 5.3

Jay L. Halio

> Such is the impulse to creativity and individuality that no major interpretation of Lear has been exactly like any other.
> —Marvin Rosenberg, *The Masks of King Lear*

How does Lear enter? What is he like? In his superbly detailed discussion in *The Masks of King Lear,* Marvin Rosenberg provides much information in answer to the latter question—the various *types* of King Lear as they have appeared onstage down through the centuries—but he says a good deal less about the staging of Lear's entrance.[1] Quarto and Folio stage directions help somewhat, but not really enough, and they are divergent. For example, as Philip McGuire reminds us,[2] the Quarto has the following stage direction: *Sound a Sennet, Enter one bearing a Coronet, then Lear, then the Dukes of Albany, and Cornwall, next Gonorill, Regan, Cordelia, with followers."*[3] The Folio omits any reference to "one bearing a Coronet," but keeps the same order of entry, though whether the characters actually proceeded in the way indicated is open to question. The stage direction simply gives the rank ordering (*pace* feminist critics who will, quite rightly, object to placing women after men—but those were Jacobean times, not ours). Usually, at least in modern productions, husbands and wives enter together, Cordelia following alone, then Lear. Gloucester, Kent, and Edmond are already onstage. But where is Edgar? And where is the Fool?

In every stage production I have seen, Edgar is omitted from the first scene.[4] Scholars have assumed that the actor playing him doubled in the role of France or Burgundy—a plausible enough explanation, given the exigencies of Elizabethan acting companies. But certainly modern productions, which can take advantage of an abundance of actors at their command, are not thus restricted. Does the original stage direction then need to be followed? Or should Edgar—in many ways the innocent gull of his scheming brother and victim of his equally gullible father—be kept away from the momentous events of 1.1? In the next scene and until the end of 3.6, he appears oblivious to those events.[5] Perhaps this is as it should be; but since 1.1, like 5.3, is a full court scene, in which even his brother Edmond is present, his omission is somewhat curious.

Similarly, the Fool is absent from the procession, according to Q and F stage directions, although some directors have brought him on.[6] In Grigori Kozinstev's great film (which, like most films of Shakespeare's plays, is a radical adaptation) Lear enters last, shown playing with the Fool. In the 1993 Royal Shakespeare Company's production at Stratford-upon-Avon, he was very much in evidence, wearing a kind of blindfold and officiously marking the divisions of the kingdom as Lear awarded his elder daughters their shares. But should he be there? In 1.4 Lear comments that he has not seen his Fool "this two days." The time scheme of the play is vague, and it may well be more than two days since 1.1, although a rigid, literalistic counting might put the action of 1.4 only a couple of days later. So the Fool may not, in fact, be present in 1.1. Doubling of roles may again offer an explanation for his absence, but there is no *necessity* for the Fool's role there. In a sense, Kent assumes that role when he challenges Lear not to divide his kingdom and banish Cordelia.

As William Ringler, Jr. and Stephen Booth have argued, the parts of the Fool and Cordelia may have been taken by the same actor, possibly one of the boy actors in Shakespeare's company and not Robert Armin, who may have played Edgar, according to Ringler.[7] The doubling of roles can be thematically effective, as Giorgio Melchiori has indicated,[8] although we see little of it today, at least in the professional theater. (Companies like the Shenandoah Shakespeare Express and the touring groups sponsored by ACTER are notable exceptions.) Possibly the doubling of France and Edgar gave Nahum Tate the idea for a romance between Edgar and Cordelia in his redaction of *King Lear,* which held the stage for well over a century, beginning in 1681. France disappears after 1.1 and is only mentioned briefly later, when his absence from the invading French army is explained in act 4. Having performed his function in the Cinderella aspect of Cordelia's story, his role is henceforward expendable, it would seem.

Edgar's is not. Moreover, he needs to be kept onstage so that he can learn how things are, how the world of *King Lear*—our world—operates. If he misses what happens in 1.1—as Shakespeare apparently intended—he makes up for it by what happens later, beginning with the very next scene. Although it takes him awhile to comprehend those experiences fully, he does finally understand them—better, perhaps, than anyone else except possibly Kent—and accordingly becomes an important commentator on events as well as an active agent in the play.

His half brother Edmond requires no such knowledge. Like Cordelia, who remains offstage from the end of 1.1 to the middle of act 4, he already has worldly knowledge, cynical though his interpretations may appear. But if he has some understanding of human nature and the way people behave, he needs to know how and when to put that knowledge to use so that it can serve his own ends. An interesting point, rarely brought out in modern productions—or the editions on which they are based—concerns his exit in 1.1. Neither Quarto nor Folio provides specifically for Edmond's departure from this scene. Although most editions have him leave with Gloucester when Lear orders the earl to bring in France and Burgundy, Q and F provide no such exit. Q is silent altogether, presumably because Gloucester's exit is clearly indicated in the dialogue; F simply marks *Exit* after Gloucester's "I shall, my Lord" (1.1.30).

What authority or justification, then, do editors have for making Edmond leave with him? Merely the fact that Edmond has nothing more to say or do in the scene, it seems. But that surely is insufficient motivation for his departure, and greater motivation exists for keeping him onstage, as Kenneth Branagh did in his 1990 Renaissance Theatre production. Remaining silent throughout the remainder of the scene, Edmond (who, let's not forget, "hath been out nine years," 1.1.27) took it all in. As the huge double doors upstage center opened to let the grand procession leave (1.1.261), they hid Edmond from view. From behind one if the doors he listened to the dialogue between the sisters that concludes the scene. Then, as the doors shut behind their departure and scene 2 began, Edmond stood revealed, exulting in what he has observed. In this attitude he then began his soliloquy.[9]

As this discussion suggests, Shakespeare's text—whether one follows Quarto or Folio—allows for various stagings, and the implications of staging are significant. They can substantially affect character interpretation and, more importantly, the overall action. One need not follow explicit stage directions literally: few directors stage the court procession in 1.1 by rank order with women last. Elsewhere, some directorial license is, I think, also permissible without distorting Shakespeare's design, though adding a silent

Edgar and/or the Fool to the scene may significantly alter that design. But keeping Edmond onstage throughout most of 1.1 does not. In my view it enhances the design and renders it more intelligible.

To turn now to the last scene of the play, which in many ways reflects or echoes events in 1.1, if with some tragically ironic twists: Edmond has risen from his status as the illegitimate younger son in 1.1—whom Gloucester was about to send "out" (1.1.28) once more—to a strong challenger for ruler of the entire kingdom. Edgar has suffered much and learned much and is now prepared to meet the challenge his brother represents. His success has often been remarked to his explain how he supplants Albany especially as the Folio alters their roles, changes that Michael Warren details in "Quarto and Folio *King Lear* and the Interpretation of Albany and Edgar."[10] But Edgar parallels and contrasts as much—or more—with Edmond and his rise to power. If Edmond had won the duel . . . but we need not speculate on that eventuality, except as it highlights parallels and contrasts between the brothers that Shakespeare I think strongly implies. Edgar's victory over Edmond not only seals the fate of the malefactors—it leads directly, for example, to Gonerill's suicide; it also ensures that a man far more capable than Albany—someone who has grown immensely in knowledge and stature throughout the play, as Edgar has done—will henceforth rule Britain after Lear dies.

And Lear dies before he can reclaim the throne. Shakespeare of course altered the old Lear story in his version, which Nahum Tate and many others refused to accept. Samuel Johnson's reflections on his death and Cordelia's are well-known, and Stephen Booth (5) has confessed to a similar reaction. The end overcame them with such powerful emotion that Johnson could not bear to read the play again until he came to edit it. But before Lear dies, some crucial actions occur that have not, I shall argue, received the full attention they deserve.

Some critics have commented on how the corpses of the daughters onstage parallel their positions in the opening scene, and indeed the daughters in death may be situated as (in 1.1) they were in life. That is, as the bodies of Gonerill and Regan are brought out (a bit earlier in F than in Q), they may be placed so that they reflect the staging of the opening scene.[11] Once again in eager anticipation the audience waits for Cordelia—and for the outcome of Edmond's attempt to do some good despite his own nature. The suspense here is very much like that generated in 1.1, where the audience awaited Cordelia's reply to Lear's questions during and after his sisters' responses.

Now, both elder sisters lie mute, death having closed their lips forever. Up to this point Edmond is also onstage, dying but not quite dead, until Albany orders him to be borne hence (5.3.230). Whether this action actually occurs before Lear enters, again neither Q nor F indicates. If he is left onstage for a while watching events unfold for which he has been responsible, it would demonstrate the circle coming full round, and his presence would parallel that in 1.1, which I have suggested both Q and F permit.[12] How soon Lear enters afterwards with Cordelia in his arms is nowhere stipulated by either text: if some attendants place Edmond on a litter and carry him off, the action would naturally take a few moments, intensifying the suspense already felt. For as Booth and others have shown, Shakespeare has repeatedly led the audience to expect, or hope for, a happier conclusion than the one he finally provides.[13]

"Enter Lear with Cordelia in his armes." This is the stage direction, identical in Q and F, that appears after line 230. Notice—as many editors and critics since Nicholas Rowe's edition in 1709 sadly have failed to do—that the direction does not say Cordelia is dead.[14] Throughout the rest of the scene Lear is torn between his fear that she is and the hope that she is not. At first he howls that "She's gone for ever" (230), but a moment later he asks for a looking glass and says:

> If that her breath will mist or stain the stone,
> Why then she lives.
>
> (236–37)

A tremendous *if,* as Rosenberg remarks, and a tremendous moment of suspense.[15] Lear's next line, as Q and F print it, is ambiguous:

> Q: This feather stirs she liues, if it be so,
> F: This feather stirs, she liues: if it be so,

Much depends upon the punctuation, notoriously unreliable in the original printed texts. As Kenneth Muir prints the line in his edition, and as Gielgud acted it, Lear believes Cordelia is still alive—that the feather has in fact stirred.[16] Is this merely an hallucination of the dying King—his deranged or wishful thinking? Or is it just possible that Cordelia gives some last fleeting indication of life? Does the feather that Lear plucks (from where?) stir, however briefly?[17] Does Cordelia faintly utter a dying breath or move her lips ever so slightly as her father busies about her limp body? If Desdemona could revive momentarily after Othello has strangled her, why not Cordelia? Lines 255–56 seems to suggest a possible cue, after Lear pleads with her to "stay a little." He thinks he hears her say something: "Ha? / What is't thou sayst?" Has Cordelia uttered a soft moan?

I submit that this possibility is not implausible and is not at variance with anything found in the text. Moreover, it heightens the dramatic tension of the close, unbearable though Dr. Johnson may have found it. As we have seen in this play, and as Philip McGuire has abundantly shown, Shakespeare's "silences" elsewhere afford latitude for interpretation, often in scenes as dramatically significant as the ending of *King Lear.* Might not Cordelia's "silence" here be such a one? McGuire's caveat is worth heeding: "Stage traditions, editorial practices, and habits of interpretation have combined in ways that drastically narrow, if they do not obliterate, awareness of the presence and the ramifications of open silences during the final moments of *King Lear.*"[18] As (in the Folio's revision) Lear dies, he seems to believe that Cordelia still lives, that his efforts to revive her have not been in vain:

> Do you see this? Looke on her? Looke her lips,
> Looke there, looke there.
>
> (284–85)

He is wrong of course. She is "dead as earth." But keeping in mind Desdemona's death, should we not at least leave open to interpretation the moment of Cordelia's final expiration?

If the actor who played the Fool also plays Cordelia, then he can hardly be represented in the final scene. But if, as in most modern productions, two different actors play those roles, he could be present at the end. Should he be? What has happened to him since 3.6? The danger in bringing him back now is, of course, that whimpering at his master's death and at Cordelia's he could precipitate an ending that descends into maudlin sentimentality or worse—bathos. But need it? Recall the effective way that Grigori Kozinstev reintroduced the Fool playing a mournful melody on his pipe, as the litter bearers carry off the bodies of Lear and the others. Recall also the kind of statement that one of the litter bearers makes when, as he passes by the Fool, he kicks him out of the way. The effect is far from sentimental, and in one gesture it summarizes much of what the play is about. On the other hand, the Fool's last line, "And I'll go to bed at noon" (3.6.41)—uttered in exhaustion after the event of acts 1–3 and rich in ambiguity as it is—may be sufficient. It seems to have been for Shakespeare. Some mysteries, after all—such as what happens to the Fool—we need not resolve.[19]

Notes

1. Marvin Rosenberg, *The Masks of King Lear* (1972, reprinted, Newark: University of Delaware Press, 1993) describes several alternative ways for Lear's entrance, and the way Mikhoels, Laughton, and Carnovsky entered in their celebrated versions (16, 30–32).

2. Philip McGuire, *Shakespeare: The Jacobean Plays* (New York: St. Martin's, 1994), 96.

3. Quotations from the "Pied Bull' Quarto and from the Folio are from the facsimiles in *The Complete King Lear, 1608–1623,* ed. Michael Warren (Berkeley and Los Angeles: University of California Press, 1989).

4. In Grigori Kozintsev's film version, Edgar enters at 1.1.28 along with the rest of the courtly procession as, presumably, one of Lear's attendant knights. See Rosenberg, *Masks of King Lear,* 14.

5. Act, scene, and line references are to my edition in the New Cambridge Shakespeare (Cambridge: Cambridge University Press, 1992).

6. Not only the presence of the Fool, but his age and even gender have aroused interest. During the long reign of Tate's redaction, the Fool's role was entirely omitted from productions. When Macready restored it in 1838, he cast nineteen-year-old Priscilla Horton in the role, and as recently as 1990 the part has very effectively been played by women (Emma Thompson in Kenneth Branagh's Renaissance Theatre production, and Linda Kerr Scott in the Royal Shakespeare Company's staging, directed by Nicholas Hytner). Though several times referred to as "boy," in the BBC television production the Fool was an elderly person, closer to Lear's age, as played by Frank Middlemass, and at the RSC in 1993 David Bradley (though not quite as elderly) played the role.

7. William Ringler Jr., "Shakespeare and His Actors: Some remarks on *King Lear,*" in *Shakespeare's Art from a Comparative Perspective,* ed. W. M. Aycock (1981), 187–93; Stephen Booth, *Lear, Macbeth, and Indefinition in Tragedy* (New Haven: Yale University Press, 1983), 129–55. Cf. Richard Abrams, "The Double Casting of Cordelia and Lear's Fool," *Texas Studies in Literature and Language* 27 (1985): 354–68.

8. Giorgio Melchiori, "Peter, Balthasar, and Shakespeare's Art of Doubling," *Modern Language Review* 78 (1983): 790.

9. This of course ignores the stage direction at the head of 1.2 for Edmond's entrance. In my edition Edmond leaves with Lear and the others at line 261.

10. *Shakespeare: Pattern of Excelling Nature,* eds. David Bevington and Jay L. Halio (Newark: University of Delaware Press, 1978), 95–107.

11. See Rosenberg, *Masks of King Lear,* 312; and C. Walter Hodges's sketches of both scenes in the New Cambridge Shakespeare, 32.

12. At some point he must be borne off, since a messenger enters 5.3.268 to announce his death.

13. Booth, *King Lear,* 11–20; Frank Kermode, *The Sense of and Ending* (New York: Oxford University Press, 1967), 82; Jay L. Halio, "The Promised Endings of *King Lear,*" in *Old Explorations, Old Texts,* eds. David Allen and Robert White (Newark: University of Delaware Press, 1992), 235–42.

14. Habits of interpretation coupled with the absence of dialogue (such as Desdemona has) conspire to lead editors and critics to assume, with insufficient textual warrant, that Cordelia is in fact dead when Lear carries her in. The bystanders—Albany, Edgar, and Kent—give no indication that she lives, either. Are they too stunned by what appears before them, provoking thoughts of the Last Judgment? But the hope that she may still be alive sustains Rosenberg's "naive spectator."

15. Rosenberg, *Masks of King Lear,* 313, also comments that his "naive spectator" hopes that Cordelia still lives, much as Shakespeare's first audiences (who knew the original story) must have done.

16. *King Lear,* ed. Kenneth Muir. The New Arden Shakespeare, 8th ed. (London: Methuen, 1959); Rosenberg, 314. In Muir's text: "This feather stirs; she lives!" G. B. Evans in the Riverside edition uses a comma instead of a semicolon but also prints the line with an exclamation point after "lives," as does G. I. Duthie in the New Shakespeare (Cambridge: Cambridge University Press, 1960).

17. Rosenberg, *Masks of King Lear,* 314, describes various ways this moment has been enacted. Hallucinating Lears, for example, imagine both the feather and the looking glass; realistic ones pluck a feather from a soldier's plume, as Salvini did, or use a strand of hair, as Redgrave and Forrest did.

18. Philip C. McGuire, *Speechless Dialect: Shakespeare's Open Silences* (Berkeley and Los Angeles: University of California Press, 1985), 97. McGuire does not refer to Cordelia's silence, but to Lear's request for someone to "undo this button" and later in his chapter to two other situations. The general point nevertheless applies.

19. Theatergoers will recall Adrian Noble's staging of 3.6 at the Royal Shakespeare Theatre in 1982, when Lear killed the Fool in his madness with the dagger he had drawn to "anatomize Regan." It was a spectacular coup de theatre, if also an example of directorial license, like much else in that production, such as the way Noble introduced the storm scene.

A Letter to the Actor Playing Lear

HUGH RICHMOND

FIRST of all: my congratulations. You have been offered the ultimate challenge for a modern actor. For centuries the goal of ambitious actors was to shine as Hamlet. In *"Hamlet" Versus "Lear": Cultural Politics and Shakespeare's Art* Reginald A. Foakes has shown why this goal has recently been replaced by that of successfully playing Lear—a challenge great enough for Sir Laurence Olivier himself notoriously to have left its acceptance so late that his own age approached Lear's without having conserved Lear's superhuman stamina.. The role is certainly an exhausting one: Paul Scofield once casually observed to me that Shakespeare's authorship, as an experienced actor, was proved when he gave Lear a necessary half-hour "tea-break" after the storm scenes, and a slow restart thereafter. Perhaps, originally, it was a "beer-break," but even so, I hope you are still very athletic, as well as over six feet tall. Most weaker Lears must insist on an anorexic Cordelia in order to have enough energy left to carry her onstage in the last scene: Gielgud required a sling and tackle. Yet the hazards extend beyond an abnormal physical stress to the violation of most aesthetic and psychological norms, which is far harder on actors, in my observation. Actually, most people don't like to look ridiculous.

Now, the first thing to do in preparation is to look at Marvin Rosenberg's *Masks of King Lear,* which will certainly give you the whole spectrum of interpretations recorded for your part's performance. On the other hand, the sheer range of earlier options he records may prove confusing, so I shall start with the current consensus about the play. Many modern critics claim that *King Lear* is the supreme achievement of the greatest of dramatists; and thus it has some pretensions to be the ultimate illustration of theatrical, not to say literary excellence. Granted this view, then its initial impact is very paradoxical. It does not require a Charles Lamb to perceive that for many interpreters it is a study in senility: an obtuse old man deservedly brings ostracism and humiliation on himself, and misery, even death, to his intimates and those he loves best. In Molière the pattern of inept patriarchy invariably proves comic rather than tragic, as in indeed was pretty much the case in *The Chronicle of King Leir,* which was Shakespeare's source and which ended happily. So much does Shakespeare's Lear invite this effect that for most of its stage history it was altered to restore the happy ending, following Nahum Tate's version, which continues to receive critical attention from distinguished scholars such as Norman Rabkin in *Shakespeare and the Problem of Meaning*. In many versions, including Kozintsev's film, modern directors also continue to find the Shakespearean text intractable enough to require heavy cutting. Kozintsev eliminated the grotesquely abortive suicide attempt by Gloucester at Dover cliff; in the opposite spirit, Peter Brook's film suppresses the amazing repentance of Edmund in the play's last scene. The fate of so important a character as the Fool is so unclear that Kozintsev repudiates the text to bring him back alive, as one among the largely proletarian survivors of the aristocratic holocaust, who will build a new world; while Adrian Noble's 1982 Royal Shakespeare Company's production shows Lear himself killing the Fool in a fit of mad rage, for which there is not the faintest textual justification.

Such vicissitudes explain but hardly justify a preliminary announcement about rest rooms by the Stage Manager before a recent production by the Berkeley Shakespeare Festival, which he ended with the remark: "and I won't wish you an enjoyable evening, because this is, after all, *King Lear.*" Perhaps you may accept the actor's supreme goal as making your audiences unhappy, and certainly much modern art seems aimed at inducing nausea. If that is your aim, then perhaps you will read no further, because I do not accept one goal of art as merely upsetting people (which is not to say that suffering cannot be therapeutic, as I hope to prove to you). So, how can you avoid fulfilling such merely negative anticipations—and make *Lear* enjoyable, perhaps even *amusing?* After all, normal people don't usually pay good money just to be depressed, and most of your audience will not consist of people as smart as modern university professors.

The critics' assumptions that the play is necessarily flawed, alienating, and negative must be recognized, because they are founded on a series of fashionable misconceptions. These views reflect a preference for negative sentimentality at the price of the repudiation of the saner, more accurate realism that normally marks the work of Shakespeare. The most current and least questioned of these sentimental anachronisms assumes that it has always been proper for a work of art to be entirely depressing, in the spirit of such moderns as Kafka or Genet or Miller. Years ago the highly orthodox critic Paul Alpers argued vehemently that *Lear* does not show us a world with any coherence or causality, but merely presents a nihilistic vision of life as brutish, violent, and hostile to humanity and humane feelings. Gloucester's blinding is not the result of any action on his part: this is just a world where any old man may have his eyes plucked out. Similarly, W. R. Elton's *"King Lear" and the Gods* finds the play devoid of providence: the gods are sadists as claimed by Gloucester (but surely not, therefore, *necessarily* so viewed by Shakespeare himself), and there can be no hope in his world. In this spirit Peter Brook's film of *Lear* showed its survivors as ineffective and dispirited: vestiges of an irretrievably ruined society. In harmony with this reading recent film versions have been shot in black-and-white, in a low lighting register; while many stage productions verge on this monochrome effect, reinforced by semidarkness. So, how can there be a cheerful way to perform *King Lear?*

Already Jan Kott has unintentionally vindicated *Lear*'s current humorous interest by associating it with Beckett's absurdist dramas in *Shakespeare Our Contemporary.* Adopting this view will make you seem agreeably avant-garde for smart reviewers. Certainly, there are parallels to be drawn between the heath scenes and *Waiting for Godot.* To many critics there seems to be a rough resemblance between the basic quartet of social outcasts in each play, for *Lear* supposedly shows us the desperate search for meaning by a quartet not dissimilar to Beckett's: a senile maniac who thinks he is a king, accompanied by an imbecilic comedian, a supposed escaped Bedlamite accused of attempted patricide, and an outlaw reduced to serving another outcast. However, anyone who has seen a really dynamic production of *Waiting for Godot* will know that it is far from being a depressing morality play—rather it is an existential farce in which, as so often in Beckett, humanity's resilience survives every disaster. If the modern play is not funny as well as just horrifying, it fails. It becomes simply a drearily existentialist sermon. Drama requires tension, such as seen in black humor, which makes deep misfortune laughable. Shakespeare finds that his horror story of *Richard III* provides frequent occasions for wit: the audience laughs and shudders simultaneously when Richard asks thanks from Lady Anne for sending her husband to heaven, in one of the most exciting scenes to play or watch that Shakespeare ever wrote.

Similarly in *Lear,* the ultimate proof of human resiliency is not mere suffering, but recourse to comedy at the worst moment.

Gloucester's blinding and self-discovery roughly parallels the fate of Greek tragedy's zenith in the sufferings of Oedipus. But Lear's humiliation is far greater: he becomes ridiculous, even a comedian—a fate unthinkable for a classical hero, who may prove to be a horrendous failure but is never comic. The authentic performance of *Lear* by contrast, requires the presence of true comedy: that the Fool be funny, not a solemn, sententious chorus; that Edmund's black humor startle us into laughter; that Lear himself achieve satirical, witty insights into society's aberrations, transcending his own subjective misery by sharing in proletarian ridicule of the pretensions of the hypocritical establishment. As an actor in any of these three roles you have an exciting chance to reverse the audience's mood, indeed, to achieve wonder and delight at the unexpected change of tone. I have seen the first half of the play full of an audience's disconcerted laughter, particularly in Adrian Noble's Royal Shakespeare Company production in which Antony Sher played the Fool and Michael Gambon played Lear.

Consider how negative values could plausibly be repudiated from the very start. Must Lear be first introduced as merely a senile incompetent, as is too often assumed? Literature abounds with analogues of the heroic patriarch as one of the great human archetypes of human potentiality and fallibility, from a Moses or Beowulf to the emperor Francis Joseph or Tennyson's Ulysses. And, naturally enough, the patriarch's role is usually focused on regulating the status of sons and the marriages of daughters, whether we think of Abraham and Isaac, Creon, or even the father of Cinderella, whose story disconcertingly parallels Cordelia's, with her missing mother, abasement, and two wicked sisters, not to mention her Prince Charming in the King of France. The love test is a folktale motif linked to the rites of passage celebrated in many fairy stories, as Bruno Bettelheim has argued in *The Uses of Enchantment: The Meaning and Importance of Fairy Tales.* Just as the prehistoric Denmark of *Hamlet*'s origins evokes the most basic ethical problems, so ancient Britain allows Shakespeare to strip off many of the accretions of civilization to expose the heart of family relationships.

Yet the issue is the exact antithesis of *Hamlet's* theme of youth's self-emancipation from coercive authority. *Lear* deals with the penultimate challenge for its hero: the trauma of withdrawal from active life that impends with age, a professional death that is prelude to the literal one, and that we now recognize as the trauma of "retirement." Marion Diamond and many other gerontologists have stressed that the tragedy of retirement lies not in the incompetence of the senior in question, but the stress of surrendering power at the peak of authority. Tyrants' refusal of this necessity is the bane of nondemocratic states such as the old Soviet Union. This great theme of the surrender of authority, power, and even autonomy, is a timeless one, which gerontologists are only now doing justice to. In his *Poetics* Aristotle has rightly said that there lies no aesthetic interest in tragedy as the punishment of mere deficiency. So Lear must be a magnificent anomaly: a dynamic octogenarian. If acting is partly surprising your audience plausibly, you should revel in challenging them by presenting Lear's swashbuckling authority in the opening scene: you should be an aging Tamburlaine, not a Willy Loman. You must show you have power, and still vividly enjoy the exercise of it!

There is ample evidence that, as usual, Shakespeare did not wish to evoke a merely archaeological awareness of prehistoric Britain, but saw *Lear* as an expression of current concerns. While the broad outlines of his story approximate to the legendary Lear of the chronicles, its archetypal validity ensures that many of the patterns in this family history correspond closely to more recent, seemingly realistic experiences in the kind of *novelle* sources favored by Shakespeare, such as those of Sercambi. In one of these (translated in Janet Smart's *Italian Renaissance Tales),* Lear's behavior is closely paralleled to that of Lord Piero Sovranzo, a rich merchant of Venice, "who had three daughters, and being an old man without a wife and not having any sons, he thought of marrying the three daughters." After these marriages, Piero lives for many years until he decides to tell his daughters and their husbands: "I am no longer likely to engage in business any more as I am old, and I don't need to keep up a household. Thus if it pleases you to feed me in your homes while I am alive, I will give you what money I have." They happily agree: "they arranged among themselves that he should spend one month with one and another month with the next and so on, continuing in this way until his death." Inevitably, he proves to be an irritation to first one family and then the next. In the first a servant advises him that he is considered "a bore" and he discovers, over a delayed dinner, that his bad treatment is "instigated by his son-in-law." Hastening to the next daughter's household, he is told: "My husband bought nothing for you this morning because you know you should be going to your oldest daughter." Finding all three families have become hostile, Lord Piero suffers "great melancholy for what he had done for his daughters and sons-in-law, that is for having given them all he had left."

At this point old Piero does not accept repudiation: "and being a wise man, he thought he would avenge himself for the betrayal done to him by his daughters and sons-in-law." He borrows fifty thousand ducats from a friend for one evening, on which he invites his children to dine with him, and he then lets them spy on him counting the money (which he returns the next day to his friend). Eager for further profit, his children respond positively when Piero says thereafter: "I will see truly which of you loves me, my children." They reply: "We all love you," and resume the most friendly behavior. However, when the old man finally dies, he requires them to distribute massive alms to the poor before opening his will, which is locked in a box with a mallet. It says: "Whoever abandons himself for others, let him be given a blow with this mallet." The story vindicates the superior cunning of the old man, and it ends on a note of amused cynicism, despite the concern for the welfare of the poor. This story of humiliated age proves darkly comic, and this is the tone for much of *Lear* seen as entertainment not emetic.

Perhaps Shakespeare picked up the alternating month's stay with each daughter from this fiction, but Geoffrey Bullough sees a more affirmative stimulus for the composition of *Lear* in a closer analogue from history in the Annesley case (see Geoffrey Bullough's *Narrative and Dramatic Sources of Shakespeare*). Brian Annesley, "a wealthy Kentish courtier and Gentleman Pensioner," had three daughters, the youngest, unmarried one being called Cordell. The others, named inappropriately Grace and Christian, tried in 1603 to have their father declared a lunatic because he was senile and "altogether unfit to govern himself or his estate." Cordell successfully defended him from the charge and ultimately inherited most of the estate despite challenges by her sisters. In 1607 she finally married the third husband of the mother of Shakespeare's patron, the Earl of Southampton, after the death of the Dowager Countess. While these Italian and English analogues may contribute realistic details to the basic story of Lear, they also confirm the universality of Lear's situation, as an aging but socially prominent figure, and certainly not one doomed to abject misery. The narratives resemble the best fairy stories as an epitome of observed reality. Like many classic authors, my gerontologist-colleague Marion Diamond considers that the decline of such an aging patriarch is one of the greatest challenges both to the central figure and to those around him. And the problems in this situation are not to be evaded easily by the now doubtful rationalization of an appeal to the explanation of senility, for this concept of axiomatic decline in seniors is no longer considered a necessary factor of all aging (as distinguished from specific diseases). So you may properly avoid the painful method of Antony Sher in developing the role of Richard III by visiting homes of the physically handicapped. We don't need a pathology of Alzheimer's Disease.

In Lear's case, the charges of senility and egotism, customarily based on the opening scene of the play, are manifestly false to the facts established by Shakespeare, which should surely affect your interpretation and behavior in the scene. First, while Lear is put at an age beyond the biblical climacteric of "threescore and ten," he remains endowed with the strength of the epic hero. He is not the puny mannequin to which Kozintsev reduces the hero in his film, an unconscious sign of the desire of modern directors to make Shakespearean heroes smaller. Indeed, few modern actors can easily sustain the physical energy required for the part, which requires Lear at the end of the play to kill offstage the youthful captain who executes Cordelia and then to carry the actress of that role onto the stage (an effect Kozintsev has to suppress). Lear must have heroic physical proportions: he cannot be a weakling, but the Beowulfian kind of warrior we identify in Old Hamlet. His behavior in the opening scene has an epic thunder that allies him to the primitive gods whom he treats as equals in the storm scenes, which also demand great emotional energy, not to mention vocal dynamics.

Moreover, if we assume that Lear is contemptible in the first scene, the play loses the catharsis of Shakespearean tragedy that comes from audience identification with the hero, for good or ill. For complex but compelling reasons (as Bertrand Evans has shown in *Shakespeare's Comedies*) audiences even project themselves into the roles of villains like Richard III and Macbeth, let alone romantic warriors like Othello and Antony. It is with the latter figures that Lear is surely allied, as "one that loved not wisely, but too well" (5.2.344). It is false that Lear at the start loves flatterers: his favorite daughter is the candid Cordelia; his favorite courtier is the blunt Kent; his favorite diversions are the subversive witticisms of the Fool. He gives minimal recognition and credit to the suave but suspect flatteries of Goneril and Regan. An interpretation founded on the idea that Lear favors such servile hypocrites distorts the play. It is clear that the "love test" is not a genuine evaluation: the distributions it occasions are predetermined, for Lear admits that before the formal ritual "We have divided / In three our kingdom" (2.1.37–38). Burgundy is shocked that his commitment to marry Cordelia should no longer be based on what "your highness offer'd" (1.1.193). Lear confesses of Cordelia that

"I lov'd her most" (1.1.123), and implies that he has allocated to her "a third more opulent than your sisters" (1.1.86). Since their "thirds" have already been assigned, the remainder must be compatible with his expectation of giving his favorite the most liberal inheritance, while it is made known in the first lines of the play that the two other portions are equal: "In the division of the kingdom, it appears not which of the Dukes he values most, for equalities are so weigh'd that neither can make choice of either's moi'ty" (1.1.3–7).

You must therefore firmly establish that the threefold division of the kingdom is predetermined and not dependent on the exact adverbial skills of your daughters—in intention at least. What then is the function of this purely ceremonial opening act? Surely it is your attempt to register the antecedent decision in the public consciousness—like any other handing over a great power. Retirement is always a recognition point that requires by custom an expression of appreciation and affection for the person withdrawing, matching a gesture of endorsement and validation from that person for his successor. In monarchies the process differs in that the person withdrawing is normally dead and honored in a state funeral, as at the end of *Hamlet,* and the successor is "recognized" formally at a coronation. But Lear is not dead, nor are you given the least suggestion that he is physically in decline and lacking in energy or determination. Why then the premature abdication? He loves power, and Kent still sees "authority" in Lear long after he has lost that power (1.4.30). Why depart from accepted practice and surrender what he values? He must value something more than power, and the slanted division of the kingdom shows what this is: the well-being of Cordelia. If we follow the map in Olivier's *Lear,* showing the divisions of Britain, the Duke of Albany (the old name for Scotland) receives the northern section; the Duke of Cornwall the contiguous lands of southwest; and Cordelia?—the richest and most powerful segment: the southeast (with the lands of his favorite Kent), which abuts both Burgundy (now Belgium and Holland in part) and France. Cordelia is associated with Kent and Dover, as Regan and Cornwall are with Gloucester, named from a town in the southwest.

In Elizabethan times, succession went by primogeniture; and this principle would make Goneril queen of all Britain, without peer after the death of Lear. But just as the private gentleman Brian Annesley rejected the claims on his estate of his two wicked elder daughters in favor of Cordell, so Lear gives the core of his kingdom to his favorite daughter, which is to be linked to one or another of the two great powers of Europe in the Middle Ages (and in Burgundy's case, even in prehistoric times). Lear is applying his personal admiration for the private worth of Cordelia to public affairs of state, against the grain of modern practice, and the only way he can repress the challenge that Goneril or Regan would be bound to make (as with York and Lancaster in the Wars of the Roses) is to make the transition while he is still in command and authoritative enough to enforce it. Conventional judgments of Lear's vanity and senility in the first scene are thus at odds with the text and with the intention of the author that they illustrate. In the love test Lear is disguising a political decision in favor of Cordelia's virtue—not exercising a whim, but corroborating the audience's own conviction of Cordelia's excellence. Lear's "flaw," if it is one, is thus truly tragic: the excessive love of virtue.

At this point you may be better able to understand and communicate Lear's bafflement and fury when the costly process of abdication on her behalf is frustrated at the last minute by Cordelia, your vast self-sacrifice and elaborate manipulations of public relations questioned by the very person whom they are designed to favor. Moreover, the spirit in which the offer is repudiated is as stiff and puritanical as any shown by Malvolio, Isabella, Angelo—or a Hamlet fresh from Reformist Wittenberg. Cordelia proves to be a real "precisian" as the Puritans were called. She perceives how dangerous your moves are, and she is also wise in not wishing to claim a "more opulent third" than her sisters', knowing the bitterness, rivalry, and confrontations that will result. More uncivilly, she will not compete in any way with her sisters' sexual terminology in professing their affection: Regan's "very deed of love" (1.1.71) and "most precious square of sense" (74) have genital overtones that affront the unmarried Cordelia. Truly loving you, she perceives an almost incestuous extreme in your intense involvement in her future and in her marital choice. Morally she is right to repudiate her sisters' preference for their father over their own husbands. What is regrettable is that in her strict and literal answer to his rhetorical and ceremonial one she allows a false impression of coldness and indifference to dominate. She is technically correct when Lear asks "But goes thy heart with this?" (1.1.104) for her response "Ay, good my lord" surely carries for her the sense: "Yes, my heart (love) for you does accompany my legalistic response." Yet she fails to convince Lear that she still has the affection for him that she later shows. In this sense she is "a heretic in the truth," or guilty of what Othello calls "hypocrisy against the devil" (4.1.6)—when virtue misrepresents itself as vice and refuses to correct the impression. Cordelia is willful in failing to help her father at his most precarious moment of self-surrender. She also is guilty here, like her father, of "tragic virtue"—of loving integrity too much. For she can hardly be justified by the consequences, which are as disastrous as Hamlet's efforts to carry out the will of the Ghost. Hamlet destroys a Danish dynasty, allowing its enemies to seize Denmark. Cordelia fuels civil war between her sisters by the resources of her own rejected kingdom. Worse, she invades Britain with a French army. French intrusion generates instinctive aversion in the English, after a millennium of such attempted invasions. Albany identifies this issue of foreign invasion against Cordelia by distinguishing it from any legal claims to the crown by Lear:

> For this business,
> It touches us as France invades our land,
> Not bolds the King, with others whom, I fear,
> Most just and heavy causes make oppose.
>
> (5.1.24–27)

By her own kind of literalism and precision, Cordelia is a traitor, campaigning against the legal and de facto government of Britain. In the world of archetypes in which *Lear* is set, no outcome inviting the King of France to become a power in Britain is acceptable. It must be to make this point that Shakespeare anticipates the creation of the kingdom of France by a millennium or so, by setting it in the time of pre-Roman Britain. In sum, Cordelia is her father's daughter: abrupt, egotistical, assertive—in many ways like her sisters. If you can, you must convince your director not to make Cordelia an implausible paragon—though I must warn you that no modern actress backed by feminist hatred for "the Patriarchy" will happily surrender to this more realistic view of her role!

The reading of the opening scene that I have proposed for you restores a true tragic tension to that scene, with a monarch unwisely sacrificing himself to the interests of virtue, and a heroine whose excellence carries with it the penalties of intransigence. As Aristotle says, only such mixed characters are fit for tragedy. A challenge to our complacency cannot come from humiliation of a senile, egotistic tyrant or from the destruction of a faultless heroine. Both figures fail because of their compulsive love of virtue and truth. Lear's preoccupation with justice verges on mania; but the modern world cannot allow that "justice for all" is the cry of a madman. Yet that preoccupation is the sole concern of Lear during his supposed "madness," which is only a passionate pursuit of the just state. Here the play reaches a level of meaning alien to modern values. For it is while Lear presses for justice that his behavior is most erratic and violent. When Goneril fails to be grateful for his abdication, he curses her and her children (1.4.275ff). When he thinks of his daughters' ingratitude, he hallucinates that they are present and undergoing formal trial, so intense is his compulsion to seek justice (3.6). In this scene he comes closest to being mad, yet his behavior is not insane, just intense and preoccupied. Similarly, in the storm scenes, Lear's excessive love of justice drives him to near-frenzy:

> Let the great gods
> That keep this dreadful pudder o'er our heads,
> Find out their enemies now. Tremble, thou wretch
> That has within the three undivulged crimes
> Unwhipt of justice.
>
> (3.2.49–53)

Yet such a proper concern for just punishment is not a stabilizing factor in Lear's consciousness. The more he concerns himself with absolute justice (like Hamlet), the more disturbed he becomes: "My wits begin to turn" (3.2.67). At the start of this scene his indignation at human misconduct is so great that he sinks to hysterical misanthropy: "Crack nature's moulds, all germens spill at once / That make ingrateful man!" (3.2.8–9).

Nevertheless, while Lear is deeply distressed, it will save you a lot of misplaced energy and ingenuity if you recognize that he is never truly mad in displaying frantic incoherence, since even when hallucinating he is dealing with objective issues and trying to diagnose the vicious behavior of Goneril and Regan. As Claudius says of Hamlet: "what he spake, though it lack'd form a little / Was not like madness" (3.1.163–64). Moreover, we tend to presume that any change in Lear reflects a decline in personality, yet what at first seems to him to be an incipient collapse of his identity proves a gain in awareness and concern for others:

> My wits begin to turn.
> Come on, my boy. How dost, my boy? Art cold?
> I am cold myself. Where is this straw, my fellow?
> The art of our necessities is strange
> That can make wild things precious. Come, your hovel.
> Poor Fool and knave, I have one part in my heart
> That's sorry yet for thee.
>
> (3.2.67–73)

This is the simplest, most considerate, and practical speech Lear has yet made. It is paradoxical that the previously compulsive Lear anticipates such a change of mood as loss of his wits. Far from being a sane man going mad, here he seems a man initially mad with rage going sane. As an actor you can achieve a legitimate dramatic reversal by giving the good sense and kindliness of these words more stress than his earlier all-too-justified but destructive fury.

This progression from justified but futile rage to existential "absurd" truth is not fortuitous. In the next scene, at the hovel, Lear has relapsed into his morbid concern for justice, which again drives his rage—but at the onset of another supposedly mad moment, he once more turns toward a sane awareness and concern for others:

> *Lear.* O Regan, Goneril!
> Your old kind father, whose frank heart gave all—
> O, that way madness lies, let me shun that!
> No more of that.
> *Kent.* Good my lord, enter here.
> *Lear.* Prithee, go in thyself, seek thine own ease.
> This tempest will not give me leave to ponder
> On things would hurt me more. But I'll go in.
> In, boy, go first—You houseless poverty.—
> Nay, get thee in; I'll pray, and then I'll sleep.
> Poor naked wretches, whereso'er you are,
> That bid the pelting of this pitiless storm,
> How shall your houseless heads and unfed sides,
> Your loop'd and window'd raggedness, defend you
> From seasons such as these? O, I have ta'en
> Too little care of this! Take physic, pomp,
> Expose thyself to feel what wretches feel.
>
> (3.4.19–34)

Here you have the power to strike right to the heart of modern concerns about our responsibility for the deprived and disadvantaged: the issue of welfare is the overriding concern of modern politics worldwide, and it is surely the heart of the play, not the earlier rantings about justice. These phrases should be the still moment at the center of the storm. Here you can show Lear learning to avoid absolute standards with the resentment that they foster, and concentrating on more practical and self-evident priorities. Stress how he begins to perceive that there is a deeper test of validity than abstract principles like justice. Physical suffering is the ultimate test of reality, and it is for this reason that Edgar is legitimately "empowered" as a "noble philosopher" (3.4.172)—because his abysmal condition defines the bedrock of human nature against which everything else must be measured. Do not make these lines mad ranting:

> Thou wert better in a grave than to answer with thy uncover'd body this extremity of the skies. Is man no more than this? Consider him well. Thou ow'st the worm no silk, the beast no hide, the sheep no wool, the cat no perfume. Ha? here's three on's are sophisticated. Thou art the thing itself: unaccommodated man is no more but such a poor, bare, fork'd animal as thou art. Off, off, you lendings! Come, unbutton here.
>
> (3.4.101–9)

Of course, much earlier the Fool had begun the education that is completed here in Lear's final acclimatization to the basic reality of human suffering, and that matches Hamlet's sardonic encounter with the figure of Death, in the form of the gravedigger and his skulls. The Fool is too clever, or too simple, to be hypocritical. He sees and takes things as they are: "The reason why the seven stars are no more than seven is a pretty reason." Lear correctly answers: "Because they are not eight"—an existential reply to which the Fool assents: "Yes, indeed, thou wouldst make a good Fool" (1.5.34–38). This earlier episode is like a little Zen training exercise, designed to encourage Lear to be less confident and assertive about human obligation and responsibility. But the role of the dispassionate "holy fool" is not merely an Eastern stereotype. Shakespeare acquired analogous inspiration from St. Paul's opening of his *First Letter to the Corinthians.* Paul censures the dogmatism, rigidity of mind, and assertiveness of the classic Hellenistic and Judaic traditions in the face of the new disruptive cult of Christianity, which challenged established principles and the authority that went with them. As Auerbach has argued in *Mimesis,* Christianity repudiated both the aristocratic, sophisticated culture of the Greek heroes from Achilles to Odysseus and the traditional theocratic Judaic social structure. Both cultures reacted negatively to primitive Christianity with its cult of the persecuted outsider, favoring the disadvantaged (not to say the proletariat). For Christianity tested intellectual and social systems not by their benefits to the elite or to the highly talented, but to the mass of repressed and suffering humanity. Paul's attitudes reflect the resulting tensions:

> For it is written I will destroy the wisdom of the wise, and will bring to nothing the understanding of the prudent. Where is the wise? where

> is the scribe? where is the disputer of this world? hath not God made foolish the wisdom of this world? . . . For the Jews require a sign and the Greeks seek after wisdom. But we preach Christ crucified, unto the Jews a stumbling block, and unto the Greeks foolishness. . . . Because the foolishness of God is wiser than men; and the weakness of God is stronger than men. . . . Not many wise men after the flesh, not many mighty, not many noble, are called. But God hath chosen the foolish things of the world to confound the wise; and God hath chosen the weak things of the world to confound the things which are mighty; and the base things of the world which are despised. (1 Cor. 1.19ff.)

In chapter 3.18 Paul reiterates: "Let no man deceive himself. If any man among you seemeth to be wise in this world, let him become a fool, that he may be wise. For the wisdom of this world is the foolishness of God. For it is written, He taketh the wise in their own craftiness." As illustration of his point, in chapter 2.1–4, Paul refers to his own awkward appearance to the oversophisticated Corinthians: "I came to you . . . not with excellency of speech or of wisdom. . . . And I was with you in weakness, and in fear, and in much trembling. And . . . not with enticing words of man's wisdom." By contrast "the natural man" considers such a posture to be "foolishness." One recalls Nature's devotee, Edmund, ridiculing this "credulous father, and a brother noble . . . on whose foolish honesty my practices ride easy" (1.2.179–82). But overall the more important issue is how the power and confidence of Lear's pursuit of what he is sure is right and virtuous is humbled to accept the less strenuous posture of the Fool. So take care that the Fool is treated with proper respect by Lear and by the other characters, not just as comic relief. Lear himself must follow a Tolstoy-like reformation, becoming a kind of "Holy Fool."

Still, what we see in *Lear* is not the overt Christianizing of Denmark in the script of *Hamlet.* Kozintsev misrepresents *Lear* when he introduces Christian symbols and ritual, in the added scene of Cordelia's marriage to France. Lear is a pagan hero, his oaths are validated by such gods as Apollo (to whose cult Herodotus ascribes the creation of Stonehenge). Throughout his career Shakespeare consciously experiments with different social models to see how well their assumptions work in practice, whether with Republican Rome in *Julius Caesar,* Imperial Rome in *Cymbeline,* or with the prehistoric Greece and Britain of Theseus and Lear. Lear is a worthier pagan hero than Old Hamlet, for his concern is with the greater issues of social justice, not with personal honor and private vengeance. Yet Lear's outlook initially is almost as incompatible with social survival as the vendetta principle. The heroic pursuit of virtue is self-destructive, and Lear has to learn to be less dictatorial, even when he pursues what seems self-evidently right: conferring authority on the virtuous Cordelia. So try to avoid gestures of overt christianizing. Such truths are at best latent, as in this pagan analogue to *Beowulf,* showing the inevitable downfall of another aging pagan superman.

At the core of this play, as with *Hamlet,* is the evolution of the hero toward an ethos that is life-enhancing rather than life-destructive. Lear learns to accept reality, as Hamlet believed Horatio did. This is what Lear achieves, as befits a powerless old man. Like ancient Tiresias and Cadmus, tripping off to the Bacchic revels under the reproaches of the puritanical Pentheus in Euripides' *Bacchae,* Lear by act 4 has become innocently unaffected. My students in the sixties held that Lear was truly as mad as Cordelia thinks at this point:

> Alack, 'tis he! Why he was met even now
> As mad as the vex'd sea, singing aloud,
> Crown'd with rank fumiter and furrow-weeds.
>
> (4.4.1–3)

But they became less confident when shown that they were delighted by the same innocent behavior of the first flower children, who shared Lear's delight in nature, and who proved as gently subversive as he does in the beach scene: "Through tatter'd clothes small vices do appear; / Robes and furr'd gowns hide all" (4.6.164–65).

Can any sensitive person consider Lear mad in this scene on the beach with Gloucester? This episode tests your will to reject noisy entropy as the key to the play's impact. Rather than make its climax the storm scenes, you may highlight the quiet moments of truth here, where Lear has the casual insight of the true sage. I saw Sebastian Shaw play this scene with Gloucester many years ago at a workshop organized by Marvin Rosenberg at the Zellerbach Theatre at Berkeley, and its quiet sanity has remained self-evident to me ever since:

> Ay, every inch a king!
> When I do stare, see how the subject quakes.
> I pardon that man's life. What was thy cause?
> Adultery?
> Thou shalt not die. Die for adultery! No,
> The wren goes to 't, and the small gilded fly
> Does lecher in my sight.

Let copulation thrive; for Gloucester's bastard son
Was kinder to his father than my daughters
Got 'tween the lawful sheets.

(4.6.107–16)

My lectures on the play ever since have had the title: "The Sanity of Lear." Every word rises naturally and wittily from Lear's calm contemplation of the pathetic groveling figure of the ruined Gloucester, with awareness of his casual adultery, announced in the play's opening dialogue. Lear still thinks that Edmund rescued his father from the "legitimate" Edgar's wicked plans, and indeed Lear echoes Edmund's sardonic speech, "Thou, Nature, art my goddess; . . . Now, gods, stand up for bastards!" (1.2.1–22), when he cries, scarcely less sardonically, "Let copulation thrive . . . for I lack soldiers." Throughout this climactic dialogue, in which the new Lear sees the world freshly, his manner may be eccentric but his perceptions are clear, unlike "the scurvy politician" who affects "to see the things thou dost not" (4.6.171–72). The as yet not fully tempered Edgar may not perceive the underlying alertness of Lear to reality, but Lear's view harmonizes too well with the final insights of Isabella and Hamlet to be dismissed as confused rambling. You must not let any postmodern director impose the trappings of lunacy on Lear at this point, as performed by the late Robert Stephens recently, flapping around with supermarket plastic bags on his feet. What you might aspire to is the quiet authority of a Zen master.

The value that we, as moderns, attach to *Lear* lies in the plausibility of Lear's transformation from a volatile if benevolent despot to a more serene sage. Our activist and destructive age may despise Lear's aspiration to quietism in his vision of peaceful imprisonment with Cordelia, but the powers of adjustment that Lear is shown to possess reflect a human adaptability of a supremely positive character, as gerontologists and brain specialists like Marion Diamond confirm. Shakespeare provocatively asserts that even as old, dictatorial, and irascible a figure as Lear can display capacities for discovery and growth. The play is full of calculated reversals, such as the parody of humility when Lear mockingly kneels to Regan (2.4.154) followed in due course by the sincere self-abasement when he again kneels, before Cordelia, accepting his role as "a very foolish fond old man . . . not in my perfect mind" (4.7.57ff). One of the play's supreme ironies is that Lear's final humility should ever be called "madness."

In conclusion, I wish to suggest an overview by which to coordinate the interpretations open to you and your colleagues: that the play is in not pessimistic, though truly tragic, in that what destroys the two principals is not innate vice, as befalls Edmund and the wicked sisters, but excessively strenuous pursuit of virtue. Even in the narrowly quantitative sense, the play is not as nihilistic as some despairing modern readers wish it to prove. At the end, the wicked characters have all met a merited death. Lear has died, but we can hardly regard the death of a character in his eighties as uniquely distressing, unless we are innocents still offended by universal mortality. The same is true with the aged Gloucester, who, instead of suicide, dies "smilingly." The event that offends idealists most is the death of Cordelia. She is one of the many innocent female victims of male assertiveness in Shakespeare: Ophelia, Desdemona, and Hermione. However, you should remember that, like Hamlet, her concerns are at odds with the autonomy and survival of her native country: she almost achieves French hegemony over Britain, just as Hamlet hands over Denmark to its dearest enemy, Norway. Moreover, Shakespeare has shifted the pessimism of her original mode of death in the sources, by suicide, to malicious execution, itself repented of by its cynical initiator Edmund, a reversal some modern directors hesitate to stage because of its affirmation of virtue's supremacy over evil. Lear may die crushed by Cordelia's death, but you might consider whether he dies despairing, for his last words suggest a hint of hope that she still breathes: "look, her lips, / Look there, look there!" (5.3.311–12). A hope is perhaps not wholly lost that Providence may intervene. If you feel this option is non-Shakespearean, recall that Shakespeare is soon to write *The Winter's Tale,* which restores to life a woman dead not for a few moments but for sixteen years. And Hermione's recovery from death is shared by another daughter of a legendary British king: Imogen in *Cymbeline.* So you have Shakespearean grounds for making Lear's death hopeful.

One other positive aspect of the conclusion lies outside your direct control, but as the most influential actor on the set you might urge your director to follow the lead of Kozintsev in stressing it after your own, now hopeful death. If Kent and Albany seem too old and exhausted to accept high office, this is not true of Edgar. While Brook's film elbows him out of the final frames, Kozintsev centers the first signs of social recovery, after the Lear family's funeral cortege, around the thoughtful survey of his new kingdom by Edgar. Edgar represents a reassuring figure like Malcolm in *Macbeth,* since he has not merely survived but learned from your sufferings, and has already intervened in the history of his society. Edgar is superior to the flawed and ineffective Cassio of *Othello*, and to the ominous Fortinbras who assumes power at the end of *Hamlet*. In *Lear* Edgar has never been less than virtuous, but at first he fails in the cunning required for survival in such a primitively competitive society. By the end of the play he is as manipulative and ruthless as Edmund, but not as cynical an egotist. He stage-manages a catharsis for his father that offends many by its grotesqueness but that restores the will to live. Edgar's supreme triumph in the play is so improbable that many modern directors cut it out: the repentance of Edmund that almost saves Cordelia. I hope you will use your influence yet again to oppose such misleading cuts, which force the script to conform to negativism. Edgar's affirmative role appears anomalous to modern critics unable to place him in their nihilistic reading of the play, but a director like Branagh chose to play Edgar in his own production as a key role, and his sense of its importance is surely correct if we look at the role more historically.

For Shakespeare inserted this Anglo-Saxon king into a legend dealing with pre-Roman Britain, just as once-pagan Denmark acquires a Hamlet from Lutheran Wittenberg. Historically, Edgar is best known as one of the most admired of Anglo-Saxon kings (A.D. 944–75), recognized in Shakespeare's mind as such when the insertion of Edgar into *Lear* drags in other Anglo-Saxons, Edmund and Oswald, associated with King Edgar (as Shakespeare knew from his own brother's name of Edmund). King Edgar's early career parallels that of Shakespeare's Edgar. Each Edgar displays a "rivalry between him and his elder brother," ending in the death of the dominant sibling and his replacement by his "weaker" rival. The career of the historical King Edgar meets your cast's need for clues about Shakespearean archetypes. His Edgar's nature is similar to that of Prince Hal in his reversal of role upon his coronation. The historical King Edgar reformed, accepting a seven-year chastity as penance for his earlier sexual sins, and feeling so repentant as "to postpone his coronation until he felt that he had come to full maturity of mind and conduct." Lear's own personality shows the same concern for modesty as Edgar's moralism: "Let not the creaking of shoes nor the rustling of silks betray thy poor heart to woman. Keep thy foot out of brothels, thy hand out of plackets" (3.4.95–97). By his coronation at Bath in 973, King Edgar became "Albiones Imperator Augustus"—the first high King of all England, accepted even by King Malcolm of Scotland. His coronation is of unique constitutional interest as "the first coronation of which we have a minute description," including the famous acclamation "Let the king live forever," and a promise to "command justice and mercy in all judgments." Lear has to learn this rule painfully.

Supposedly persuaded of Edgar's greater wisdom, six kings including Malcolm rowed a boat under his captaincy as a gesture of submission, as most English schoolchildren have been taught ever since. King Edgar showed such skill as a diplomat and administrator that his reign is frustratingly uneventful for historians: "It was a period of national consolidation, peace, and orderly government." One of his key traits was the opposite of Lear's confidence in his own love of virtue and justice, for Edgar was careful to support existing officers, institutions, and laws to a degree that earned him censure from one nationalist for "his love of foreigners and of foreign fashions and evil ways." For example, "he seems to have carefully forborne from interfering with the customs and internal affairs of the Danish district," which thus achieved its special status as "the Danelaw." His own laws were few, and "the words that stand at the head of his ordinances commanding that every man should be worthy of folk right, poor as well as rich, show the spirit of his administration." With such discreet policy "The peace of the years between 955 and 980 left a permanent impression on English history in the sphere of religion and culture" for which "King Edgar was a decisive factor." This high reputation of King Edgar proved enduring:

> Ancient scholars . . . regarded Edgar with veneration, and modern historians, realizing the significance of the ideals to which he gave his patronage, have tended to include him among the greatest of Old English rulers. . . . It was a notable achievement to keep England secure against foreign enemies for sixteen years and to maintain a standard of internal order which set a pattern for later generations. . . . It is his distinction that he gave unreserved support to the men who were creating the environment of a new English culture.

From his own time down to the present, Edgar's "personal character, the events of his life, and the glories of his reign made a deep impression on the English people. Not only are four ballads, or fragments of ballads, relating to his reign preserved in the different versions of the national chronicle, but a large mass of legends about him, originally no doubt contained in gleemen's songs, is given by William of Malmesbury." The Chinese curse is: "May You Live in Interesting Times," matched by the European aphorism, "Happy Is the Country that Has No History." Historians concur about

King Edgar: "It is a sign of Edgar's competence as a ruler that his reign is devoid of recorded incident."

My account of the historical King Edgar's anachronistic role as Shakespeare's matured *ingenu* presents him to you and your fellow actors as the key to the underlying rhythm of the whole play: as a prefiguration of the kind of kingship that might be learned by more recent, historical figures from the legendary vicissitudes of Lear's reign. The historical King Edgar's remarkable development validates Edgar's staged progression, and King Edgar's diplomatic finesse and temperate pursuit of justice also provide the norms for judging the pagan Lear's passionate but self-defeating obsession with virtue and justice. The parallel of an erratic youth evolving into a wiser ruler is a recurrent one in Shakespeare, which explains why King Edgar appealed to him, as an analogue for Prince Hal and Malcolm. Like them, Edgar is not a wry recluse or a feeble pacificist: as with Lear, to the end Edgar can still fight and kill in the true pursuit of peace and justice. Edgar's expertise and the powerful resonance of his name offer another positive that offsets the seeming negation of hope at the end of *Lear.* I hope that you and your colleagues will defy critics' belief that this is a nihilistic play and follow Kozintsev and Branagh, who show how it looks forward to the providential world of *Cymbeline.* If your troupe follows your lead in a positive reading of Shakespeare's supreme role, favorable audiences may require Marvin Rosenberg to add a reference in the next edition of *The Masks of King Lear.*

References

Alpers, Paul J., 1962. "King Lear and the Theory of the 'Sight Pattern'" *In Defence of Reading: A Reader's Approach to Literary Criticism,* edited by Reuben A. Brower and Richard Poirier. New York: Dutton.

Aristotle. *Poetics.* 1987. Translated and edited by Stephen Halliwell. Chapel Hill: University of North Carolina Press.

Bettelheim, Bruno. 1976. *The Uses of Enchantment: The Meaning and Importance of Fairy Tales.* London: Thames and Hudson.

Bullough, Geoffrey. 1966–75. *Narrative and Dramatic Sources of Shakespeare.* London: Routledge and Kegan Paul.

Diamond, Marion. 1984. "The Advantages of Aging." *Psychology Today,* no. 27, 104.

Dictionary of National Biography. Vol. 6:365–70 (King Edgar).

Elton, W. R. 1966. *"King Lear" and the Gods.* San Marino: Huntington Library.

Evans, Bertrand. 1960. *Shakespeare's Comedies.* London: Oxford University Press.

Foakes, Reginald A. 1993. *"Hamlet" Versus "Lear": Cultural Politics and Shakespeare's Art.* Cambridge: Cambridge University Press.

Kott, Jan. 1966. *Shakespeare Our Contemporary.* New York: Doubleday.

Lamb, Charles. 1946. "On the Tragedies of Shakespeare." In *Shakespeare Criticism: A Selection,* edited by Nichol Smith. London: Oxford University Press.

Rabkin, Norman. 1981. *Shakespeare and the Problem of Meaning.* Chicago: University of Chicago Press.

Richmond, Hugh M. 1989. *Shakespeare in Performance: King Richard III.* Manchester: Manchester University Press.

Rosenberg, Marvin. 1972; reprint, Newark: University of Delaware Press, 1994. *The Masks of King Lear.*

Sher, Antony. 1985. *The Year of the King: An Actors Diary and Sketchbook.* London: Chatto and Windus (Hogarth Press).

Smart, Janet I. 1983. *Italian Renaissance Tales.* Rochester, Mich.: Solaris Press (Sercambi).

Stenton, F. M. 1977. *Anglo-Saxon England.* Oxford: Clarendon Press.

Gleanings: The Residue of Difference in Scripts: The Case of Polanski's *Macbeth*

BERNICE W. KLIMAN

ARTISTS in all media may revise, but the lengthy and collaborative process of filmmaking makes the work of art susceptible to change at every level of development—from first conception to videotape redistribution. Purposeful difference usually denotes intent; a new version somehow approaches the artist's desired goal better than the original was able to do. But in filmmaking (and probably also in theatrical production) unintended or incidental differences couple with deliberate revision to produce the final effects. The records of changes from inception to conclusion are seldom open to inspection, but for Roman Polanski's *Macbeth* several scripts expose layers of effort, revealing false starts and revisions, distinguishing Polanski's conscious choices in his finished film.[1] Comparing Polanski's scripts and film is especially fruitful because he is not a filmmaker who leaves matters to chance on the set; he writes and sketches what he wants.[2] In a long career, he has demonstrated that he attempts to impose his concept on the collaborative and sometimes recalcitrant medium of film. With his precision and his need to plan meticulously, his changes in several scripts of *Macbeth* open a unique window into his creative process.

When he co-wrote the script with Kenneth Tynan in 1970, Polanski spent six or seven arduous weeks working out details.[3] Well before shooting his films, he knows how he wants them to look. So precise is his exactitude that he uses cameramen no taller than he (5 feet 5 inches) so that they will see through the lens what he sees. While the visual texture of his films is primary, he also works hard to construct realistic characters, making sure that they behave as he would expect.[4] His frequent question is, "Would a person like that react that way?"

While many more scripts in various stages of development may have existed for *Macbeth,* those that are available show that there were at least three overlapping levels represented by four scripts.[5]

Polanski sent me a copy of an early script marked up with cancellations, insertions, corrections, and taped-on changes. I call this document "the first script," a misnomer because it obviously is not the first script. It is, though, the earliest available. It marks a particularly significant change from an earlier version, the palimpsest concealed beneath the taped-on and handwritten revisions. A script at a slightly later stage I call the "intermediate script." With a few interesting exceptions, it is a clean copy of the first script, recording the changes neatly; its differences are too few, however, to consider it a new stage in Polanski's script development. A somewhat later script I call "the Ross script" for reasons that will become obvious. On it, a few erasures and some retyping signal further changes—changes that are especially notable when they occur in the same places Polanski revised the first script—when, in other words, the revision in the first script was a step toward still further revision in the Ross script. The layers in these two main scripts are tantalizing—with cancellations or erasures that sometimes completely and sometimes partially obscure the underlying state. All these scripts divide the play into 140 scene-segments but without splitting the scenes into all the shots that we see in the final film (the Ross script, however, divides several scenes into segments, labeled a, b, etc.). Polanski also sent me 35 pages of vivid, urgent sketches—each page with several frames capturing key narrative moments—that indicate his visual aim for almost all 140 scenes.

After twenty-five weeks of shooting, in 1971 Polanski began editing the film. This work must have been rigorous because he films many long-takes usually with one camera rather than with the very shot takes that can be pieced together more easily.[6] The last level of script development is a release script, a technical postproduction script[7] that records the intersection of sound and image and describes every shot (i.e., every start and stop of the camera) in a finished version of the film. This *Macbeth* release script lists several hundred shots in 16 reels, as compared to the 140 scene-elements in the working scripts. The release script records what is on the film, which is somewhat different from what is on the videotape—because the different aspect ratios force some cropping of the video frame. Thus, though my descriptions from the release script often apply to both film and videotape, at times enough material variation exists between film and video to give them different effects. Clearly, Polanski had nothing to do with the creation of the videotape; yet this postproduction revision is part of the film's history, part of its story as a work of art, and the version that audiences from now on are most likely to see.

Knowing the control Polanski insists upon, having his first and second thoughts on paper, I infer that whatever is in the film is closer to what he wanted even when it differs from the preproduction scripts. Film editing accounts, most likely, for the fact that the film eliminates many little narrative bridges found in the first three scripts: one among many is Lady Macbeth's rushing along the corridor to ring the bell that invites Macbeth to commit the murder (scene 44). Instead, the camera cuts directly from Macbeth to the shot of her delicately ringing the bell. Another is a shot of Malcolm and Donalbain, on horseback, one wheeling toward England, the other to Ireland (scene 57). The visual is not necessary because the film includes their lines from the play that reveal their plans. Circumstances, of course, forced some changes upon Polanski, the most well-known probably being the scene of the bearbaiting, which was unfilmable with the resources Polanski had at hand. When bears and dogs would not "hit their marks," Polanski reluctantly omitted the shot of the baiting in process, settling for shots before and after to suggest the whole. These are all expected adjustments that produce a tightly paced film, running two hours and twenty minutes.

More interesting, however, are Polanski's changes that help him express his purpose: virtually every change in the scripts strengthens the idea that the film expresses, that society rather than any one individual is tragically flawed; it is a tragedy with neither a specific tragic hero nor a specific villain.[8] It is not unreasonable to suppose that Polanski had this purpose from the beginning, but the first scripts do not achieve this interpretation as compellingly as do the Ross script and the film. Polanski surmounted three hurdles before he could get an audience familiar with *Macbeth* to see his vision: the view that the witches, Lady Macbeth, or Macbeth are the centers of the tragic action. Though he had read the play many times, he had never seen a production of *Macbeth* on stage and thus perhaps only gradually realized that he would have to enforce his view on those (like Tynan) already familiar with the play from countless productions that center the tragedy on anything other than society.[9] A modification in the witches, who from first to last are not supernatural powers, and distinctions among several minor characters helped Polanski clarify his purpose.

Before I had the opportunity to examine these scripts, I had already written about the film (in a study on *Macbeth* in performance). At that time, somewhat embarrassed, I stumbled into a kind of feminist reading of the film. "Embarrassed"—because how could I consider the dedicated womanizer to be a feminist filmmaker?[10] Many of Polanski's female characters are victims (a condition that some early feminists were prone to expose and that many later feminists are loath to admit), and his sympathy for their pain is remarkable. Lady Macbeth, for example, with her childlike vulnerability becomes a sympathetic character through her suffering. Lady Macduff is a strong and tender woman. The gentlewoman, whose role Polanski expands in the Ross script, lovingly nurtures Lady Macbeth. These women are part of the scheme of making society, not individuals, culpable; Polanski removes any power from Lady Macbeth in particular, but to intensify the point, makes all the women virtual ciphers in the male society and thus not implicated in the males' antler butting. A good example of a material difference in the video that obscures Polanski's depiction of Lady Macbeth's role occurs in the play's first scene. While the bloody sergeant (who will later appear as Menteith with a scar over his eye) relates Macbeth's victories, Donalbain is as delighted as Duncan, but Malcolm scowls. The video, because of the aspect ratio, omits Donalbain and Malcolm from the scene entirely. Polanski's film establishes a competition between Malcolm and Macbeth that reaches its fulfillment when Malcolm unsmilingly thrusts his wine goblet at Macbeth and thus changes Macbeth's mind about not murdering Duncan after Lady Macbeth's pleas have been ineffectual.

Polanski also shows women who absent themselves from a society corrupted by ambition and who control their own lives. Thoroughly rooted in grime and domesticity, his witches are women, not demonic forces. In spite of naturalism, Polanski maintains dramatic interest in their scenes establishing them as a countercommunity, separate from the contentious Scottish court. He contrasts them in their easy camaraderie to the males, jostling for position. I have argued that his witches use spells to ward off the evil of warriors lusting for power: spitting over shoulders has long been a symbol for guarding against evil. They might throw herbs over a severed hand as protection from the violence of the men. They divine the future, perhaps relish the self-destructiveness of the warriors, but do not cause it. The witches change very little in the scripts I have seen but one difference is telling.

The first, intermediate, and Ross scripts describe The Young Witch as "pudgy, ugly, and vacant-looking" (scene 9b in the Ross script). Even so, it's surprising how many observers of the film miss Polanski's point. Jack J. Jorgens, who has written perceptively about the film, cautiously remarks that the Young Witch might be pretty under her stringy hair (162). Marvin Rosenberg and many others, however, declare her beautiful (16).[11] Yet Polanski not only describes her as ugly in the script but also has her made up with sores on both cheeks and directs her to let her lower lip hang. An audience's interpretation may, of course, vary from what the filmmaker wants. Though Polanski with his tight control over every aspect wants to prevent just such accidents in interpretation, ultimately, people will see what they want to see. Polanski's scripts make clear that he wanted his witches all to appear foul in contrast to the warriors who look, in the main, fair (with the exception of a scruffy Macduff played by Terence Bayler).

A change in the Young Witch suggests his accommodation to misreading of her as attractive (possibly during rushes): the film's Young Witch is dumb, able only to mouth words and grunt, whereas in the preproduction scripts she does speak. Why bother to change her from a speaker to a silent participant? It could have been an accident of the casting, the inability of the twenty-year-old actor Noelle Rimmington to speak the lines as Polanski wanted.[12] But it is also possible that by making her vocally deficient he substitutes for the ugliness his scripts called for and that the viewers of his rushes, like many viewers of his film, did not see. With her vacant silence, he enlarges the community of the witches where the—as we might put it today—"verbally, mentally, temporally, and visually challenged" all have full standing, in contrast to the male warrior society, where Donalbain, who has a heavy limp, is not Duncan's choice as heir. (Much to Donalbain's disgust, for at Duncan's announcement, he is at least as angry as Macbeth is, as Rosenberg points out [154]. The script says that Malcolm is the eldest; however, the visual picture is of a Donalbain who looks older than Malcolm). Making the witches into the Other helps Polanski shape his design: and we can infer why if he could not convincingly make his Young Witch ugly, he might have settled for making her dumb: he interprets the play as the tragedy of a society blemished in soul yet beautiful in surface. His witches allow him to center the paradox of fair and foul within the warrior society.

The film is tragic (rather than simply an appalling story of violence and evil) because one can sense something better in Banquo, Seyton, Lennox, and even, at the end, Malcolm.[13] By minor changes in the scripts Polanski reinforces a positive view of these characters. Though Shakespeare's Banquo is problematic since he suspects that Macbeth has murdered Duncan yet pledges his loyalty to him, Polanski's Banquo—played by Martin Shaw—seems to be an honestly righteous man. The film insists on his detachment from Macbeth by keeping him silent—from the Ross script on—as others hail Macbeth king at Scone, in contrast to the first script that has him initiate the hail. The film is careful to shoot him in profile so that we can see his tightly closed lips. Later his awkwardness with Macbeth when leaving with Fleance to hunt before the banquet implies a moral difficulty, his ambivalence about Macbeth. In the first three scripts and in the film, Banquo gives a signal for hanging prisoners, while in the video, because he is cut out of the frame, he does not signal; there is no signal. These changes make Banquo a better man, particularly (though presumably inadvertently) in the video.

The weak Seyton (Noel Davis), simpering behind Macbeth and Lady Macbeth in the bear scene, is a despicable sycophant who does not question anything Macbeth tells him to do. But he is loyal to the end, facing down a hoard of deserting servants and soldiers, and one may, perhaps, see something hopeful in that loyalty; led by a better person he might have been a better man. From the Ross script on, Polanski expands benign aspects of his role. For example, Seyton is the first person Macbeth sees when entering Inverness, and there is easy affection between them (scene 24). The Ross (scene 34) and release scripts (reel 4, shot 12) have him carving the meat at the banquet for Duncan, and the release script adds the role of royal taster to Seyton's other offices (reel 9, shot 57), an adroit touch that suggests Macbeth's paranoia.

Rebellion against evil is also potentially noble: Menteith as the bloody sergeant grew from pride at Macbeth's valor to cynicism about Macbeth's crimes. Lennox, while he remains with Macbeth after ceasing to trust him, finally does leave openly, tendering his resignation as chamberlain. Soon followed by Menteith and Caithness, Lennox joins Malcolm not so much for self-interest as from disgust with Macbeth.[14] In contrast, the murderous thugs who remain with Macbeth exit ignominiously, looting as they go, after they see the woods of Birnam approaching. The scene of Lennox's resignation (not shown in Shakespeare) is another way Polanski suggests that there is some hope for the society within its own warrior code, which prizes loyalty, brutal violence against enemies, and domestic harmony. All the possibly noble thanes contribute to a sense that though the society is corrupt something better struggles to emerge.

Most importantly, perhaps, Malcolm, though still proud, gains in stature in a few late scenes; an audience can overlook his earlier arrogance because exile has somewhat chastened him and he does not lie to Macduff (most of 4.3 is omitted). Polanski's view seems to be that society has a share both of evil and good men and that a society might be healthy in its own terms if good were to predominate. He is skeptical, though, about the possibility—and none of these "good men" is unproblematically virtuous.

Further changes intensify the differences between these characters and those remaining. Neither the first nor the Ross script identifies the murderous looter in the beach scene as one of Duncan's men, as the film explicitly does by having him interrupt his attack on the wounded soldier and kneel to the King riding by (in a segment following the credits).

Duncan's response to the supine Cawdor, tied on a litter, changes so as to point up Duncan's cruelty. In the first and Ross scripts upon learning from Ross about Cawdor, Duncan turns away and then as an afterthought wheels around and calls to someone offscreen to bestow Cawdor's medallion on Macbeth (scene 6). In the film, he menacingly lifts the medallion with the point of his sword, the first instance of the motif that continues through the film: a sword's point at a victim's throat, often a helpless person. Macbeth kills Duncan finally with the point of his sword in the jugular, later kills Young Seyward the same way, and then declines to finish off Macduff similarly, though his dream vision hints that he would. Polanski makes Duncan suspect by linking him, if retrospectively, with Macbeth's point-of-sword maneuvers. Polanski's Duncan, as played by the manly Nicolas Selby (then forty-five), is strong and pitiless. We hear his ruthlessness when he says "greet Macbeth," and we hear it later when he chides his sons for being surprised that Cawdor died so bravely. "Don't you know," his tone asks cynically, "that men's honor cannot be measured by what they seem" (scene 17). His words of course say, "There's no art / To find the mind's construction in the face. / He was a gentleman on whom I built / An absolute trust." These lines are usually said rather sentimentally and immediately usher Macbeth in to ironic effect. Polanski instead cuts to the letter scene, 1.5, right after Duncan's harsh words, ending the segment with a point about Duncan.

Though ugliness is no guarantee of moral rectitude, many of Polanski's handsome creatures are hard-hearted (as well as charming when they need to be), not only Duncan, but also Lady Macbeth, Macbeth, Malcolm—and especially Ross, whose characterization is arguably the most significant material Polanski added to the first film script. Kenneth S. Rothwell, Jack J. Jorgens, and others have noted the prominence Polanski gives Ross, weaving his machinations into the fabric of the Shakespearean narrative.

With the development of Ross as a pivotal character, Polanski emphasizes the evil-in-beauty that he sees in the society—and that concept retains centrality when Ross, played by handsome John Stride (who ten years before had played a young Romeo in Franco Zeffirelli's Old Vic stage production),[15] hands the crown over to Malcolm. Visually, Ross is the kingmaker. But that wasn't the case in the first script, which does not envision a key role for Ross. It's shocking to think that an element of the film that seems so integral to Polanski's purpose should have entered the creative process so late. The concept is a brilliant stroke that captures efficiently the interplay of personality and society.

As in the Shakespeare script, in Polanski's first script Ross functions mainly as a messenger. In a revision inserted in Polanski's first script, however, a red-haired thug surfaces at Macbeth's side, a step toward the conception of Ross. Called the Bodyguard, the red-haired thug first appears during the prelude to Banquo's exit from Macbeth's court, a scene that the script adds in a taped-on piece (scene 61): "At Macbeth's side is a new character, his BODYGUARD, a muscular thug with bright red hair." He and others are looking at a caged bear being prodded with sticks by children. The first script inks him in again as the scene continues (scene 61) and then again as Macbeth's entourage proceeds toward Macbeth's apartment where Macbeth will meet the two soldiers who will assassinate Banquo (scene 62). We are, it seems, to notice the Bodyguard and recognize him as a retainer, though not in the trusted position of Seyton. He next appears as the Third Murderer (scenes 66–69). In an insertion in the first script, the Bodyguard joins Seyton to help dispose of Banquo's two soldier assassins, who had been lacking in enthusiasm for their task. In the first script, the Bodyguard and Seyton each "bundles" an assassin through a door that leads down into a watery dungeon (scene 73). The film, however, distances Seyton somewhat from this brutality because it does not show him physically thrusting the men into the dungeon. Ross in the film, not Seyton (as in the Ross script), is the one who relieves the younger murderer of his crutch and uses it to push him into the dungeon. The film also increases the horror by making two guards willing assistants in the disposal: the more that anonymous men do Macbeth's bidding, the better Polanski enforces his idea about society.

The Bodyguard is not present during the banquet: he's not the sort one invites to dinner. The first script next inks him in at the head of armed men who enter Macduff's castle (84), allowed in by a treacherous servant, who had been playing blindman's buff with the children. In the film, the murderer with a large mole, played by Ian Hogg, asks "Where is your husband?" and casually breaks a vase. In the first script the red-haired Bodyguard plays that part (scene 87).[16] The first script (as revised) and the intermediate script make the Bodyguard the messenger who reports that the woods move.[17] The last time the first script mentions the Bodyguard, again in a taped-on piece (scene 129), he is leading a group of looters out through the gate of Dunsinane past Seyton's dead body; in the intermediate script, the Bodyguard before leaving shoots Seyton with an arrow to the forehead. Thus, after introducing this character in the revision recorded in the first script, Polanski continued to add details in the intermediate script. At one point, in the scene that begins with Macbeth saying "Bring me no more reports," Polanski in the first script had placed the Bodyguard among the other thanes but then crossed him out (scene 95). He evidently toyed with the idea of making him a nobleman and then rejected that notion: the bodyguard could only be a servant.[18] In essence Polanski picked up again the idea of making him a thane when he revised the script once more.

The Bodyguard is the objective correlative for the evil person that Macbeth, whom Polanski first describes as "open-faced," has become. Macbeth's last moment of humanity surfaces when, after Duncan's murder, he regrets what he has done. Once he butchers the drugged guards and plans Banquo's murder, Macbeth is lost. Admitting into the script this Bodyguard is Polanski's sign that Macbeth has made evil his good. Polanski then eliminates this excellent visual emblem who is too much associated with Macbeth alone.

In the Ross script, Polanski replaces the Bodyguard with Ross, erasing imperfectly one name and replacing it with the other—thus leaving the faint tracings of the change. When Polanski transmutes the Bodyguard into a vicious Ross, who is with the English forces, he has an anonymous soldier kill Seyton. Whether by accident or design, this spreading of casual evil increases the sense that the society rather than any one or two individuals is flawed. Except for the Macduff carnage, where Ross will play the role of traitor rather than murderer, this Ross script slots Ross into most of the positions formerly held by the Bodyguard, but it also develops his motivation more thoroughly. In the scripts, Ross travels with two servants. In the film, however, he is alone, emphasizing his minor status, and making his ambition all the more intelligible, making him, as it were, hungrier for advancement than he would seem if he had a following of his own. As one of Duncan's thanes and then as one of Macbeth's thanes, Ross appears, of course, in the background of many scenes. He is thus more of a presence than a bodyguard can be. With his connections to Duncan, Macbeth, Macduff, and Malcolm, Ross is an integral part of the society, more significant than the marginal Bodyguard brought in only to serve Macbeth. By changing the Bodyguard into Ross, Polanski intensifies his point about Scottish society.

The Ross script repeatedly differentiates Ross from other thanes. Polanski's first significant change is to have his new Ross kneel to help Macbeth, the rising man, the newly made Cawdor, mount a horse (scene 14). In the first script, when Ross meets Macduff leading Duncan's meager funeral procession, Polanski clarifies the men's feelings (scene 58). Ross says, "Is't known who did this more than bloody deed?" to which Macduff replies, "Those that Macbeth hath slain." Polanski adds: "Ross raises his eyebrows. *They* are talking in ironic deadpan tones and it is clear where *their* suspicions lie" (emphasis mine). Polanski had some trouble settling on "ironic," with two other choices crossed out; he clearly wanted to get the tone right. In the Ross script, instead of joining Macduff in suspicions of Macbeth, "Ross," says Polanski, "is probing him to find out his sympathies. *Macduff* replies in ironic, deadpan tones and it is clear where *his* suspicions lie" (emphasis mine). Ross in this script and in the film does not join with Macduff in irony at Macbeth's expense.

In the Ross script, Polanski has Ross "enthusiastically" hail Macbeth king at Scone. In the videotape, with its revisionary technology, the frame focuses on Banquo's silence rather than on Ross's initiative in hailing Macbeth. Though the release script mentions Ross's voice, the videotape version, in reducing the horizontal dimension to fit the television frame, does not reveal him or expressly make it his voice. The film, however, shows him in left profile facing Banquo in right profile; Banquo's seriousness wipes the smile from Ross's face. Ross's intimate knowledge of Banquo's feelings, expressed through grim silence, arguably allows Ross to inveigle his way into Macbeth's inner circle through informing on Banquo, a subtle point of which the video audience will be unaware.

Though the Ross script, the release script, and the film also place Ross in the Bodyguard's position in the bear scene before Macbeth's meeting with the two soldier assassins, the videotape eliminates Ross here as it had at Scone, gaining in shock and surprise by suddenly showing him later as the third murderer without any prelude to indicate his connections to Macbeth (taking him directly from the scene with Macduff to the role of Third Murderer).[19] In this presumably accidental way, the videotape creates an effect—admirable in its own way—different from the one Polanski shaped in scripts and film. Since Polanski in a *Playboy* interview affirms that an essential element for him is not allowing the audience "to anticipate what is going to happen next" (96), the revision forced by the technicality of aspect ratios satisfies his principles.

As befits Ross's new role, Polanski also modifies his part in the banquet scene. In the first script, Ross is simply one of the thanes present at the table, and we hear nothing of him until he says, "Please it your highness To grace us with your royal company" (scene 74). In the Ross script and film, however, Ross enters somewhat late, and he and Macbeth "exchange glances." In the first script, when he is still just a messenger, Ross is the one to ask "(inquisitively) 'What sights, my lord?'" Since that question will not at all do for the new Ross, who must protect rather than expose Macbeth, the Ross script overlays the name of Lennox here. Soon after, in the Ross script and film, Ross is the betrayer of his kin, the Macduff family. The servant still plays a part, opening the gate to the armed men, but now at Ross's signal. In the Ross script, Ross bribes the man with money while in the film nothing so overt motivates the man's treachery. The murders are familiar hangers-on in Macbeth's court, where they will return, and they also had been part of Duncan's court. Instead of the attempted rape of the nursemaid by three soldiers as in the first and Ross scripts, the film's servant rapes her while two soldiers hold her. Though Polanski multiplied abominations with these revisions of the Macduff scene,[20] his drawings show the central image that appalled audiences, the two bloody babies; the essence of the scene is unchanged.

In the first script it seems that, as in Shakespeare, the Macduff murders motivate Ross's defection to the English court—after he left his cousins unprotected in Fife. In both, Ross appears next in England. In the Ross script, however, Ross, having returned to Dunsinane after betraying Macduff, intercepts Seyton, to whom Lennox has thrown his chain of office and letters of resignation. Cowing Seyton into given these to him, Ross, followed by a scurrying Seyton, brings them to Macbeth. After reading one letter and burning the other, Macbeth bestows Lennox's medallion of office on the surprised Seyton. The two Macduff murderers, who are also watching the medallion intently, want it too, but they follow Macbeth off-frame. The camera remains on Ross, whose mouth twists (scene 96 says, "ROSS smiles") and whose glance follows the departing Lennox.[21] Next Ross is in England. He carries off his part there with practiced hypocrisy. His next moment is at the end, during the climactic match between Macbeth and Macduff, a moment absent from both the first and Ross scripts but described in the release script (reel 16, shots 12–13). Leaving Macduff after declining to kill him, Macbeth hurls his ax at the crowd of soldiers watching. A cut to Ross shows him reacting as the ax hits him and knocks off his helmet. His surprised reaction yields one of the film's few chuckles—but Ross is unscathed. The first script (scene 134) had Macduff removing, with some difficulty, the crown from Macbeth's severed head, and hailing Malcolm king. The Ross script has Ross with similar difficulty use a dagger to lever "the crown off MACBETH's head," then hand it to Malcolm and hail him King. The film is almost the same except the crown easily slips into Ross's hands. Overall, in the film Ross moves up in the world, a chilling thought.

With this Ross, Polanski reinforces his notion of a diseased society at the center of the play, chipping away through these means and others the concept of the nobly ambitious Macbeth gone bad poised against righteous thanes and a sacred king. The latter interpretation depends on clearly malevolent witches and a powerful and domineering Lady Macbeth—both of which Polanski declines to depict. Instead, with the ambitious Ross, the thuggish thanes, and the Macduff servant to swell the scene—treacherous murder and rape are an inevitability; they would have happened one way or another; Macbeth is the one who murders the King only because opportunity presents itself. At first Polanski called his film "The Tragedy of Macbeth," but his new title, "Macbeth," better reflects his interpretation: if society is the tragic figure, then it is not the tragedy of Macbeth. The realistic witches and the diminished stature of both Macbeth and Lady Macbeth from the beginning prove that the film's view of society fulfilled Polanski's vision, but through the new Ross as well as numerous local changes he pushes his audience to accept his vision. If Polanski's view is bleak, it is because he gives us no sense that the society understands itself sufficiently to purge its rotten elements. At the end, Donalbain stumbles upon the witches' cave as had Macbeth and Banquo, and will presumably, as in the Chronicles, begin again the cycle of destruction.

If by "Polanski," we mean the product (scripts, film, and videotape) rather than the individual, then we do not have to trouble about who executed the changes in various forms. While Polanski's known strong personality and his desire to control his projects suggest that he is the source of most revisions, there is no way to know this certainly or determine when in the process they occurred. Some changes come with filming: the artist accommodates to ineffectual bears and dogs. When he must, he moves on before he gets precisely what he wants; he went 20 percent over budget as it was. A journalist who covered some of the filming (by acting in the scene of prisoners being hanged) reports that Polanski shot the sequence many times, taking great pains with details, though the camera was thirty-five feet away from the action. Finally, he turned to something else, promising to continue later with the hanging. But he never did.[22] On the other hand, the changes that take form in his mind before camera setups start eating up his budget before his film can develop fully. Such revisions include the cascade of changes that led him from anonymous thanes to the red-haired thug to Ross, the changes in the Young Witch, and the other minor characters that so coherently capture the interpretation that he achieved.[23] Like all artists, Polanski shapes his material, both chance and planned, to emphasize or diminish parts in service of the whole. His scripts show him in the process of performing this artist's task. Fragile and incomplete ephemera provide a glass through which we can glimpse his task in progress.

Notes

1. An astounding feature of the script is how much was there from the beginning; all sorts of little details from the early script make their way into the final film. A few examples—the opening on the predawn sandy beach, the witches' rites before the credits; the sound of battle under the credits; a looter's killing of a wounded soldier; the king riding by; the defeated being hanged under the supervision of Macbeth and Banquo; Macbeth glancing down at Cawdor's medallion on his chest after Ross has given it to him; the blind witch rubbing the young witch's back—detail after detail from every aspect of the film. Still, there are many differences; for example, the early scripts describe the two murderers of Banquo as about thirty, in the film they appear to be father and son; the preproduction scripts describe "Two YOUNG BROTHERS" in Macbeth's 4.1 fantasy, while the film shows Malcolm and Donalbain in white. While the first, possibly adventitious, variance, contributes to the pathos of Macbeth's use of the men as pawns, some viewers cannot make sense of the latter choice. I can explain neither change with the materials at hand.

I am grateful for their help to Roman Polanski, Andrew Newman, Kenneth S. Rothwell, and to John Golder, organizer of the Australian and New Zealand Shakespeare Association Conference, who invited me to present a version of this paper, January 1996. The audience contributed questions and comments that helped clarify the issues.

2. While planning meticulously, he does allow for creative inspirations and decisions by actors (especially minor actors), and he does not spell out every nuance in the scripts, not often naming the emotional effect he seeks.

3. Kenneth Tynan kept a journal during the year he was connected with Polanski's project, first as coauthor of the script starting in April 1970, and then as literary advisor during twenty-five weeks of filming from November 1970 to April 1971. He or someone else may have saved other documents. Tynan says it took six weeks to develop the script (Tynan 122); another source says seven weeks (*Playboy* 79).

4. Tynan, 187, mentions that at one point the "first scene—only eight lines long—has already gone through a dozen revisions" to get the realism Polanski wants. Tynan remarks, "Sometimes I get impatient with the way he frets over minute details of description—even of layout on the page."

5. Scripts are located, in order of composition, in Polanski's private collection, at the libraries of the University of Southern California and the Ohio State University, and at the Library of Congress.

6. Tynan describes the way Polanski works: "He hardly ever uses more than one camera, and he favors long takes on which he must stake everything, since this method makes it impossible to delete anything without causing an unacceptable jump-cut. Having committed himself to a single camera setup, he lets the takes multiply" (189).

7. The cover page contains the following information: "*~~THE TRAGEDY OF~~*^ MACBETH | RELEASE SCRIPT | MAI HARRIS | 26 D'ARBLAY STREET | LONDON W. 1. January 1972. A similar postproduction script, but without a cover page, submitted to the Library of Congress for copyright purposes is dated 19 December 1971 but was received at the library 14 December 1973. Release scripts, which specify the number of feet in each shot, describe only enough of a scene to link the visual and aural elements; the Library of Congress Motion Picture Collections has one.

8. Roger Greenspun in a *New York Times* review (21 December 1971) saw immediately that the film is about a corrupt society rather than about Macbeth and Lady Macbeth.

9. Tynan shows that he never did "get it"; he maintains that Lady Macbeth had to be young and attractive to persuade her husband to murder Duncan. Polanski makes very clear through his filming of the so-called persuasion scene (1.7) that Malcolm's arrogance rather than Lady Macbeth's persuasive powers settles Macbeth. See below.

10. Of course, in being thus embarrassed, I am showing myself guilty of the biographical fallacy. A recent long profile by Lawrence Weschler in *The New Yorker,* however, describes Polanski, as hesitantly as I do, as a feminist: Weschler characterizes the 1965 *Repulsion* as a film "virtually protofeminist in the intensity of its identification with the inner experience of a beautiful young woman . . ." (95, but see Tynan 124). For a view of Polanski's range, see the now outdated filmography in Bisplinghoff.

11. Weschler also calls her "a beauty alongside two wrinkled hags" (99), locating, as does Rosenberg, the paradox of "Fair is foul and foul is fair" within the community of witches.

12. Welles, for example, had just such difficulties with his witches in his 1948 film. See Kliman, "Welles," 31.

13. Without entering into definitions, whether Aristotelian or not, I suggest that regret for something wasted is one element of tragedy.

14. Shakespeare affords multiple possibilities for the named thanes. See Kliman, "Thanes."

15. See Levenson, 82–104.

16. Polanski says his filming "was based on a childhood experience. . . . I suddenly recalled how the SS officer had searched our room in the ghetto, swishing his riding crop to and from, toying with my teddy bear, nonchalantly emptying out a hatbox full of forbidden bread. The behavior of Macbeth's henchmen was inspired by that recollection" (Polanski 333).

17. The Ross script changes the speech prefix from "BODYGUARD" to "SECOND MINOR THANE" (except, in error, for his first speech, still calling him "BODYGUARD").

18. Later Polanski shows the Bodyguard and Seyton both at Macbeth's side in a set of four scenes (scenes 97–100) watching soldiers grimly fortifying Dunsinane, a sequence the film omits.

19. A moment-by-moment perusal of the videotape does indeed show a glimpse of Ross in 3.1, but one could easily miss him. The videotape does not feature him at the side of Lady Macbeth as does the film.

20. See Weinraub for Polanski's view of violence. See also DuBois.

21. Polanski brilliantly uses long shots from castle ramparts: from Inverness, Lady Macbeth watches the approach of Duncan; later, Macbeth shouts his "Then fly false thanes . . ." (5.3.7–8) at the retreating figures of Lennox and his party.

22. Freud, 28.

23. Parker is particularly good on differentiating an author's intentions from both accidental and purposeful revisions that interfere with an author's clearest vision (10). He asserts that revision, even by the author alone, can lead to "unintended, uncontrolled effects" (75). But Polanski's scripts and film are amazingly free from "stubs," leftovers from early versions that disrupt artistic unity. There is, of course, a difference between revision long after a work is complete and revision that is part of the composing process; though Polanski worked on the film for over a year, one may consider the whole long process his effort to discover, explore, and reinforce his vision.

References

Bisplinghoff, Gretchen, and Virginia Wright Wexman. 1979. *Roman Polanski: A Guide to References and Resources.* Boston: G. K. Hall.

DuBois, Larry. 1971. "*Playboy* Interview: Roman Polanski." *Playboy* (Dec.) 93–126.

Freud, Clement. 1971. "An Odyssey in Wales: Roman Polanski's *Macbeth*," *Show* (June) 24–28.

Greenspun, Roger. 1971. "Polanski's and Tynan's 'Macbeth,'" *New York Times,* 21 December, 51.

Jorgens, Jack J. 1977. "Roman Polanski's *Macbeth.*" In *Shakespeare on Film.* Bloomington: Indiana University Press.

Kliman, Bernice W. 1982. *Macbeth: Shakespeare in Performance.* General Editors J. R. Mulryne and James Bulman. Manchester: Manchester University Press Paperback version, "Visionary Director on Film: Roman Polanski."

———1991. "Thanes in the Folio *Macbeth.*" *Shakespeare Bulletin* 9, no. 1 (winter):5–8.

———"Welles's *Macbeth,* A Textual Parable." In *Screen Shakespeare,* ed. Michael Skovmand. Aarhus, Denmark: Aarhus University Press.

Levenson, Jill L. 1987. *Romeo and Juliet: Shakespeare in Performance.* Manchester: Manchester University Press.

Parker, Hershel. 1984. *Flawed Texts and Verbal Icons: Literary Authority in American Fiction.* Evanston, Ill.: Northwestern University Press.

Playboy 1972. Pictures, Background, and Quotations. (February): 77–82.

Polanski, Roman. 1984. *Roman by Polanski.* New York: Morrow.

Rosenberg, Marvin. 1978. *The Masks of Macbeth.* Newark: University of Delaware Press.

Rothwell, Kenneth S. 1983–84. "Roman Polanski's *Macbeth:* The 'Privileging' of Ross." *CEA Critic* 46, nos. 1 and 2 (fall and winter):50–55.

Tynan, Kenneth. 1971. "The Polish Imposition." *Esquire* (September):122–25, 180–89.

Weinraub, Bernard. 1971. "'If you don't show violence the way it is,' says Roman Polanski, 'I think that's immoral and harmful. If you don't upset people then that's obscenity.'" *New York Times Magazine* (12 December):36–37, 64–82.

Weschler, Lawrence. 1994. "Artist in Exile." *The New Yorker.* Illustrated (5 December):88–107.

Macbeth at the Turn of the Millennium

BARBARA HODGDON

Two recent *Macbeths*—Michael Bogdanov's English Shakespeare Company production (1992) and Robert Lepage's staging with Québec's Théâtre Répère (1993)—raise a series of questions about reading current configurations of performed Shakespeare. Although the most obvious distinctions between the two are between an English-language production and one based on Michel Garneau's 1978 Québecois "tradaptation," and between a production situated within Anglo-European theatrical culture and one occurring outside that culture, on its margins, each staging also resonates with different notions of playing or replaying Shakespeare—whether as reprisal or as exploration. Clearly, the linguistic and locational histories and politics of each remain central in assessing how different conceptions of the use or exchange value of Shakespeare's authorial property drive a production's re-textualization—and re-texturization—as performance. But I want to widen that idea to focus on the relations between "Shakespeare" and "performance" in the phrase "performed Shakespeare."

In this regard, *Macbeth* is an especially apt choice, for tension between the two has from the outset shaped its textual and theatrical histories as well as the critical discourses describing both.[1] According to the prevailing view, the Folio represents a palimpsest—an "original" text (1606) that caught up allusions to the 1605 Gunpowder Plot and James I's fascination with demonology and was written over, post-1609, with material from Middleton's *The Witch* (1612–17?).[2] Whereas the play so meticulously described by Simon Forman appropriated Scots history to serve James's spectacle of rule, the text was then subjected to theatrical (or performative) practices that transposed scenes, cut lines, and interpolated songs and dances, a process further heightened in Thomas Davenant's seventeenth-century operatic adaptation, which Samuel Pepys described as "one of the best plays for a stage, and variety of dancing and music, that ever I saw."[3] But if *Macbeth*'s earliest identity could trope a linkage between history (or tragedy) and spectacle, its later theatrical and cultural destinies reveal an increasingly uneasy engagement between the two that surfaces most perceptibly in accommodating the play's supernatural or visionary features. Such a representational strain can, of course, be attributed to historical differences in belief systems; even so, those differences continually return to questions of *appearance* and *embodiment*. Although I have been referring implicitly to the witches, a perennial representational crux for any performed *Macbeth,* they are only one instance of this phenomenon, and the issues I want to address extend beyond them. Here, then, I am interested in reading the Bogdanov and Lepage stagings through several categories of analysis: conceptual environment or mise-en-scène; relation to theatrical as well as critical tradition; borrowings from, and representation of, other cultures (including what I will call "citational history"); use of actors' performative bodies; and each production's claim to "the new."[4]

* * *

Like the ESC's signature production, *The Wars of the Roses* (1987–89), its *Macbeth* foregrounded "history" as the conceptual "real" for the performance. Viewing Shakespeare as our postmodern contemporary, Bogdanov worked in a territory that joins Kott's vaguely Marxist Grand Mechanism, which endlessly reproduces itself, subjecting individual identity to its flow, to a neo-Brechtian desire to dismantle power's ideological fables. This *Macbeth* urged an engagement with late twentieth-century military culture, seen through the obsessive lens of a Tom Clancy techno-thriller in which wars and warriors become symbols of masculine virility and virtues. The production's central set piece, a massive cranelike steel construction, fused the phallocentrism of high-tech weaponry to Kott's staircase of power. A commando's corpse slung from its turret, it dominates the opening spectacle, in which bursts of machine-gun strafing and the noise of circling helicopters (borrowed from *Apocalypse Now?*) drown out Shakespearean "thunder and lightning" to establish an entirely recognizable milieu that could be anywhere from Rwanda to Beirut to Sarajevo. At Malcolm's investiture as Prince of Cumberland, it reappears, a red velvet carpet at its foot, a silvered ramp leading up to a golden replica of Edward I's throne (complete with the Stone of Scone): one with the battle machine; the seat of power is built on and from it. Draped in black for interior scenes, its dragonlike presence hovers over the banquet table: spotlit, Banquo's Ghost materializes there; and Macbeth conjures the witches from its top, connecting the two "visions." Later, the crane becomes the tallest tree in Dunsinane's forest. Amid smoke, helicopter noise, and searchlight spots, Malcolm, assault rifle in hand, appears atop it, like a vision of Rambo's return; and (of course) Macduff descends from its struts to kill Macbeth. Finally, its image stands behind the production's final show of power, which like many of Bogdanov's closural spectacles, occurs outside *textual* boundaries, taking on the status of directorial or auteur commentary. Following Malcolm's invitation to his coronation, the ceremony itself is staged. In a tunnel of light, a woman dressed in bright blue appears with Duncan's crown and places it on Malcolm's head. Waving away a servant carrying Duncan's golden cape, Malcolm summons another who, at his signal, invests him with the ermine-collared red velvet robe of English royalty as Elgar's *Pomp and Circumstance* celebrates a "land of hope and glory" now ruled by a self-made "foreign" king.

If Macduff, standing by Macbeth's body, looks a bit stunned at this (re)vision of a New World Order, the spectacle also may have puzzled audiences at Chicago's International Theatre Festival, even those whose memory of the ESC's *Wars* would invite them to read *Macbeth* as extending the company's—and the director's—critique of imperialist postures. Graham Holderness's program notes clarify the interpretive ground:

> Duncan's system of trust and loyalty, so effective in disguising the true violence of his power, is replaced by a remote and cautious vigilance, exercised by the calculation of a king who will not expose himself to the protection of those on whose power he relies. The relationship between authority and force is now in the open. Now the knives are really out.
>
> The moral order is not restored in its original form, since it was never in the first place presented as a moral order, but as a violently self-divided society, whose basis in naked power is ultimately demystified and exposed. So the play cannot be an Aristotelian tragedy: the destructive fury it unleashes is not assimilated into any pattern of reassurance or consolation. Nor does the tragedy of Macbeth appear as a moving and instructive case-history of a good man undermined by his fatal flaw; since Macbeth is not in any sense "evil," but only too good in those qualities his society most values. The individual cannot be blamed for the self-destructive contradictions of a divided society: and so *Macbeth* is not an individual tragedy in the Bradleian mold.[5]

Repositioning the play as "a history of feudal society, a study of militarism and an analysis of the passions and ambitions dominant within a political ethic," Holderness parallels its term with those of contemporary cultural theory—power, punishment, and the body. Like Caryl Churchill's *Softcops, Macbeth* was to be read as Bogdanov's meditation on Foucault, with Shakespeare as middleman. Indeed, the *textual* body this staging most closely resembles is that of Holderness's program notes: it is his "authority" that replaces Aristotelian and Bradleian paradigms, that is up there on the stage, marking a traffic between recent cultural materialist readings of Shakespeare's texts and theatrical practice. When it came to reading *performance,* however, the invited symmetry was less with feudal social systems (or even any allusion to King James) than with an ironic regeneration of a late 1980s American worldview where the warrior as a male gender ideal (re)gained cultural hegemony, where blood sacrifice was redeemed by further blood sacrifice, and where the problems posed by "evil" were solved by technology.[6]

If Bogdanov emphatically envisioned *Macbeth* as a militaristic fable, that totalizing idiom also deflected traditions of reading character "in" (or through) actors' performances.[7] For the most part, character appeared subservient to the production's central conceptual element, the steel crane. While it produced some stunning visual effects, the machine took on the status of star actor; haunting the staging, it became a high-tech substitute for the witches, a visual sign of the "fate"—or fatalism—of millennial, power-driven cultures. Although neither critical discourse nor theatrical practice attributes "character" to the witches, they do represent a force to be reckoned with, one that was extraneous, even extratextual, to this *Macbeth.* Bundled in layers of cast-off clothing, one huddled outside the theater door, begging; ignored by most, it was only when she crawled onto the stage from the audience during the opening spectacle that she became someone-to-be-looked-at. Although figuring the witches as homeless street people attempted to align early modern and contemporary histories, situating them with this degree of specificity diminished their supernatural soliciting, reducing them to mumbling scavengers making chains of paper dolls and stick mannequins to feed the fire burning in a trash can, around which they hunkered. But the clearest instance of the production's inability to accommodate them came in the conjuring scene where, after disappearing into a huge vat with a mirrored lid, they emerged, transformed by red wigs, heavy makeup, and black leather bras and miniskirts into garishly sexualized whores, one of whom was a cross-dresser. Reminiscent of Ionesco's *Macbett* (1972), whose weird sisters (together with the Lady) appear in bikinis, bitching up the witches not only evoked yet another demonized social stereotype but also furthered the production's rigorously masculinist emphasis.

Just as both the witches' reembodiment and Malcolm's coronation rely on changes of costume and theatrical properties, such exterior signs were, throughout, the dominant register of "character." And just as the emperor's new clothes are always important (especially when they are "borrowed robes"), so is the cloth they are cut from. Camouflage fatigues, commando berets, Macbeth's silvered leather trenchcoat, the bulletproof vest he puts on and then discards, the murderers' "terrorist" stocking masks, the British railway trolley carrying rifles and the throne that Seyton drags onstage: all the signs of Bogdanov's notorious eclecticism, which so enlivened and illuminated *Wars,* gets drawn into this *Macbeth*'s citational history. At the level of the linguistic sign, consider the Porter's speech, in which farmer, equivocator, and English tailor got discarded for politician, lawyer, and moneylender—present-day professions that, by updating early modern references, indicate a conception of Shakespeare's text as porous, open to historical change.[8] Similarly, costumes pinned social identities onto actors, marking them with badges of gender, class, and nationality. The Lady's first appearance, in a bloodred gown and carrying a candle, links her with the conventional "scarlet woman" as well as anticipating her sleepwalking; at the banquet (a white-tie affair), she wears white satin and elbow-length gloves. Initially, Malcolm and Donalbain are dressed like public schoolboys; later, Malcolm puts on a club tie and blazer and drinks white wine with a kilted Macduff. Tartans, kilts, bagpipes, sporrans, and knee socks are absolutely de rigueur at Inverness, and Lady Macduff appears to have consulted Martha Stewart on dining-room decor: when surprised by the murderers, the family is having a tea of (Scotch) oatmeal at a table covered with a tartan cloth, all wearing plaids. While these particular signs frame *Macbeth* a bit insistently as the Scottish play, they can be read as part and parcel of an overall strategy that deliberately disarticulates the ESC's staging from past performative traditions privileging characters' psychological coherence. If this results in flattening characters into social or national icons, rendering them in an almost allegorical fashion that will inevitably disappoint spectators accustomed to acting predicated on modernist notions of interior selfhood, it also serves to mark character, in a specifically Brechtian sense, as a social, historical, and political *construction* and to hollow out Stanislavskian language-driven performative traditions.[9]

Traces of that distinction were most easily available in Michael Pennington's Macbeth, a performance in which the introspection long celebrated as the tragic hero's hallmark gave way to a rapid delivery that denied rhetoric, as well as any Bartonian notions of relishing the language for its own sake,[10] in favor of seizing on narrative signals that pushed thought—and action—forward. When, for example, he sees the air-drawn dagger, he immediately readies himself for "the deed" by rolling up his sleeve, so that the ensuing speech supports the resolve already manifest in his gesture. Elsewhere, the strategy of playing character as sign calls particular attention to class and gender difference. After stabbing Macduff's son and garroting his daughter, two men force Lady Macduff down on the table as though to rape her; giving his accomplices a dismissive look, as though reminding them of the basic training slogan (This Is My Rifle; This Is My Gun; This Is for Killing; This Is for Fun), their leader shoots the Lady point-blank.[11] And this slaughter brings a charged perspective to the ensuing England scene where, as domestic dining gives way to a sophisticated café setting, an insolent, upper-class snob of a Malcolm plays a Machiavellian game of testing Macduff's naive idealism that seems as brutal as the assassins' "violent delights."[12] Moreover, thinking character less in terms of an overarching structure than as existing from moment to moment throws the contradictions posed by gender into bold relief. Had Macbeth not heard the cry of women, which momentarily unmans him, he might have attacked; although he then seems to regain (or be forced into) maleness by the Lady's death and is about to kill Macduff, upon hearing that he is not of woman born, he offers himself up as a sacrifice.

Some (though not all) of these character effects can be attributed to found symmetries with, or reference points in, other representational and cultural forms that give Shakespeare's texts competitive value in a mass-culture marketplace, but they also invite a revision of emphasis that marks *Macbeth*'s embodiment with a different ideological identity. Despite such (welcome) frissons of appearance, however, traces of more traditional or conventional notions of character intruded upon my own reading of the ESC's staging. My notes record cross-comparisons with other *Macbeth*s, among them Trevor Nunn's Other Place production (1977), in which the performances of Judi Dench and Ian McKellen hold something like patents or copyrights. These memories surfaced especially for moments that evoked "private imaginings": Dench's terrified, and terrifying, invocation of the spirits; her anguished cry in the sleepwalking scene; McKellen's powerful execution of the soliloquies, his masterful manipulation of the hired assassins. One factor that enables such comparisons, of course, is that both stagings have common reference points within Anglo-European theatrical culture. But since all are primarily verbal or auditory reminiscences, it might be more accurate to say that they mark my (long internalized) duty as a *textual* reader. And because all describe an emotive investment present in one production and lacking in another, they also betray my embeddedness within, and my nostalgic desire for, the return of (repressed) performative traditions. In saying this, I acknowledge—and fall into—the gap Brecht opens up between dramatic and epic theater, an "in-between" position resembling, though reversing, his own "not . . . but." What is at stake, then, in negotiating between traditions of performed Shakespeare and stagings that may resist, or refuse to bear the weight of, its past appearances and embodiments?

That question is central to Robert Lepage's *Macbeth*—in the sense that such negotiation becomes one *subject* of that performance.[13] For Lepage, Shakespeare represents both the strange and the essential: strange because his texts come from another culture; essential because those texts, crucial to theatrical culture, offer a company like Théâtre Répère the means to legitimate its work, much as the early silent cinema sought, by filming Shakespeare's plays, to gain entry to high culture. Lepage also conceives of "Shakespeare" as a pre-text—a starting point for theatrical experiment and exploration, not a point of arrival; moreover, Garneau's "tradaptation," which resituates "Shakespeare" in a Québecois idiom, resembles Peter Brook's ideal text for his Paris experiment: "a new play, written in French, and written by Shakespeare."[14] Significantly, this puts "Shakespeare" in the same marginal position as Lepage, licensing his (partial) ownership of a colonial text in a postcolonial society. As a critic consciously situated within what Homi K. Bhabha calls the "ideological ambivalence" of the "nation-space,"[15] Denis Salter writes provocatively about the potentially alienating effects of "Shakespearean textuality" on the subjectivities of the postcolonial director and actor attempting to discover how to perform the plays from a position on the margins.[16]

Position also, of course, affects a critic seeking to re-perform the performance. Whereas Salter is alert to these politics, I am much less embedded in the linguistic histories he details. My own position differs markedly from that I described in relation to Robert Lepage's *Midsummer Night's Dream,* a postcolonial performance brought back into Empire that not only critiqued dead(ly) performance traditions but precipitated a national identity crisis for its British reviewers.[17] In the case of *Macbeth*, I no longer can occupy what Michelle Cliff calls a condition of "in-between-ness": I am much more an outsider, neither a Québecoise nor a French-speaking "English" Canadian but an American, familiar enough with French yet not with pre–1950s Québec French or the even older idioms upon which Garneau relies. Spectatorship for me, then, is tied less to auditory than to specular traces, less to product than process, less to textual fidelity than to performative bodies.

Serving Shakespeare through Garneau is only the most obvious sign of how Lepage's *Macbeth* moves at a tangent to traditional, "end-product" stagings that know (perhaps all too well) exactly who their author is and, by memorializing or fetishizing his language, indulge in what Gilles Deleuze aptly calls a process of "magnification-normalization."[18] Lepage's notorious impatience with the languages of the stage and the limitations of Western theatrical traditions has repeatedly led him to raid other cultures, gathering up their signs and reworking them through parody or pastiche. Rejecting an Anglo-European image vocabulary for a pervasive orientalism that laminates ritualistic borrowings drawn from Japanese, Indonesian, and Balinese theater onto classical texts, his stagings often appear to approach pure image. Yet Théâtre Répère's *Macbeth* is not entirely a media(e)scape from "Shakespeare," for it slips into Asian cultures through cinema—specifically, by quoting the most celebrated film "tradaptation" of *Macbeth*, Akira Kurosawa's *Throne of Blood*, or *Castle of the Spider's Web*, a masterpiece in its own right.[19] Taking Kurosawa's filmic vocabulary into the theater not only acknowledges cinema's competition with Shakespearean textuality but moves an entity grounded on text, word, and the conventional relation between signifier and signified into a different sign system, grounded on the visual—a move that blurs oppositions among text, film, and performance.[20]

Re-imagining *Macbeth* through Kurosawa's film renders the stage as a flat or iconic surface. Made of upright blackened timbers lashed together and arranged serially, with wide gaps between them, across the whole width of the stage, the set creates a series of frames for the action. The spaces between the timbers permit only partial depth perspectives into an upstage area, and the timbers themselves, built into hinged frames, can be flipped up, over, and then down to form an additional acting platform on top of the monumental arborlike construction.[21] In this mannerist geometry of horizontal space, perception is severely controlled, even restricted: passing from one frame to another, actors' bodies often appear fragmented, and one view or emphasis pans, cuts, fades, dissolves, or wipes into the next, as though imitating film editing. Admitting to an obsession with the language of the frame and its effect on storytelling, Lepage speaks of how it enables him to juxtapose a downstage character to an upstage icon that counterpoints what the character says: "putting a frame *around* the theatrical action allows me to create filmic effects . . . to create intimate close-ups, blowups of small details, and ways to isolate things, to concentrate fully on them."[22] Yet if cinema functions throughout this *Macbeth* both as a means of rethinking dramatic focus and as a theatrically re-mediated memory trace, Lepage also raids Kurosawa's cultural capital more precisely by cutting out certain frames and sequences and by reinserting them into his own spectacle.[23] Moreover, these are not just random choices, but two of Kurosawa's signature visions, which bracket the performance in cinematic parentheses.[24]

As the performance begins, three figures draped in black veiling stand in front of the timbered arcade, spinning small drumlike instruments attached to arrow shafts around their heads, while four others kneel, facing the arbor, and beat on it with batons to produce a hollow drumming. A shout punctuates the drumming, now fallen into the rhythm of hoofbeats, and follow-spots pick out Macbeth and Banquo, seated high on the crossbeams behind the arcade, "riding horseback" through a swirling mist, as in Kurosawa's famous ride through the forest maze. And toward the end, veiled figures atop the platform swing crossbows over their heads as Macbeth, below them on the forestage, is caged in a shower of arrows, which are snapped out through the gaps in the timbers and then drawn back by disembodied hands, so that it appears (and sounds) as though they have been shot. In *Throne of Blood,* Macbeth dies in Grand Guignol fashion, his throat pierced with an arrow that appears, as if by magic, from offscreen right; similarly, Lepage relies on theatrical sleight of hand. After Macduff corners Macbeth atop the platform and cuts his throat, the frame holding his body is swung down so that only his disembodied head remains visible. Just as these two moments frame the production, they also frame Macbeth's spatial journey: seen first in an open space where he can move freely and then, with the Lady, atop the platform, once he descends to and enters the timbered structure, his movement becomes increasingly cabined, cribbed, and confined until at the end he is dismembered, his staring head fixed in space, an icon of the fragmented human body.

In discarding the traditional property head, this image insists on the *real* physicality of the body as *Macbeth*'s, and Macbeth's, an inescapable *theatrical* fact. Yet the production consistently re-sights—and resites—theatrical bodies as cinematic bodies. The dagger speech, for instance, becomes a nightmare vision that encloses Macbeth in the space of his own mind. As he speaks on the forestage, isolated as if in close-up, a procession of other figures—Banquo, Fleance, Lennox, the Lady, her waiting woman, the Porter, and Malcolm—pass behind him within the timbered structure, walking backward in slow motion: the ghosts of whom he speaks? the troupe of friends he is in danger of losing? The figures appear as both real and unreal, apparitions he has conjured up, moving ritualistically away from him as he moves irrevocably toward Duncan's murder. Later, the banquet—staged, like Banquo's murder, as a shadow play—evokes the phantasmagoric associated both with cinema and orientalism.[25] Enlarged silhouettes of those at the banquet are projected on white canvas sheeting that descends in front of the timbered frames, producing the illusion of a nightmare dream-screen from which Macbeth and the Lady emerge only briefly, to talk apart, before transforming back into shadows again: as the others leave, only Macbeth's silhouette remains, isolated, evanescent, in danger of disappearing altogether. When he visits the witches, hands reach through the spaces between the timbers to caress him, so that he turns into Siva's many-armed figure, floating in foreground space. But when he tries to enter the witches' cage, the hands withdraw, and as he looks through the gaps, he sees Fleance, grinning like a skull, laughing, and holding a mirror; turning away from the vision, Macbeth howls in anguish as the crown held over the apparition's head uncoils with a snap and remains suspended over the arcade where, just before the battle, Macbeth strides back and forth, his movements outlined by strobe lighting that produces an effect similar to Eadweard Muybridge's zoetropic projections of animals and humans in motion. Though he moves forward, he also appears to be standing in place: if the future exists in the instant, that future is also impossible—hindered, stopped, forever locked in one place.

Frame, fragment, fracture: all are especially suited to configuring the disintegration of masculine subjectivity. His body contoured by side lighting, Gerald Gagnon's bearded, squarely built, half-naked Macbeth reels from frame to frame; rarely perceived as whole, he at times appears as much a stalking animal as human, like a figure drawn from fable. While Kurosawa relocates Macbeth in terms of an historically specific seventeenth-century samurai culture, Lepage puts him at the center of a dark, archaic milieu in which recurring spatial patterns recuperate his story as myth—the feature of Kurosawa's film that Peter Brook found most compelling. And just as Kurosawa's forest spirit, enclosed within a bamboo cage, spins out Macbeth's fate on her ever-turning wheel, Lepage's witches, doubled by the Lady, Lady Macduff, and the Gentlewoman, perform "his" music, scoring out his destiny with a droning hum each time he is seen or when his name is mentioned. If one effect of reinventing theater through cinema is to ritualize Macbeth's body, that is also the case with the Lady. However, she not only inhabits space differently but, unlike Macbeth, is perceived as *whole,* rather than fragmented; still and contained, rather than restlessly seeking to escape enclosure—and closure.

Perhaps even more than Macbeth, the Lady is an always already ideologically overdetermined subject: hers is a body that carries more entrenched signs, critical as well as performative, than most theatrical bodies. Indeed, the idea of the Lady as virago operates as a kind of fetish that can not only imprint, and thus obscure, the actor who plays her but also play into reading her performance. A century ago, A. C. Bradley, influenced by the aura of Sarah Siddons's famous portrayal, called her "the most commanding and perhaps the most awe-inspiring figure that Shakespeare every drew"[26]—a line that could also describe Marie Brassard's Lady, whose presence—and performance—alters the production's specular economy, giving it a decentered locus of corporeal authority. She first appears sitting—naked—on top of the platform after reading Macbeth's letter by the light of a single candle, she burns it in a golden basin. Small and delicate, her white skin appears luminous against the darkened timbers, the formal eloquence of her body riveting all attention; as she speaks, she caresses her thighs and breasts, then turns on one side, facing the audience, her hands behind her head in a classic statutary pose. When Macbeth enters, he attempts to turn her into a sexualized object, but it is she who determines when—and how—they will make love, during which she urges him to murder, climbing atop him briefly before rising to dress.

Here, Brassard's physical delicacy and her nudity work to erase or, at the least, to destabilize the Lady's image as virago by bringing into view another image track of her body. Put succinctly, her performance re-authors the role. Yet once again, it does so through—and *against*—cinema. Or, more precisely, against the potentially voyeuristic perspectives of Roman Polanski's *Macbeth* (1971), produced with *Playboy* funding in the wake of Kenneth

Tynan's *Oh, Calcutta!* (popular culture's *Dionysius 69*, Joseph Chaikin's adaptation of Euripides' *The Bacchae*), just a year after Sharon Tate, Polanski's pregnant wife, had been murdered in the Manson cult killings. In Polanski's film, the Lady also invites Macbeth to murder while lying in bed beside him; she also appears nude, but only in the sleepwalking scene, where her nakedness figures her extreme vulnerability, her loss of power.[27] Brassard's nudity, however, escapes such cinematic citations to trope her dominance, autonomy, and *self*-possession. Showing—and showing up—the illusions associated with the role, Brassard's performance surpasses them, sets up a representational tension between self and other in which "other" stands both for other performances of the role and for the idea that "character" can be thought of as a kind of passing narrative that becomes written onto, and transmitted by, the body.

Brassard herself situates her performance—and her body—in relation to that of Orson Welles's Lady, Jeanette Nolan, who falls into the "tall, dark, strong, evil" paradigm. Because of her own size, Brassard decided to "give [the Lady] a lot of spiritual strength contained within one small body": she speaks of the decision to make her naked in key scenes as "a way to convey her fragility through a balanced image pattern." Naked at the beginning, she has nothing; she becomes regal, powerful, but loses her strength and authority once Macbeth isolates himself and acts less and less with her assistance; finally, when she sleepwalks and as she dies—scenes in which she also appears nude—she again has nothing.[28] But while Brassard sees her work in visual, relational terms, her performance exceeds the symbolic trajectory she describes. What she says aligns with Janet Adelman's reading of the Lady's sleepwalking: "her own subjectivity denied her, she is the broken object of others' observation, [one who] has become entirely absent to herself."[29] Though psychoanalytically smart and useful in thinking how the Lady's body is diagnosed and read by the Doctor and the Gentlewoman, that fractured subjectivity is not necessarily what *appears* in performance, where the Lady—especially when her nude body tropes her earlier mastery and ambition—is intensely, vitally present. Watching Brassard's Lady, this moment created a disturbance of reading, an instance where "text," troubled by a competing *performative authority,* cracked open to reveal her as the historian of "the deed" in a play—and a production—where history is a male province. If the only way to tell such a history, in which narrative and time become discontinuous, is to become absent to oneself, it is a curious coincidence that Simon Forman concludes his description of *Macbeth* by bracketing off this scene in a separate paragraph: "Observe Also howe mackbets quen did Rise in the night in her slepe, & walke and talked and confessed all, & the docter noted her wordes."[30] In 1611 as in 1993, the Lady's body, and her words, earn her special notice.

Textually, the sleepwalking scene marks the end of the Lady's role. As far as I know, it is only film, not theater, which records her death, bringing into representation what the text leaves inchoate, assigns to report. In Orson Welles's film, Nolan's Lady plunges screaming from a cliff; Polanski shows her broken body, covered with a rude shift and lying in the castle courtyard, largely ignored in the battle preparations. Here, however, Lepage stages her death: just after the sleepwalking scene, she appears, her legs wrapped around the rungs of a ladder, which leans forward in slow motion, parallel to the edge of the stage; she falls slowly from it, crumpling onto the forestage in front of the arcade. Yet the moment is not, as with its cinematic referents, simply an image of masochistic self-destruction that offers a gratuitous (and misogynistically satisfying) explanation of her death. After all, even a represented dead body counts for very little when it is not discovered, or when it is discovered only to the spectator, then reported within the fiction. Here, however, the Lady's nude body becomes a *substitute* for Macbeth's "Tomorrow" soliloquy, which (according to my notes) was not spoken. Instead, when Macbeth hears the women's cries and learns that the Lady is dead, he collapses just behind her body; then, following a blackout (during which Brassard leaves the stage), he rises to meet his death. Marking a point of change, her dead body is the (unseen) site over when he reconfigures his masculinity.[31] Even if the soliloquy was spoken, substituting the Lady's body for Macbeth's text does more than register my own perceptual fantasy. It marks a locus of displacement where theatrical realization reveals ideological contours that surpass textual knowledge—a locus where the performing body determines its own authority.

* * *

What can be said in conclusion? So far, I have avoided considering these two productions in relation to each other, or reading one through the other, primarily because doing so risks falling back on performance-to-performance paradigms that revolve around the articulation, or rearticulation, of "Shakespearean" textual authority. If anything, both of these *Macbeth*s testify to a dispersal of that authority. In each, though in very different ways, "Shakespeare"—

understood as "his" text—competes with other authors or auteurs: for Bogdanov, Kott, and Holderness; for Lepage, Kurosawa, and, in the deep background, Peter Brook. The presence of such (not entirely) "new" father figures embody several trends apparent in the work of (re)producing performed Shakespeare and of (re)situating his plays as artifacts of theatrical culture. Impatient with heavily institutionalized revivals that serve up a universally magnified, elitist Shakespeare, Bogdanov stages a collision between past and present histories, jamming the channels between the two. Equally impatient, both with a Shakespeare-who-belongs-to-somebody-else and with the limitations of the proscenium stage, Lepage not only works from Garneau's "tradaptation" but reinvents the spatial economy of the stage by making it readable through and against cinema. For both, "Shakespeare" becomes the ground or pretext for performative inquiries that explore the porous nature of boundaries between critical and theatrical discourses and between cinematic and theatrical forms of spectacle. Such resitings and dispersals, of course, align with, and can be understood through, poststructuralist and postmodernist frameworks, but they also extend a process begun in the early seventeenth century, once Middleton's *Witch* became inscribed onto *Macbeth* to alter forever both its textual display and performative array. Competing textual and performative authorities have always been instrumental to *Macbeth;* it is our perennial desire for "Shakespeare-as-culture" that has absorbed them under his name.

"Shakespeares" that escape from text-as-theater, or theater-as-text, to embrace other sign systems signal an emergence (or re-emergence?) of a *material* theater in which language is only one—and perhaps not the most hegemonic—signifying practice. Although less obvious in Bogdanov's work, which remains based in (surgically altered) language, this trend is especially evident in Lepage's production, where the performing body consistently works to destabilize its more traditional textual other. Where the 1970s neo-Elizabethan nostalgia spawned productions which, by privileging the actor and placing him (or her) at the center, pretended to serve up a "pure" Shakespeare based on actors-speaking-text, that movement seems, in retrospect, more an outgrowth of formalism than an archaeological rediscovery of early modern theatrical practices.[32] Our most current critical and performative rediscovery, of course, is the body. And Lepage's work, which begins by attempting to *see* how to *do* Shakespeare, not necessarily to hear "his" voice, and to transmit theater physically, rediscovers the valorized body of the late 1960s experimental theater.

Do these two *Macbeths* tell a "new" story? Not, I would say, a new Macbeth story, though they do point toward the need for new stories (or histories) about how performance and performance studies take on the cultural work of reconfiguring "Shakespeare." Each of these *Macbeths*, for instance, invites renewed attention to issues of subjectivity—both in terms of theatrical subjects as well as reading or spectatorial subject positions. Whereas Bogdanov's work produces "characters" as social or national icons, in Lepage's production, actors' performing bodies resite character, become complicit with reauthoring roles. Neither of these strategies for dispersing Shakespearean authority, however, participate in anything that could be called the "Death of the Character." Instead, what emerges, at least for me, is the sense that something like a new characterology is in process, taking place through, and being shaped by what we call "Shakespeare." In this "new" characterological project, "Shakespeare," the director, his imaginative ancestors, the actor, and the spectator-reader-critic play out flexible, multiple, collaborative roles. It is tempting to say that such a project begins to resemble circumstances we imagine existing in the early modern theater, before the Birth of the Author. If that is indeed the case, it is equally likely that the reauthorized appearances and reembodiments to which we bear witness are simply our own, peculiarly postmodern, reinvention of an old theatrical game.

Notes

1. My argument differs substantially from that of Harry Berger Jr. in "Text Against Performance in Shakespeare: The Example of *Macbeth,*" in *The Power of Forms in the English Renaissance,* ed. Stephen Greenblatt (Norman: University of Oklahoma Press, 1982), 49–80, since refined in Berger's *Imaginary Audition: Shakespeare on Stage and Page* (Berkeley: University of California Press, 1989). In setting text *against* performance, Berger argues that because performance confines text to particular, local bodies and to narrative demands, it limits critical reading, obscures psychoanalytic insights, and blunts the possibility of Derridean play.

2. See Stephen Orgel, "What Is a Text?" in *Research Opportunities in Renaissance Drama* 24: 3–6. See also Jonathan Goldberg, "Speculations: *Macbeth* and Source," in *Shakespeare Reproduced: The Text in History and Ideology,* eds. Jean E. Howard and Marion F. O'Connor (New York and London: Methuen, 1987), 242–64. Kenneth Muir's Arden edition (1951) has the most in-depth discussion of textual problems. That 3.5 and 4.1 show evidence of interpolation, has in this century become the orthodox view. See also Stanley Wells and Gary Taylor, *William Shakespeare: A Textual Companion* (Oxford: Clarendon Press, 1987), 128–29, 543–44.

3. Forman's description of a 1611 performance can be found in Muir's Arden edition, xvi–xvii. *The Diary of Samuel Pepys,* eds. Robert C. Latham and William

Matthewes (Berkeley: University of California Press, 1974), 8: 171, entry for 19 April 1667.

4. I adapt these categories from Patrice Pavis, "Wilson, Brook, Zadek: An Intercultural Encounter," in *Foreign Shakespeare: Contemporary Performance,* ed. Dennis Kennedy (Cambridge: Cambridge University Press, 1993), 271.

5. Graham Holderness, "Macbeth: Tragedy or History," *Stagebill* (June 1992): 12d.

6. See J. William Gibson, in "The Return of Rambo: War and Culture in the Post-Vietnam Era," in *America at Century's End,* ed. Alan Wolfe (Berkeley: University of California Press, 1991), 376–95.

7. See, for instance, W. B. Worthen, "Staging 'Shakespeare': Acting, Authority, and The Rhetoric of Performance," in *Shakespeare, Theory, and Performance,* ed. James C. Bulman (London and New York: Routledge, 1996), 12–28.

8. Insofar as this practice makes old texts do fresh work, such rewriting resembles the scholarly practice of footnoting.

9. See, for instance, Alan Sinfield, "When Is a Character Not a Character? Desdemona, Olivia, Lady Macbeth, and Subjectivity," in his *Faultlines: Cultural Materialism and the Politics of Dissident Reading* (Berkeley: University of California Press, 1992), 52–79. See also my unpublished essay, "Where Have All the Early Modern Subjects Gone?" read at the Shakespeare Association of America, April 1995.

10. See John Barton, *Playing Shakespeare* (London and New York: Methuen, 1984).

11. Although the Macduff killings have been considered gratuitous, Lynda Boose tells me that since the time of Robert the Bruce, custom has it that the Lady of Fife (i.e., Lady Macduff) crowns the Scots king. Killing the Lady as well as her children, then, would be politically expedient.

12. The juxtaposition resembles that in the ESC's *Henry V,* where Pistol and company's departure for France, amid horns and football slogans, opens onto a serene, Manet-like tableau of the French, all in white and sipping champagne.

13. W. B. Worthen is currently completing a study of the subject(s) of Shakespearean performance. I am much indebted to his work.

14. Peter Brook, quoted by Dennis Kennedy, "Shakespeare Without His Language," in Bulman, *Shakespeare, Theory, and Performance,* 145.

15. See Homi K. Bhabha, "Introduction: Narrating the Nation," in *Nation and Narration,* ed. Homi K. Bhabha (London and New York: Routledge, 1992), 1–3.

16. See Denis Salter, "Between Wor(l)ds: Lepage's *Shakespeare Cycle,*" *Theater* 24, no. 3 (1993): 61–70. For Garneau's "tradadaptation," see *Macbeth de William Shakespeare,* trans. Michel Garneau (Montreal: VLB Editeur, 1978).

17. See my article, "Looking for Mr. Shakespeare After 'The Revolution': Robert Lepage's *Dream* Machine," in Bulman, *Shakespeare, Theory, and Performance,* 68–91.

18. Gilles Deleuze, "One Manifesto Less," in *The Deleuze Reader,* ed. Constantin V. Boundas (New York: Columbia University Press, 1993), 204–22, esp. 208.

19. This is not the first time that Lepage has relied on another directorial auteur. Peter Brook's famous "white box" *Dream* offered a visual source that Lepage turned upside down in his own *Dream* for the Royal National Theatre. See my article, "Looking for Mr. Shakespeare." Salter raises the question of "foreign domination" in Lepage's tendency to mimic others and so to do work that is "a reflection of Somebody Else." See Salter, "Between Wor(l)ds," 66. But

I might say that Lepage is, at least in the case of *Dream,* simply turning the colonizer's work back on itself.

20. The practice is not limited to Lepage. The RSC's 1994 *Henry V* also incorporated quotes from two films, those by Lawrence Olivier (1945) and by Kenneth Branagh (1989).

21. I rely here on Salter's description in "Between Wor(l)ds," 65, as well as my own notes.

22. Robert Lepage, quoted in Denis Salter, "Borderlines: An Interview with Robert Lepage and Le Théâtre Repère," *Theater* 24, no. 3 (1993): 76.

23. Cf. Roland Barthes, "Diderot, Brecht, Eisenstein," in *Image-Music-Text,* trans. Stephen Heath (New York: Hill and Wang, 1977), 72.

24. When asked by Denis Salter why he and his company place "borders" or "frames" both around and within the three cycle plays (*Coriolanus, Macbeth,* and *The Tempest*), Lepage answered, "The frame is a way of putting *everything*—including the fragmented body—into parentheses." Such bracketing off evokes, as Salter writes, "the process by which marginalized societies are allowed to capture part—but of course only part—of a Cultural Object, since they don't have an inalienable right to take over the whole thing." See Salter, "Between Wor(l)ds," 65.

25. On the links between cinema and orientalism, see Antonia Lant, "The Curse of the Pharoah, or How Cinema Contracted Egyptomania," *October* 59 (winter 1992): 87–112.

26. A. C. Bradley, *Shakespearean Tragedy,* 2nd ed. (1905; reprint; New York: St. Martin's, 1992), 322.

27. Macduff's son, his two murdered babes, and the Fellini-esque witches also appear naked. See Bernice Kliman, *Macbeth: Shakespeare in Performance* (Manchester: Manchester University Press, 1992), 138–43.

28. Marie Brassard, quoted in Salter, "Borderlines," 78–79.

29. Janet Adelman, *Suffocating Mothers: Fantasies of Maternal Origin in Shakespeare's Plays, "Hamlet" to "The Tempest"* (London and New York: Routledge, 1992), 145.

30. For Forman's account, see Muir's Arden edition, xvii.

31. See Elisabeth Bronfen, *Over Her Dead Body: Death, Femininity, and the Aesthetic* (New York: Routledge, 1992), x–xv.

32. One result, at least in critical discourse, has been to foreground and celebrate the practices of the Royal Shakespeare Company. See, for instance, Cary M. Mazer, "Historicizing Alan Dessen: Scholarship, Stagecraft, and The Shakespeare Revolution," in Bulman, *Shakespeare, Theory and Performance,* 149–67.

Who "Has No Children" in *Macbeth*?

TOM CLAYTON

He has no children.

Macbeth 4.3.216

He that has no children knows not what love is.

Tilley, Dent C341

THE *Masks* of Shakespeare's plays demonstrate throughout that Shakespeare's ways make a settled view of his proceedings impossible to maintain unaltered so long as one continues to return to the scene of his playwrighting. The view I hold of Shakespeare's Macbeth at this writing is that he is a villain-hero—more than a mere protagonist—fatally ambitious but once full enough of the milk of human kindness to require letting by his wife in order to dare do more than may become a man, and so become none. He lives just long enough to know himself, too well, a regicide and worse, and to die in action by another's deed of the kind that made him a hero in the first place. He thus restores in a measure, however high his head upon a pole at play's end, something of the sometime man in place of the type and title of his reign, The Tyrant. He is throughout the observed of all observers, like Hamlet in this and in his vividness of imagination. His hope shattered in "success," he passes through security to desperation. The Weird Sisters gave him the first two, by his subjective piecing out of the first alone and taking the second too trustingly for granted—until he hears the word of promise of his ear broken to his hope in the word of Macduff's birth from his mother's womb untimely ripped. The better parts of even a desperate Macbeth are both there in the end, as traces of the man of milk as well as of defender's blood he was and fleetingly becomes again:

> Of all men else I have avoided thee [Macduff].
> But get thee back, my soul is too much charg'd
> With blood of thine already.
>
> (5.8.4–6)[1]

His initial lack of fear is due to his "security," but even when that proves to have been a delusion he accepts Macduff's challenge with alacrity:

> Though Birnam wood be come to Dunsinane,
> And thou oppos'd, being of no woman born,
> Yet I will try the last. Before my body
> I throw my warlike shield. Lay on, Macduff,
> And damn'd be him that first cries, "Hold, enough!"
>
> (5.8.30–34)

Famous last words, matter for an epitaph.

In 1.3 with fortune-teller's trifles like "hail to thee, Thane of Cawdor" (a transfer of title already declared by Duncan in 1.2.64–65 but news to Macbeth) and "hail to thee, that shalt be King hereafter," the Weird Sisters marshalled Macbeth the way that he was going. When he goes of his own volition to visit *them* in 4.1, the dramatic (and literary) design, as foreshadowing, converges with motivation, mimetic action, and significance as prophetic truth itself, the power of which Macbeth seems to have conferred upon the Weird Sisters by killing Duncan and sealing his own fate. Each of their three prophesying caveats comes true—in reverse of the order in which they were given, and Macbeth dies to his deep damnation when he tries "the last"—that is, the first—of the Weird Sisters' caveats:

> Macbeth! Macbeth! Macbeth! Beware Macduff,
> Beware the Thane of Fife.
>
> (4.1.71–72)[2]

2

"He has no children." The half-line is declarative, metrical and limpid, and apparently without depth or guile on anyone's part—until one asks who "He" is. And thereby hangs a tale. More hangs on the answer than appears at first glance, and the question requires referring not to those two familiar, mild-mannered misleaders, preemptive paraphrase and tendentious description, but to the primary evidence of word and other action of the context, for an answer. There is an unwritten standing law that quotations should be few and brief; when this law is combined with the fact that readers seldom have a copy of the subject texts open at their side, a not uncommon result is some critical slippage between text and reader, occasionally including slippage between text and critic that is compounded in the reader. The pertinent local context follows, with my interpolations (of 1, 2, and 3) marked by < >. In 4.3, the first subscene consists in the long duologue between Macduff and Malcolm on the latter's fitness for rule that is terminated when the Doctor enters for the subscene concerned with the miracles of Edward the Confessor, which in turn gives way to the third subscene with Ross's entrance (at 160) and arrival from Scotland with news that he is understandably loath and slow to deliver.[3] Asked by Macduff, "Stands Scotland where it did?" he replies,

Alas, poor country,
Almost afraid to know itself! It cannot
Be call'd our mother, but our grave; where nothing,
But who knows nothing, is once seen to smile;
Where sighs, and groans, and shrieks that rent the air
Are made, not mark'd; where violent sorrow seems
A modern ecstasy. The dead man's knell
Is there scarce ask'd for who, and good men's lives
Expire before the flowers in their caps,
Dying or ere they sicken.
Macduff. O relation!
Too nice, and yet too true.
Malcolm. What's the newest grief?
Ross. That of an hour's age doth hiss the speaker;
Each minute teems a new one.
Macduff. How does my wife?
Ross. Why, well.
Macduff. And all my children?
Ross. Well too.
Macduff. The tyrant has not batter'd at their peace?
Ross. No, they were well at peace when I did leave 'em.[4]

. . . .

Ross. Your castle is surpris'd; your wife, and babes,
Savagely slaughter'd. To relate the manner,
Were on the quarry of these murther'd deer
To add the death of you.
<1> *Malcolm.* Merciful heaven!
What, man, ne'er pull your hat upon your brows;

Give sorrow words. The grief that does not speak
Whispers the o'er-fraught heart, and bids it break.[5]
Macduff. My children too? *<to Ross, ignoring Malcolm>*
Ross. Wife, children, servants, all
That could be found.
Macduff. And I must be from thence!
My wife kill'd too? *<to Ross>*
Ross. I have said.
<2> *Malcolm.* Be comforted.
Let's make us med'cines of our great revenge
To cure this deadly grief.
Macduff. **He has no children.** All my pretty ones? *<to Ross, ignoring Malcolm>*
Did you say all? O hell-kite! *<i.e., Macbeth>* All?
What, all my pretty chickens, and their dam
At one fell swoop?
<3> *Malcolm.* Dispute it like a man.
Macduff. I shall do so; *<finally, to Malcolm>*
But I must also feel it as a man;
I cannot but remember such things were,
That were most precious to me. Did heaven look on,
And would not take their part? Sinful Macduff,
They were all strook for thee! naught that I am,
Not for their own demerits, but for mine,
Fell slaughter on their souls. Heaven rest them now!
Malcolm. Be this the whetstone of your sword, let grief
Convert to anger; blunt not the heart, enrage it.
Macduff. O, I could play the woman with mine eyes,
And braggart with my tongue! But, gentle heavens,
Cut short all intermission. Front to front
Bring thou this fiend of Scotland and myself;
Within my sword's length set him; if he scape,
Heaven forgive him too!
Malcolm. This [tune] goes manly.
Come go we to the King, our power is ready,
Our lack is nothing but our leave. Macbeth
Is ripe for shaking, and the pow'rs above
Put on their instruments. Receive what cheer you may,
The night is long that never finds the day.
Exeunt.

(4.3-164–180, 205–40)

In this triologue, Malcolm is mostly silent but three times speaks briefly to Macduff as prompted by his verbal reactions to Ross's answers. Macduff does not respond to Malcolm, speaking only to Ross, formally and as much or more to himself, finally responding directly to Malcolm only the *third* time Malcolm speaks to him (4.3.219, 220).[6]

So who "has no children" in line 216? Malcolm, who is present, or Macbeth, who is not? The gloss in David Bevington's Bantam edition (1988) reads, "i.e., no father would do such a thing (*?*), or he (Malcolm) speaks comfort without knowing what such a loss feels like (*?*)" (4.3.217n). If "no father" is as presumably meant to be Macbeth, this note levels opposing solutions to the problem of ambiguity of reference—the "indeterminacy" or "indefinition" of a sort—and the differences of interpretation attending it. To my present way of thinking, the immediate context and the whole scene quite readily disambiguate by themselves, but the local reference in this case is also germane to *Macbeth* and Macbeth in relation to the meaning and significance of the whole play.[7]

When such critical questions arise—about the parental status of the Macbeths, for example—it is natural for students of all kinds to turn from the script itself to diverse authorities, such as current scholarly and reading editions; studies of the play in performance and performances themselves; perennials like A. C. Bradley's *Shakespearean Tragedy* (1904) and later discussions like Geoffrey Bullough's *Narrative and Dramatic Sources of Shakespeare* (1975); and classic essays on or near the subject, notably L. C. Knights's celebrated (and for its title notorious) "How Many Children Had Lady Macbeth?" and Cleanth Brooks's equally celebrated "Naked Babe and the Cloak of Manliness." The respective collections of their own essays reprinting these came out in the same year, 1947, two years after the end of World War II, appropriately enough, nearly half a century ago but still—or again—worth reading, along with Bradley and many studies now out of print.

For its comprehensiveness and circumspection the first of all resorted to—and also the last, often enough and for good reason—might well be Marvin Rosenberg's masterful *Masks of Macbeth* (1978), which makes a case both persuasive and (in an appendix) genially speculative for the Macbeths' parenthood. He sums up the critical position at the time as represented by the Variorum edition of 1901–3, which, "canvassing a spectrum of criticism, cites about as many who refer the *He* to Macbeth as to Malcolm" (554). Perhaps that is still the case at this end of the century, but it is not easy to tell, because when the half-line is not glossed in place or somewhere else it is impossible to know the editor or critic's view further than to suppose that he must have thought interpretation obvious and a gloss redundant.[8] And if obvious, then by implication Shakespeare's unambiguous intention. Editorial silence seems to mean that "He" is Macbeth. The lengthier the gloss, the more likely is identification of "He" as Malcolm, who is technically eligible as "yet / Unknown to woman" (126–27), if he is telling Macduff the truth at that point; but such a contrast suggests that his proponents may protest too much, Occam's razor-wise.

Perhaps the most self-assured recent case for Malcolm is given by Nicholas Brooke in his Oxford/World's Classics edition (1990, 4.3.216n):

> 1. Malcolm would *not offer such a simplistic cure* if he had children of his own; 2. Revenge on Macbeth's children is impossible because he has none; 3. If Macbeth had children, he would not have slaughtered others. The first sense seems to me *an inevitable snub to Malcolm's glib haste*. See proverb "he that has no children knows not what love is," Dent C341 (emphasis mine)

—which proverb applies as well—and better—to Macbeth.

The locus classicus of modern critical reasoning on the subject is Bradley's Note EE, beginning "Three interpretations have been offered of the words 'He has no children'" (399). Brooke (1990) naturally follows Bradley's exposition there with his own "spin," as does Kenneth Muir without spin in the New Arden edition (1962, 4.3.216n), whose neutral description reads,

> There are three explanations of this passage. (i) He [Macduff] refers to Malcolm, who if he had children of his own would *not suggest revenge as a cure* for grief. Cf. *John* III.iv.91: "He talks to me that never had a son." This was supported by Malone and Bradley. (ii) He refers to Macbeth, on whom he cannot take an appropriate revenge. . . . (iii) He refers to Macbeth, who would never have slaughtered Macduff's children if he had had any of his own. Cf. *3 Hen. VI* V. v. 63: "You have no children, butchers if you had, / The thought of them would have stirred up remorse." (Delius). *I adhere to (ii).* (emphasis mine)

Bradley had cited in more detail the parallels in *King John* and *Henry VI, Part Three* (5.5.63): in *King John,* "Pandulph says to Constance, 'You hold too heinous a respect of grief,' and Constance answers, 'He talks to me that never had a son'" (399), a parallel supporting Malcolm. In *3H6* "Margaret says to the murderers of Prince Edward, 'You have no children, butchers! if you had, / The thought of them would have stirred up remorse'" (400), a parallel supporting Macbeth; but Bradley "see[s] no argument except that the words of Macduff almost repeat those of Margaret; and this fact does not seem to have much weight. It shows only that Shakespeare might easily use the words in the sense of (*c*) if that sense were suitable to the occasion" (400).

Bradley's reasoning in favor of Malcolm is sound, as far as it goes, and I do not slight it here in quoting only his conclusions and primary reasons. Unlike Muir later, Bradley could not "think interpretation (*b* [= ii]) the most natural," partly because

> Macduff is not the man to conceive at any time the idea of killing children in retaliation; and that he contemplates it *here,* even as a suggestion, I find it hard to believe. . . . Macduff listens only to Ross. . . . When Malcolm interrupts, therefore, he puts aside his suggestion with four words spoken to himself, or (less probably) to Ross (his relative, who knew his wife and children), and continues his agonised questions and exclamations. (400)[9]

There are two main arguments *against* Macduff's referring to Malcolm. The first and most obvious is the immediate dramatic context itself. The difference between Bradley's neutral and Brooke's indignant characterizing of Malcolm's attempted interventions demonstrates the latitude and subjectivity of perception here, but the primary emphasis should be not on Malcolm's "glib haste" (or whatever it is) but on what Macduff's dialogue shows of himself: he is in shock, preoccupied with his loss and its causes, his guilty absence as he sees it and the murderer acting in his absence. He gives no hint that he even hears Malcolm until his third try; and, while an actor's delivery could easily effect a glancing reference to Malcolm, such reference is gratuitous, the more so in reproach of Malcolm. In the lines in question, 216–19, his concentration alternates between his murdered children and their murderer—"*He*" (Macbeth), all his children, "hell-kite" Macbeth, his children and their mother:

> *Macduff.* **He has no children.** All my pretty ones? <*to Ross, ignoring Malcolm*>
> Did you say all? O hell-kite! < *i.e., Macbeth*> All?
> What, all my pretty chickens and their dam
> At one fell swoop?

This intense concentration does not change direction until Malcolm's "Dispute it like a man." From there to the end of the scene Malcolm and the just retribution in prospect carry his attention and his animus, which includes his self-rebuke to "sinful Macduff" and his invoking "gentle heavens" to

> Cut short all intermission. Front to front
> Bring thou this fiend of Scotland and myself;
> Within my sword's length set him; if he scape,
> Heaven forgive him too!
>
> (4.3.231–35)

The scene ends on a stirring martial note that heralds the coming end of oppression and the Tyrant, advancing the "Western" aspect of *Macbeth* toward the showdown and the morality play that combines poetic justice with the tragic finale.

I should add that I think—not everyone does—that Malcolm's character in the entire play and in this scene as King-in-waiting is that of a worthy successor to Duncan very like his father, one whose attempted interventions with Macduff seem intended to be seen as sympathetic, and tentative and inexperienced in such cases rather than as gauche, callow, and deserving of rebuke.[10] Within the earlier part of the scene there is little enough to go on, however, which partly justifies Bradley and others' confining their attention to the immediate context alone: earlier Macduff was first shocked by Malcolm's confession of his vices of lust and avarice, and then stunned by his abrupt change when convinced of Macduff's integrity. Not surprisingly, to Malcolm's "Why are you silent?" then, he replies laconically, "Such welcome and unwelcome things at once / 'Tis hard to reconcile" (137–39).

3

The second argument and the more telling is the connection of him who "has no children" with the play as a whole. With Malcolm as "He," there is no connection of consequence, and the effect is local and the line an ephemeral throwaway. With Macbeth as "He," there is profound and reverberating resonance, and the line articulates a theme of the play and tacit motive of the protagonist hinted at elsewhere but made explicit—and succinctly so—here. As L. C. Knights describes one aspect of it (*Explorations* 40n), "The Macbeth-Banquo opposition is emphasized when we learn that Banquo's line will 'stretch out to the cracke of Doome' (4.1.117). Macbeth is cut off from the natural sequence, '*He has no children* (4.3.217), he is a 'Monster' (5.7.54). *Macbeth's isolation* is fully brought out in the last Act" (emphasis mine).

The ambiguous question of parental status is forced tantalizingly upon any interpreter's attention, critical or theatrical, at several points. Presumably we are meant to believe that Lady Macbeth has "given suck" (1.7.54), as she says she has;[11] and though Macbeth tells her to "Bring forth men-children only!" (1.7.72), there is no evidence in the received text of when she might have had this experience of breast-feeding (a Scottish practice not shared by upper-class English women), and no explicit reference made to a child or children dead or alive begotten by Macbeth *or* born to Lady Macbeth. In the sources Lady Macbeth had at least one son (Lulach) by an earlier marriage (to Gillecomgain, Bullough 433), and those may well explain the origin of "I have given suck"—but cannot explain its significance and effect in the play as we have it, where the details in context are

> I have given suck, and know
> How tender 'tis to love the babe that milks me;
> I would, while it was smiling in my face,
> Have pluck'd my nipple from his boneless gums,
> And dash'd the brains out, had I so sworn as you
> Have done to this.
>
> (1.7.54–59)

In a play in which others' children figure so prominently by themselves and in relation to their parents—Banquo's, Duncan's, Macduff's and Lady Macduff's, Old Siward's, and one might add the second and third Apparitions as well as Banquo's royal descendants—this is a curious oversight. Certain it is that Macbeth is haunted by his fear of Banquo, for "'Tis much he dares" (3.1.50), despite the fact that he might well find reason for security in Banquo's further strength, that "He hath a wisdom that doth guide his valor / To act in safety" (52–53), except that "under him / My genius is rebuked, as it is said / Mark Antony's was by Caesar" (54–56). He immediately recalls of the Weird Sisters that speaking to Banquo,

> prophet-like,
> They hail'd him father to a line of kings.
> Upon my head they plac'd a *fruitless crown,*
> And put a *barren sceptre* in my gripe,
> Thence to be wrench'd with an unlineal hand,
> No son of mine succeeding. If 't be so,
> For Banquo's issue have I fil'd my mind,
> For them the gracious Duncan have I murther'd,
> Put rancors in the vessel of my peace
> Only for them, and mine eternal jewel
> Given to the common enemy of man,

To make them kings—the seeds of Banquo kings!
Rather than so, come fate into the list,
And champion me to th' utterance!

(58–71, emphasis mine)[12]

"No son of mine" stillborn or otherwise dead, or living now, or to be born hereafter. But one thing is very clear about the play as we have it, that we see no Macbeth child, son or daughter, and we hear no unequivocal reference to one. It would be reasonable (if idle) therefore to infer that Macbeth offspring were little if at all on Shakespeare's mind, as they well might not be, since he had none in the sources. "Following" sources in silence leaves ambiguous traces (propter hoc or only post hoc?), but the play as it is concentrated on Macbeth, the relationship between wife and husband, and to a lesser extent Lady Macbeth herself.[13]

It is surprising that in his classic essay on the play Cleanth Brooks says nothing at all about these matters, but as his title implies his interest was especially in the contrasting symbolism of pity, as with "the naked babe" of 1.7, and with the mere "cloak of manliness" of one who dressed but could not act the part ("Now does he feel his title / Hang loose about him, liked giant's robe / Upon a dwarfish thief," 5.2.20–22ff.)

It is not surprising that L. C. Knights in his ironically witty title did not address his own question, because his purpose in discussing "a re-orientation of Shakespeare criticism" (*Explorations* 15, "How Many" part 1) was to discourage the study of Shakespeare's characters as persons in their own right beyond the limits of the plays in which they are articulated.

> [T]he bulk of Shakespeare criticism is concerned with his characters, his heroines, his love of Nature or his "philosophy"—with everything, in short, except with the words on the page, which it is the main business of the critic to examine. I wish to consider . . . how this paradoxical state of affairs arose. To examine the historical development of the kind of criticism that is mainly concerned with "character" is to strengthen the case against it. (20)

Concluding, with the polemical exclusiveness usual to theoretical claim-staking, that "the only profitable approach to Shakespeare is a consideration of his plays as dramatic poems, of his use of language to obtain a total complex emotional response" (20), in part 2 he asks "How should we read Shakespeare?" and gives as example a detailed analysis of *Macbeth* (ii), beginning "*Macbeth* is a statement of evil" (32)—"but it is a statement not of a philosophy but of ordered emotion" (45). In keeping with his method, he says nothing of the "I have given suck" speech in relation to character or action, but finds it an instance of "the violence of the imagery" that complements "explicit references to the unnatural" (37).[14]

Both essays seem to me salutary for and beyond their day, and I see little enough to fault in either their orientation or their particular treatment, insofar as both were very much interested in the play as written, and attending to important aspects of the play previously neglected or ignored altogether. Because they are critical and text/script-centered, such addresses translate readily enough into the terms of theatrical performance and criticism.

4

The local (in 4.3) and the global (the whole play, its world and its action) reciprocally affect each other according to the reader's interpretation or the actor's expression of their relationship and may also be said to effect each other, according to how either is interpreted and given priority, entailing a correlative significance in the other. If the Macbeths have children, or at least a child, then it would be nonsense for Macduff to say Macbeth "has no children." If there is no evidence that the Macbeths at the time of the play's action have children, for all practical purposes they have not. And it matters especially that Macbeth "has no children."

Closest to his wife in our perception when she reads his letter aloud before we see them together and again when they plan and execute their regicidal plot, Macbeth is by degrees cut off first from her, as he becomes progressively more depressed, fearful, and finally desperate; and then from virtually all but Seyton, by which time he has

> . . . liv'd long enough: my way of life
> Is fall'n into the sere, the yellow leaf,
> And that which should accompany old age,
> As honor, love, obedience, troops of friends,
> I must not look to have; but in their stead,
> Curses, not loud but deep, mouth-honor, breath,
> Which the poor heart would fain deny, and dare not.
> (5.3.22–28)

There is no mention of the unique solace of children, here, and the prospect of living progeny, greater than the earlier greatest, is behind. Macbeth is alone to face his future—his death and his damnation.

Finally, Macbeth's barrenness is significant as an unspecified but implicit motive for his killing others and their children, and it is significant in another—perhaps more—important way as symbolizing a moral desiccation and a spiritual sterility contrasting with the symbolic green thumbs (or fingers) of the "gardener"-kings, both Duncan the unfortunate and too trusting, who in 1.4.28–29 says he has "begun to *plant* thee [Macbeth], and will labor / To make thee full of *growing*"; and his son and heir, Malcolm, who, summing up his immediate obligations and responsibilities at the end of the play, says,

> What's more to do
> Which would be *planted* newly with the time,
> . . . .
> . . . This, and what needful else
> That calls upon us, by the grace of Grace,
> We will perform in measure, time, and place.
> (5.9.30–31, 37–39, emphasis added)

5

Although the play, scene, and dialogue require identification of "He" for performance and for audience (and reader) understanding, a stage direction so refined might well seem impossible, Shavian, or absurd: easy enough as "glances at Malcolm" or "he means Macbeth" (SDs no editor understandably has seen fit to supply), but inevitably somewhat Shavian, and therefore not Shakespearean, if meant to indicate Macbeth and, more, suggest an array of nuances in action and verbal expression scarcely to be scored. It seems doubtful whether many stage or screen Macbeths can have referred "He has no children" to Malcolm, and I can say with certainty that Colum Convey did not in the most recent *Macbeth* I have seen, not at least on the evening of 21 August 1996 at the Royal Shakespeare Theatre.[15]

I admire unabashedly a view that humanizes a protagonist increasingly desperate and cornered by entertaining as his motive his natural concern for his son's patrimony, and on that account I warmly applaud "Lady Macbeth's Indispensable Child" (Rosenberg, *Masks* 671–76), the more so when the author's witty caveat is over the entrance to qualify his generosity:

> Every Shakespearean is entitled to an imaginative speculation now and then, as long as he labels it speculation. This appendix speculates on an *extra-textual* possibility in the staging of *Macbeth.* Anti-speculationists are warned. (671, author's emphasis)

No anti-speculationist I, just a pro-inferentialist, to whom 4.3 and the play say and show that Macbeth is the man of the hour in his play until he is out of time, a giant even as a "dwarfish thief," the Tyrant whose assassins have indeed battered at the peace of Macduff's wife and children (and also brought them the peace that passeth all understanding), and the King of fruitless crown and barren scepter accordingly on Macduff's distracted—hypothetical—mind as "He" who "has no children" and has been driven to desperation and libericide to try to prevent a future that comes upon him pari passu with his striving. That seems to be what makes *Macbeth* a tragedy, what made Macbeth Macbeth.

NOTES

1. Quotations from *Macbeth* are from G. Blakemore Evans's *Riverside Shakespeare,* 2d ed. (1997).

Modern editions differ in the number of scenes in act 5. Hunter has six scenes. The Folio (followed by Brooke) has seven, occupying TLN 2395–2529 on a single opening at nn3^v–4^r (758–59 of Charlton Hinman's *Facsimile*). Editions with eight scenes (e.g., Bevington, Foakes, Harbage) begin scene 8 at TLN 2435 ("Why should I play the Roman fool, and die"). Editions with nine scenes (e.g., Dent, Evans, Muir) begin 9 at TLN 2477 ("I would the friends we miss were safe arriv'd"). Wells and Taylor (and after them Greenblatt) have eleven scenes, distinguishing two scenes at TLN 2415 ("That way the noise is. Tyrant, show thy face!") and 2427 ("This way, my lord, the castle's gently render'd").

There are typographical and formal reasons (e.g., "Exeunt" and "Exit") in F itself for nine or eleven scenes, but the practical effects on the stage or in the reading are slight indeed; and, since fewer than 100 lines are involved, passages are easily located in any text.

2. For "the last" as fulfilling *the first* of the Weird Sisters' caveats, see my note, "Macbeth's 'Yet I will try the last' What?" The *last* caveat given in 4.1 is the *first* to be realized in a moving Birnam wood in 5.5; the second ("none of woman born") remains second, leaving the first given as "the *last*" to be tried.

3. Stephen Booth (106–11) gives detailed and witty attention both to 4.3 and "to Malcolm's behavior" as "the most perverse element in a perverse scene" (107), concluding that "Malcolm and Macduff are and remain our allies, but in the morally insignificant terms of our likes and dislikes as audience to an entertainment they are—because this scene is—irritating to us" (111). "Shakespeare develops the socially and emotionally awkward exchange between Ross and Mac-

duff in such a way that it resembles the work of a clumsy playwright. Not only does Macduff have to prod Ross, he does so in lines that lack verisimilitude and seem prompted by the despair of a writer who does not know his trade" (110). One doesn't have to share this view to find it thoughtfully and productively provocative.

4. Similar circumlocutory dialogue continues until Ross gives the awful news, beginning in line 204.

5. Lines 208–9 may go some way to explain the apparent design of Lear's last speech—a single half-line—and death in the 1608 Quarto version of the play, "Breake hart, I prethe breake" (L3), *if* the line in Q is Lear's by design and not by misplaced speech-heading: it is Kent's line in the Folio.

6. Evans and Muir make a single line of blank verse of the part-lines (220). Bevington, and Wells and Taylor (+ Greenblatt), treat both Malcolm's speech of three iambic feet and the two feet of the first line of Macduff's reply as short lines aligned with the left margin, like the ambiguous Folio (TLN 2069–70), in which part-lines of blank verse are all so aligned. Brooke leaves "I shall do so" as a short line, joining "Dispute it like a man" with "At one fell swoop?" (219). The distinction among the three would be lost in the theater and is of mainly editorial significance—there being some justification for all three—on the page.

7. Most undergraduates, in my experience, infer without hesitation that "He" is Macbeth, which I accordingly take to be the natural, spontaneous reading and often assume without comment in discussing the play in the classroom—where in spring 1996 Oliver Thoenen, a history major originally from the United Kingdom, who had done *Macbeth* on his A levels, rightly drew me up short with the note in Bevington s Bantam edition (just quoted). The present essay germinated from class discussion of the matter.

8. Among post-1950s editors silent on "He" are Dent, Evans, Harbage, Hunter, and Greenblatt. I sympathize with this exercise of editorial restraint.

9. Noting that Bradley "strongly supported the view that this refers to Malcolm," R. A. Foakes (1968) continues that "it is more often taken as a reference to Macbeth" and that he "think[s] Macduff has Macbeth in mind" (4.3.216, 127).

10. Garry Wills has recently expressed the view that

> Malcolm becomes a physician to Macduff's grief for his wife and children. . . . It is true that Malcolm is manipulative here, as in the testing scenes. He is fashioning Macduff into an instrument of his purpose. . . . The shrewd manipulator is far closer to James's image of himself than is the wimp or milksop Malcolm so often seen on the stage. Malcolm only takes his proper station in the play if we see him as the great counter-witch pitted against Macbeth. He has "purged" and strengthened Macduff. Now he launches him at the target, "devilish Macbeth." (123–24)

11. There is in fact no way of knowing whether she remembers or fantasizes—as well as no reason to doubt her. Thus it is easy to see why some might argue that Shakespeare fulfilled his dramatic intentions in the contextual impact of this speech, without giving further thought to the child or children alluded to, presumably because not part of his envisioning and design. Stephen Booth writes that "Lady Macbeth's mysteriously missing children present an ominous, unknown, but undeniable time before the beginning" (94); and that's true, too.

12. It is significant that while Macduff invokes "gentle heaven" to related purposes, Macbeth invokes "fate" and brings it on himself, not unassisted but of his own will in a special application of the idea that "character is fate" (Novelis), which George Eliot (*The Mill on the Floss*, 1860) thought "one of his questionable

aphorisms" (6.5) but Thomas Hardy approved (*The Mayor of Casterbridge,* 1886, chap. 17). The idea is expressed first in the West by Heraclitus: ἦθος ἀνθρώπῳ δαίμων

13. In round numbers supplied by Marvin Spevack's Character Concordance (in vol. 3, *Tragedies*) based on the first edition of Evans's *Riverside Shakespeare,* Macbeth has 32% of the dialogue to Lady Macbeth's 12%, ranking fifth in percentage of dialogue behind Hamlet (of course; 39%), Timon (36%), Henry V (33%), and Iago (33%—.02% less than Henry).

14. It follows that his treatment of 4.3 looks beyond character: "the conversation between Macduff and Malcolm has never been adequately explained" (42). It has three functions, "but the main purpose of the scene is obscured unless we realize its function as choreic commentary. In alternating speeches the evil that Macbeth has caused is explicitly stated, without extenuation. And it is stated impersonally" (43)—and he quotes in illustration. Since in much of the scene "the impersonal function of the speaker is predominant, . . . [t]here are only two alternatives: either Shakespeare was a bad dramatist, or his critics have been badly misled by mistaking the *dramatis personae* for real persons in this scene" (44).

15. Tim Albery, director; Roger Allam as Macbeth. Cf. Rosenberg:

> In the theatre some Macduffs have alluded to Macbeth, some to Malcolm. The *New Monthly Magazine,* in 1828, complaining about one stage Macduff's implication that Macbeth was meant, argued for Malcolm," who is so forward with his counsel to a heartbroken father." . . . [Leigh] Hunt, too, saw Macduff turning away from Malcolm as "unable to understand a father's feelings," rather to Ross, for sympathy. When a Macduff of Kean's played it as Hunt suggested, the critic was impressed at the "deep and true effect . . . far beyond that which can be produced by any denunciation of impotent vengeance." (554)

References

Booth, Stephen. 1983. *"King Lear," "Macbeth," Indefinition, and Tragedy.* New Haven: Yale University Press.

Bradley, A. C. 1904; reprints *Shakespearean Tragedy.* New York: Meridian, 1960.

Brooks, Cleanth. 1947. "The Naked Babe and the Cloak of Manliness. In *The Well-Wrought Urn: Studies in the Structure of Poetry.* New York: Reynal.

Bullough, Geoffrey. 1957–75. *Major Tragedies: "Hamlet," "Othello," "King Lear," "Macbeth."* Vol. 7, *Narrative and Dramatic Sources of Shakespeare.* New York: Columbia University Press. *Macbeth* 423–527.

Clayton, Tom. 1997. "Macbeth's 'Yet I will try the last' What? (*Macbeth* V. Viii. 32)." *N&Q* 247, no. 4 December.

Dent, R. W. 1981. *Shakespeare's Proverbial Language: An Index.* Berkeley: University of California Press.

Hinman, Charlton, prep. 1968. *Norton Facsimile: The First Folio of Shakespeare.* New York: Norton. *Macbeth* 739–59.

Knights, L. C. 1933; rev. ed., 1947; New York: New York University Press, 1964. "How Many Children Had Lady Macbeth?" In *Explorations: Essays in Criticism Mainly of the Literature of the Seventeenth Century.*

Rosenberg, Marvin. 1978. *The Masks of "Macbeth."* Berkeley: University of California Press.

Shakespeare, William. *Macbeth*. Edited by David Bevington, 1988. Bantam Shakespeare. New York: Bantam.

———. 1992. *The Complete Works of Shakespeare*. New York: Harper.

———. 1997. *The Complete Works of Shakespeare: Updated Fourth Edition*. New York: Longman.

———. Edited by Nicholas Brooke. 1990. Oxford Shakespeare/World's Classics. Oxford: Oxford University Press.

———. Edited by R. W. Dent. 1969. Blackfriars Shakespeare. Dubuque: Wm. C. Brown.

———. Edited by G. Blakemore Evans. 1997. *The Riverside Shakespeare*. 2d ed. Boston: Houghton. *Macbeth* 1355–90.

———. Edited by R. A. Foakes. 1968. Bobbs-Merrill Shakespeare Series. Indianapolis: Bobbs-Merrill.

———. Edited by Stephen Greenblatt. 1997. *The Norton Shakespeare Based on the Oxford Edition*. New York: Norton. *Macbeth* 2555–2618.

———. Edited by Alfred Harbage. 1956; rev. ed. 1971. Pelican Shakespeare. New York: Penguin.

———. Edited by G. K. Hunter. New Penguin Shakespeare. Harmondsworth: Penguin.

———. Edited by Kenneth Muir. 1962. New Arden Shakespeare. 9th ed. Cambridge: Harvard University Press.

———. Edited by Stanley Wells and Gary Taylor. 1986. *William Shakespeare: The Complete Works*. Oxford: Clarendon.

Spevack, Marvin. 1968. *A Complete and Systematic Concordance to the Works of Shakespeare*. Vol. 3, *Tragedies*. Hildesheim: Olms. *Macbeth* 663–750.

Tilley, Morris Palmer. 1950. *A Dictionary of the Proverbs in England in the Sixteenth and Seventeenth Centuries*. Ann Arbor: University of Michigan Press.

Wills, Garry. 1995. *Witches and Jesuits: Shakespeare's "Macbeth."* New York: Oxford University Press.

II
Language, Politics, and History

Site-Reading Shakespeare's Dramatic Scores

JOHN F. ANDREWS

DURING recent decades we've learned from art curators that paintings by Old Masters such as Michelangelo and Rembrandt become much more vibrant once centuries of grime have been removed from their surfaces—once hues that have been obscured by overlays of extraneous matter are permitted to radiate again with something approximating their pristine luminosity. In music, meanwhile, we've learned from conductors like Neville Marriner and Christopher Hogwood that there are aesthetic rewards to be obtained from a return to the instruments and arrangements with which Renaissance and Baroque compositions were initially presented. In theater we've learned from twentieth-century experiments in the revival of Elizabethan and Jacobean plays that an unadorned thrust stage, analogous to the performing spaces on which these works were originally enacted, will do more justice to their dramaturgic intricacy than will a proscenium designed for modes of representation that evolved later in the annals of Western drama. In archaeology we've learned from excavations in London's Bankside that playhouses such as the Rose and the Globe were configured in ways that look quite different from what historians had long induced from documentary evidence. And now in textual analysis we're learning from a fresh scrutiny of the first printings of Shakespeare's scripts that they too look different, and function differently, when we attempt to view them through early-modern eyes and resist the urge to "normalize" or rectify features that have struck later readers as ill-considered, inconsistent, or unsophisticated.

I'm producing *The Everyman Shakespeare,* a paperback set of the author's plays and poems,[1] and one of the edition's hallmarks is an effort to restore traits a seventeenth-century booklover would have enjoyed in contemporary issues of these titles.[2]

We all know that spelling and punctuation were only beginning to become standardized by the time that dramas like *The Winter's Tale* were being completed, and thus that some words and phrases could vary a good deal from one stylist, or one situation, to another. Because we've long been aware that "accidentals"[3] such as orthography were subject to scribal and compositorial proclivities, however, as well as to the evolving house styles of Renaissance printing shops, we've been hesitant, when confronted with many of the peculiarities we observe in late Tudor and early Stuart publications, to attribute specific features to the authors whose scripts lay behind the various stages of textual transmission. We've been particularly reluctant to ascribe authorial design to any of the accidentals we observe in works for which there is a paucity of manuscript evidence to draw upon as a control.[4] And we've been even more careful in our approach to the accidentals in books whose progenitors are believed to have been unconcerned about indifferent details, especially when we have no indication that they were involved in preparing or proofreading the volumes that were typeset from holographs or from transcripts of their compositions.[5]

But is it possible that we've been too cautious in our treatment of the spelling and punctuation practices in early-modern printings? Could it be that we've been so anxious to avoid paying too much attention to seemingly inconsequential matters that we've trained ourselves to pay too little attention? With regard to Shakespeare at least, I'm persuaded that the answer is yes, and that many of us have unwittingly rendered ourselves incapable of perceiving, let alone appreciating, characteristics that are more than likely to be authorial and that are often rhetorically or semantically expressive.

At the risk of being "damned" for falling into "Caribdis your mother" while I "shun Scilla your father" (*The Merchant of Venice,* 3.5.16–18)—at the risk of reading too much into what may sometimes be nothing more than incidental variations, and variations that reflect copyists and compositors rather than the poet whose artistry we seek to elucidate—I'm prepared to argue that the original printings of Shakespeare's plays and poems contain orthographic patterns that are so conspicuous, so pervasive, and so appropriate to many of the contexts they inform that they are almost certain to be the result of the dramatist's own deliberations. I'm willing to assert, in effect, that for Shakespeare spelling was analogous to a trope, a tool that could be put to a broad range of figurative uses, and one that he habitually employed in conjunction with other spins on a language that in his time was still amenable to an almost limitless application of English.

On the inference that, in a manner that would have endeared him to James Joyce and a company of the more adventurous stylists of our own epoch, Shakespeare reveled in the flexibility that a largely unanchored orthography and grammar afforded[6] and on the assumption that a good deal of the poet's verbal playfulness proved impervious to sea change and successfully weathered a hazardous voyage into print, *The Everyman Shakespeare* adheres to early-modern spelling form—or adaptations of those forms that conserve their fundamental distinctions from current usage—whenever there appears to be any possibility that what we'd now classify as archaisms or anomalies might have some bearing on how given words were intended to be pronounced, or on what they meant, or could have meant, in the playwright's day. When there is a strong likelihood that alternate versions of the same morpheme could be significant, moreover, the *Everyman* text replicates the diversity to be discovered in the pages from which all later editions derive.[7]

In many cases this procedure is relevant to the identities of individual dramatis personae. One of the heroine's most familiar questions in *Romeo and Juliet* is "What's in a Name?" For a quarter of a millennium, readers—among them prominent actors, directors, producers, and commentators—have been led to believe that Juliet was addressing this query to a Romeo called "Montague." In fact "Montague" (or "Montagew") *was* the spelling Shakespeare would have found in the poem from which he drew the bulk of his material for the play. For reasons that will become apparent to anyone who examines the tragedy in detail, however, the playwright changed his male protagonist's surname to "Mountague," a coinage that alludes suggestively to a combination of *mount,* a noun and a verb with both erotic and spiritual associations, and *ague,* a violent, quiver-inducing fever.[8] Setting aside an editorial practice that began with Lewis Theobald in the first half of the eighteenth century, *Everyman* resurrects the sound and sense of the appellation that Elizabethan audiences heard Juliet speak.

Readers of *The Merchant of Venice* in the *Everyman* collection may be surprised to see that the character other editions identify as "Lancelot" is actually "Launcelet," a sobriquet that calls attention to the Clown's lusty "little lance." Like Launce in *The Two Gentlemen of Verona,* Costard in *Love's Labor's Lost,* Peter in *Romeo and Juliet,* Bottom in *A Midsummer Night's Dream,* and Dogberry in *Much Ado about Nothing,* to cite but five of the other bumpkins who served as earthy vehicles for an irrepressible Will Kempe, Launcelet is an upright "member of the common-wealth"; in due course we hear that he's left a pliant wench "with child."[9]

Readers of the *Everyman Hamlet* will note that "Fortinbras"—as the name of the Prince's Norwegian opposite is rendered in the First Folio and in most modern editions—never appears in the

1604–5 Second Quarto of the drama. There Hamlet's foil is "Fortinbrasse." In the opening scene of Q2 a surname that meant "strong in arms" or "strong-armed" in French is lengthened and inserted into the dialogue to the accompaniment of puns on *brazen,* in the phrase "brazon Cannon," and on *metal,* in the phrase "vnimprooued mettle, hot and full." Later in the same title readers of the *Everyman* set will chuckle over "Ostricke," the ostrich-like courtier who invites the Prince of Denmark to participate in a fencing match that will draw the action to its close. Only in the final entrance direction for this fastidious fop does Q2 dub the young lord "Osrick," the name a more dignified character bears in all of the Folio's references to him and in even those twentieth-century editions of *Hamlet* that claim to base their texts primarily on the Second Quarto.

Readers of the *Everyman Macbeth* will wait in vain for the fabled "Weird Sisters" to arrive; instead they'll encounter the "weyward" or "weyard" women. Shakespeare knew that in his *Chronicles of England, Scotland, and Ireland* Raphael Holinshed had used the adjective *weird* to describe the "goddesses of destinie" who accost Macbeth and Banquo on the heath; but, no doubt because he wished to quibble on *wayward,* the dramatist altered the epithet for these deceitful hags to *weyward.* Like Samuel Johnson, who thought punning vulgar and lamented his predecessor's proclivity to seduction by this "fatal Cleopatra," Lewis Theobald saw no purpose in the playwright's weyward spelling of an adjective that reflects the guile of Macbeth's misleading charmers. He therefore reinstated the "correct" form from Holinshed, and editors ever since have followed suit.[10]

In many instances Renaissance English had a single spelling for what we now regard as two separate words. One example is *humane,* which embraces the definitions that modern English would come to supply for both "human" and "humane." In the Folio printing of *Macbeth* the protagonist's wife expresses a concern that her husband may be "too full o'th' Milke of humane kindnesse" to undertake a deed that will crown his ambition. As she phrases it, *humane kindnesse* can denote several things, among them "humankind-ness," "human kindness," and "humane kindness." The Lady's words are thus a reminder that to be true to his own "kind," a human being in Shakespeare's era was expected to be kind in the sense we now limit almost entirely to "humane." To disregard this logic, as the title character and his "Partner of

Greatnesse" will discover to their everlasting regret, is to ignore a principle as fundamental to the cosmos as the laws of gravity.[11]

In a way that parallels *humane, bad* could mean either "bad" or "bade," *ere* either "ere" (before) or "e'er" (ever), *least* either "least" or "lest," *lye* either "lie" or "lye,"[12] *nere* either "ne'er" or "near" (though the usual spellings for the latter were *neare* or *neere*), *right* either "right" or "rite," *sow* either "sew" or "sow,"[13] *tide* either "tide" or "tied,"[14] and *vaine* either "vain" or "vein."

There were a number of word-forms that operated in Renaissance English as interchangeable doublets. *Travaile (travail)* could mean "travel," for example, and *travell (travel)* could mean "travail." By the same token, *deere (deer)* could mean *deare (dear)* and vice versa, *dewe (dew)* could mean *due, hart* could mean *heart,* and, as we've already noticed, *mettle* could mean *mettall (metal).*

An intriguing instance of the equivocal force some word-forms carried in Shakespeare's day is *loose,* which oscillates between "loose" and "lose" when we translate it into modern English. In *The Comedy of Errors* when Antipholus of Syracuse likens himself to "a drop of water, / That in the Ocean seekes another drop" and then says that he will "loose" himself in his quest for a long-lost twin, his words tell us both that he will release himself into a vast unknown and that he will lose his own identity, if necessary, to be reunited with the sibling for whom he searches. On the other hand, in *Hamlet* when Polonius says he'll "loose" his daughter to the Prince, he little suspects that by so doing he will also lose his daughter through a gesture that recalls the folly of Jephtha.

In some cases the playwright employs word-forms that can be construed multifariously, and frequently as words we wouldn't think of at present as being in any respect akin. *Sowre,* for instance, can mean "sore," "sour," "sorrowful," "sower," or "sure," depending on how it is employed.[15] In other cases Shakespeare uses word-forms that have individual modern counterparts, but not counterparts with the same potential for multiple denotation or connotation. Thus, although *onely* invariably means "only" in the usual twentieth-century sense, Shakespeare occasionally gives it an extra, figurative twist that would require a deconstructive nonce adverb such as "one-ly"—often symbolizing a virility that is assertively "man-like"—to paraphrase in today's idiom.[16]

In a few instances Shakespeare employs word-forms that have only seeming equivalents in present usage. For example, *abhominable,* which meant "inhuman," "non-human," or "sub-human" to the poet and his contemporaries (who traced it, however incorrectly, to the Latin *ab,* "away from," and *homine,* "man"), is not the same word as our *abominable* (ill-omened, abhorrent). In his advice to the visiting players in the Second Quarto *Hamlet,* the Prince satirizes incompetent actors who imitate "humanitie so abhominably" as to make the characters they depict implausible as real-life men and women. Modern readers who are unfamiliar with the disparity between Shakespeare's word and our own, and who see *abominably* on the page before them, are ill equipped to register the full import of the Prince's sarcasm.

Current English treats as single words a number of forms that were usually represented as two words in Shakespeare's era. What we write as *myself,* for example, and use solely as a reflexive or intensifying pronoun, is almost always *my self(e)* in Shakespeare's works; so also with *her self, thy self, your self,* and *it self* (where, as usual, *it* does duty as a forerunner of today's *its*). Often there is no decipherable difference between Shakespeare's usage and our own. At other times there is, however, as we realize when we come upon "our innocent selfe" in *Macbeth* and ponder how affected such an expression would sound in modern parlance, or as we note when we see how naturally the self is objectified in the balanced clauses of the balcony scene in *Romeo and Juliet*:

> Romeo, doffe thy name,
> And for thy name, which is no part of thee,
> Take all my selfe.

Yet another distinction between Renaissance orthography and our own can be exemplified with words such as *today, tonight,* and *tomorrow,* which—unlike *yesterday*—were conceived as two-word phrases in Shakespeare's time. In *Macbeth* when the Folio prints "Duncan comes here to Night," the unattached *to* can function either as a preposition (with *Night* as its object, and at this juncture as the King's destination) or as the first part of an infinitive (with *Night* masquerading tropically as a verb). These interpretive possibilities resonate tellingly with the question Lenox asks the title character shortly after the monarch's assassination: "Goes the King hence to day?" And they anticipate the irony a seventeenth-century playgoer or reader might have detected in one of the most moving of all the protagonist's meditations:

> To morrow, and to morrow, and to morrow,
> Creeps in this petty pace from day to day,
> To the last Syllable of Recorded time:

And all our yesterdayes, have lighted Fooles
The way to dusty death.

Here, by virtue of the playwright's deft use of parallelism, the route "To morrow" is shown to be identical with "The way to dusty death," a relationship we miss if we don't know that for Macbeth, and for the audiences who first heard these lines spoken, *to morrow* was not a discrete word but a potentially multivalent word-pairing.[17]

When we forget that the verbal nuances in Shakespeare's scripts were initially conceived as words and phrases for people to listen to in the theater, we sometimes overlook a fact that is central to the artistic coherence of a work like *Macbeth*: that the messages a sequence of sounds transmit through the ear are, if anything, even more significant than the signals a succession of letters, punctuation marks, and white spaces convey through the eye. A fascinating illustration of this truth, and of the potential for ambiguous or polysemous implication in practically any Shakespearean passage, may be discerned in the dethronement scene of *Richard II*. After Henry Bullingbrook asks the King if he is ready to resign his crown, Richard replies "I, no no I; for I must nothing be." Here the pointing in the 1608 Fourth Quarto, the earliest publication to incorporate this multifaceted line into what modern editions designate as 4.1, permits each *I* to indicate either "ay" or "I" (*I* being the normal spelling for "ay" in Shakespeare's day). Understanding *I* as "I" permits corollary wordplay on *no,* which can be heard, at least in its first occurrence, as "know." At the same time the second and third soundings of *I,* if not the first, can also be heard as "eye." In the situation in which this speech occurs, that construction echoes a thematically pertinent exhortation from Matt. 18:9—"if thine eye offend thee, pluck it out."

But these are not all the meanings *I* can have here. *I* can also represent the Roman numeral for "1," which will soon be diminished, as Richard explains, to "nothing" (0), along with the speaker's title, his worldly possessions, his manhood, and eventually his life. Shakespeare was ever mindful that to become "nothing" was inter alia, to be emasculated, to be reduced to an effeminate "weaker vessel" (1 Pet. 3:7) with "no thing" or at best "an O-thing." As the Fool in *King Lear* warns another monarch who has abdicated his appointed station, a man in want of an "I" is impotent and sterile, "an O without a figure."[18] In addition to its other dimensions, then, Richard's response is a statement that can be formulated mathematically, and in symbols that adumbrate the binary system behind today's computer technology: "1, 0, 0, l, for 1 must 0 be."

Modern editions usually print Richard's reply "Ay, no; no, ay; for I must nothing be." Displaying it in this fashion makes good sense of what the title character is saying. As we've seen, however, it doesn't make total sense of it, and it doesn't emphasize the King's paradoxes in the same way that hearing or viewing three undiscriminated *I*'s is likely to have done for attentive observers in Shakespeare's own age.

English Renaissance society was more attuned than is ours to the oral and aural manifestations of language, and if we want to comprehend, and reify, the drama a diversified culture created we must train ourselves to "hear" the word-forms we see on the pages that supply our most reliable evidence of what Elizabethan and Jacobean theater was like. We must condition our imaginations to acknowledge that for many of what we regard as stable ties between morphemes and meanings—between the letter *I,* say, and the first-person pronoun—there were different linkages—such as the connection between a long-*i* sound and the concepts "ay" and "eye"—that could be just as pertinent to what the playwright was communicating at a given moment.[19]

As the word *audience* may help us to remember, people who frequented the Globe usually spoke of "hearing" rather than "seeing" a play. If we're serious about analyzing and reanimating the works we know to have been composed for that magic circle, we will learn to do likewise. We'll reacquire the capacity to listen with our eyes. We'll do everything we can to renew a skill that atrophied within a few decades of the playwright's exit: the ability to sight-read a Shakespearean score.

Let us now sample a few sites in *Macbeth* to determine how an activity of this nature might be applied to the artistry in a play with which we're well acquainted. In 1.3.51–55, Banquo tells the weyward Sisters

> My Noble Partner
> You greet with present Grace, and great prediction
> Of Noble having, and of Royall hope,
> That he seemes wrapt withall. . . .

A short while later (line 140), Banquo says "Looke how our Partner's rapt." Then in a missive the title character's wife allows us to overhear at the opening of 1.5, Macbeth himself recounts the effect the witches' message had on him: "I stood rapt in the wonder of it."

Within the compass of three brief scenes we hear the same sound thrice. In the first instance, the Folio's "wrapt" relates Banquo's salutation to a clothing image he has introduced with the question "Are ye fantasticall, or that indeed / Which outwardly ye shew?" A similar context informs the second instance. The protagonist having soliloquized about a "rapt" state in which "Function is smother'd in surmise," Banquo comments that "New Honors come vpon him / Like our strange Garments, cleaue not to their mould, / But with the aid of vse" (1.3.136–44). So also in the third instance. When we examine the clause extracted from 1.5, we see that a thane who describes himself as "rapt in the wonder" of what the witches have predicted for him has been enveloped in the "Ayre, into which they vanish'd."[20]

To reinforce the sound that associates these passages with one another, Shakespeare has employed an apt convergence of semantically distinct senses.[21] He has thereby portrayed a soldier so wrapped in rapture—so shrouded by the fantasies into which the wayward Sisters have thrust his confused cogitations—that for a pregnant interval he is rendered incapable of normal discourse.

Unfortunately, owing to the ministrations of an influential eighteenth-century editor, only a fraction of the multitudes who have produced or written about *Macbeth* since 1725 have fully appreciated the brilliance with which Shakespeare depicts a hero's susceptibility to temptation. In 1.3.55 Alexander Pope emended the Folio's *wrapt* to *rapt*. As a consequence, the purchasers of Pope's six-volume edition and virtually all subsequent readers of "The Scottish Play" have been shortchanged. They've been denied a pivotal clue to a drama whose enigmas demand constant attention to the perils of "double sence" (5.7.49).[22]

Thanks to Pope and to all the editors who've sanctioned his disambiguating modification of Shakespeare's script, anyone whose experience of these three passages has been confined to the masks in which *The Tragedie of Macbeth* is habitually attired in post-Folio reductions of the play has been led to focus on one development—the onset of a nobleman's "rapt" condition—to the exclusion of another theme of equal if not greater importance—the process by which a magnificent warrior becomes inextricably "wrapt" in the lure of "borrowed Robes" (1.3.107).

Let's now proceed to a few of the other homonyms that figure in the Folio *Macbeth*. During the soliloquy in which he attempts to decide whether "This supernaturall solliciting" is "ill" or "good," the title character asks

> why doe I yeeld to that suggestion,
> Whose horrid Image doth vnfixe my Heire,
> And make my seated Heart knock at my Ribbes,
> Against the vse of Nature?
>
> (1.2.132–35)

Since 1709, when Nicholas Rowe altered *Heire* to *hair,* editors have assumed that the Folio spelling in line 133 is either inadvertent or inconsequential. The context calls for "hair," which is almost certainly what the speaker intends, and "heir(e)" is recorded in the *Oxford English Dictionary* as a variant of that morpheme. But is it not conceivable that Shakespeare went out of his way to challenge our expectations here with a form whose weirdness would be seen in retrospect as an "earnest" of the "successe" Macbeth achieves by yielding to a "suggestion" that goes "Against the vse of Nature"?[23]

In 3.4.12–14, the Folio prints the following exchange between the title character and the First Murtherer:

> *Macbeth.* . . . There's blood vpon thy face.
> *Murtherer.* 'Tis Banquo's then.
> *Macbeth.* 'Tis better thee without, then he within.

Here, without giving the matter a second thought, most of today's editors silently correct the second "then" to "than" and drop the comma that precedes it. Since *then* is the normal spelling in the early texts for the morpheme we know today as *than,* and since "than" is obviously what Macbeth means, the routine procedure is perfectly understandable. In this instance, however, the Folio version of the line is open to an unanticipated and ironically apt secondary construction that will almost immediately come back to haunt the speaker. Once again, in short, there are significant benefits to be gained from an editorial willingness to "vnfixe" a line that is much more interesting—because much more Shakespearean—in its seventeenth-century apparel.[24]

In 5.3.18–20, the title character says

> *Seyton,* I am sick at hart,
> When I behold: *Seyton,* I say, this push
> Will cheere me euer, or dis-eate me now.

In this passage, drawing upon a conjecture by Charles Jennens (1773), most of today's editors replace the Folio's "dis-eate" with "dis-seat." In keeping with this substitution, a few twentieth-century actors, if not many editors, have been won over to a second alteration, "chair" for "cheer," which was proposed by Alexander Dyce in 1857. What almost no one seems to have noticed is that *dis-eate,* which can refer to indigestion, malnutrition, or regurgitation, operates in this clause as an antonym to *cheer,* which pertains not only to a sense of well-being but to nourishment and to hospitality.[25] Macbeth will soon describe himself as "supt full with horrors" (5.5.13), and he may now be disclosing that what makes him "sick" is a surfeit that has resulted in nausea. In the words of Menteth:

> Who then shall blame
> His pester'd Senses to recoyle, and start,
> When all that is within him, do's condemne
> It selfe, for being there.
>
> (5.2.22–24)

Even without the *s* that editors now add to the Folio spelling of "dis-eate" in 5.3.20, many theatergoers are likely to infer that Macbeth either says "dis-seat" or evokes it. That is by no means inappropriate, because the "push" that threatens to "dis-eate" the tyrant will eventually "dis-seat" him too. Bearing this in mind, a performer who wishes to help audiences apprehend two strands of implication simultaneously might be able to do so with a pronunciation of "cheer" that edges it toward "chair."

Now for another passage in which Jacobean playgoers might have responded in diverse ways to a verbal pattern with the potential for multiple senses. In act 1, as Macbeth is weighing his options, he says:

> If it were done, when 'tis done, then 'twer well,
> It were done quickly: If th' Assassination
> Could trammell vp the Consequence, and catch
> With his surcease, Successe: that but this blow
> Might be the be all, and the end all. Heere,
> But heere, vpon this Banke and Schoole of time,
> Weel'd iumpe the life to come. But in these Cases,
> We still haue iudgement heere, that we but teach
> Bloody Instructions, which being taught, returne
> To plague th' Inuenter.
>
> (1.7.1–10)

In his text of this speech—having decided that the through line from "Schoole" in line 6 to "teach," "Bloody Instructions," and "taught" in line 9 was less emphatic than the leap from "Bank" to "iump" in lines 6–7—Lewis Theobald changed "Schoole" to "shoal." It's a small but bold emendation, and surprisingly few of the editors who have dealt with *Macbeth* since the eighteenth century have ventured to question it.

Theobald assumes that when Macbeth speaks the word *Bank* he means either "sandbank," a synonym for "shoal" (a bar or shallow in a body of water), or "embankment" (a steep shoreline of the type that might parallel a shoal). But *Bank* can also mean a number of other things, among them "bench" (both in a scholastic sense of the word that refers to a classroom bench, and in a legal sense that refers to a seat of justice and to the judicial system generally), "rank or tier of oars" (a nautical sense), "moneylender's office" (a financial sense that anticipates the modern use of the term for a more complex monetary institution), and "pile of money" (a gambling sense from the game of hazard, where the amounts wagered on a bet were stacked on the card table). Most of these definitions can be paired with pertinent meanings for *School,* among them "classroom," "school building," "school of thought," "academic discipline," and "experience" (a sense that survives in the expression "school of hard knocks").

Meanwhile it turns out that *school* and *shoal* were word-forms that overlapped in certain respects, with *shoal* as a variant of the morpheme *school* and *school* as a variant of the morpheme *shoal.* Then as now, for example, both forms could refer to fish who swam together as a "school" or "shoal." And in all likelihood, depending upon the dialect of a particular speaker, each form could commence with either an "sh" sound or an "sk" sound. In this respect *school* and *shoal* would probably have resembled *schedule,* a word that is now pronounced "shedule" in the United Kingdom and "skedule" in the United States.

A word-form that editors for the last two centuries have perceived as defining one pole of a distinction, then—the sound, if not all the meanings, of *school*—would probably have been accepted in Shakespeare's time as yet another instance of those linguistic units—like *travaile* and *travell*—that possessed more variability and latitude than their successors were permitted to retain once eighteenth-century dictionaries began "fixing"—both repairing and rigidifying—the protocols of English usage.

How would Richard Burbage have pronounced *Schoole* when he created the role of Macbeth in the early years of the seventeenth century? Is it possible that he gave it a Germanic flavor and said *shule*? Might he have said something that sounded more like *shole*? Or could it be that he spoke it in our fashion—*skool,* or perhaps something closer to *skole*—but did so in the awareness that at least some of those who heard him would associate an *sk*-pronunciation not only with "school" but with an earlier form for "shoal"? We can't say. But perhaps a modern actor[26] could experiment with various ways of splitting the difference—for example, by rendering the Folio word "shool"—in an effort to offset some of lamentable results of a "dissociation of sensibility."[27]

Let's draw these reflections to a close with the soliloquy that Macbeth's Lady delivers earlier:

> What thou would'st highly,
> That would'st thou holily: would'st not play false,
> And yet would'st wrongly winne.
> Thould'st haue, great Glamys, that which cryes,
> Thus thou must doe, if thou haue it;
> And that which rather thou do'st feare to doe,
> Then wishest should be vndone. High thee hither,
> That I may powre my Spirits in thine Eare,
> And chastise with the valour of my Tongue
> All which impeides thee from the Golden Round,
> Which Fate and Metaphysicall ayde doth seeme
> To have thee crown'd withall.
>
> (1.5.22–33)

Here the first word that will impress most of us as wayward is "High" in line 28. Why should we not follow the editors of the 1685 Fourth Folio and read it as "Hie"? Because "High" plays on "highly" in line 22 to suggest that the "great Glamys" who hies—hastens—his wife's side will do so in a "high" way that befits his excitement over the exaltation the witches have forecast.[28]

But surely the most provocative phrase in this speech is "powre my Spirits in thine Eare" in line 29. The Lady's syntax encourages us to construe *powre* as "pour," and of course that is what we read in all modern editions. That interpretation is supported by 4.1.63, "Powre in Sowes blood," and by 1.3.96–98, where we read that

> euery one did beare
> Thy prayses in his Kingdomes great defence,
> And powr'd them downe before him.

Before we conclude that *powre* was Shakespeare's sole spelling for "pour," however, we need to consider 5.2.27–29, where we come across *poure* in Cathnes' call to

> Meet we the Med'cine of the sickly Weale,
> And with him poure we in our Countries purge,
> Each drop of vs.[29]

To complicate the issue further, we have 4.1.78–80, where the Second Apparition tells Macbeth

> Be bloody, bold, & resolute:
> Laugh to scorne
> The powre of man. . . .

Here *powre* appears to mean "power" and only "power"—though the earlier instances of the same spelling for "pour" make us pause for a double take.

And then, as if to deride us for trying to sort *pour* and *power* into categories that are completely proof against contamination, the Folio serves up 4.1.17–18. There the Second Witch enumerates the ingredients to be mixed into a cauldron that will ensure "a Charme of powrefull trouble." Every modern edition treats *powrefull* as an idiosyncratic but otherwise unproblematic spelling for "powerful." But surely the playwright expects us to compare the "trouble" the witches are brewing with the "Spirits" that Macbeth's Lady has conjured up in 1.5 to "powre" into her husband's ear.[30]

Here and elsewhere the early printings of Shakespeare's texts point to a powerful dramatist, an artist whose other gifts were inseparable from the way in which he prompted his actors and encouraged his audiences to pour full any receptacle that could accommodate a rich medley of verbal associations. In the words of Caliban, he was—and for those who read him aright,[31] he remains—"a braue God, and beares Celestiall liquor."[32]

Notes

1. *The Everyman Shakespeare* (1993–) is published by J. M. Dent—originator of The Everyman Library, and now a subsidiary of the Orion Group in London—and copublished by the Charles E. Tuttle Company of Boston. The first four sections of this article are adapted from "The Text of The Everyman Shakespeare," a preface that appears in each volume.

2. Here I refer primarily to the Octavos and Quartos that appeared between 1593 and 1622, and to the 1623 memorial collection we now label the First Folio. I recognize that the reading experience the Quartos provided was far less formal than the one that would have been afforded by a more elaborate, "literary," and expensive Folio.

3. This term is normally applied to those attributes of a text that are regarded as semantically insignificant—that is, qualities with respect to which inessential variations will have no bearing on the sense of a given passage. In his chapter on "The Treatment of Accidentals" in *Principles of Textual Criticism* (San Marino: Huntington Library, 1972), James Thorpe discusses spelling, capitalization, italicization, and punctuation, "as opposed to the 'substantives' or verbal readings that directly communicate the essence of the author's meaning" (133). As Thorpe and others are quick to point out, however, many of the items that go into "the formal presentation of a text" are anything but immaterial in their import, because something so seemingly trifling as "the lowly comma is capable of moving mountains of meaning" (131). For one of the most thorough considerations of this much-debated topic, see the essays in *Play-Texts in Old Spelling,* edited by G. B. Shand with Raymond C. Shady (New York: AMS Press, 1984).

4. For Shakespeare, of course, we are limited to half a dozen signatures and to a three-page section that is widely, but by no means universally, regarded as his in a single dramatic manuscript. See the analysis of "Hand D" by Scott McMillin in *The Elizabethan Theatre and "The Book of Sir Thomas More"* (Ithaca: Cornell University Press, 1987).

5. There is a broad consensus among Shakespeare scholars that the dramatist was meticulous about, and must have taken part in the proof-correcting of, the two narrative poems he issued with florid dedications in 1593 (*Venus and Adonis*) and in 1594 (*Lucrece*). There is an equally broad consensus that Shakespeare had little or no interest, and probably no active role, in the publication of even such scrupulously produced dramatic texts as the 1600 First Quartos of *The Merchant of Venice* and *A Midsummer Night's Dream.* I find it difficult to believe that a poet who spoke so poignantly about the immortality his sonnets would confer had no desire to see that his dramatic scripts were conveyed to posterity in accurately printed editions. For this reason I suspect that he did take some care for the morrow when opportunity presented itself—to supplant a deficient 1603 Quarto of *Hamlet,* for example, with "a true and perfect Coppie" in 1604—and that after he retired from the theater, had he but "liu'd to haue set forth, and ouerseen his owne writings," he would have followed Ben Jonson's precedent and supervised a folio edition of his works.

6. For a valuable discussion of this topic, see Margreta de Grazia's "Homonyms Before and After Lexical Standardization," in *Shakespeare Jahrbuch 1990* (Bochum), 143–56. For a broader overview of the eighteenth-century approach to sixteenth-and seventeenth-century English dramatic texts, see de Grazia's *Shakespeare Verbatim: The Reproduction of Authenticity and the Apparatus of 1790* (Oxford: Clarendon Press, 1991).

7. Like every other post-Folio redaction of Shakespeare's works, the *Everyman* set is based upon a sequence of compromises. By comparison with the kind of text that Stanley Wells advocates in *Modernizing Shakespeare's Spelling* (Oxford: Clarendon Press, 1979), it looks like an old-spelling edition. By comparison with the sixteenth-and seventeenth-century printings upon which it is founded, it looks like a modern-spelling edition. It is perhaps best described as a hybrid, an exercise in partial modernization that retains more features of the

original printings than does the *The Riverside Shakespeare* (Boston: Houghton Mifflin, 1974), but shares with that superb compilation an effort "to preserve a selection of Elizabethan spelling forms that reflect, or may reflect, a distinctive contemporary pronunciation, both those that are invariant in the early printed texts and those that appear beside the spellings familiar today and so suggest possible variant pronunciations of single words." As the *Riverside* editor G. Blakemore Evans notes, "Although the forms preserved may in many cases represent scribal or compositorial choices rather than Shakespeare's own preferences, such an approach nevertheless suggests the kind of linguistic climate in which he wrote and avoids the unhistorical and sometimes insensitive levelling that full-scale modernization (never consistent itself) imposes" (39). Ultimately, of course, it is impossible for even the most meticulous editors to recognize every instance in which they are guilty of "insensitive levelling," because any textual intervention, no matter how minor, is bound to be distorting.

8. The playwright's principal source was *The Tragicall Historye of Romeus and Juliet* (1562) by Arthur Brooke. We can never be positive that it was Shakespeare, rather than a scribe or compositor, who supplied the *Mountague* spelling, but the odds in favor of the playwright would seem to be enhanced by the fact that this is the form the surname takes in all of the early printings, from the 1597 First Quarto through the 1623 First Folio. For anyone who doubts that an alteration of Romeus' family name was part of a conscious plan, it may be worth pointing out that "Capulet"—spelled "Capelet" and "Capilet" in Brooke—like "Capilet" in *Twelfth Night* (where it applies to Sir Andrew Ague-cheek's mare) and *All's Well That Ends Well* (where it identifies the Diana whom Bertram believes himself to have ridden) means "small horse."

9. See *The Merchant of Venice,* 3.5.28–45. All act, scene, and line citations refer to the *Everyman* edition. Each passage is quoted, however, as it appears in the Quarto or Folio printing that lies behind a given text.

10. The word *weird* is to be found nowhere in Shakespeare's works. There is one *wayward* in *Macbeth,* at 3.5.11 in a Hecat speech that many scholars assign to a playwright other than the author of the rest of the tragedy; further uses of the word or its derivatives appear in thirteen other Shakespearean titles. Only in *Macbeth* do the forms *wayward* and *weyard* occur. We would be required to hypothesize a most unusual scribe or compositor if we were to conclude that one of them, rather than the playwright, was responsible for such a bizarre deviation from Holinshed's *weird.*

11. For another instance of *humane* that is thematically resonant, see *The Tempest,* 5.1.17–20, where Ariel tells Prospero "your charm so strongly works 'em / That if you now beheld them, your affections / Would become tender." Prospero asks "Dost thinke so, Spirit?" And Ariel replies "Mine would, Sir, were I humane." Compare 1.2.265, 284, 345, and 3.3.33 in the same play.

12. Many of the Porter's jests in *Macbeth,* 2.3.24–48, pun upon distinctions that we now allocate to the spellings *lie* and *lye.* Compare the Clown's wordplay in *Othello,* 3.4.1–17.

13. In *Coriolanus,*1.3.55–57, Valeria asks Volumnia and Virgilia "How do you both? You are manifest house-keepers. What are you sowing heere? A fine spotte, in good faith. How does your little Sonne?" Here the dialogue suggests that either the mother or the wife of the title character is sewing, and probably that both are doing so. But the phrasing of Valeria's question, and the remarks about Martius' child that ensue, would also have reminded Renaissance audiences of biblical commonplaces about sowing and reaping: see Job 4:8, Prov. 6:16, Jer. 12:13,

Hos. 8:7 and 10:12, and Gal. 6:7. Compare *Othello,* 2.4.72, and see *Hamlet,* 2.1.73–80, where Ophelia's reference to "sowing" (sewing) introduces a narrative about some unhappy consequences of the figurative planting her father has done in 1.3.

14. In *The Two Gentlemen of Verona,* 2.3.37–45, the Folio word *tide* provides the occasion for several exchanges about a "tied" dog who threatens to make Launce lose the "tide."

15. See *Julius Caesar,* 1.2.177 (where Cassius refers to Casca's "sowre fashion," his sour and sore-headed disposition), *Macbeth,* 2.1.55 (where the protagonist addresses a "sowre and firme-set Earth"), and *Othello,* 4.3.95 (where Aemilia speaks of "Palats both for sweet, and sowre"). Compare *Love's Labor's Lost,* 1.1.318 ("therefore welcome the sower Cup of prosperitie"), *Romeo and Juliet,* 2.4.24 ("so sower a face") and 3.2.116 ("if sower woe delights in fellowship"), and *The Tempest,* 4.1.20 ("Sower-ey'd disdaine").

16. In *Much Ado About Nothing,* 3.4.74–76, the bawdy Margaret tells Beatrice "Get you some of this distill'd *carduus benedictus,* and lay it to your heart, it is the onely thing for a qualme." Earlier (in 3.1.92, during the comedy's second eavesdropping scene) Hero has referred to Benedick as "the onely man of Italy." Compare *Julius Caesar,* 1.2.153–54, where Cassius says "Now is it Rome indeed, and Roome enough / When there is in it but one onely man." This passage prepares us for the irony of 3.1.59–74, where a Caesar who prides himself upon his stoic firmness says that "Men are Flesh and Blood, and apprehensive / Yet in the number, I do know but One / That unassayleable holds on his Ranke." In *Macbeth,* 1.7.72–74, after the hero's Lady has persuaded him to "screw" his "courage to the sticking place," he tells her "Bring forth Men-Children onely: / For thy undaunted Mettle should compose / Nothing but Males."

17. As one might expect, there is touching, and usually unintended, ambiguity in the various references to *night* during the balcony scene of *Romeo and Juliet.* See 2.1.127–29, where Juliet tells the youth who has just overheard her nocturnal soliloquy "Thou knowest the mask of night is on my face, / Else would a maiden blush bepaint my cheeke, / For that which thou has heard me speak to night." Later in the same scene (line 159) the heroine admits "I haue no Joy of this contract to night"; soon we hear her utter "sweet goodnight," however (line 162), and those words reverberate shortly thereafter in Romeo's "O blessed blessed night" (line 181). Eventually (line 195), in a promise that might be construed as an unconscious attempt to protect herself against, or atone for, all that she and Romeo have pledged "to night," Juliet says "To morrow will I send."

18. See the notes to 1.4.195–207 in *Everyman King Lear.*

19. In *Othello,* 4.2.60–62, the Folio reads "Turne thy complexion there: / Patience, thou young and Rose-lip'd Cherubin, / I heere look grim as hell." The final line is usually rendered "Ay, here look grim as hell" in modern editions. A similar crux occurs in *The Merchant of Venice,* 4.1.290–91, where the 1600 First Quarto reads "I would loose all, I sacrifize them all / heere to this deuill, to deliuer you." Most of today's editions render the first line "I would lose all, ay, sacrifice them all, / Here. . . ." Compare *A Midsummer Night's Dream,* 3.2.237, where the 1600 First Quarto prints "I doe. Perseuer," the Folio prints "I, doe, perseuer," and most modern editions print "Ay, do, persever." For a few of the scores of additional *I/Ay* ambiguities in Shakespeare, see *Antony and Cleopatra,* 3.13.172–73, *Hamlet,* 3.2.79–80, and *Julius Caesar,* 1.2.122–23.

20. In this setting, as frequently elsewhere in *Macbeth,* "Ayre" hints at "Heire"; see 1.3.132–35 (discussed in the next section), and compare 3.4.58–60,

where Macbeth's Lady rebukes her husband's infirmity with a reminder of "the Ayre-drawne-Dagger which you said / Led you to Duncan." In 3.5.20, Hecat announces "I am for th'Ayre: This night Ile spend / Vnto a dismall, and a Fatall end." In 4.1.137–38, where he unwittingly curses himself with the imprecation he hurls after the witches, Macbeth says "Infected be the Ayre whereon they ride, / And damn'd all those that trust them."

21. For related play on *rapt/wrapt* see *Timon of Athens,* 1.1.19 ("You are rapt, sir, in some work, some dedication. . . . ") and 5.1.64 ("I am rapt and cannot couer. . . . "), and *The Tempest,* 1.2.177.

22. This phrase comes from the speech Macbeth mutters after he hears that Macduff was "from his Mothers womb / Vntimely ript." What the title character has just discovered is that his adversary was not borne—carried—to full term, and was thus not brought into the world entirely by his mother's own agency. In this instance, the protagonist suddenly realizes, "th' Equiuocation of the Fiend / That lies like truth" (5.5.42–43), has taken advantage of an overconfident usurper's failure to reckon with the potential for duplicity in *borne,* an early-modern word-form that encompassed the meanings a later era would file separately under the headings *born* and *borne.* "I beare a charmed Life, which must not yeeld / To one of woman borne." When twentieth-century editions change *borne* to *born,* imposing an orthographic order that was yet to be codified in 1623, they deny today's readers an opportunity to experience the kind of "Equiuocation" a buyer of the First Folio would have understood—and enjoyed—with at most a moment's pause for rumination.

23. In 4.1.111–14, in a passage where the Folio's *haire* is strongly associated with *heire,* the title character addresses the apparitions who parade before him: "Thou art too like the Spirit of Banquo: Down: / Thy Crowne do's seare mine Eye-bals. And thy haire / Thou other Gold-bound brow, is like the first: / A third, is like the former." Near the end of the tragedy, in a speech (5.5.9–13) that recalls 1.3.132–35, Macbeth says "I have almost forgot the taste of Feares: / The time ha's beene, my sences would haut cool'd / To heare a Night-shrieke, and my Fell of haire / Would at a dismall Treatise rowze, and stirre / As life were in't." Finally, in 5.7.77–78, in a remark that implicitly identifies *haires* with *heires* and echoes both 1.3.132–35 and 5.5.9–13, Seyward consoles himself by saying "Had I as many Sonnes, as I haue haires, / I would not wish them to a fairer death." For an example of *hair/heir* wordplay in another work, see *Antony and Cleopatra,* 1.2.194–96.

24. For other instances in which *then* can mean both "then" and "than," see *Antony and Cleopatra,* 4.2.44, *Hamlet,* 3.1.79, *Julius Caesar,* 5.4.29–29, *Macbeth,* 1.5.27–28 and 3.2.4–7, *The Merchant of Venice,* 3.2.160-62 and 3.5.42–45, and *Twelfth Night,* 5.1.370–73.

25. Compare 3.4.30–33, where Macbeth's Lady says "My Royall Lord / You do not give the Cheere, the Feast is sold / That is not often vouch'd, while 'tis a making: / Tis given with welcome."

26. When Stacy Keach played the title role of *Macbeth* in a 1995 production for The Shakespeare Theatre in Washington, he said "school" rather than "shoal" in 1.7.6. During a question-and-answer session that took place near the end of the show's sold-out run, a member of the audience asked Mr. Keach what books, if any, he had read in preparation for the part. Among the titles he singled out for special commendation was *The Masks of "Macbeth"* by Marvin Rosenberg, a professor whose course, Keach said, had been very helpful to an aspiring actor during his undergraduate days at the University of California at Berkeley.

27. T. S. Eliot was referring to something other than the topics in this article when he coined this phrase in a famous essay on "The Metaphysical Poets"—see *Selected Essays, 1917–1932* (New York: Harcourt, 1932)—but many of his observations are nevertheless germane to the present discussion.

28. For an instructive counterpart to this quibble on *hie,* we might turn to the 1599 Second Quarto of *Romeo and Juliet,* for 3.4.69–97 where the heroine's Nurse says, "Then high you hence to Frier Lawrence Cell, / There stayes a husband to make you a wife: / Now comes the wanton bloud vp in your cheekes, / Theile be in scarlet straight at any news: / Hie you to Church, I must an other way, / To fetch a Ladder by the which your love / Must climbe a birds neast soone when it is darke." Juliet's reply completes the pairing: "Hie to high fortune, honest Nurse farewell." Here again it would seem that Shakespeare used variant spellings to qualify, if not nullify, the semantic distinctions we might otherwise insist upon as our ears take in the word-forms *hie* and *high.*

29. Here *poure,* a spelling that is to be found in several other passages in Shakespeare, occurs on a page that appears to have been set by Compositor B or another *do-go-heere* speller; it is thus possible that this is that typesetter's spelling for "pour" rather than Shakespeare's. The same compositor seems to have set the page that contains 4.1.63 ("Powre in Sowes blood") and 4.1.80 ("powre of man"), however, so even if he had a mild preference for *poure* he must have been quite tolerant of *powre* forms when he encountered them in his copy. A different Folio workman, either Compositor A or another *doe-goe-here* speller, appears to have set the text for 1.5.29 ("powre my Spirits in thine Eare"). For a study of the Folio compositors that has stood the test of time with remarkable endurance, see Charlton Hinman's *Printing and Proof-Reading of the First Folio of Shakespeare,* 2 vols. (Oxford: Clarendon Press, 1963). For a valuable update on and corrective to several aspects of this monumental achievement, including its roster of compositorial attributions, see Peter Blayney's introduction to the revised edition of Hinman's 1968 facsimile of *The First Folio of Shakespeare* (New York: Norton, 1996).

30. Perhaps the most fascinating illustration of the malleability of *powre* in Shakespeare occurs in *Antony and Cleopatra,* 2.2.234–38, where Enobarbus says "I saw her once / Hop forty Paces through the publicke streete, / And hauing lost her breath, she spoke, and panted / That she did make defect, perfection, / And breathlesse powre breath forth." In most of today's editions line 238 is printed "And, breathless, power breathe forth." Since *breath* occurs as often as *breathe* in positions that call for a verb, this reading is entirely defensible. But so is "And, breathless, pour breath forth." In the *Everyman* text of the play, the line is left indeterminate: "And breathless powre breath forth." For other provocative instances of *powre* and its derivatives in *Antony and Cleopatra,* see 1.1.22, 2.5.32–34, 53. For additional Folio instances of *powre* and its derivatives, compare *Othello,* 1.3.102–5, 2.1.78, 2.3.368, 5.2.155, *The Tempest,* 1.2.3, 4.1.38, and *The Winter's Tale,* 1.2.200, 4.4.363–65. For *powre* and its derivatives in Quarto printings, where the transmission of Shakespeare's texts would have been influenced by factors other than those that affected the shop where the First Folio was printed, see *Titus Andronicus,* 2.3.61 (where *powre* means "power"), 2.3.163 (where *powr'd* means "poured"), and 3.1.299 (where *powre* means "power"), *2 Henry IV,* 4.4.46 (where *powre* means "pour"), *Hamlet,* 1.5.62 (where *powre* means "pour"), Sonnet 55, line 2 (where *powrefull* means "powerful"), Sonnet 94, line 1 (where *powre* means "power"), Sonnet 100, line 4 (where *powre* means "power"), and Sonnet 150, line 1 (where *powre* means "power").

31. Among the advantages of an editorial practice that preserves as many as possible of the "accidentals" in Shakespeare's earliest publications is the light those details sometimes shed on semantic relationships that would otherwise be difficult to perceive. During the penultimate scene of act 4 in *Coriolanus*—4.7 in the forthcoming *Everyman* edition and in Volume 17 of its precursor, *The Guild Shakespeare* (New York: Doubleday [Guild America Books], 1989–92), but 4.6 in most of today's other editions—as news spreads that a vengeful Caius Marius is leading a Volscian army against a now-defenseless Rome, two Senators upbraid the Tribunes who incited the plebeians to demand the banishment of Rome's haughty champion. "We lou'd him," Menenius tells Brutus and Sicinius, "But like Beasts, and Cowardly Nobles, / Gave way unto your Clusters, who did hoote / Him out o'th' City." A moment later the "Clusters" themselves enter, and Menenius excoriates them: "You are they / That made the Ayre vnwholsome, when you cast / Your stinking, greasie Caps, in hooting / At Coriolanus Exile." Nowhere else in the canon do we encounter the word *Clusters*. What are we to make of it? And why does Menenius twice employ it to identify a crowd of commoners? A helpful clue is to be found in the Folio text of *Othello*, where the compound the 1622 Quarto renders as "Clisterpipes" is spelled "Cluster-pipes." Notwithstanding his "small Latine, and lesse Greeke," Shakespeare evidently knew that the word we now spell *clyster* derived from κλυστήρ, the Greek word for a cathartic. Recognizing that the Greek upsilon could be represented in English by either a *u* or an *i/y* character, the playwright probably realized that *cluster* offered possibilities for wordplay that would not be available to him if he opted for a form like *clister* or *clyster*. So what are the "Clusters" that "did hoote" Coriolanus out of Rome? They are purgatives: foul-smelling, noisy agents of evacuation who acted upon Rome's unhealthy body politic as diarrhetics. As a consequence of their labors a flatulent "Citty," having reduced its former savior to a piece of excrement, discharged him in an explosive movement of its urban bowels. For other scatological imagery in *Coriolanus*, see 2.1.46–82 (where *faces* plays on *faeces*, the Latin root of "feces"), 2.3.202 (where *pass* hints at defecation), and 3.1.50–55 (where *y'are bound* alludes to constipation).

32. *The Tempest*, 2.2.126.

History-Making in the Henriad

MICHAEL GOLDMAN

THEN and now are not so far apart, as my reader may confirm by trying to think back to when this sentence began. When did that *then* cease to be *now*? For that matter, when did the sentence really begin? Perhaps two weeks ago when I first drafted it, perhaps in kindergarten, perhaps as part of a gleam in my father's eye, perhaps in the Renaissance, to which we shall soon be going. Or perhaps the *then* we are seeking will not exist till a moment from now—or was it a moment ago?—when, troubled by some distracting twist in my argument, you looked back and began what I have called "this sentence" again.

I'm trying to evoke really two points in this riff on now and then. First, that the present moment is not a dimensionless point on the time line, but a temporal space of ambiguous duration. Second, that the past, even when, for all practical purposes, it may be clearly distinguished from the present—as when we speak of our childhood or the childhood of Prince Hal—the past is subject to a similar ambiguity. I am not referring to the familiar proposition, by now rather overworked, that we write and rewrite the past from the position of the present. Rather, I mean that the experience of the present, of living and acting in the present, involves a continual history-making activity. That is, it involves a redrawing, a reexperiencing of the borders between then and now, a beginning of the sentence again.

It's my notion, which I hope to explore in this essay, that for Shakespeare's audience in the *Henry IV* plays, the process of experiencing the drama—of undergoing, construing, fighting with, surrendering to the play as it unfolds—becomes in many ways the process of history-making itself. It creates a rhythm of instability, of perpetual realignment that we come to associate with the process of political action and decision-making we see on stage—a process that Shakespeare portrays as itself a process of representation, of struggling among and with representations like his and ours and those of people, past and present, in power over us. It is a process of aligning past and present, then and now, and one of the ways it works on us is by exposing us to many folds and wrinkles and ambiguities in our awareness of time.

I was led to notice this aspect of the *Henry IV* plays by the sense I'd had for some time of a certain recurrent texture, a complicating strangeness never adequately accounted for even among the wealth of wonderful criticism that the plays have elicited. Indeed, I first began to think along the lines I'll be following here when I found myself trying to make sense out of *1 Henry IV*'s own beginning, the address "So shaken as we are. . . . " with which Henry opens the play.

> So shaken as we are, so wan with care,
> Find we a time for frighted peace to pant
> And breathe short-winded accents of new broils
> To be commenced in stronds afar remote.
> No more the thirsty entrance of this soil
> Shall daub her lips with her own children's blood,
> No more shall trenching war channel her fields,
> Nor bruise her flow'rets with the armed hoofs
> Of hostile paces. Those opposed eyes
> Which like the meteors of a troubled heaven
> Did lately meet in the intestine shock
> And furious close of civil butchery
> Shall now in mutual well-beseeming ranks
> March all one way and be no more opposed
> Against acquaintance, kindred, and allies.
> The edge of war, like an ill-sheathed knife
> No more shall cut his master. Therefore, friends,
> As far as to the sepulcher of Christ—
> Whose soldier now, under whose blessed cross
> We are impressed and engaged to fight—
> Forthwith a body of English shall we levy,
> Whose arms were molded in their mother's womb
> To chase these pagans in those holy fields
> Over whose acres walked those blessed feet
> Which fourteen hundred years ago were nailed
> For our advantage on the bitter cross.
> But this our purpose now is twelvemonth old,
> And bootless 'tie to tell you we will go.
> Therefore we meet not now.[1]
>
> (1.1.1–30)

The problem I faced was basic—how can this relatively long speech be performed effectively, and by that I simply mean interestingly. I had never heard it come across as anything but an inert block of oratory, and the reason seemed to be that performers had trouble sustaining a sense of purpose. What was the King doing here? Why was he telling his closest advisers—and at length—something that after twenty lines he admits they already know and in fact have known for a year?

Most actors treat the speech as a kind of extension of the familiar offstage music with which modern productions of the histories usually begin—a sort of prolonged trumpet blast meant to suggest regal pomp and ceremony. Unfortunately, dramatic interest doesn't thrive on anything so static. The problem is heightened because the speech is *about* purpose—Henry's purpose in calling his counselors together, Christ's purpose in walking the earth, the purpose of a strangely personified Peace in gasping out a promise of new war. The problem of understanding and dramatically correlating all these purposes is the same as that of finding a purpose the actor can latch onto in the speech itself. It's a problem about going back in time and aligning a lot of information about the past, more specifically about a variety of pasts, rather irregularly defined, into a coherent relation with the present.

The speech poses a problem about time even in its very first words. It begins with a curious disruption in the audience's sense of time, which is worth dwelling on, for a number of reasons.

> So shaken as we are, so wan with care,
> Find we a time for frighted peace to pant.

What does "find we a time" mean? Is this an order? A description of what is being done now? A pious hope? The phrase is rarely glossed, but most critics would seem to agree with Kittredge that it's an imperative of sorts—*let us find a time.* Yet if it's an imperative, it has a peculiar spin, especially if one thinks of it as an imperative issuing from a king speaking in public at the beginning of a play. It's not a very commanding command, and it suggests a questioning or entreating note very hard to omit in speaking, even if one wants to. It can be read, possibly, to suggest that *we have just found a time,* or, contrastingly, *by all means we must find a time.* As we shall see, neither of these, nor any paraphrasable reading on the spectrum between them, can make completely coherent sense in terms of the entire scene that follows. The speech keeps us vibrating between these possibilities, as if we couldn't decide what time it was. For there is an even greater problem: exactly *where* is this time that we—or is it he—are being urged to find?

Finding a time is different from, and more complex than, simply finding time. It means opening up a space in which certain things can happen, a certain kind of time. One of the things history does is to describe what kind of a time this time or that time was; one of the things politics does is to convert time into *a* time, an era, a period in which forces can be marshaled, the Era of Good Feeling, the hundred days, the Cold War. The time that Henry describes is a time shaken and ravaged by war, but it is a space in which peace can act. And yet the space is as imaginatively elusive as the description of peace itself, for it is a frightened, exhausted peace, which speaks of war. Or is it that it *will* speak of war as soon as it can catch its breath? Is this time that Henry invokes *now,* or rather, what kind of now is it? Are we—is Henry's England—in the midst of it or has it just begun; is it about to begin or are we searching, shaken as we are, for a way to make it happen—to realign its components, to make them, as Henry says "march all one way?" It is an opening, then, which, even as it plunges us into political planning and into an impassioned effort to sum up the past, immediately makes us feel uneasy about getting a purchase on time.

This uneasiness will be compounded twenty-odd lines later, when the audience receives a more violent disruption to its sense of time. Henry turns from contemplating Christ's divine purpose to rather more abruptly defining his own.

> But this our purpose now is twelvemonth old,
> And bootless 'tis to tell you we will go.
> Therefore we meet not now.

This is a surprise. Henry's purpose—his vision of a crusade—has seemed to open up directly from the finding of a time in line 2, open up with a manifest insistence on urgency and connectedness. Temporal and logical sequence have been almost pedantically emphasized ("lately . . . therefore . . . now . . . forthwith . . . therefore") It is an at least subliminal jolt to discover that Henry has been finding this time, if not actually repeating this speech, for a year.

These temporal disruptions work to establish a counterpoint with the problems Henry faces governing England and with those faced by Shakespeare and his audience in construing history. If we look more closely at the speech we notice that the sudden reference to a "twelvemonth-old" purpose is but one of several openings into the past that occur in it, evocations of distanced sources and origins of historical action. The first such source is the earth of England, a cruel mother who "daub[s] her lips with her own children's blood." There are also the English mothers in whose wombs the arms of English soldiers were moulded, specifically for the purpose of chasing the pagans from Jerusalem. And there is Christ himself, described in terms that heighten our awareness of both sacred and secular action at a distance:

Therefore friends,
As far as to the sepulchre of Christ—
Whose soldier now, under whose blessed cross
We are impressed and engag'd to fight—
Forthwith a power of English shall we levy,
Whose arms were moulded in their mother's womb
To chase these pagans in those holy fields
Over whose acres walk'd those blessed feet
Which fourteen hundred years ago were nail'd
For our advantage on the bitter cross.
But this our purpose now is twelvemonth old. . . .

The sepulchre is a point in space that is also a point in and out of time, a then that is eternally now, redefining the future. We are given the particular detail of Christ's feet, again at a particular location in space but also at a very specific distance (1400 years ago) in time. Christ's historical force has a traditionally apolitical dimension—it leaps over time to offer us individual access to eternal safety, but in the context of the scene and in the immediate context of the speech, we are urged to see it in its political dimension. "Our advantage" (a word Henry will later use in an urgently political sense: "Advantage feeds him fat while men delay," 3.2.180) suggests not only personal salvation but also the redemption of England and the consolidation of Lancastrian power.

To see what is unique about this opening scene we would do well to remember a point that has been very well made by David Kastan. Discussing *1 Henry VI,* he notes that in the opening scene of his first tetralogy, Shakespeare stresses the fact that we are in the midst of "an ongoing temporal process." A past exists, whose impact on the present requires our consideration.[2] Now, this is an important feature of all Shakespeare's histories, as it is, say, of the *Oresteia,* and it's certainly true of *1 Henry IV.* But in the latter play, something very different is happening as well. We are being forced to *find a time,* to wonder where in time we are coming from, to ask what is in fact anterior, what is present. How are we to situate ourselves in the face of the many ongoing thens out of which an uncertain now must be rescued? Yes, we are once more in the midst of a temporal process, but the midst is not easily located or described. *Finding* the midst is a political question, a history-making one, for it is a space from which to act.

Henry Bolingbroke is in the midst of a political situation that he is trying to control. He is attempting to align past and present, to project a purpose into the future. And now, as the scene moves on, we experience a further instability, related to those that have come before, about his control over the present—or is it the immediate or not so immediate past? Just as earlier we asked, where does Henry locate the time he is finding, we must now ask, what does he know and when did he know it? As Henry turns to Westmoreland and asks him to make his report, the audience faces mounting uncertainty about history and time.

Westmoreland brings news of civil war. Mortimer has been defeated by Glendower, and the crusade must be postponed. This is news to us, but is it news to Henry?

> It seems then that the tidings of this broil
> Brake off our business for the Holy Land.
>
> (1.1.47–48)

Henry's response mimes surprise, but he casts it in the past tense of narrative ("brake") and introduces it by a phrase ("It seems") that suggests control, a presentation to his on-stage audience. But it is only after the news gets worse and more uncertain, that Henry suddenly seems to have known not only Westmoreland's news but even more recent facts:

> Here is a dear, a true-industrious friend,
> Sir Walter Blunt, new lighted from his horse. . . .
> And he has brought us smooth and welcome news.
>
> (62–66)

For the past thirty lines, Westmoreland's narrative has been invested with a feeling of present unfolding. Now it is abruptly placed in a superseded past.

We quickly realize, moreover, that the news Blunt brings is neither smooth nor entirely welcome. Once we think about past and future, as Henry soon forces us to do, we realize that the news only points to more trouble, which again Henry must struggle to control. Hotspur's victory raises the problem of Henry's son; would they had been exchanged at the point of origin! (*That* would have been a convenient realignment.) It also brings with it new signs of rebellion, over which Hotspur and Worcester must be confronted. And so the scene ends, with a heightened sense of busyness, of new purpose, and of greater urgency. Both time and the effort to organize time are speeding up. Rapid movement in time and space are insisted on:

> Cousin, on Wednesday next our council we
> Will hold at Windsor. So inform the lords;
> But come yourself with speed to us again. . . .
>
> (102–4)

It is important to notice that this has been a behind-the-scenes scene. Henry is setting up a meeting of the full council, into which much planning must go if it is to be manipulated properly. But it is also a public scene. Even with his inner circle Henry must always be shaping, controlling, and history-making. As we watch the news shifting from bad to good—as we watch the *same* news shifting from bad to good, to advantage or disadvantage, we too become involved in a constant realignment and redefinition of present and past. To take a final example from Henry's last words in the scene:

> For more is to be said and to be done
> Than out of anger can be uttered.
>
> (105–6)

What is the source of Henry's anger—in both the temporal and logical sense? When and at what did he become angry? Logically, he has known of Hotspur's defiance since the scene began, but does he begin the scene showing this anger and at this cause?

My point in referring to the question of Henry's anger is not to discuss a particular performance solution, but to draw attention once more to the way in which the audience is being bombarded with unsettling invitations to temporal realignment. There are of course many different performance arcs that can be cut through this scene, but even if the actor plays something like anger in the opening lines, the anger shown at the end must be different both in tone and attribution than at the beginning. The effects are not crude, but they are numerous and have a cumulative destabilizing effect, no matter how the scene is performed. In this brilliant opening, we experience history-making by negotiating a series of subtle jolts in which origin and experience, purpose and event, past and present are continually, simultaneously realigned.

About the scene that follows, it might well be said that the transition to Falstaff and the tavern provides the most famous contrast in all Shakespeare—so famous that nothing more need be said about it. But the perspective we are pursuing here suggests a significant point that seems to have been ignored. For it's not only that in 1.2. we are projected into the antitemporal holiday world of the tavern, or that we begin an alternating rhythm of high and low, but that we first see the tavern world—which, remember, is from the Elizabethan audience's point of view, the *familiar* one of a popular historical play, *The Famous Victories*—that we come to what is apparently this more familiar version only after the historiographically charged treatment of the opening scene.

So the tavern scene is both new and old at once, and the more unexpected first scene has set up a context in which this new/old scene must be weighed and appreciated. Today we know Shakespeare's play so well that it may seem to tick along all too smoothly between court and tavern. But for Shakespeare's original audience—and, I would suggest, for us in an optimal production—the dive to the tavern is vertiginous. These worlds are not going to be neatly insulated and kept apart, anymore than the irresponsible Hal and the heroic Hal are to be the utterly distinct personae of *The Famous Victories*. And the leaking of one world and one characterization and one attitude to time into another will be reinforced by our felt concern with Shakespeare's own historiographical problem—how to keep these two worlds, with their very different relations to event and situation, simultaneously before us, how to hold onto both these conflicting truths about experience in the forward rush of time?

I want to continue scene by scene just once more, because the next scene, 1.3, is a very good example of how Shakespeare presents political struggles as contests in history-making, struggles over and with history. The King begins harshly:

> My blood hath been too cold and temperate
> Unapt to stir at these indignities
> And you have found me. . . .
>
> (1.3.1–3)

The anger—whose origin seemed curiously veiled when we encountered it in the first scene—is now produced or reproduced by Henry as a well-managed effect.

We watch not the King's anger but its use and political significance. Then we move on to a battle of historical descriptions (all versions of "how the quarrel between Hotspur and the King came about,") ending when Worcester redescribes Mortimer and Richard's history in order to convert Hotspur into a rebel. The most interesting description in the scene is of course Hotspur's brilliant narrative of the effeminate courtier who pestered him at the battlefront, but the key point about this narrative is that it has no political effect, except to make Hotspur attractive.

Here and elsewhere, Hotspur fails to grasp the difference between telling a good story and making history. All his narratives have a curiously *literary* quality, which I associate with their remoteness from the political; they tend to break off from the historical into the legendary. They do not carry their weight as parts of a sophisticated struggle for power, though they are exercises of personal charisma. That charisma of course has a political potential; Henry fears it and Worcester knows how to manipulate it. But Hotspur confuses history with what he calls "chronicle," which he sees as part of a permanent literary canon, a stable repository of truth:

> Shall it for shame be spoken in these days,
> Or fill up chronicles in time to come,
> That men of your nobility and power
> Did gage them both in an unjust behalf . . .
> To put down Richard, that sweet lovely rose,
> And plant this thorn, this canker, Bolingbroke?
> (1.1.3.168–74)

This response of course has been cynically elicited by Worcester from his excitable nephew. Those in the audience who have been following Shakespeare's version of the story since *Richard II* know it is not so simple as that.

It's not easy to make historical drama feel like the reality of historical action, to organize a narrative and yet render the complexities of the uncertain political moment. But Shakespeare finds ways in *Henry IV* to make even this difficulty contribute to the destabilizing texture I've been discussing. Hal's famous "I know you all" soliloquy calls attention to Shakespeare's elegant solution of a narrative problem, keeping Hal's hands clean and his story clear, though at the possible expense of some verisimilitude. Similarly, Henry's "But this our purpose now is twelvemonth old" may suggest that he has yielded to the demands of exposition, again by sacrificing some probability. But the most interesting use of this tension has to do with the large-scale organization of Part One.

To explain this, one must first recognize that the most common oversimplification of historical analysis is the pattern most natural to drama. One might call it the "single-climax pattern." It views history as a version of the simplest private drama—the biorhythm of tension-climax-release. It's a story we like to tell about all kinds of life, including public life. It's what makes elections so satisfying to follow, at least when your side wins. Unlike, say, following the other events in the news, all the tensions go in one direction and are resolved thrillingly in a single day. This pattern also enjoys the advantage of being the simplest shape that will lend itself to the effective disposition of large theatrical forces. In *1 Henry IV* this pattern leads to Shrewsbury.

From the first, everything presses toward the climactic encounter on the battlefield. Shrewsbury offers the appearance of a simple test of political morality: is the character in question doing what's necessary to win? Hal yes, Falstaff no, Hotspur not enough. Characters are seen orienting their own sacrifices or self-indulgences toward that climax. The conduct of the play itself becomes a metaphor of government—the plot, like Harry, triumphs and orders all our feelings, however varied. We would like to linger with Falstaff and Hotspur, but we need to move on. Nevertheless, the variety and the profusion of slight slidings, delays, and doublings under the arc of the plot point to the truer complexity of history. The single-climax model, for all the pleasure we get out of it, is inadequate, except as a usefully deceptive metaphor, a politically inspired fiction.

The immense clarity of Hal's rescuing the king and defeating Hotspur in one prolonged *aristeia* is undercut, and not only by the figure of Falstaff, with his own narrative and parody of Hotspur's death. All the preparations for battle, with their emphasis on calculation, betrayal, and spin-doctoring, give us a different angle on the history we are watching from that of the "long hour by Shrewsbury clock"—Falstaff's phrase, we remember, for a fight that never happened in a time that never was. Behind the scenes in which the noble son articulately rescues the noble father, we are aware of the hidden drama of numbers in which, among other things, Hotspur's father silently betrays his son.

These slidings grow more pronounced in the Second Part. Remember I'm concerned here not with irony as such, with the puncturing of legends or propaganda, but with a kind of bifocalism, which takes many forms, including the play with and against the single-climax pattern. It's actually something between bifocalism and binocularism, since it produces neither unresolvable alternatives nor seamless depths. Its effect, in any case, is to reinforce the sense of what I've been calling "history-making." In *2 Henry IV,* one of the most notable examples of this bifocalism is the relation of the two parts themselves.

Much has been written about this relation, almost all of it in terms of an historical question about Shakespeare—what did he intend in writing a sequel and when, in the history of writing Part One, did he start to intend it? I would like to suggest that Part Two provokes such concerns because, in its relation to the first part, it fosters the impression of time being stopped and moving on at the same time.

Part Two continues narratively out of Part One, but in many ways it seems to be retelling the same story. Are we advancing or going over familiar territory? Are we moving ahead or marking time? We find ourselves in a curiously suspended moment, as if we had stepped back to Part One and were hanging there waiting for Henry to die, while at the same time the rebellions of Part One were being acted again. This of course is partly a requirement of the sequel genre, but this sequel seems to go further, to incorporate this aspect of sequelhood into its own texture, to make a dramatic point out of what today we would call its "belatedness."

Hal seems palpably to be marking time while he waits for the play to make its now familiar stops on his journey to legitimation. Playing a joke on Falstaff, Northumberland's defection, the reconciliation with the King—haven't we seen all this before, faster and younger and funnier? It's a virtuosic achievement, to give the audience what it has expected from Part One and yet to get on with the history—to fill up what seemed like a tiny space left over after Shrewsbury with an equally long historic narrative, and the resultant structure accomplishes many things. But one of them is to heighten our sense of history as a perpetual readjustment of the relation between now and then. Even the most important new character in Part II, who has no source either in the chronicle or in the structure of Part One—Justice Shallow—is most vivid as a narrator and re-narrator of the past, a past of inconsequential pastimes placed in a dim prepolitical backward before the crises of Richard II's reign, when Mowbray and Gaunt were merely names on the lips of would-be fashionable gentlemen.

One might remember, too, how scenes from the life of Richard II—scenes we never quite get to see in *his* play—are re-narrated in both parts of *Henry IV.* Especially dwelt on are moments when Bolingbroke and Richard appear in succession:

> Thou that threw'st dust upon his goodly head
> When through proud London he came sighing on
> After th'admired heels of Bolingbroke,
> Criest now, "O earth, yield us that king again."
> (*2 Henry IV,* 1.3.103–6)

And always the concern is with the realignment of present and past, with reinterpreting the past to gain political advantage in the present.

Probably the most striking reminder, however, of how the narrative relations between present and past can constitute the very material of political action comes at the beginning of *2 Henry IV*;

> Open your ears, for which of you will stop
> The vent of hearing when loud Rumour speaks?
> (Induction, 1–2)

I wonder if justice has been done to the boldness, the strangeness of this extraordinary choice on Shakespeare's part—to begin his sequel with Rumor. And there's perhaps no moment stranger, more puzzling than when Rumor suddenly interrupts himself:

> But what need I thus
> My well-known body to anatomize
> Among my household?
> (20–22)

We are addressed as rumor's household, a slightly aggressive note of intimacy. But why is the theater, in particular, the home of rumor? There are several possible answers, all important for Shakespeare's treatment of history. First, it may have to do with the appetite of any theatrical audience for intimate knowledge. Furthermore, rumor sets up a curious glancing relation with the factual information it purportedly conveys—it seems unusually close to the fact by virtue of its vividness and unofficial provenance, but distant from it by virtue of its unreliability. It reminds us of a gap even as it deceptively, pleasingly appears to leap it. It thrives on a gap of representation, which is also a gap of time.

There is also the matter of rumor's speed. Rumor spreads from an event with legendary rapidity, faster, it sometimes seems—and certainly seemed in Shakespeare's day—than any other mode of communication. Indeed in preelectric times, rumor had an exemplary metaphysical function rather like that of the speed of light since Einstein. It reminds us that even apparent instantaneity involves a gap. There is an event, a radiation of rumor from it, and out of that radiation, after an interval, needing interpretation, it reaches us.

We will return shortly to the specifically theatrical aspect of rumor, but first more needs to be said about rumor's historical and political significance. In *2 Henry IV,* rumor is acknowledged as a material fact of history, to be evaluated and wielded with care by the hopeful politician. Perhaps rumor is most emphatically connected both to high politics and historical narration at the beginning of act 3. There, Henry despondently imagines what it would be like to read "the book of fate" in which historical events could be seen before they happen. This reminds him of Richard's prophecy that has rung through the Henriad:

> "The time will come that foul sin gathering head
> Shall break into corruption"—so went on
> Foretelling this same time's condition
> And the division of our amity.
>
> (3.1.76–79)

Henry is haunted by Richard's uncanny prescience. Warwick, however, moves quickly to demystify this superstitious—and politically demoralizing—view by explaining Richard's prophecy in materialistic terms. Historical prediction, he says, is a form of rational political calculation:

> There is a history in all men's lives,
> Figuring the nature of the times deceased;
> The which observe'd a man may prophesy,
> With a near aim, of the main chance of things
> As yet not come to life. . . .
> King Richard might create a perfect guess
> That great Northumberland, then false to him,
> Would of that seed grow to a greater falseness. . . .
>
> (3.1.80–90)

With that, King Henry pulls himself together, and the discussion shifts into a practical mode—into an evaluation of rumor as a method of calculating rebel forces:

> *Henry.* They say the Bishop and Northumberland
> Are fifty thousand strong.
> *Warwick.* It cannot be, my lord.
> Rumor doth double, like the voice and echo,

> The numbers of the fear'd. . . .
> To comfort you the more, I have receiv'd
> A certain instance that Glendower is dead.
>
> (95–103)

Glendower, who like Hotspur also confused legendary narration with history making, charisma with political effectiveness, is dead indeed. History is made by those who can grasp the real forces alive in the flux of the moment, who can swim, as Shakespeare will soon put it, in the tide that governs the affairs of men.

Warwick's rational analysis of rumor reminds us that the issue of representation as it is raised in these history plays is not merely an aesthetic or epistemological one. It goes to the root of politics itself, where understanding and action intersect. The serious political actor must fight to sift, control, manipulate a bundle of constantly changing representations. As Part Two draws to a close, Hal acts to take charge of his kingdom in an atmosphere that seethes with rumor, with a cynical understanding of the past that constitutes an expectation for his future. We watch him overcome rumor—he calls it "rotten opinion"—with his rejection of Falstaff.

Now, there is one more way in which the historico-political significance of rumor is connected to the phenomenology of theater and that is also foregrounded by *2 Henry IV.* This is the peculiar proximity that the play affords us to action as a source of rumor. In a number of places, but especially at the rejection of Falstaff, I think we feel—influenced as we are by busy preparations, public outcry, multiple audiences, crowds, and the general buzz around the rejection scene—that we're watching the propagation of rumor as if at the first microsecond after the big bang of an event. The play indeed makes us alert to an "event" as a letting loose of rumor in the world. Indeed, the release of rumor is itself an event, a political action, part of the fluid power-negotiation to which politicians must train themselves to respond and that history attempts to represent. Action becoming theater becoming action. The household of rumor, Shakespeare understands, has special though sobering access to the process of history.

Thinking about rumor brings home to us the intimate connection between history, action, and theater. Action always involves the representation of action, its performance, as it were, before an audience. Action in this sense requires an historical attention—an attempt at aligning then and now with an eye on the future. The historicizing attitude attempts to describe an event in vectored terms—what is the direction of this process? In this sense, the problem of history is entwined with the problem of action. And theater allows us peculiar access to this linkage of history and action, because in the theater we construe even the most entertaining moments into what we call the "action" of a play. If they don't construe—if we can't feel in some way that this activity is coming from somewhere and going someplace, they quickly bore.

Again, we must not confuse the issue here with the familiar poststructuralist critique of history. The point is not that, because representation involves a gap, history must involve one too, but rather that the existence of this gap means that we always live with one foot in the historical. Our experience is rooted in the ambiguous proximity of then, the "complex temporality" of now.[3] Every moment involves the construction of a past that gives the the present its momentary stability. *History,* in the usual sense of the term, magnifies the basic problems of representation, because it attempts to settle the past. But if we are, as we always are, shaken and wan with care, *getting* the past to settle is difficult and provisional. It involves finding a time, stabilizing a now from which to act. All action, but particularly what we think of as political action, involves a species of instantaneous critical historiography.

At this point, keeping the phenomenology of drama in mind helps with another problem, which might at first seem to blur the picture of history we have been developing. Isn't there, or at least wasn't there in Shakespeare's day, a concern with history as moral evaluation—not the vector of the scene, but its eternal valence? In the theater, however, all the moral revelations of a scene, interesting as they may be, are subject to the question: where does this new knowledge mean the action is going? Yes, in the prayer scene of *Hamlet* we are very interested to learn that Claudius is indeed guilty and would go to hell if killed at this moment, but above all we are aware that we must adjust to the fact that this confrontation, so appropriate to a fifth act, is being thrown at us in the third. Similarly, our inner debate about whether Henry IV is a good king is always involved with adjustments of the vector. We watch Prince John in Gaultree forest, and the instability of our response reflects our sense of the complexity, the bifocal/ binocularity of the process that is unfolding—where does this mean England is going now? Not under the aspect of eternity, but contingently, as they all move on, rebels and rulers, winners and losers, schlemiels and schlemozzels, to further contingencies. The moral bouncing, like the temporal realignments, is something the play forces us not to sum up, but to live through. Not, that is, are the Lancasters in the right, or more right than wrong (though we are free to contemplate such questions) but, more pressingly, how are we to *grasp* this cross-hatch of taint and virtue, of competing interests, of power and problem and maneuver? Grasping it is the truly *historical* activity, by which the reality of political action in the flux of time may be apprehended.

Where might we go from here? Is the texture I've been exploring an isolated feature of one pair of plays, or can we locate it in some larger Shakespearean universe? Let me conclude by suggesting, very briefly, a possible avenue for further exploration. The focus we have been observing—on rumor and realignment at the point of origin, the point somewhere beyond the shimmering border where *now* shades off into *then*—this focus may shed some light on one of Shakespeare's favorite motifs: let's call it "the theme of the Questionable Father."

Who is my father? Where and what is he? Is he, for instance, the self I must be true to, the absent judge who has deputized me, the forgiveness I must pray for, the law I must enforce, or is it escape, or is it rescue him from? Is he Father Christmas, our Father in Heaven, or more enigmatically, Father Time? From the ever-wandering Antipholus of Syracuse and his father Aegeon, to Hal and Henry IV, to Hamlet and Old Hamlet's ghost, to Angelo and the Duke of dark corners, we see young men (and young women, too, think of Viola and Portia) haunted, burdened and holding themselves back from action under the shadows of an obscurely fostering paternal or quasi-paternal imperative, a source of strength and weakness, of virtue and taint, a past that commands them but that they must uneasily redefine and re-present. Who are you, father? How did my sentence begin? Nay, answer me, stand and unfold yourself.

What we feel, then, on the scale of national history-making in *Henry IV* may have its counterpart, for Shakespeare, in the instabilities of personal life. Time, that pleases some, tries all, but not only because we grow old and die. It tests us because its structure is unfixed, depending on human action and negotiation. We move uneasily and irregularly within time, because time is the only dimension in which we can never locate ourselves with confidence. Which of . . . and here I want to conclude by quoting a phrase that brings my argument full circle by returning it to Shakespeare's method in the Henriad. It is the phrase he uses in his epilogue to close the circle at the end of the second tetralogy—to close, not with a smooth progression to a stable finish, but with yet another unexpected temporal disruption. For he concludes his chronicle of the rise of the House of Lancaster by making a bidirectional leap in time that, altering the meaning of its own sentence, abruptly cuts short the celebrations of Henry V's triumphs, harking back simultaneously to the promising theatrical past of Shakespeare's early days and to the tragic historical future of Henry's son, concentrating that movement into a surprising, bluntly impassive half-line:

> Small time: but in that small, most greatly lived
> This star of England. Fortune made his sword;
> By which, the world's best garden he achieved;
> And of it left his son imperial lord.
> Henry the Sixth, in infant bands crowned king
> Of France and England, did this king succeed;
> Whose state so many had the managing,
> That they lost France, and made his England bleed:
> Which oft our stage hath shown.
>
> (*Henry V*, epilogue, 5–13)

Very likely some of the original dramatic force of this passage came from flinging a late Elizabethan audience, which might well be concerned with the succession to an aging Queen, back to a bloody future. But certainly it continues to work, as so much in the Henriad does, by reminding us—forcing us to experience the fact—that to make history is to find oneself moving with dizzying, indeed frightening uncertainty in time. Which oft our stage hath shown.

Notes

1. All Shakespearean citations are to *The Complete Signet Classic Shakespeare,* ed. Sylvan Barnet (New York: New American Library, 1972).
2. David Kastan, *Shakespeare and the Shapes of Time* (Hanover: University Press of New England, 1982), 24.
3. See Homi Bhabha, *The Location of Culture* (London: Methuen 1994).

The Historical Subject as *Roman* Actor and Agent of History: Interrogative Dramatic Structure in *Julius Caesar*

GÜNTER WALCH

(APRIL 1989)

OUR time is characterized by rapid social and political changes, growing concern about the future, and an increasing awareness of the individual's precarious situation. This has been made clear by the pivotal role of power relations in scholarship and the arts from such contemporary theoretical discourses as structuralism, post-structuralism, the New Historicism, some forms of psychoanalysis, and Marxism. The GDR's current lively interest in the anniversary of the French Revolution, for instance, has not been limited to a handful of specialized historians, but involves artists and musicians and, above all, the general public. History is traditionally a strong component of this country's intellectual and cultural life and seems now to be acquiring a new significance. Methodologically this calls for an open approach and for a richer understanding of history. Humankind will not survive the onslaught of the scourges of armament, hunger, and environmental destruction, so the argument goes, if a world different from the one we now live in is no longer imaginable. History along with the theater and the arts are thus important sources for the (necessary) social imagination. And Marxists should, for these reasons, turn to history for a study without illusions about its real contradictions, and try to comprehend it as a complex sequence of decision-taking situations rather than looking at it primarily as an affirmation of political ideology.[1]

The fortunes of the historical subject in the throes of fundamental historical change is a concern shared by scholars, readers, directors, actors, and theater audiences. But *Julius Caesar*, even though it has been referred to as a play about revolution, has yet to play a major role in any recent national or international discussion of the stage or in literary criticism. This point is underlined by reference to the choice of plays by Shakespeare critics interested in power relations, social contradictions, and resulting political conflicts. At the center of the canon that has developed in recent years are *Hamlet, Coriolanus, Henry IV, Measure for Measure,* and *The Tempest.* Other plays include *Henry V, King Lear,* and *Troilus and Cressida* as well as a few of the comedies. The latter are especially evident within various trends in feminist Shakespeare criticism. Some other plays are occasionally referred to or at least mentioned, but very rarely *Julius Caesar.*[2]

One reason for this is that *Julius Caesar* is Shakespeare's apparently most pronouncedly neoclassical play. Ever since the later seventeenth century the theatrical and critical reception of *Julius Caesar* has tended toward the neoclassical representation of rounded characters and, above all, of a closed narration of events that are largely of a public nature. This does not necessarily mean that internal contradictions in the characters have been consistently ignored. But there has been a marked tendency to consider these prerequisite for lifelike characters. People harbor internal contradictions. So do characters. Characters are like people. Depending on the critics' or directors' political, philosophical, and aesthetic views, either Brutus or Caesar has been extolled as the tragic protagonist, and embarrassing passages have been faded out. As a result, the play's characters have seemed highly stable. As seemingly true-to-life personages they have developed a degree of persuasive pressure that has led to an urge to rid them of traits marring their seemingly "natural" character.

Thus Granville-Barker, to give just one example, like Pope and others before him, attributed Brutus' important speech accompanying the blood ritual, "Stoop, Romans, stoop, / And let us bathe our hands in Caesar's blood, / Up to the elbows, and besmear our swords" (3.1.105–9) to Cassius as unfitting to Brutus' noble character.[3] In the same spirit, all T. S. Dorsch can find to say about this particular theatrical scene is that it "merely disgusts us." Also, Brutus' association of Caesar with pillage in his quarrel with Cassius—Caesar, he says, was slain "but for supporting robbers" (4.3.23)—is, to Dorsch in the introduction to his influential Arden edition (1975), simply an "inexplicable statement," a "careless" mistake on the part of Shakespeare, who happened to be following Plutarch very closely but was deplorably lacking in consistency at this point (xxxvi).

The impression of exceptionally stable meaning consolidated by such moves seems to have been aided by the remarkable stability of the printed text itself. Unlike, notoriously, *King Lear* or (considering the texts chronologically closest to *Julius Caesar*) *Hamlet* and even *Henry V, Julius Caesar* raises few exciting textual problems. There is, of course, no Quarto, let alone several. The only authoritative text is in the First Folio. This does contain what seem to be a few absurdities that most probably result from doubling at least one actor's part (Cassius/Ligarius) and from a few contradictory stage directions. Or there is the famous illogicality (if it is an illogicality) of the two passages telling us about Portia's death (4.3.143–61; 4.3.180–94), probably the result of different stages of work with the text. Such traces of theatrical textual activity as these have been, it appears, too faint to inspire fresh readings of a play exceptionally well printed from a well ordered and legible copy text.[4] Or again, if we look at *Coriolanus* for a comparison with a Roman play favored by modern critics and writers interested in problems of power and authority, we find that to Bertolt Brecht, for example, this play appeared significant because of the fundamental class conflict at its base. He was interested in staging, in a new and topical way, the political and economic strategies of the patricians defending the profits accruing from their usury, and the resistance by the plebeians in which we can surmise echoes of the first stirrings in 1607 of the Levellers and Diggers.[5] Leaping forward to the most recent critical work, *Coriolanus* is analyzed in terms of a political legitimation crisis,[6] or of the failure of entrenched authority,[7] or, as part of an examination of the dialogic-mimetic speech act structure of Shakespeare's oeuvre; attention is also drawn to *Coriolanus'* open form of representation in which the dramatist, after previous experiments in breaking up firmly established significations of authority in his textual work, from the turn of the century makes that approach a compositional principle.[8]

In all of these instances, the angry plebeians, and the political, linguistic, and aesthetic issues that have been raised in connection with them, then as now, are at the center of interest. But compared with the active plebeians in *Coriolanus,* those in *Julius Caesar,* almost prototypically dirigible objects of political manipulation, and, no doubt largely for that reason, generally have not been attractive to recent critics endeavoring to understand more carefully the complex causes and consequences of historical and textual contradictions in the terms just indicated. Yet, as I propose to demonstrate, *Julius Caesar,* written in 1599, is as much part of Shakespeare's turn of the century theatrical exploration of power as *Henry V* and *Hamlet,* its closest chronological neighbors to which the same historical, political, and aesthetic conditions of theatrical signification apply. In these plays particularly, as on the Shakespearean stage as an emerging mode generally, authority is both a represented object of, and a representing agency in, theatrical production. An historically new type of theater, a commercially funded, secular, professional, shareholding enterprise represents the established authorizing types of political, ecclesiastical, and juridical discourse dominant in Elizabethan England within its texts and productions. But at the same time, generating and sustained by, and helping to generate, a modern type of authority, itself unrepresented, and now openly embracing "as authoritative the provision of pleasure, the efficacy of communication, the distribution of information and news-value, and the functions of social release and collective memory,"[9] this theater in its synthesis of textual and theatrical signification breaks with the fixed correlation of signs of officially sanctioned ideological meanings. It thus engenders "a new discursive paradigm" contributing to "the project of modernity . . . for which new modes of negotiating and appropriating authority were indispensible and, indeed, constitutive."[10] Considering the prominence of the English Renaissance theater as a medium of communication, its contribution to that project, which is of undiminished relevance to this time, is of considerable significance.

All of this is emerging more clearly in our own time. As we begin to penetrate post-Enlightenment appropriations and adjustments of Shakespearean drama and its wealth of theatrical means and devices that undermine the authorized representation of power, we can also appreciate that drama's affinity to indeterminate interrogative textual structures. This certainly applies to *Henry V* and *Hamlet* that are chronologically closest to *Julius Caesar,* written and performed at a time of sharpening crisis during the last years of the aging Queen's reign. In *Henry V* Shakespeare uses the natural analogy of the honeybee along with its rich Renaissance intertextuality. It is one of several time-honored contemporary topoi drawing on *natural* phenomena for their *ideologically* stabilizing effect. This makes it particularly hard to de-essentialize Canterbury's imperative discourse of power. Furthermore, Shakespeare's handling of the Chorus character makes evident the difference between what is said and what is shown on the stage, between the officially sanctioned patriotic ideology and the actual political situation. In *Hamlet,* first performed between 1599 and 1601 but probably composed after *Julius Caesar,* Shakespeare employs a variety of approaches and devices contributing to the degree of intensity to which the problem of the historical individual caught between the necessary and the possible, obedience and desire, is dramatically explored. The popular characters of the philosophical gravediggers illustrate this, as does at the level of official culture, neoclassical poetic theory itself, that the Prince, while prescribing it in his advice to the actors, contradicts in his own actions.[11]

My point of departure for the subsequent reading of *Julius Caesar* is that, through this text, Shakespeare unfolds on the public stage a political alternative to imperial *tyranny.* This feudal term, along with *tyrant(s)* (and accompanied by the relevant register generally), appears seven times in key positions and is used very much through Marcus Antonius' apologetic language to associate absolutist ancient regime thinking and practice on- and off-stage. However, although the play possibly sympathizes with republicanism, it does not seem able or willing to take sides in the struggle of constitutional systems as early as 1599. Shakespeare keeps his distance from both systems and their ideologies. Yet to allow the comparison to unfold dramatically meant, and still means, moving it into the sphere of what is becoming thinkable, this being always specified by meaning in circulation; and, possibly, to suggest by implication a third alternative: instead of the rule by one (Caesar) or a privileged elite (Brutus' republicanism), the determination of public affairs by the many or even by all. In this way the play excels in raising questions rather than in being able to answer them. Catherine Belsey asks two such questions: "Perhaps the play condemns usurpation rather than tyranny? Or tyranny but not absolutism?"[12] Since the play, sustained by the self-authorization of the new theater for which it was written, foregrounds this process of questioning, it is here discussed in terms of an interrogative text.[13] As an interrogative text, *Julius Caesar* urges the reader or auditor to venture answers to questions that are raised or, more typically, suggested. Furthermore, it operates as an interrogative text by drawing attention to its own textuality, for instance, the appropriation of classical material, and by inviting questions concerning itself, that can undermine dramatic illusion where it emerges. At crucial points the audience is distanced from stage events. And it is an interrogative text since, on the strength of its distancing interrogative structure, it does not permit any single and privileged discourse to contain and situate the others.[14] Shakespeare develops a specific interrogative structure in which several discourses work together and against each other. This undermines the control of any of them by a single discourse—primarily the imperative discourse of established authority. The dramatist works toward an altogether new discourse the object of which involves a problem of representation, the problem of representing something as yet undeveloped, something historically new just then emerging, and something without precedent.

Why does Shakespeare turn from writing English history plays to writing Roman tragedy? What explains this radical generic break? The classical material and mode were of course anything but new to him. But *Julius Caesar* was a far cry from *Titus Andronicus* (1589–90) and, in a different genre, from *The Rape of Lucrece* (1594). Above all, for the first time Shakespeare turned to Plutarch, a highly political writer, in his search for suitable material. If we think of the dramatist's writing process in terms of historical activity and thus as an integral part of history itself (rather than as an act of inspiration passively outside history and at best merely reflecting some of its aspects) to ask, for example, what might possibly explain that generic change is not only legitimate but becomes indeed indispensable. A connection may be presumed with *Julius Caesar* as one of the first plays, if not the very first, opening the Globe. The superior new building and its favorable position on the Bankside may also have attracted more refined people with more elevated classical tastes.[15] It seems possible that the Lord Chamberlain's Men were worried by the bishop's order of 1599 which, although it did not ban English history from the stage, subjected it to prior licensing by the Privy Council. However, other companies went on performing history plays for at least another half dozen years. If abandoning national history as a subject for its stage by Shakespeare's company signals extreme caution and the wish to avoid clashes with the censor, this stands in curious contrast to their willingness to perform *Richard II* on the eve of the Essex Rebellion. That example, including Elizabeth's much quoted remark—"I am Richard II, know ye not that"—tells us how sensitively the authorities did, and could be expected to, react to any suspected form of subversive activity. (The stumbling block in this case, however, may not have been Shakespeare's play at all but—as Barroll (1988) has tried to show—John Hayward's *The first part of the life and raigne of King Henrie the III* of 1599.)[16] Whatever the external reasons may have been, it now appears fairly certain that the history play, which in the late sixteenth century had given to the theater such an excellent opportunity to communicate Tudor historiography with its audience about the need for national unity both at home and abroad, was around the turn of the century becoming more and more of a liability since, as Shakespeare had consistently done, political issues were raised through the agency of the genre.

The ideological boundaries of plays representing English history, a discourse always already interpreted by establishment historiography, were now being more and more jealously guarded. Compared with the growing constraints imposed by writing and staging English histories, the new historical, philosophical, linguistic, gestic, and visual material provided by the classical discourse offered a number of creative advantages. Above all, the exploration of contemporary reality[17] could be continued with stage characters less encumbered by domestic accretions, with great figures that could display what appeared to be exemplary civic virtues in a spirit of free humanity, and whose pathos communicated a concentrated historical experience and bestowed on stage events a dimension of universal history. In political terms highly topical at that point in English history and for the "project of modernity" generally, Shakespeare, in Harry Levin's words, "[i]n transferring his venue from the English monarchy to the Roman republic . . . shifted his emphasis from kingship to citizenship, and from the duties of the subject to the rights of the citizen."[18] In turning to Rome and *Romanitas,* Shakespeare was, however, dealing with a thoroughly ambiguous discourse. Its potential for self-representation had long since been appropriated by Renaissance monarchies, the Tudors among them. Public displays of the representatives of authority and their insignia became an indispensable method of wielding power. Classical mythology was central to public spectacles, court celebrations, and royal progresses. King James's style of government and representation was conceived wholly in terms of *Romanitas,* his court theater as well as his (and Elizabeth's) understanding of the royal personage as an actor always on public display, setting his own standard right up to the construction of a royal pedigree, invariably including Hercules as the ancestor of all European monarchs.

The ambivalence of the Roman discourse allows associations with both republican civic virtues and free humanity on the one hand, and with absolute power on the other; its differences and contradictory functions constitute the tragedy and particularly the dramatically decisive scene, 3.2, in which first Brutus, then Antony carry on their rhetorical struggle for power. Antony presents Caesar, who had kept "the general coffers" (91) filled, as the people's benefactor. He has left the citizens seventy-five drachmas each and his "private arbours, and new-planted orchards, / . . . To walk about and recreate yourselves" (250, 252–53). Above all, Antony identifies Caesar with Rome. The common weal is identical with Caesar's welfare, and now with that of his party. Therefore the conspirators' crime was not merely directed against Caesar, but against Rome. Their reasons can only have been personal:

> What private griefs they have, alas, I know not,
> That made them do it.
>
> (215–16)

Since realm and ruler are identical, opposition against the regime is opposition against the realm itself. Consequently the conspirators are "traitors" (199, 203, 207, 257; Antony first skillfully elicits the word from the Fourth Plebeian at 155). This is the language and the strategy of absolute power[19] as we also find them in Shakespeare's other dramatic genres, from the early histories to the late romances. The native discourse of absolute power merges easily with the Roman discourse. On the other hand, Brutus' discourse, because of his republicanism, is more narrowly associated with *Romanitas*. Among Brutus' civic virtues his honor is most prominent, clearly no longer a discredited feudal concept of honor but that of a free and proud citizen. This is a significant conceptual change pointing toward, perhaps, the ultimate causes for Shakespeare's decision respecting genre. Brutus' honor safeguards his credibility, certainly to the conspirators and to his own thinking. In accordance with dramatic requirements his speech relies on logical, although finally tautological, arguments. Its conspicuous lack of manipulative intent is indicated by its prose form, and it foregoes all concrete detail. There is nothing in this speech to answer the will, the drachmas, or the gardens. He, too, speaks on behalf of Rome. As republican Rome it is a Rome of liberty that has to ward off the absolutism of the individual tyrant.

But this speech, so thoroughly informed by an emancipatory program shockingly opposed to any kind of absolute power, contains a significantly empty space. It originates in Brutus' silence about the particularity of the claim to power by these republican patricians, themselves a small privileged elite. Historically, democratic rule can hardly become a forthright subject of drama in 1599. Yet the possibility that it is suggested even at that point by the play of differences within the dialogues cannot altogether be excluded. The actual republican particularity, which in Shakespeare's play does not contradict the facts from ancient history, is veiled in this text by the subjective honesty of Brutus' ideas as submitted in his speech and then by the conspirators' assertive slogans proclaiming their own understanding of their cause:

> Liberty! Freedom! Tyranny is dead!
> (Cinna, 3.1.78)
>
> Liberty, freedom, and enfranchisement!
> (Cassius, 81)
>
> Peace, freedom, and liberty!
> (Brutus, 110)

Accompanying the blood ritual immediately after the killing, these slogans are pragmatically adequate. But neither here nor anywhere else in the play, in a situation of less excitement, are they filled with any kind of programmatic content. What the liberty threatened by Caesar was like politically, what republican liberty is meant to be like, even the assessment of Caesar as a tyrant, and of absolutist rule itself, all remains entirely unresolved and is (as I shall demonstrate) deliberately opened up for questioning.

The language of *Romanitas,* particularly close, but by no means limited, to Brutus, seems to favor a tendency toward rhetorical abstractness. At the same time Shakespeare uses this very discourse to break up a closed dramatic representation of traditional material. In other words, he does this to achieve something similar to that achieved by the use of, say, an anachronistic chorus or natural analogies in *Henry V.* In *Julius Caesar,* as at roughly the same time in *Hamlet,* he avails himself of the metaphors of his profession, the theater, to literally dramatize, and thus direct attention to at a most prominent point in the play the sense-generating function of the discourse of *Romanitas.* The crucial moment comes in the second scene of act 2 when the great conspirators' conference has been concluded and the necessary arrangements made. Speaking last, Brutus dismisses the others by admonishing them to dissemble—a piece of advice entirely out of character by conventional standards and justifiable only by the noble aim they aspire to:

> Good Gentlemen, look fresh and merrily.
> Let not our looks put on our purposes,
> But bear it as our Roman actors do,
> With untir'd spirits and formal constancy.
> And so good morrow to you every one.
> [*Exeunt. Manet Brutus.*
> (2.1.224–28)

This is much more than a piece of indirect characterization. Shakespeare, to use Homann's term in making "the theater turn to itself"[20] as he so often does, is quite specific. Brutus refers to Roman actors as conceived by an Elizabethan, with stylistic characteristics of the histrionic representation of *Romanitas*. Their style of performance is determined by a "formal constancy" that elevates it beyond all common human weakness, by a rigidly formal and ceremonial regularity, unity, and immutability. *Romanitas* has endowed these actors with the timeless constancy and grand harmonious stance of a classical statue.

There is a fascinating aspect to these surreally statuesque Roman actors, whom the dramatist here evokes on the stage for his agents of history, as the standard of demeanor adequate to a most crucial situation. Brutus refers to them to conceal from himself that empty space in his long speech. To quote Marx on the needs of the French revolutionaries, they have been summoned by the "world-historical necromancy . . . in order to conceal from themselves the bourgeois limitations of the content of their struggles and to maintain their passion on the high plane of great historical tragedy."[21] The ghosts from the days of Rome already haunted the Renaissance stage and because of the ambivalence of classical discourse, served aristocratic as well as bourgeois interests.

Although the historical situations, the earlier English prerevolutionary and the later French revolutionary situation, are quite different from each other, the representational coincidence is not accidental as long as we do not limit our concept of revolution just to the change of political hegemony, but conceive of it in the far more comprehensive terms of a change in historical formation.[22] As a site where, in one dimension, illusions are produced, the public stage is a most adequate place for classical actors in their Roman robes and once—again in Marx's words about the agents of history—"their dramatic effects."[23] In the play, Cassius, standing by Caesar's dead body, reminds his fellow conspirators and the audience of the theatrical nature of the "lofty scene" that has just taken place by his famous anticipation of future revivals as theater shows:

> *Cassius*. Stoop then, and wash. How many ages hence
> Shall this our lofty scene be acted over.
> In states unborn, and accents yet unknown!
> *Brutus*. How many times shall Caesar bleed in sport,
> That now on Pompey's basis lies along,
> No worthier than the dust.
> *Cassius*. So oft as that shall be,
> So often shall the knot of us be call'd
> The men that gave their country liberty.
>
> (3.1.111–18)

The dramatic ironies involved in the dramatic characters' assessments of themselves have been commented on so often that there is no need for repetition. What concerns us here is that at this moment they have reached the climax of their historical action. As late as at 2.1.101–11 the conspirators were shown to be unable to agree even on the direction in which the Sun rises, a point on which an argument would seem to hold little promise in any situation. Now, after having been admonished to emulate the perfect actors of antiquity, the "lofty scene" just then performed can be celebrated as exalted and perfectly achieved. The historical act of the liberators can now be reviewed like a premiere: a huge success. Cassius and Brutus quite unambiguously associate the historical act represented with its representational form as a theatrical performance during the blood ritual. Brutus had earlier defined the murder itself as a sacral scenic event: "Let's be sacrificers, but not butchers, Caius" (2.1.166). What has thus been achieved is that, at the climax of their historical act, for a brief passing moment, "the most boldest and best hearts of Rome" (3.1.121) are shown, during the ritualized sacrifice and now during the blood ritual, to live up to the high demands made by the classical discourse. Such agreement of classical norm and dignified "lofty" action will only be reached again by Cassius, Titinius, and Brutus after Philippi by their classically heroic suicides. But even then a high price has to be paid. It consists in the relinquishment by Cassius of his Epicurean philosophy (5.1.77–79), and by Brutus of his Stoic philosophy (101–8).

Yet even in act 3 Shakespeare's use of the classical discourse as theatrical language at the moment of that climax contains the implication of the element of illusion that is inherent in the events shown. At that moment, at the height of the task, the characters are simultaneously agents of world history and "Roman actors." But from now on they will be measured against the standard raised by *Romanitas*. The discourse of *Romanitas* has helped to bring together in one great moment both history and human endeavor as authorized by universal history, but has not eliminated their difference. On the contrary, after the production and performance of "our lofty scene" by these Roman actors, that very difference breaks open and begins to take command of the action. And this is precisely the function of the theatrically marshaled discourse of *Romanitas* in *Julius Caesar*: to make visible the difference between expectations and their fulfillment, between what is said and what is done, between theory and practice, between the normative "formal constancy" of the "Roman actor" and the actual activity of historical subjects under the conditions and constraints of social crisis. *Romanitas* informs and provides orientation for this dramatic text. It enables strategy to be organized as a process.

In conclusion, let me indicate at least some of the problems, and consequences for *Julius Caesar* as a whole, of Shakespeare's dramatic use of the discourse of *Romanitas.* Setting up, for emulation on the stage of the theater and on the stage of history, the ideal type of the "Roman actor" in acts 2 and 3 entails the consequences of raising, through both declaration and the stage events, a classicist expectation among the audience. But his expectation is fulfilled only incompletely. The fact that the reason is a critical distance from Roman values on the part of Shakespeare, increasing from *Titus Andronicus* to *Julius Caesar,* is substantiated by Robert Miola's analysis in *Shakespeare's Rome* (1983) of Shakespeare's representation of misogyny from which female characters suffer in this and other works. All Romans, women as well as men, are expected to behave heroically according to "our fathers' minds," as Cassius insists, and definitely not according to "our mothers' spirits" (1.3.82–83). Miola comments: "Any civilization founded on principles such as these, Shakespeare suggests, is strange, unnatural, inhuman, and doomed" (96–97). From a different point of view, Shakespeare's critical distance from *Romanitas* is thus corroborated. It allowed Shakespeare to use the discourse of *Romanitas* not only as a representing discourse, which was after all dominant in Renaissance culture, but also as a discourse critically represented for dramatically functional purposes.

But that makes the play much less stable than has commonly been assumed. Instability is indeed, as such, one of its central motifs, a fact that has, however, more often than not been interpreted in terms of formal dramatic irony rather than as a result of different discourses working against each other. One further consequence of that function of discourses is that the aesthetic determination of the "Roman actors" is inscribed in the text of Caesar himself, of the man nourishing the plain belief, "for always I am Caesar" (1.2.209):

> But I am constant as the northern star,
> Of whose true-fix'd and resting quality
> There is no fellow in the firmament. . . .
> I do know but one
> That unassailable holds on his rank
> Unshak'd of motion; and that I am he,
> Let me a little show it, even in this,

> That I was constant Cimber should be banish'd,
> And constant do remain to keep him so.
>
> (3.1.60–62, 68–73)

The "constancy" Caesar claims for himself at this point appears eight times in the play, as "constancy" / "constant(ly)." He is made to lay claim to the "constancy" of the "Roman actors" so highly commended by Brutus as their essential formal characteristic in his last words, a few lines before his fall. The many apparent disparities or breaks in the other characters can also be interpreted in the light of this sort of textual activity. If, for instance, the noble Brutus keeps rejecting, with a kind of stubborn constancy, the politically and strategically reasonable alternative suggestions submitted by Cassius, a character with a low measure of "formal constancy," the audience's attention is very deliberately directed toward the contradictions of the political process unfolded by the activity of historical subjects. Furthermore, from a different perspective, the famous line, "Caesar did never wrong, but with just cause," ridiculed by Ben Jonson and obviously changed in the First Folio (3.1.47–48), might be considered as a signal of textual activity rather than dismissed as sheer nonsense. To the classicist ear this line must needs be devoid of all ethical consistency and, as an allegation mentioned nowhere else in the play, seems to infer logical instability of the worst order, which can only sound aesthetically ludicrous. But as a form of utterance originating in a representational crisis of absolutist power, it generates political sense. It disrupts the tendency toward closure instinctively seized upon and made essential by critics who can only explain the line by seeing it as a leftover from Plutarch and something Shakespeare neglected to tidy up. That political sense is generated by making the crisis of legitimation appear in a paradox. After all, attempts to justify an exercise of power that has become doubtful with arguments meant to sound just, reasonable, and natural are common practice among representatives of established authority. What makes the example of Caesar never doing wrong "but with just cause" stand out is its paradoxical directness. We should be wary of dismissing it too lightly; all the evidence, chiefly the attacks on it by Ben Jonson, himself a member of that company, repeated over many years, indicates that the actors went on using the original version of that line apparently unperturbed.

There is yet another indication that *Julius Caesar* is less stable than has been assumed. Caroline Spurgeon demonstrated many years ago that the imagery in *Julius Caesar* is peculiar in that it does not come from any one single dominant area, even though images of civil strife are prominent in the first half and animal imagery has contributed with some consistency to building the main characters.[24] Such relatively open audience response guidance, which can encourage auditors to increase their efforts of making sense of what they hear and see, has been corroborated by E. A. J. Honigmann's analysis generally of "a steady move away from the notion that character is fixed, defined, an object, a formula, an ascertainable humour, a ruling passion" so that the result is a strategy of "mixed" audience response guidance reaching a climax in *Julius Caesar.*[25] For Honigmann, as for Dr. Johnson before him, who was uncomfortable with the play's relatively cool atmosphere, Shakespeare's mixture of the tactical means guiding audience response is "very slightly wrong." If illusion is impeded by that coolness, it is of course the result of a procedure creating distance to the stage events by which Shakespeare "wished the audience to respond in an entirely new way to his hero."[26] This, I suggest, is one of the principal reasons why Shakespeare should have abruptly, as it may appear, resorted to classical discourse. Only in the context that this makes possible can attention be wholly directed, in Honigmann's words, to "Brutus' muddles."

Placed at the center of attention, along with their activity, are the intellectual and emotional problems of historical subjects in a situation that, contrasting with the traditional story of antiquity, can be discerned as historically new; it is a situation involving unprecedented tasks for the solution of which the previously acquired, traditionally authorized patterns of thinking and behavior suddenly no longer provide adequate orientation. Thus they are subjected to inquiry. In *Hamlet* this will happen most obviously in the monologues, from which their essential instability derives. In *Julius Caesar* the text's interrogative strategy becomes thematic through the work of interpretation that is performed—in the double sense of the word—by the characters: "During the fearsome night many men try to construe events according to their own ends and desires. Brutus interprets murder as a sacrifice; many try to interpret Caesar's dream."[27] Cicero is given only nine lines in the whole play, most of them actually of a phatic nature. He seems to have been put in the play specifically to dramatize that emphasis on interpretation:

> Indeed, it is a strange-disposed time:
> But men may construe things, after their fashion,
> Clean from the purpose of the things themselves.
>
> (1.3.33–35)

Cicero's reading of "portentous things" is by no means the only example. Passages probing the differences between "seeming," "appearing," "acting," "fashioning," "construing," and the world of reality occur thirty-five times in the text.[28] They are part of an exploration that is directed, not at the subjectivity generally of human perception and the limits of all human understanding,[29] but at a specific historical situation. The various devices used by Shakespeare for the purpose are too numerous to be accidental. From a distance, Cicero puts the gnoseological problem as such in words but remains even more passive and ineffective than the many other intellectuals in the play—the soothsayer, Artemidorous, Cinna.[30] This may reflect the way in which Elizabethan intellectuals felt in the face of the breakdown of the traditional alliance between intellectuals and the crown, forged during the Reformation. *Julius Caesar*'s activity as interrogative text is in search of the aesthetic object to be appropriated, that is, the historical subject working at historical change. Text is generated accordingly. Brutus has 720 lines. We are being continually reminded of Caesar even when he does not himself speak, but 150 lines are sufficient for all he has to say in the play. He represents what is equally well-known to Romans and Elizabethans, absolutist authority. What the text directs attention to is the process of countering Caesar's power along with its consequences, and hence to the character of Brutus. Leaving the programmatic details of the political struggle as vague as they are helps audiences to concentrate on the underlying process.

The plebeian scenes, so often discussed primarily in terms of timeless psychology, can also be read as part of the exploration of the historical activities involved in that process. In 3.2., little is left of the intelligently aggressive wordplay of the citizens, especially of the cobbler, right at the beginning of the play. In the end, law and order are restored, but initially the plebeian wit of Shakespeare's carpenters and cobblers (and, elsewhere, gravediggers) clearly triumphs. As can be shown by dialogue analysis, a considerable though ultimately illusory power base is built for the cobbler by the calculated granting or withholding of information. But why does Shakespeare introduce such self-assured plebeians at all if at their reappearance all their self-assurance has evaporated, and they are shown to be such easy prey to rhetorical manipulation? The answer is implicit in the question: the first scene on "A Street" is needed not merely to open up right at the beginning a representation signaled to the audience as closed by the very genre of the play, but also as a precondition for the later ones. Such guided audience response is aimed less at representing changes in the psychology of the masses than at the process they inevitably help to constitute. Another problem is thus raised, new certainly as far as the way and context of posing it is concerned. In this theatrical situation unprecedented in Elizabethan England, in which the republican revolutionaries become active, it is shown, over and above what the masses may actually be like, that there is no choice but to mobilize them if the political power struggle is to be won. This part of a new dramatic discourse is emerging slowly under the conditions of the Elizabethan popular theater where patricians have to share the stage with plebeians and where closed forms of representation can be opened at significant moments by a host of theatrical signs.

It was characteristic of Samuel Johnson that he should have been affected by Shakespeare's opposition of discourses, but only as a disturbance causing him deep anxiety. "A quibble was the golden apple," he wrote in his *Preface to Shakespeare* "for which he would always turn aside from his career, or stoop from his elevation."[31]

Notes

1. See Wolfgang Klein, "Ungebundene Menschlichkeit," *Sinn und Form* 41 (1989): 463 concerning our study of history without illusions; and Thomas Metscher, "Geschichte, Humanität, Utopie," in *Gulliver 6: Shakespeare inmitten der Revolution* (Berlin, 1979), 26, for *JC* as a play about revolution.

2. My tentative description of the new canon is based on the following publications: J. Drakakis, ed., *Alternative Shakespeare,* (1985); J. Dollimore and A. Sinfield, eds., *Political Shakespeare: New Essays in Cultural Materialism* (Manchester, 1985); T. Hawkes, *That Shakespearian Rag. Essays of a Critical Process* (London, 1986); P. Parker and G. Hartman, eds., *Shakespeare and the Question of Theory* (N.Y.: Methuen, 1985); J. Howard and M. F. O'Connor, eds., *Shakespeare Reproduced: The Text in History and Ideology* (N.Y., 1987); and L. Tennenhouse, *Power on Display: The Politics of Shakespeare's Genres* (N.Y., 1986).

3. See Ernst Th. Sehrt, "*Julius Caesar*: Brutus," in *Sympathielenkung in den Dramen Shakespeares,* eds., W. Habicht and I. Schabert (Munich: Fink, 1979), 65–71, esp. 65, who correctly criticizes the previous critical neglect of the blood ritual as stage spectacle—All references are to The Arden edition, ed. T. S. Dorsch (London: Methuen, 1975).

4. See Stanley Wells and Gary Taylor with John Jowett and William Montgomery, *William Shakespeare. A Textual Companion* (Oxford: Clarendon Press, 1987), 386–91.

5. See Christopher Hill, "The Many-Headed Monster," in *Change and Continuity in Seventeenth Century England* (Cambridge: Harvard University Press, 1975), 182.

6. Michael Bristol, "'Lenten Butchery': Legitimation Crisis in *Coriolanus,*" in *Shakespeare Reproduced,* 207–24.

7. See Thomas Sorge, "The Failure of Orthodoxy in *Coriolanus,*" in ibid., 225–41.

8. Robert Weimann, "Bifold Authority in Shakespeare's Theatre," *Shakespeare Quarterly* 39 (1988): 403–4, esp. 402.

9. Ibid., 402–3.

10. Ibid., 402.

11. See Robert Weimann, "Mimesis in *Hamlet*: Spiegel und Wirklichkeit," in *Shakespeare und die Macht der Mimesis* (Berlin: Aufbau, 1988), 219–55.

12. Catherine Belsey, *The Subject of Tragedy* (London: Methuen, 1985), 90.

13. Our approach draws on Emile Benveniste's linguistic distinction between declarative, imperative, and interrogative statements in *Problems in General Linguistics* (Coral Gables, FL: University of Miami Press, 1971).

14. Belsey, *Critical Practice* (London: Methuen, 1986), 92.

15. Walter Cohen, *Drama of a Nation. Public Theater in Renaissance England and Spain* (Ithaca: Cornell University Press, 1985), 302–3.

16. Leeds Barroll, "A New History for Shakespeare and His Time," *Shakespeare Quarterly* 39 (1988): 441–64.

17. The continuity of the project is emphasized, for example, by Paul N. Siegel, *Shakespeare's English and Roman History Plays. A Marxist Approach* (London: Associated University Presses, 1986).

18. Harry Levin, "General Introduction," in The Riverside Shakespeare (Boston: Houghton-Mifflin, 1974), 20.

19. See Belsey, *Subject of Tragedy,* 101–3 for a similar interpretation.

20. Sidney Homann, *When the Theater Turns to Itself: The Aesthetic Metaphor in Shakespeare* (London: Associated University Presses, 1981).

21. Cf. Karl Marx, "The Eighteenth Brumaire of Louis Bonaparte," in *Collected Works,* vol. 11 (Moscow: Progress Publishers, 1979), 104–5.

22. See Wilfried Schröder, "War die französische Revolution auch eine Epochenzäsur in der kulturellen, künstlerischen und literarischen Entwicklung? Probleme und Problemfelder," *Weimarer Beiträge* 34 (1988): 37.

23. Marx, "Eighteenth Brumaire," 104, 106.

24. Caroline Spurgeon, *Shakespeare's Imagery and What It Tells Us* (Cambridge: Cambridge University Press, 1935), 346–47.

25. E. A. J. Honigmann, *Seven Tragedies* (New York: Barnes & Noble, 1976), 12.

26. Ibid., 30.

27. Jean Howard, *Shakespeare's Art of Orchestration. Stage Technique and Audience Response* (Urbana: University of Illinois Press, 1982), 145.

28. Robert Miola, *Shakespeare's Rome* (Cambridge: Cambridge University Press, 1983), 79–80.

29. That is the approach of René E. Fortin in "Julius Caesar: An Experiment in Point of View," *Shakespeare Quarterly* 19 (1968): 341–47.

30. Honigmann, *Seven Tragedies,* 38.

31. "Preface to Shakespeare," in *Criticism: The Major Texts,* ed., W. J. Bate (New York: Harcourt, 1970), 213.

POSTSCRIPT (1995)

"The Historical Subject as *Roman* actor and Agent of History: Interrogative Dramatic Structure in *Julius Caesar*" goes back to an article in German that originally appeared in *Shakespeare Jahrbuch* 126 (Weimar, 1990).[1] Most of the work on the text was done in 1988. The world around us was still apparently what it had been for over forty years, the superpower blocs separated by walls and curtains of iron, concrete, and bamboo. Nobody in their right mind anticipated the political turmoil that was to change Europe and indeed the world within merely a year. And yet one had been sensing changes in the atmosphere beneath the quiet surface for some time, causing restlessness, some anxiety, and a little hope. To an "Anglicist" engaged in studying English Renaissance literature in East Germany, the atmosphere suggested certain structural similarities to that feeling of crisis reverberating through Shakespeare's turn-of-the-century plays. Like one or two other scholars working in the German Shakespeare Society, I had for some time been assimilating international developments in literary theory, otherwise largely unknown in the country and anything but privileged, for their epistemological and heuristic potential. In the case at hand I had turned a little further back to Emile Benveniste's concept of the interrogative text of 1971 to try and, perhaps, get a little closer to understanding how historical change becomes palpable in texts, and how something intimidatingly new gradually may become thinkable.

I had suggested to the board of the Shakespeare Society, in 1986 I believe, to make the Renaissance reception of classical antiquity generally and in particular Shakespeare's transition from his English history plays to the more immediately political Roman history plays the subject of the society's annual conference in 1989. Everywhere in the country outstanding anniversaries of various kinds always had to be solemnly celebrated, the idea being of course to bolster the system's official ideology. Over the years this had involved a long chain of recurring public rituals. But when the French Revolution came up for celebration, the parallels offered by my suggestion, by great political crises in Roman, Elizabethan, French, and now increasingly German history, parallels not only between regimes in social distress and beyond reform but also of cultural forms and rituals, seemed to me to offer fruitful opportunities for discussion.

My suggestion was turned down by the party controllers on the society's board for reasons not entirely clear to me to this day. Instead, the time-honored subject of individual and society was chosen. My keynote lecture was thus never written. In the paper that I did submit to the conference I tried to convey what had been on my mind for some time by an analysis of a single play, *Julius Caesar,* a text not figuring prominently in the theoretical discussions of the eighties in both the East and the West in spite of its overtly political character and the scandalous tyrannicide, with the "Subject" of the title as a textual trace of the official program. There was now no room for any discussion of the general issues involved.

The English version adapted from the German original was completed in September 1989 amid a tense and exciting political situation. It has not been changed since. Not written with hindsight, it may perhaps stand as a text shaped by the conditions of dictatorship and the censor, although the very first paragraph of the English version reflects the amazing pace of the chaotic thaw by now taking place: a study of history "without illusions about . . . real contradictions" and not "as an affirmation of political ideology" was of course precisely what was and had always been impossible, and was contributing to the downfall of the GDR, although no one could as yet see it at the time. While I was thus stating my paper's concern directly, quoting from an unusual essay by an historian, the bulk of the chapter remains indebted to Aesopian textual strategies. As a consequence it subsequently turned out in my exchanges with some American colleagues that they were wondering about the relevance of my text. They thought it a perfectly normal academic text that might be printed in any scholarly journal, but what about its GDR specificity?

To me that question was both reassuring and sobering. Retrospectively reassuring, because the Aesopian discourse was still proving its efficacy. Sobering, because it was proving its efficacy rather too well, hindering communication even where it was desired.

I should have been warned, though, by what happened at the Weimar conference in 1991. My next offer for a keynote lecture on "Reason and Chaos in Shakespeare,"[2] submitted in early 1989, had been accepted by the board meanwhile, and the lecture was duly delivered in April 1991, well over a year after the fall of the Wall. No need for Aesopian language this time. I addressed my topic of the misappropriation and linear abuse of Enlightenment rationalism by Western culture and in particular by Marxist ideology in the "normal" straightforward academic manner. But it turned out that several newcomers to the Weimar conference from the West, in particular one extremely famous German scholar, simply could not understand what the seemingly liberating excitement over chaos theory, a theory appropriated once again for strategic discursive purposes during the GDR's Götterdämmerung as a paradigm critical obviously of linear and static thinking, was all about. There was some spectre haunting the hall that he could feel but that he could not see, and he advised the conference to pursue a different critical paradigm—his own.

It was a blindness not at all shared by GDR colleagues used to Aesopian discourse that was, after all, by this time only a residual presence in my text, a sort of hangover, as it were. And several of them would not have had the difficulty with my earlier interpretation of *Julius Caesar* either. At any rate quite a few did understand what the project was, that is, to throw into question, having defined the method applied as "interrogative," "the rule by one (Caesar)" or by "a privileged élite" (Brutus' republicanism), and then to suggest as "a third alternative" as "becoming thinkable . . . the determination of public affairs by the many or even by all." These people well versed in Aesopian discourse realized immediately that to suggest in public a program of democratic reform was only possible by establishing an historical, literary, and theatrical discourse with reference to Caesar and Brutus that safely related to the Renaissance.

But that in itself would of course not have sufficed for a piece of academic criticism. What had attracted my critical attention in the first place was the play's theatrical imagery, often noted but not before explored in this manner. It brings out the basic instability of character and circumstance, the gulf between expectations and fulfillment, theory and practice, what is said and what is done, the working of ideology, in other words. What set my stage for displaying my Aesopian analogy was Marx's *Eighteenth Brumaire of Louis Bonaparte* through which I proposed to read *Julius Caesar.* Everyone was familiar with this satirical account of Louis Napoleon's coup in December 1851. Marx qualifies Hegel's dictum that "all facts and personages of great importance in world history occur, as it were, twice" by adding that what occurs the first time as tragedy, happens the second time as farce. In a customarily ritualistic situation in which historical periods like the Renaissance with its appropriation of classical culture, or events like the French Revolution, had always been celebrated as events climaxing in the revolution in Russia of which the East German ancien régime declared itself a part, setting up as a frame that text by Marx in which he describes how it becomes possible, in Marx's words, "for a grotesque mediocrity to play a hero's part," left it to the audience to draw its own conclusions.

Adumbrating the discursive strategy of one's own text is the kind of very personal auto-metacriticism one would wish to avoid, if only to avoid the trap of premature generalization at the end of a century whose events have made suitable skepticism of grand narratives, even potential ones, appear more than justified. That is why I am restricting myself to my own writing experience, in one particular case, in this postscript. It was agreed upon by editors and author simply because of the strong possibility that tactical invisibility might remain chronic with readers inexperienced in deciphering the kind of culture produced under conditions of absolute authority. For that blindness is not the kind of productive partial blindness we associate with Paul de Man's work, the kind of blindness that provides the originating locus of such insight as it achieves. It can only read the surface, although, like de Man's blindness, it is not simply a form of ignorance or neglect. It is the unavoidable condition of intercultural encounters, the kind of problem anthropology, and literary anthropology, is trying to understand. It is also far more than merely an academic issue. It can be experienced every day in contemporary Germany, where the two parts of the country, West and East, that have been so luckily reunited continue to be separated by a common language, even where there is a generous measure of goodwill. The cultural difference we accept as normal when there is a language barrier, or in the case of past civilizations, this cultural difference, which in present-day Germany includes vast differences in the accumulation of experiences, values, judgments, and assets, remains invisible under the deceptive surface of a common language. The resulting misunderstandings characteristic of the present situation in this country seem all the more mysterious and can therefore be painfully frustrating.

This may suggest another, somewhat profounder justification of this postscript. It comes from an attempt to understand better the working of absolute authority in the texts that have come down to us. That is why Michel Foucault and the New Historicism's interest in power, and particularly in the containment of its subversion, became so important concerns to me in the late 1970s and in the 1980s. However, Annabel Patterson's mostly historical studies on *Censorship and Interpretation: The Conditions of Writing and Reading in Early Modern England*[3] and on *Reading Between the*

Lines[4] are the only in-depth work I am aware of specifically concerned with such textual strategies. The masses of first-hand experience with texts structurally similar to, but specifically different from, hers that are now available may prove useful to this kind of historical research the significance of which we may be only beginning to understand.

What, however, it might well be asked, was the use of writing texts that their author wanted to be published and yet at the same time wanted to become really visible only to a small circle of initiates? Essays in criticism that their author wanted, and did not want, to be read? Apart from the cheerful admission that under the circumstances writing such texts was an exhilarating experience, my answer would be that one can only try.

Notes

1. "Das Historische Subjekt als 'Roman Actor' und Geschichtlicher Akteur. Zur Interrogativstruktur des *Julius Caesar.*"

2. Günter Walch, "Vernunft und Chaos bei Shakespeare," *Shakespeare-Jahrbuch* 128 (1992).

3. Annabel Patterson, *Censorship and Interpretation: The Conditions of Writing and Reading in Early Modern England* (Madison: University of Wisconsin Press, 1984).

4. Annabel Patterson, *Reading Between the Lines* (Madison: University of Wisconsin Press, 1993).

Marlowe and Shakespeare's African Queens

MAURICE CHARNEY

LET me begin with some of my assumptions about Shakespeare's relation to Marlowe before speaking specifically about Shakespeare and Marlowe's *Dido Queen of Carthage.* It is obvious that Shakespeare is deeply indebted to Marlowe, the Rival Poet of the Sonnets. One of the difficulties in demonstrating this influence is that Shakespeare seems to avoid verbal imitation. He goes out of his way, for example, to make Shylock's speech very different from that of Barabas, even though *The Merchant of Venice* and *The Jew of Malta* are close to each other in many other ways.[1] This is also true of Marlowe's *Edward II* in relation to Shakespeare's *Richard II.* Clearly Shakespeare's play is acutely conscious of Marlowe as a model rather than as a source.[2] The whole study of sources, much developed by Germanic scholarship of the late nineteenth century, tends to skew the meaning of sources to verbal resemblances. Many of the extensive similarities claimed are pure fantasy and wishful thinking, along the lines of the disintegrators, who tend to recognize the styles of Kyd, Peele, Heywood, and others wherever they think they ought to find them. The many volumes of Geoffrey Bullough's monumental *Narrative and Dramatic Sources of Shakespeare*[3] sum up this method of source hunting at its best.

For Shakespeare in relation to Marlowe, however, this approach doesn't work very well. When Shakespeare is really close to Marlowe in conception, he seems to go out of his way to conceal and obscure the verbal similarities. Sometimes, of course, the opposite is true, and the resemblance is so close that it verges on parody. An excellent example is Aaron's first speech in *Titus Andronicus,* "Now climbeth Tamora Olympus' top" (2.1.1),[4] where Aaron echoes the grandiloquent style of Tamburlaine:

> I will be bright and shine in pearl and gold
> To wait upon this new-made empress.
> To wait, said I? To wanton with this queen,

> This goddess, this Semiramis, this nymph,
> This siren. . . .
>
> (2.1.19–23)

Aaron can't continue in this Tamburlainean style, yet he can't resist giving the audience one sample of his quality. Shakespeare seems to be indulging himself in a delicious moment of parody. In Pistol the parody of Tamburlaine is more direct: "Shall packhorses / And hollow pampered jades of Asia. . . . / Compare with Caesars, and with Cannibals, / And Trojan Greeks?" (*2 Henry IV* 2.4.166–70). Shakespeare seems to be using parody to relieve himself of the grievous anxiety of Marlowe's influence.

I want to look at Marlowe's *Dido Queen of Carthage* in relation particularly to two plays of Shakespeare, *Hamlet* and *Antony and Cleopatra*. For convenience I will call *Dido* Marlowe's play; although it is actually a collaboration with Thomas Nashe, most critics find Nashe's role minimal. In Marlowe's play, as in Vergil's *Aeneid* book 2, Aeneas' narration is a rhetorical set piece, a kind of formal classical oration. Aeneas speaks in answer to Dido's question: "May I entreat thee to discourse at large, / And truly too, how Troy was overcome?" (2.1.106–7).[5] It is a speech of about 160 lines, broken four times by single lines of Dido. It is an heroic and passionate speech, but extremely formal, without any character interplay with Dido. In this sense, it is like Othello's grand wooing speech of "the story of my life" (*Othello* 1.3.128) by which he wins Desdemona. At the end, the breathless Dido says, "I die with melting ruth: (2.1.289), and before she exits she is already speaking words with amorous connotations:

> Trojan, thy ruthful tale hath made me sad.
> Come, let us think upon some pleasing sport,
> To rid me from these melancholy thoughts.
>
> (2.1.301–3)

The erotic sense of "some pleasing sport" looks forward to Tamora, Queen of the Goths, in *Titus Andronicus,* whose wooing of the all too willing Aaron echoes Dido and Aeneas.

"Aeneas' tale to Dido" (*Hamlet* 2.2.457) was a rhetorical set piece, established by Vergil's *Aeneid* in a speech in book 2 that probably every Elizabethan grammar school student had to translate. In *Titus Andronicus,* which has more Dido and Aeneas allusions than any other play of Shakespeare, Titus' frantic speech about his ravished and handless daughter uses Aeneas' tale to Dido to provide the perfect tragic context:

Ah, wherefore dost thou urge the name of hands,
To bid Aeneas tell the tale twice o'er,
How Troy was burnt and he made miserable?

(3.2.26–28)

At the end of the play after the deaths of Lavinia, Tamora, Titus, and Saturninus, a Roman Lord addresses Lucius, Titus' son, who will be the next Emperor of Rome:

Speak, Rome's dear friend, as erst our ancestor,
When with his solemn tongue he did discourse
To lovesick Dido's sad attending ear
The story of that baleful burning night,
When subtle Greeks surprised King Priam's Troy;
Tell us what Sinon hath bewitched our eares,
Or who hath brought the fatal engine in
That gives our Troy, our Rome, the civil wound.

(5.3.80–87)

Titus Andronicus is conceived in terms of the events of Aeneas' tale to Dido in Marlowe's play rather than directly from Vergil's *Aeneid.* The emphasis here is Ovidian rather than Vergilian, and although Tamora is a Gothic and not an African queen like Dido, she is nevertheless represented as a foreign temptress of otherwise virtuous Romans. This is the same context as the Troy tapestry in *The Rape of Lucrece,* a narrative poem from around the same time as *Titus,* with its strong emphasis on Sinon's betrayal.

When we come to *Hamlet* via *Titus Andronicus* and *The Rape of Lucrece,* we should not be surprised that Hamlet picks out "Aeneas' tale to Dido" for a taste of the Players' quality and for "a passionate speech" (2.2.441–42) related to his own overwhelming passions of the moment. It seems obvious to me[6] that Hamlet's "excellent play, well digested in the scenes, set down with as much modesty as cunning" (2.2.449–51) is Marlowe's *Dido Queen of Carthage.* As the only play of Marlowe written for a private theater performance by the Children of the Royal Chapel,[7] it is not unusual that Hamlet should refer to it as something out of the ordinary, written in a style more choice than Marlowe's other public theater plays for adult companies. "Caviary to the general" (2.2.447) represents Hamlet's refined taste as opposed to that of Polonius and the groundlings. The basic question is what other Dido play besides Marlowe's could Hamlet be referring to? There are two references in Henslowe's *Diary* for 1598 that are probably to a revival of Marlowe's play. Other than this, it is unlikely that Hamlet is referring to the obscure *Dido* play by Halliwell, acted at Oxford in 1583 and now lost, or to the equally obscure *Dido* play by William Gager, written in Latin, and performed in the same year at Christ Church, Oxford, at the entertainment of Count Alasco of Poland.[8] If I am correct in my assumptions, Hamlet's speech is Shakespeare's most extensive discussion of Marlowe. It is a kind of displaced hero worship with many characteristically grudging disclaimers.

It is odd, therefore, to find Harold Jenkins in his Arden edition of *Hamlet* saying that Aeneas' tale to Dido echoes the Marlowe play "at one or perhaps two points, though I think not more."[9] In his "Explication of the Player's Speech," Harry Levin states categorically that "*Dido* does not seem to have influenced *Hamlet*."[10] This is to interpret influence in a purely verbal way. Although there are a few similarities of expression, as if Shakespeare is parodying the old play, the basic speech and its function are similar in both plays. It is a "ruthful tale," as Dido says (2.1.301), designed to arouse powerful emotions. The Player in *Hamlet* turns color and "has tears in's eyes" (2.2.531) and cannot go on, which is perhaps an indication of how Aeneas should speak in Marlowe's play. It is a passionate speech like that of the "bleeding Captain" in *Macbeth*—"But I am faint; my gashes cry for help" (1.2.42).

Of all the speeches that Hamlet could remember, why does he focus on Aeneas' tale to Dido? He needs that speech desperately at this point in the play to provide biting analogies for his own tragic situation. The savage slaughter of Priam is a re-creation of the Ghost of Hamlet's father's description of his own murder, and the intense grief of Hecuba both here and in *The Rape of Lucrece* links her ironically with Gertrude. Could we continue on to Ophelia as Hamlet's unexpressed and unexpressible Dido? The sorrowful story of the destruction of Troy offers an intensely tragic matrix.

That Dido was a classical exemplar of forsaken love is seen most clearly in Lorenzo's catalogue at the beginning of the fifth act of *The Merchant of Venice*. Dido and Aeneas as a pair of lovers are among Troilus and Cressida, Pyramus and Thisbe, and Medea and Jason:

> In such a night
> Stood Dido with a willow in her hand
> Upon the wild sea banks, and waft her love
> To come again to Carthage.
>
> (5.1.9–12)

This is Desdemona's symbolic willow of forsaken love. In *Titus Andronicus,* Tamora projects an erotic tryst with Aaron in the forest specifically modeled on the Dido and Aeneas story. Listening to the hounds and the hunting horns, Tamora anticipates an amorous fulfillment that never occurs:

> And after conflict such as was supposed
> The wandering prince and Dido once enjoyed,
> When with a happy storm they were surprised
> And curtained with a counsel-keeping cave,
> We may, each wreathèd in the other's arms,
> (Our pastimes done) possess a golden slumber. . . .
>
> (2.3.21–26)

But Aaron is more intent on revenge than on lust.

In *A Midsummer Night's Dream,* Hermia swears to Lysander by Cupid's bow, Venus' doves, "And by that fire which burned the Carthage queen, / When the false Troyan under sail was seen" (1.1.173–74). Incidentally, Jackson I. Cope sees in the mixture of farce and romance in this play "Marlowe's most significant gift to Shakespeare."[11] In *The Taming of the Shrew,* Lucentio, in the guise of Dido confiding in her sister Anna, swears to his servant Tranio that he is in love with Bianca:

> And now in plainness do confess to thee,
> That art to me as secret and as dear
> As Anna to the Queen of Carthage was,
> Tranio, I burn, I pine, I perish, Tranio. . . .
>
> (1.1.152–55)

The wealth of allusions to Dido and Aeneas in Shakespeare shows that they were familiar, classical exemplars of love. In *The Tempest,* "Widow Dido" (2.1.83,104) is part of the amusing banter of Adrian, Gonzalo, Sebastian, and Antonio. "Widower Aeneas" (81) is even more incongruously domestic, and Tunis, from where the shipwrecked royal party is coming after the marriage of Claribel, is identified with ancient Carthage (and therefore Dido). Dido is specifically linked with Cleopatra in Mercutio's slighting references to Romeo's Rosaline: "Laura, to his lady, was a kitchen wench, . . . Dido a dowdy, Cleopatra a gypsy, Helen and Hero hildings and harlots, Thisbe a gray eye or so, but not to the purpose" (*Romeo and Juliet* 2.4.40–44). Incidentally, Hero is from Marlowe's poem, *Hero and Leander,* which has many stylistic affinities with *Dido* in the genre of mock heroic. Hero and Dido figure often in the catalogue of traditional lovers, especially forsaken lovers.

In *Antony and Cleopatra,* when Antony learns of Cleopatra's supposed death, he disarms and prepares for his own death, when he will meet Cleopatra in Elysium, "Where souls do couch on flowers" (4.14.51). Here, Antony and Cleopatra, like Dido and Aeneas, are finally united: "Dido and her Aeneas shall want troops / And all the haunt be ours" (53–54). This is like the Marlovian figure of invidious comparison, in which Antony imagines that he and his Cleopatra are superior to classical exemplars of love like Dido and Aeneas.

Most critics do not see much relation between Marlowe's *Dido* play and Shakespeare's *Antony and Cleopatra,* but Barbara J. Bono conceives Shakespeare's play as the natural culmination of his preoccupation with Vergil's *Aeneid,* and especially with the Dido and Aeneas story.[12] There are some striking verbal similarities between Marlowe's and Shakespeare's plays, but they are few, and the real relationship is essentially one of conception and style. J. B. Steane speaks most eloquently (and most extensively) about the imaginative link between these two plays:

> But above all *Dido* suggests *Antony and Cleopatra.* Here it is not so much a matter of local similarities or general resemblances of plot but essentially of a similar "feel" in the substance of the poetry. Marlowe's imagery here is very like Shakespeare's.[13]

Steane is vigorously supported by Brian Gibbons: "the quality and dramatic effect of Dido's sublime erotic rhetoric informs the inner life and movement of Cleopatra's poetic imagination."[14]

Cleopatra and Dido are both African queens,[15] and they are clearly set apart from the world of Rome. The deep-seated conflict between the values of Rome and Egypt in *Antony and Cleopatra* echoes the conflict between Trojan (and Roman by implication) and Carthaginian values in *Dido.* This is analogous to the conflict between Roman and Gothic (or "barbarian") values in *Titus Andronicus*—Tamora is an exotic, non-Roman queen like Cleopatra and Dido. In all three of these plays, love as an absolute, intense state of being is identified with the women. The men waver, especially Aeneas, and even Antony knows that "I must from this enchanting queen break off" (1.2.129). In both plays, love challenges the masculine, heroic values associated with Rome (and also with Troy as an intermediate kingdom that will be re-created in Rome.)

Aeneas' military colleagues have much the same disdainful attitude toward their leader as Antony's associates, including Enobarbus. *Antony and Cleopatra* begins with Philo's moral revulsion at Antony's "dotage":

> His captain's heart,
> Which in the scuffles of great fights hath burst
> The buckles on his breast, reneges all temper
> And is become the bellows and the fan
> To cool a gypsy's lust.
>
> (1.1.6–10)

Enobarbus is more moderate but he doesn't at all understand that Antony is in love with Cleopatra and trying heroically to break off with her. When Antony says, "Would I had never seen her!" (1.2.154), Enobarbus can only reply: "O, sir, you had then left unseen a wonderful piece of work, which not to have been blest withal would have discredited your travel" (155–57). This is totally to misconstrue what Antony is saying.

Similarly in Marlowe's play, Aeneas' chief associate, Achates, speaks like a Roman soldier against the unmanly enticements of love:

> Banish that ticing dame from forth your mouth,
> And follow your foreseeing stars in all;
> This is no life for men-at-arms to live,
> Where dalliance doth consume a soldier's strength,
> And wanton motions of alluring eyes
> Effeminate our minds inur'd to war.
>
> (4.3.31–36)

Harry Levin notes how important that curious word "ticing" is in Marlowe's play.[16] This is exactly the speech that Aeneas wants to hear to steel him against Dido's charms:

> Her silver arms will coll me round about
> And tears of pearl cry, "Stay, Aeneas, stay!" . . .
> I may not dure this female drudgery:
> To sea, Aeneas, find out Italy!
>
> (4.3.51–52, 55–56)

Antony would never have used the derogatory phrase, "female drudgery," for Cleopatra's attractions. The conflict in the two soldiers is analogous, but Aeneas never rises to tragic stature.[17]

A much closer link exists between Dido and Cleopatra. Both of them conceive love in passionate, godlike, transcendental terms.

To Dido love conveys immortality, and her speech prepares us for Doctor Faustus' more famous lines to the shade of Helen:

> If he forsake me not, I never die,
> For in his looks I see eternity,
> And he'll make me immortal with a kiss.
>
> (4.4.121–23)

Cleopatra seems to echo these lines in her speech to Antony:

> Eternity was in our lips and eyes,
> Bliss in our brows' bent, none our parts so poor
> But was a race of heaven. . . .
>
> (1.3.35–37)

An even stronger example of the imaginative affinity of Dido and Cleopatra is in Dido's invidious comparison of her love with the heavenly powers:

> Heaven, envious of our joys, is waxen pale,
> And when we whisper, then the stars fall down,
> To be partakers of our honey talk.
>
> (4.4.52–54)

"Honey talk" is a real Cleopatraism, both lofty and homely at the same time, like Cleopatra's line: "Pity me, Charmian, / But do not speak to me" (2.5.118–19). In Cleopatra's dream of Antony after his death, the lover's imagination is represented as superior to mere reality, no matter how grandiose:

> His legs bestrid the ocean: his reared arm
> Crested the world; his voice was propertied
> As all the tunèd spheres. . . .
>
> (5.2.82–84)

Again, there is Marlowe's favorite figure of invidious comparison with the inevitable conclusion: "nature wants stuff / To vie strange forms with fancy" (94–95). In love, art and fancy are always superior to mere nature.

Hyperbole, a favorite figure of both Marlowe and Shakespeare, provides one of the stylistic links between *Dido* and *Antony and Cleopatra*. Borrowing from George Puttenham, *The Arte of English Poesie* (1589), Levin calls his book on Marlowe *The Overreacher: A Study of Christopher Marlowe,* in which hyperbole is defined as "the Ouer reacher, otherwise called the loud lyer."[18] In my book on Shakespeare's Roman plays, I argue for hyperbole as the principal figure of *Antony and Cleopatra*.[19] Beyond hyperbole itself, there is an extravagance and wildness in the style of *Dido* and *Antony and Cleopatra* that T. S. Eliot was among the first to observe: the style of *Dido* "secures its emphasis by always hesitating on the edge of caricature at the right moment."[20] This idea is expanded in Clifford Leech's essay on "Marlowe's Humor," in which he speaks of "the pervasively comic tone" of *Dido*. Perhaps "comic" is not quite the right word. Brian Gibbons employs a more subtle vocabulary in words such as "mock heroic," "unstable," "farcical," and the kind of "rich artifice" associated with the boy actors.[22] It all seems to come down to the fact that both Marlowe and Shakespeare have more temperamental and stylistic affinities with Ovid than with Vergil. Vergil's "pius Aeneas" and the gravity and sober dignity and destiny of Rome are not in the Marlovian or Shakespearean mode.[23]

This is just a stab at a large topic, but I hope I have been able to sketch some of the paradoxical qualities of Shakespeare's complex relation to Marlowe. From all we can tell, Marlowe's *Dido* play must have meant a lot to Shakespeare, and he remembers Aeneas' tale to Dido and Dido's tragic love affair throughout his career. Shakespeare undoubtedly knew Vergil's *Aeneid,* but Marlowe's *Dido* vividly dramatized the tragic encounter of forsaken love. If Hamlet is indeed speaking of Marlowe's play, nowhere else is Shakespeare so effusive about a contemporary play that "pleased not the million" (2.2.446) but was "as wholesome as sweet, and by very much more handsome than fine" (455–56). These are the characteristics of "an excellent play" (449), one that might serve as a model.

Dido was clearly imprinted in Shakespeare's mind as an exemplar of forsaken love, and although Cleopatra seems to be reconciled with Antony in death and imagines strolling with him in the Elysian Fields, she too is ultimately unfulfilled. But Cleopatra and Dido share a conception of love that is luminous and transcendent. Both are imperious African queens, something like the ideal image of Humphrey Bogart's African Queen, who share a vision of the overwhelming powers of love, even if it remains only a glorious vision. Once the topic of influence is removed from its narrow base in verbal similarities and parallel passages, then we can see Marlowe exercising an abiding fascination for Shakespeare. There are inevitably verbal echoes but that is not the main point. We see Marlowe working so powerfully on Shakespeare's imagination that he can transmute his models and sources into something characteristically his own.

Notes

This essay was first presented at a meeting of the Marlowe Society at the Modern Language Association convention in Chicago, 29 December 1995. I am grateful to the many comments and suggestions of the audience, especially to Diana E. Henderson, who sent me the chapter on *Dido* from her excellent book, *Passion Made Public: Elizabethan Lyric, Gender, and Performance* (Illinois: University of Illinois Press, 1995).

1. See Maurice Charney, "Jessica's Turquoise Ring and Abigail's Poisoned Porridge: Shakespeare and Marlowe as Rivals and Imitators," *Renaissance Drama,* n.s., 10 (1979): 33–44.
2. See Charney, "Marlowe's *Edward II* as Model for Shakespeare's *Richard II,*" *Research Opportunities in Renaissance Drama* 23 (1994): 31–41.
3. Geoffrey Bullough, ed., *Narrative and Dramatic Sources of Shakespeare,* 8 vols. (New York: Columbia University Press, 1957–75).
4. All quotations from Shakespeare are from *The Complete Signet Classic Shakespeare,* ed. Sylvan Barnet (New York: Harcourt, 1972).
5. All quotations from *Dido Queen of Carthage* are from the Revels edition, ed. H. J. Oliver (London: Methuen, 1968).
6. It also seemed obvious to Frederick S. Boas in *Queen Elizabeth in Drama and Related Studies* (London: Allen & Unwin), 1950), 85. Oliver in his Revels edition of *Dido* says that there is "almost certainly an allusion to *Dido* in Shakespeare's *Hamlet,* II.ii" (xxxii). See also Henderson, *Passion Made Public,* esp. 164 n. 30.
7. See Jackson I. Cope, "Marlowe's *Dido* and the Titillating Children," *ELR* 4 (1974): 315–25.
8. See Brian Gibbons, "Unstable Proteus: Marlowe's *The Tragedy of Dido Queen of Carthage,*" in *Christopher Marlowe,* ed. Brian Morris, Mermaid Critical Commentaries (New York: Hill & Wang, 1968), 33.
9. Harold Jenkins, ed., *Hamlet,* The Arden Shakespeare (London: Methuen, 1982), 479.
10. Harry Levin, *The Overreacher: A Study of Christopher Marlowe* (Boston: Beacon, 1964), 144.
11. Cope, "Marlowe's *Dido,*" 325.
12. See Barbara J. Bono, *Literary Transvaluation: From Vergilian Epic to Shakespearean Tragicomedy* (Berkeley: University of California Press, 1984).
13. J. B. Steane, *Marlowe: A Critical Study* (Cambridge: Cambridge University Press, 1964), 59.
14. Gibbons, "Unstable Proteus," 43.
15. See Emily C. Bartels, *Spectacles of Strangeness: Imperialism, Alienation, and Marlowe* (Philadelphia: University of Pennsylvania Press, 1993), esp. chap. 2, "Reproducing Africa: *Dido, Queen of Carthage* and Colonialist Discourse." Bartels is at work on a book on Renaissance views of Africa. See also Margo Hendricks, "Managing the Barbarian: *The Tragedy of Dido, Queen of Carthage,*" *Renaissance Drama,* n.s., 23 (1992): 165–88.
16. Levin, *The Overreacher,* 16.

17. See John P. Cutts, *The Left Hand of God: A Critical Interpretation of the Plays of Christopher Marlowe* (Haddonfield, N.J.: Haddonfield House, 1973), who mounts a withering attack on the heroic stature of Marlowe's Aeneas.

18. Levin, *Overreacher,* 23.

19. See Maurice Charney, *Shakespeare's Roman Plays: The Function of Imagery in the Drama* (Cambridge: Harvard University Press, 1961), esp. 79–80.

20. T. S. Eliot, *Selected Essays 1917–1932* (New York: Harcourt, 1932), 105.

21. Clifford Leech, "Marlowe's Humor," in *Essays on Shakespeare and Elizabethan Drama in Honor of Hardin Craig,* ed. Richard Hosley (Columbia: University of Missouri Press, 1962), 70.

22. See Gibbons, "Unstable Proteus." Jackson Cope's argument about the boy actors is very relevant to this discussion of the special style of *Dido.*

23. Bono in her impressive book, *Literary Transvaluation,* seems disappointed with Marlowe's lack of seriousness in his imitation of Vergil. For the Ovidian emphasis of Marlowe see Gibbons's exciting article, "Unstable Proteus." See also Matthew N. Proser, "*Dido Queene of Carthage* and the Evolution of Marlowe's Dramatic Style," in *"A Poet and a Filthy Play-maker": New Essays on Christopher Marlowe,* ed. Kenneth Friedenreich, et al. (New York: AMS Press, 1988), 83–97. See also the unpublished essay by Robert A. Logan, "Making the Haunt His: *Dido Queen of Carthage* as a Precursor to *Antony and Cleopatra.*" Of course, we have to take account of the fact that Ovid and Vergil come to Marlowe and Shakespeare through many intermediate sources. For the significance of Lydgate's *Troy Book* and popular accounts of the Fall of Troy see Ethel Seaton, "Marlowe's Light Reading," in *Elizabethan and Jacobean Studies Presented to Frank Percy Wilson,* eds. H. Davis and Helen Gardner (New York: Oxford University Press, 1959), 17–35. Marlowe translated Ovid's *Amores* and the style and tone of *Hero and Leander* is very Ovidian.

III

Actors and Acting, Directing and Staging

On the Aesthetics of Acting

STEPHEN BOOTH

FOR reasons of tactical convenience, I want to start on the topic of the aesthetics of acting by leaping *in medias res* to tell you about some unusually awkward exchanges I had with colleagues a few summers ago.

Since so much of this collection's appeal is likely to be to college professors, few of its readers will need to be told that, threatened with time free from teaching, college professors get nervous about the fact that, although they have not perished, they have—lately at least—not published either. When two of them meet in the summertime, they usually race each other to say "Well, what are you working on?" or "What are you *do*ing now?"

There is no perfectly satisfactory answer, but one of the best is "Nothing much"—which is satisfying because, in "Nothing much," the questioner receives the comforting news that the person questioned isn't doing anything much *either.*

The trouble with that answer is that the guilty questioner can suspect that his or her colleague is either *(a),* modest or *(b)*—what amounts to the same thing—lying. By autumn, the questioned colleague may be in a position to stun the scholarly world with his or her long-awaited monograph on the uses of *apud* in Ovid. Or, he or she may be nine-tenths of the way through a big colon-hinged book: *The Carthaginian Spring: A Saline Solution to the Problem of the Dead Sea Scrolls.* Therefore, since one is certain not to be doing enough to make a tree sloth feel lazy, the kindest course is usually just to tell a questioner what one is indeed doing.

I was following that course a few summers back, when I noticed that I was getting strange, embarrassed reactions. People would ask me "well-what-was-I-doing," and I would say, "Well, I've been thinking about acting," and they would get slightly flustered and say that that was nice—and quickly change the subject to some more cheerful topic like the Dean's recent heart attack.

After I got that response a couple of times, I realized that the people to whom I had said, "Well, I've been thinking about acting," thought I was considering going on the stage. (However slow-witted, an English teacher will eventually spot the presence of a syntactic ambiguity.)

The people to whom I'd said that I was thinking about acting were understandably concerned. They knew I had a wife, two children, and a garden to look out for, and they didn't want to be parties to a folly. They knew about Gauguin, of course, but that kind of abandon and abandonment rarely works out well. I was making a good living dazzling children, and they could not in conscience encourage me to run off to make my fortune as a waiter.

What interests me more than any of that is this: all of my much-relieved colleagues who stayed to find out that "well-what-was-I-*do*ing-now" was "thinking about the *art* of acting" leapt casually from the abandoned assumption that I was going on the stage to a new assumption—namely that I was studying the methods and techniques by which actors act.

The reason I am so struck by the confidence and consistency with which my colleagues interpreted the variously ambiguous statement "I have been thinking about acting"—and the reason I endeavor to make that confidence and consistency strike you too—is that they exemplify a surprising fact that, surprisingly enough, doesn't seem to surprise anybody.

We live in a period when more people in Europe and North America spend more time thinking and talking about acting than ever before in the history of the world. I don't find that surprising. But I do find it surprising that we are so very concerned with the art of acting that—although we give a lot of attention to evaluating acting—we give our most careful attention to thinking about acting *from the actor's point of view.* When we do that, we are as a restaurant critic would be if he thought of dinner from the point of view of the entrée.

I don't mean to suggest that I scorn or ask you to scorn actors' views on acting. Nor do I think we should scorn to be as fascinated as we are with those views. But I do find our fascination surprising. The fascination suggests that as consumers we are so totally devoted to the pleasure acting gives us that we take its worth for granted and have energy left over for peripheral reminders of the beloved agency of delight.

Having inadvertently submitted my colleagues (who, after all, only asked what I was doing because they feared—and doubted—that I might in fact *be* doing something) to two separate and unprofitable journeys through a peculiarly uninteresting field of ambiguity, I settled upon an answer to the "Well-what-are-you-*do*ing-now" question that approached adequacy: "Well, I've been thinking about the aesthetics of acting."

That was clearer, but it still generated reasonable but ill-made assumptions—namely that I was concerned to determine which actors or sorts of actors are good and which are bad.

As a culture, twentieth-century Western civilization gives a lot of time and energy to that topic too. People you overhear at bus stops and in coffee shops talk about which actors they like best and why. About ten years ago I appeared in federal court in Los Angeles in a tax fraud case; I was there as an expert witness on Shakespeare (don't ask). My testimony required me to meet with the prosecutor at 7:00 A.M. before court. The courthouse is in a tough neighborhood. At about 6:30 I was walking down a short side street when five motorcycle people appeared at the other end of the street, walking toward me fast. They were wearing black leather jackets and belts studded with spikes. They were very big. One of them was a young woman. She too was very big and dangerous looking. She was walking backwards in front of the fast-moving others and appeared to be shouting at them. When the group was close enough for me to hear her, it turned out that what had her so perturbed was her companions' ludicrous failure to see that Angela Lansbury was the best actress in the world.

Comparative acting is, of course, only a branch of the larger topic, drama in general.

Western culture has had three great ages of drama: one in ancient Athens, one in the Renaissance (in particular, the English and Spanish Renaissances), and now. Our period is probably the greatest of the three—not only for quality and quantity but for the pervasiveness of drama as a mode. Consider the fact that comic strips are plays and the fact that most people in the industrialized—read "rich"—world see and hear an hour or so of drama every day of their lives and the fact that in an average week American commercial television presents more first-class drama in English than the whole nineteenth century did before Oscar Wilde ('92) and Bernard Shaw ('98) came up in the bottom of the ninth.

But I digress.

I was about to say that, when I say "Well, I've been thinking about the aesthetics of acting," I mean not that I'm concerned with good acting as opposed to bad acting, but with the basic, usually unasked question, "Why do we like acting?" (That too is ambiguous—so ambiguous that, after I laid the question out carefully for an actor-friend of mine, he *still* told me why he liked to act.)

So, back to basics.

Why do people like to see and hear people pretend to be other people?

That's an odd thing to like, particularly so because—however unlike reality the pleasurable acting of any period inevitably is—we praise actors for being realistic.

If it's reality we want, there's any amount of it available all around us—for free.

Remember, I'm talking about our pleasure in watching and hearing actors—not our pleasure in drama in general. We take distinguishable pleasure in the acting itself: "It wasn't much of a play, but the acting was great." "It was something about a man who always wears black and broods about his family, but Johnny Cash was in it, and he's always good."

Why do we delight in being audiences to acting?

I was fussing away at this particular tip of the paradox whereby we value artifice for seeming natural, when I got a letter from a friend who wanted to get up a conference panel on Shakespearean repertory companies—the kind of companies put together for Shakespeare seasons like the ones at Ashland in Oregon; San Diego and Orinda in California, Madison in New Jersey, and Stratford in Ontario. They are like—but smaller, traditionally more specialized, and in most cases less permanent than—the Royal Shakespeare Company in England.

The letter focused not on the aesthetics of acting but on the aesthetics of repertory casting, and from it I saw that I could think more efficiently about acting in general by thinking about the narrower subject of *repertory* acting.

In the course of describing the session he had in mind, my friend gave some examples of "effects of repertory casting on the interpretation of Shakespeare's characters." He pointed to an instance of repertory casting by which an actor played Angelo in *Measure for Measure* in the afternoon and Petruchio in *The Taming of the Shrew* that night and was paired with "a rather tough middle-aged actress" as Isabella, the harassed maiden at the center of *Measure for Measure,* and as Kate the shrew. He also mentioned an actor whose Falstaff "lingered on" when he played Othello.

It is reasonable to infer that those examples were intended to illustrate negative results of repertory casting. It is even more reasonable to guess that—whatever my friend's intentions may have been in citing these particular cases—such examples will seem negative to anyone who follows common sense to the assumption that, since illusion is obviously of the essence of all theater, the effect of anything that diminishes or complicates an audience's acceptance of the actor's identity as the character he or she portrays is always and of necessity bad.

It is easy and comfortable to be led astray by common sense; it is particularly so when the object of one's thought is the theater.

I submit (1) that collision between, on the one hand, actors' own identities and/or their previous stage identities and, on the other, the identities they assume in the particular fiction in which we see them at a given moment on a given stage is a positive artistic good; (2) that that virtue is simply and merely an extension of the essential virtue of theater, which, in turn, is the most extreme of all manifestations of the common denominator of all aesthetic pleasure: double identity (being something and not being it too; being something and having one or more other, independent, and independently defined identities as well); and (3) that, whatever common sense may say, common experience bears me out.

To start with number three, let me report—or rather, I hope, remind you of—the following theatrical phenomena, phenomena not obviously related to one another but, I think, all capable of informing a discussion of the aesthetics of repertory casting. Each testifies in one way or another to audience delight in collisions of identities and of realities.

1. The most popular feature of souvenir programs for Shakespeare festivals is the scorecard-like grid on which each actor's several different parts are listed. As evidence of that popularity, consider what happened to Hilary Tate, who writes and edits for the Oregon festival, in the summer of 1991—the first and last time she left the grid out of a program. After all, the actors' current roles were listed under their photographs. That should have been enough. It was not. A bereaved public was at once heartbroken and enraged. It scolded Hilary Tate relentlessly all summer. Several people even wrote in to say that they had drawn and filled out their own grids.

2. People sitting down front in a theater and off to one side enjoy being able to see exiting actors for a step or two after they have left the stage. I have spent an improbably large percentage of my life listening to what audiences say during performances and in lobbies between acts. And, on the basis of sustained, quasi-scientific eavesdropping, I conclude (a) that seeing exiting actors go out of character when they think they are safely out of sight of the audience (and are in fact still in full view of part of it) is pleasur-

able to the people who catch them; (b) that seeing exiting actors *stay* in character after they reach the supposed safety of the wings and another reality is also pleasurable—and is pleasurable in exactly the same way as seeing actors drop the illusion too soon; and (c) that convincing illusion and unconvincing illusion are equally pleasing, pleasing in the same way, and, in fact, equatable.

3. Audiences are similarly and eternally delighted both with coincidences of onstage fact with offstage fact (Laurence Olivier as Antony and his wife Vivien Leigh as Cleopatra; Richard Burton as Petruchio and his wife Elizabeth Taylor as Kate; Kenneth Branagh and his wife Emma Thompson as Benedick and Beatrice), and with onstage contradictions of offstage fact (consider Laurence Olivier and his wife Vivien Leigh as father and daughter in Brook's *Titus Andronicus* or Laurence Olivier and his wife Joan Plowright as Shylock and Portia in a television *Merchant of Venice* or Kevin Kline as Benedick and his wife Phoebe Cates as Hero in Central Park in New York in 1987. Above all, consider a Berkeley Rep production of Noel Coward's *Private Lives. Private Lives* begins with two mismatched honeymooning couples and ends up with the pairs reassorted. In the Berkeley Rep production the four honeymooners were played by two pairs of married actors. During the first interval the audience busied itself giving and receiving notice that the actor playing husband A in the play was in fact married to the actor laying wife B, and so on. The plot thereupon contrived to align the onstage pairings with the offstage ones, and all of us liked that a lot.

4. Late in her career Sarah Bernhardt played a particularly lively redheaded fourteen-year-old boy. I think that one can safely assume that her success in the role depended equally upon her success in superseding the reality in which (a) she was a woman, (b) she was a woman over seventy years old, and (c) she was a woman in her seventies who had a wooden leg *and* upon her failure to supersede that reality.

(While I am on the topic, I might also mention the more complex issue of Herbert Marshall—another actor with a wooden leg, a wooden leg that apparently generated such an itch in the minds of Hollywood casting directors in the '30s and '40s that I know of no actor outside musical comedies who danced in a higher percentage of his films than Marshall did.)

This list should include the always delightful occasions where an audience is not sure whether an onstage accident has happened to a character or to the actor playing him. Such dubious accidents are theatrically invaluable and are worth generating.

For example, Jerry Kilty—a marvelously entertaining actor who doesn't appear to be working anymore—usually contrived to have his characters take large bites of apples just before they had to talk fast; the characters almost, but never quite, choked. Kilty also fell backwards over footstools whenever possible.

The classic account of the classic example of such calculated interplay of realities is the appreciative account of the "real bully circus" in chapter 22 of *Huckleberry Finn.*

The most extensive stage use of merely apparent stage accident occurs in Anthony Shaffer's *Sleuth* (a play generally powered by its audience's urgent awareness of two realities). The first-act curtain comes down just after one of the play's two characters shoots the other at point-blank range. Audiences thereupon go out in the lobby to savor their keenness in noticing that the actor playing Milo fell dead a half second before the other actor fired his prop gun. About five minutes into the second act the two characters (who, it turns out, are both in excellent health) discuss exactly the fact the audience has discussed—discuss it as a fact not of the performance but of the fiction.

Whenever a role is cast against type, the double reality inherent in drama is automatically enhanced. I will end this discussion of the pleasures of perceiving in multiple realities by illustrating the delight that casting against type appears to generate in the voting members of the Academy of Motion Picture Arts and Sciences.

In April 1961 Shirley Jones, the peach-cheeked soprano-next-door in a series of big but homey movie musicals of the 1950s, won the 1960 Academy Award for playing a nonsinging whore in *Elmer Gantry.* Seven years earlier Frank Sinatra won for playing the definitively un-crooner-like Angelo Maggio in *From Here to Eternity.* Bing Crosby got the 1944 Academy Award for playing a priest (albeit a singing priest). In 1988 Cher joined the list for *Moonstruck*—placed there in part, I think, by a public perennially and eternally struck by the long-established fact that Cher's half of Sonny and Cher can act as well as sing and clown and fall out of dresses. Susan Sarandon—whose career, though she did play Marmee in the 1994 version of *Little Women,* has been largely devoted to playing worldly, sexy, sexually available women—won the 1995 Academy Award for playing a nun. A perfect instance is Linda Hunt, who got an Academy Award for *The Year of Living Dangerously* (1983) in which she so successfully played a man that audiences gasped when, at the end of the movie, the credits said that the role of Billy—a man—had been played by someone named Linda. Tom Hanks (Hollywood's latest Jodie Foster) made his name in light comedy, and that probably helped him to the two statues he won for deeply unconvincing performances as damaged persons—performances, by the way, that demand constant, intense audience awareness that Hanks is acting, and very well too.

In fairness, however, I should admit that people used regularly to win Academy Awards for playing parts that might have been written for them at Central Casting: Marie Dressler for *Min and Bill,* Wallace Beery for *The Champ,* Charles Laughton for *The Private Lives of Henry VIII,* Thomas Mitchell for *Stagecoach,* Greer Garson for *Mrs. Miniver,* Charles Coburn for *The More the Merrier,* Judy Holliday for *Born Yesterday,* Gary Cooper for *High Noon,* Yul Brynner for *The King and I,* and so on. The only recent examples I can think of are Jack Palance for *City Slickers* (1991) and Nicholas Cage for *Leaving Las Vegas* (1995).

The most interesting specimen of both kinds of winner is John Wayne, who in his middle sixties got the 1969 Academy Award for *True Grit.* He played a John Wayne hero who, because he was a fat man in his middle sixties, was no longer a John Wayne hero and also, as he amply illustrated in the gunfight at the end, still was.

I want now to expand on my first two propositions. Those were (1) that collision between, on the one hand, actors' own identities and/or their previous stage identities and, on the other, the identities they assume in the particular fiction in which we see them at a given moment on a given stage is a positive artistic good, and (2) that that virtue is simply and merely an extension of the essential virtue of theater, which, in turn, is the most extreme of all manifestations of the common denominator of all aesthetic pleasure: double identity (being something and not being it too; being something and having one or more other, independent, and independently defined identities as well).

All representational art depends for its effectiveness on the essential fact that the representation is not the thing represented and—in a way—is. Dramatic art exaggerates both sides of that paradox. A fiction physically enacted before us is necessarily less questionable than one we read about. (Peter Pan *can* fly; we see him flying; Iago's scheme is workable because we see it work; so in *Much Ado about Nothing* is the Don John charade by which Margaret (whom we never get to hear wonder why she calls Borachio Claudio or why he calls her Hero), is successfully mistaken for Hero. We don't see that, but we see people who have seen it and evidence that it worked.

In *Richard III* we are witness to Richard's successful courtship of the widow of one of his victims over the corpse of another who was both her father-in-law and her king. His success is amazing but believable: we see and hear Richard maneuver, and we see and hear Anne as she weakens and succumbs. The medically unlikely deaths of Enobarbus and Iras in *Antony and Cleopatra* are undeniable: we see Enobarbus and Iras fall over.

Conversely, however, we are always aware that we are in seats at one end of a big room and that the people at the other end of the room *are* at the other end of that room and not in Never-Never Land or pre-Christian Britain or Illyria or a mile without prehistoric Athens in a Warwickshire wood.

In the theater everybody believes in Tinkerbell (no one can help it), and nobody does (no one could).

The essence of theater is not success in passing illusion off as reality but in enabling an audience to cope with two realities at once. And, as long as the balance between the two is maintained, any element in any dimension that reasserts such doubleness is likely to be to the good.

Moreover and on the other hand, some diminishment in audience pleasure usually results from too great a oneness between actor and character. I think that is always true when an actually deformed actor plays Richard III. Victor Buono—a very fat Falstaff who played the part without padding—was (until the summer of 1995 when I saw John Goodman), the best Falstaff I had ever seen, but I suspect that Victor Buono's Falstaff would have been even better if he had been built like Roddy McDowell. The key phrase in what I've just been saying has been "as long as the balance . . . is maintained." As this essay progresses, it may seem increasingly probable that I lust to see Mae West as Viola, Michael Jackson as Othello, Madonna as Cordelia, and Arnold Schwarzenegger as Puck. I do not. I mean only to suggest that the greater strain an illusion bears without breaking, the better we like it. The better we like it—not the better we *should* like it.

That brings me to what may seem to be a digression but is not: the difference between actors and stars.

By "actors" I mean performers whose own identities and previous theatrical identities do not impinge upon, or linger in, their performances. For example, even though he gets star billing, Richard Pasco is not a star but an actor; back in 1979, his (excellent) Brutus in the BBC *Julius Caesar* did not—at least for me—echo in, or color, his (absolutely *superb*) Jacques in the BBC *As You Like It* two weeks later. Nor did his Hamlet or his Angelo or the newspaperman he played in *Room at the Top*.

Much the same was true of Edward G. Robinson and Rosalind Russell, who by all standards but the one I am using here were obviously stars. You wonder why they never got Academy Awards? Because, I think, they were so good at acting that they did not invite audiences to notice—and thus to enjoy—their achievement in "being" people they were also and urgently *not.* Remember Rosalind Russell as the neurotic schoolteacher in the 1955 movie version *Picnic*? It was embarrassing to be in the same theater with the strips of film she was on. She was pathetic and painful—and not just *in the way* the character would be in real life. In practical effect, she *was* the character, and there was no joy in spending time with her. There would have been considerable joy for an audience that, from moment to moment during the performance, could have remembered and enjoyed the fact that this gallant, frustrated, petty, disgusting schoolteacher was *also* Rosalind Russell, a once and future leading lady.

Edward G. Robinson—perhaps the best actor of the twentieth century—was, despite his distinctive appearance (he looked like a second-hand plum), so good at acting that he never even got *nominated* for an Academy Award. In 1935 in *The Whole Town's Talking* Robinson played two characters—Public Enemy Number One and a meek little clerk whose co-workers thought he looked like the gangster, but who could not himself see any likeness. The movie was obviously designed to exploit the theatrical energy available from Robinson's identification with gangster parts. Robinson, however, was so good an actor that he perfectly removed that whole dimension of the film and of its audience's pleasure. For instance, in one early scene, Robinson as the clerk sat by a mirror in a lunchroom and tried to look like a newspaper photograph of Edward G. Robinson. He failed. Moreover, Robinson played the two characters—who of course successfully masqueraded as one another—without recourse to any distinguishing quirks (for instance, facial tics or speech mannerisms), and the audience never for a moment doubted which was which.

Stars, of course, can be very good actors indeed. (If you care to see what the greatness of a great star who is also a very good actor consists in, I recommend a double bill of Charlton Heston disaster movies. The Charleston Heston of *Earthquake* and the Charlton Heston of *Airport 75* are both so much Charlton Heston that even the scriptwriters have probably long since forgotten what names his two characters had. But—if one goes to one of those theaters that do most of their business as places for drunks to sleep and sees both films as I once did at one delirious, five-chocolate-bar, four-hour sitting—one discovers that the two Hestons are different, deeply different, different beyond the surface differences dictated by the two scripts.)

Nonetheless, the distinguishing characteristic of stars is that they are always *both* themselves and any particular character they play. And that capacity in stars makes us capable of an effortless, magical double-think. Consider our truly amazing capacity to tell one another the plot of a movie calling the main characters by the actors' names and mixing those names with character labels: "The whore who brings Clint Eastwood the reward money casually mentions that Morgan Freeman is dead."

The great stars never let us forget that they are acting, *and* they also succeed in engaging us in the particular fictional lives they adopt and present to us. To do that is to do something much more miraculous than what Edward G. Robinson did and Ralph Richardson did, what Richard Pasco, Harvey Keitel, Jean Smart, and suchlike other great actors do. To do what stars do is to duplicate the essence of theater and to multiply its essential pleasure. The experience of a star performance is more complicated than the experience of a performance by an ordinary journeyman actor, or by an ordinary master actor, or by an ordinary great actor.

A star performance is particularly hard to think about and to praise because it does not square well with the reasonable but wrong assumption that the success of a successful theatrical illusion will be commensurate with its perfection. I suggest, however, that stars deserve the adulation and money they get, that, in this matter, low, easily scorned, popular tastes are right—profoundly right—and echo the deepest, the most basic, element of theatrical aesthetics.

I suggest that the overlapping identities that result from repertory casting can be, and usually are, positive assets for the audiences who perceive and wrestle with them—assets even for audience members who, in dutiful obedience to their common sense and in all honesty, complain that today's Othello reminds them of yesterday's Falstaff or that Kate looks like Petruchio's former drill sergeant. Repertory casting allows audiences the pleasure of watching stars where they would otherwise be watching mere actors.

What Huckleberry Finn likes best about the real bully circus in chapter 22 is the hoary routine in which a drunk stumbles out of the audience and demands to be allowed to perform. Huck is not only delighted when the surprisingly able drunk reveals himself to be another circus performer but is so far deceived as to pity the ringmaster for being fooled by one of his own men. Let me conclude by saying about the pleasure all acting offers audiences and about the heightened version of that pleasure that results from repertory casting what Huckleberry Finn says in concluding his account of the bully circus: "it was plenty good enough for me; and whenever I run across it, it can have *my* custom every time."

Killing Mercutio: Or, Is There Such a Thing as an Actor-Playwright?

LOIS POTTER

THE actor playing Mercutio is having an amazingly good day. The audience falls silent as he speaks the first words of the Queen Mab speech: "Who shall attempt to describe their impression upon the hearers? Who shall describe the manner—the look—the utterance of him who then gave them? Shall we go too far if we say the world had since nothing to compare with that representation? The life, the brilliancy, the style of the character was suited to the actor. He was all fire, energy, and spirit."[1] Who is this actor—apart from being one of the few that Marvin Rosenberg has never described? He is the author of the lines he speaks so eloquently: William Shakespeare, the actor-playwright.

This account, needless to say, comes from a work of fiction. *The Forest Lad* (1838) by "Captain [Henry] Curling" describes the world premiere of *Romeo and Juliet* as a success beyond a playwright's wildest dreams. It is graced by the presence of most of the famous Elizabethans, including the Queen herself. Although Shakespeare's writing is "too exquisite for the rudeness of the age in which they lived" (246), the audience, with the wonderful hindsight sometimes granted to characters in historical novels, recognizes that it is hearing immortal words. "They came from the tongue of him who composed them, now uttered to an audience for the first time . . . Mercutio was Shakespeare's self,—the most mercurial and spirited of the production [*sic*] of his comic muse; and the impressive manner in which he gave the words of the character and their fire and brilliancy, his exquisite intonation, nay, the every dash of his look was irresistible."[2] This identification of the author with his creation, and the fascination with the actor-author relationship, extends to the Queen herself. After the play, she sends for him, excited both because someone who has just died on the stage will live again in her presence and because "we will have both the character and the creator of the character before us."[3] For a comparable experience one might look at Rosenberg's perceptive account of the moment when Hamlet, an amateur actor, attempts to recite a speech that the First Player then proceeds to interpret in the manner of a trained professional: "An actor acts Hamlet, but once we are involved in his story, we don't think of him as an actor, but as indeed Hamlet. . . . Hamlet will do his part of the speech differently from the Player, to establish contrast: he may simply remember the words intelligently, with no pretense of acting; he may recite them as a talented amateur; he may attempt a great declamatory effect, that he himself recognizes as inadequate." Rosenberg adds, drawing on Nevill Coghill, "another Chinese-box irony: the best player in Shakespeare's company, Burbage, would be playing the amateur Hamlet; some lesser actor, the model Player."[4] Muriel Bradbrook has complicated the irony by suggesting that the First Player might have been made up to look like Burbage;[5] in a still further *mise en abîme,* many scholars have speculated that this Player would have been played by Shakespeare himself.[6]

If I have begun with the "evidence" of a novel, it is because Captain Curling differs so much from most modern writers in imagining an audience able to respond to Shakespeare simultaneously as actor and playwright. Of course, most twentieth-century writers know, as Curling did not, the meager evidence—all of it late, and based on hearsay—about the nature of the roles actually played by him (Adam in *As You Like It;* the Ghost in *Hamlet*).[7] In addition, we can cite Henry Chettle's reference in 1592 to having seen him "exelent in the qualitie he professes" (presumably acting)[8] and an epigram by John Davies (published in 1610) which says that he "played some kingly parts in sport."[9] Though Aubrey knew a tradition that he (by contrast with Ben Jonson) "did acte exceedingly well,"[10] by the end of the seventeenth century oral tradition had demoted him to one who "as I have heard, was a much better writer than an actor."[11] Forty years later, Colley Cibber enthusiastically developed this view into a theory: "How many shining Actors have the warm scenes of his genius given to Posterity? Without being himself, in his Action, equal to his Writing! A strong Proof that Actors, like Poets, must be born such. Eloquence and Elocution are quite different Talents. *Shakespear* could write *Hamlet;* but Tradition tells us, That the *Ghost,* in the same Play, was one of his best Performances as an Actor." By now, this "tradition" has become a cause for disparagement. Because Shakespeare did not play leading roles, he must have been, not a good supporting actor, but a second-rate one.

Not surprisingly, then, no novelist since Curling has imagined Shakespeare playing a bravura role like Mercutio. In the well-known Brahms and Simon spoof, *No Bed for Bacon,* he is shown as a terrible actor who plays only small parts (the Bishop of St. Asaph's in *Henry VIII;* Fabian in *Twelfth Night*).[12] More sympathetically, Marchette Chute, re-creating the first night of *Romeo and Juliet* in a book for young readers in 1954, imagines him as Benvolio and director (or co-director) of the play.[13] Anthony Burgess in *Nothing Like the Sun* (1964) depicts him as an actor mainly of small parts that demand no creative involvement on his part (Philostrate in *A Midsummer Night's Dream;* Antonio in *the Two Gentlemen of Verona*). Burgess also knows and uses the tradition about Shakespeare's having played the Ghost in *Hamlet.* It is during his performance of that role that, riddled with venereal disease, he shrieks and collapses mid-speech, unable to remember lines.[14] The most capable actor among novelistic Shakespeares seems to be the one who makes two brief but memorable appearances in John Arden's *Books of Bale, A Fiction of History* (1988). Though on the final occasion he is drunk, it is obvious that he is also a consummate professional, and he sobers up as soon as he starts to prepare for his first entrance.[15]

If it is surprising to find so many writers drawing negative conclusions about Shakespeare's acting simply because there is no evidence about it; it is even more surprising to find widespread acceptance of the idea that he had a poor memory, clearly a serious handicap for any actor. Bernard Shaw makes this a running gag in *The Dark Lady of the Sonnets,* where the poet is constantly complaining of his memory and mangling the fine phrases that he is trying to write down. When Shakespeare is onstage, Burgess imagines, the prompter must be in readiness, "for Will is not always reliable, even with lines that he himself has written."[16] Though Sonnet 23 contains a reference to an "imperfect actor" forgetting his lines because of stage fright, this seems too slight a basis for such a legend. I think it can be traced to another source. In 1910, the year of Shaw's play, C. W. Wallace published an account of the Belott-Mountjoy lawsuit in *Harper's Monthly Magazine.* This was a controversy, in 1612, over a verbal promise to do with the financial arrangements in a marriage negotiation for which Shakespeare had acted as go-between and about which he was therefore called as a witness when relations between father and son-in-law turned nasty. The main feature of his testimony was his repeated inability to remember any of the details about which he was asked. Never mind that, as Samuel Schoenbaum points out, the Belott-

Mountjoy marriage negotiations had taken place eight years previously and none of the other witnesses could remember them either.[17] What seems to have become part of the collective Shakespeare myth was simply the idea that, while still in his forties, he already had a failing memory. This could certainly explain his early retirement from the stage, even if one did not, as Burgess later did, attribute it to the effects of syphilis.

And so the matter has rested until two recent developments. The first is the ongoing work of Donald Foster with the database SHAXICON. On the hypothesis that Shakespeare's vocabulary as a writer was influenced by the words he had to memorize and repeat as an actor, Foster has used the computer to study the correlation between—on the one hand—performances and revivals of plays in which Shakespeare is known to have acted and—on the other—the increase in rare vocabulary in plays written during this time. Because the sources of these rare words can be traced not merely to plays in the company's current repertory but to particular roles in those plays, he argues that it is possible to determine which parts Shakespeare played and even to date premieres and revivals through this pattern.[18] His findings confirm most of the traditional views, since he attributes to Shakespeare a number of kingly roles (Navarre in *Love's Labor's Lost,* Henry IV, the King of France in *All's Well That Ends Well,* Antiochus and Simonides in *Pericles,* and Jupiter in *Cymbeline*). The statistics also give him the roles of Adam in *As You Like It* and the Ghost in *Hamlet* (doubling with the First Player, the Messenger/Gentleman of 4.5, and perhaps Lucianus). While most of these roles are reassuringly like those most scholars assume Shakespeare played—that is, solid supporting roles that are unlikely to make anyone famous—they also include a few that Foster himself finds puzzling, such as Aaron in *Titus,* Ulysses in *Troilus,* and both Ford and the Host in *Merry Wives.* Foster suggests that in some cases the reason for Shakespeare's familiarity with a role may simply have been, not that he played it himself, but that he had to drill someone else in it. As Foster himself intends to publish further on this subject, it would be premature to add much to what he has written to date. But it is worth pointing out that his evidence, if it can be accepted, would make nonsense of the argument about the dramatist's poor memory. The parts attributed to him (particularly Henry IV) contain some extremely long speeches, and the Shakespeare depicted by Burgess would have been insane to write such roles for himself.

The other important redirection of attitudes to Shakespeare the actor is suggested in Meredith Skura's fascinating book, *Shake-*

speare the Actor and the Purposes of Playing. Unlike most of the writers I have mentioned, Skura assumes that Shakespeare had a real talent for his profession. On the evidence both of her research into the psychology of actors and of some of the plays' images, she imagines an actor with a more complex relationship to the theater. On the one hand, Shakespeare is fascinated by the figure of the clown, perhaps something of a comedian himself (she notes Aubrey's anecdote about the high style in which he "killed a calf") with "a natural gift for making comedy out of violence."[19] On the other, he is terrified by the thought of the hostile audience. It is from his experience as an actor, she argues, that he derives his numerous recurring images of the single figure hunted down by a pack, the baited bear and the hunted animal.[20]

Since we are unlikely ever to find the answers to the questions we should like to ask about Shakespeare the actor, it is perhaps more interesting to ask why we seem, despite the lack of evidence, so stubbornly to cling to the myth of the dramatist who couldn't act. Perhaps the simplest explanation, and one that certainly accounts for Colley Cibber's remarks, is the common desire to find feet of clay. But it may be possible to get a little further than this by extending Skura's interesting study of the actor-personality to look at the personality of that still rarer type, the actor-dramatist.

Actor-dramatists often begin writing either because they want to create better roles for themselves than they are ordinarily allowed to play, or because they want to play, in imagination, *all* the roles in their plays. Cibber in his *Apology* is frank about his motives: as a young actor, constantly cast in roles that bored him, "I was at last reduc'd to write a Character for myself."[21] Coward, writing a play to order, carefully created a good part for himself to ensure himself a place in the cast;[22] later, he was still more open about his intentions, as he argued himself into the part of Sholto in his own *The Young Idea,* since, "as I had taken the trouble to write the part specially for myself, it would be both illogical and foolish to allow anyone else to get so much as a smell of it."[23] Kenneth Branagh wrote *Public Enemy* with himself in mind.[24] Alan Alda claims that writing plays gave him a sense of control over his life: "If people wouldn't give me a part, I could at least write myself a part."[25] The nineteenth-century actor-dramatist Dion Boucicault, cast as Rolla in a school production of Sheridan's *Pizarro,* recalled, "I wanted to play every part himself, but had to content myself with teaching all the rest how their parts should be given."[26] As a child, John Mortimer acted in Shakespeare's tragedies for his parents: "Unfortunately I was an only child and so had to act all the parts."[27]

What kind of part would an actor be most likely to write for himself, if his first aim is to further his own acting career? Initially, no doubt, the kind that offers greatest emotional range, a chance to dominate the stage and be noticed. These need not be large parts: Cibber, who disliked learning lines, gave himself interesting characters who appear in only a few scenes. In later plays such an actor may choose to emphasize a familiar type (a Cibberian fop, a "Noel Coward character"). But he may equally well choose to play with the very expectations he has created, as when Coward created lower middle-class roles for himself. Molière gave himself parts in which, as a silly ass (*La Critique de l'Ecole des Femmes*) or dim-witted hypochondriac *(Le Malade Imaginaire),* he railed at that disrespectful playwright Molière. If Kitty Clive actually wrote *The Rehearsal, or Bays in Petticoats* (1753)—and it is hard to see who else could have had the nerve to ask her to perform in such a play—she experimented quite daringly with her double identity, casting herself as the obnoxious but wealthy would-be playwright, Mrs. Hazard. Hazard goes to see her play rehearsed at Drury Lane with, among others, Mrs. Clive in the cast. Needless to say, Mrs. Clive fails to turn up to the rehearsal and Mrs. Hazard, livid at this lack of civility, finally decides to play the role herself. The theater prompter (who is playing himself) suggests that she wear Clive's stage costume: "I believe it will fit you exactly, as you're much of her size"—to which Hazard retorts angrily, "I happen to be a Head taller, and I hope something better made."[28] Like Cibber's mock-vanity in his *Apology,* Clive's mock-vanity in the play appears to satirize her while really containing the satire within the audience's knowledge that it is the actress herself who has written the lines.

Self-referential jokes of this type have been detected in Shakespeare's plays—for instance, in the depiction of naive characters called William—but one would first need to show that Shakespeare had developed a stage persona like Molière's or Clive's. "A star," John Lahr has written, "is his own greatest invention. . . . Coward was a performer who wrote, not a writer who happened to perform."[29] That is, he wrote plays with a view of performing in them before an audience who knew that he was the author, and sometimes (as in *Private Lives* and *Present Laughter*) exploited the audience's knowledge of his offstage existence. Leading roles in Elizabethan drama tend to emphasize performativity: characters impersonate others, take on disguises, go mad, sing and dance. But the notion of playing "in one person many people"—as Richard II does in imagination and as Bottom is laughed at for wanting to do—is much more possible in the Elizabethan theater, with its doubling of parts, than in most subsequent stage traditions. And Foster's statistics cannot tell us about the hypothetical Shakespeare who played a number of brilliant one-scene cameos, since these are unlikely to offer enough distinctive vocabulary to be noticed as an influence in later plays.

Nevertheless, as the depiction of both Bottom and Richard suggests, an actor-dramatist may well be aware of his own danger as a focus of envy, not merely from non-acting playwrights like Robert Greene, but from non-writing actors in his own company. Molière's *Impromptu de Versailles* stages a confrontation between the author and disgruntled members of his company who complain that they cannot possibly learn their lines at such short notice; they add that his situation is different from theirs: "Vous n'êtes pas à plaindre; car ayant fait la pièce, vous n'avez pas peur d'y manquer." ("No reason to feel sorry for you; since you wrote the play, you don't have to worry about forgetting the lines.") Then his wife sarcastically proposes that "Vous deviez faire une comédie où vous auriez jouê tout seul." ("You should write a comedy where you could act all by yourself.")[30] The situation is comic, of course, and is designed to justify a series of brilliant impersonations where Molière does, in a sense, play all the parts himself. But it is possible that the appearance of such total control on the part of the actor-dramatist has something to do with the exceptional degree of hatred that was directed not only at Molière but at others who had what Colley Cibber called "the superfluous Capacity of writing myself the characters I have acted."[31] When Kenneth Branagh's play was produced, he recognized that he had been "hoisted by my own petard in having written a great vehicle for myself. . . . I came in for an inevitable bashing over my presumption in having both written and performed in the play. . . ."[32] It is possible, of course that we need to reverse cause and effect. Even allowing for the fact that envy and malice seem to go along with all kinds of outstanding success, there may be a necessary element of presumption in the actor-dramatist that arouses dislike. Dion Boucicault received such scathing reviews at the beginning of his acting career before he had become known as a playwright, that his biographer is forced to hypothesize "something in his personality which marked him out for attention."[33] In any case, the very fact that his power is apparently so totalizing is what, paradoxically, makes the actor-dramatist vulnerable. For the one thing that he cannot control is the audience response, and there is no more complete a rejection than an audience's refusal to accept an actor who is performing in his own play.

Finally, it is possible that we play down the importance of Shakespeare the actor to Shakespeare the playwright because we do not really believe that the two roles can coexist. At least as important as the War of the Theaters is the War within the Theater itself—that is, the war between actors and playwrights. A long tradition of theatrical satire from *The Rehearsal* (Buckingham et al.) and *The Female Wits* (anonymous) to Sheridan's *The Critic* shows bumbling playwrights demanding the impossible from bewildered or rebellious actors who take revenge by cutting the text or by refusing to learn it in the first place. As late as 1961, Sir Cedric Hardwicke referred to "this everlasting distinction between the actor's art and the playwright's." After quoting Ellen Terry—"'My boy,' she said to me, 'act in your pauses'"—he adds, approvingly, "At those moments, you are a creator, not a servant of playwrights."[34] One is reminded that the phrase "to create a role" traditionally means to be the first actor of a part, not to be its author. Of course, there is usually an element of partnership in this creation, and Ellen Terry's remark is the product of an age when authors expected the actor to be a co-author. H. C. Merivale tells of a French author who complained to an actor in rehearsal, "Mais Monsieur, vous n'ajoutez rien!" ("But, sir, you are adding nothing!") On the other hand, he recognizes that, with Shakespeare, he is confronting a writer who preempts all possible creativity on the part of the actor: "What is there to add? But it is the actor's work to add not by the unwholesome thing called gagging—though even that is sometimes not without its use—but by interpretation and by thought. . . . With Shakespeare, *on n'ajoute pas.*" Burgess transforms Hamlet's dislike for the ad-libbing of clowns into a dramatic scene where Shakespeare gets Will Kemp fired from the company—a fictitious moment that at least one modern writer has reported as if it had really happened.[35]

It can also happen, though less frequently, that the author becomes a rival actor. Before the typewriter and the photocopier, there was a brief period in the history of every play—before the parts had been copied for rehearsal purposes—during which its author was also its only possible interpreter. Sybil Thorndike said of Shaw, who read the part of St. Joan aloud to her: "he could have played it better than any of us."[36] Peter Holland's fascinating account of the author's "Reading to the Company," a practice that lasted into this century, shows that there was at least one occasion when the actor actually did have the opportunity to play all the parts himself. "If performance is a sphere of displaced intentionality in which the voice of the playwright is unheard except revoiced, reading to the company may have retained the last vestigial assertion of intention, even as the playwright, like a version of Lewis Carroll's Cheshire Cat, vanishes leaving only the play-text behind."[37]

So perhaps there is never really an actor-playwright; only a person who passes from being a playwright to being an actor. Even Coward has said, "I always forget, when I'm playing in my own plays, that I'm the author. . . . Not at rehearsals, when I'm after the others. But when I'm actually doing it I can't remember thinking 'I've written the play.' I think, of the two, I really prefer playing other people's plays to my own."[38]

Criticism of the plays is equally schismatic. How often is there a really successful fusion of the literary approach with the theatrical one? Marvin Rosenberg clearly states the need for a cutoff point in any discussion of performance; as he says early in *The Masks of Hamlet,* he will not deal with versions of the play unless they "illuminate Shakespeare's text."[39] Though—partly as a result of Rosenberg's own work—many scholars have come to believe that such illumination is possible, many others remain conscious of the tension between the theatrical experience and the literary one. They feel that performance inevitably shuts off options, emphasizing the visual at the expense of the verbal, the anecdotal at the expense of the universal. Philip Edwards notes the paradox: Shakespeare's plays are only half alive if they are not acted in a theater, and yet they are not only too long but also too complex for any but a theater of the mind.[40] Richard Dutton recently offered an explanation for this paradox, suggesting that the dramatist, restrained from publishing by his arrangement with the King's Men, may have written his plays with a view both to stage abridgment and to the chance of circulating a full text in private among choice readers.[41] Eric Sams suggests that Shakespeare spent his years of retirement in revising his plays for publication.[42] Though I should be sorry to replace Shakespeare the man of the theater with Shakespeare the literary man who feels so little at home in it, it may be that we simply need to acknowledge the existence of both: the actor who expects his plays to be cut for performance and the playwright who aims his work at the thoughtful reader. It would seem that the actor and author are like those other pairs of "equal opposites" that Shakespeare so often depicts; equally powerful, equally valuable, they cannot coexist and eventually recognize that one must destroy the other. It is to Dryden (an author who, according to Cibber, read his own works aloud without any attempt at performance),[43] that we owe the claim that Shakespeare was forced to kill Mercutio, who otherwise would have killed him.[44]

Incidentally, just who do you think did play Mercutio?

Notes

1. "Captain Curling" [Henry Curling], *The Forest Youth, or Shakespere as He Lived, an historical tale* (London: Eli Charles Eginton & Co, 1838), 245.
2. Ibid., 246.
3. Ibid., 248.
4. Marvin Rosenberg, *The Masks of Hamlet* (Newark: University of Delaware Press, 1992), 426–27.
5. Muriel Bradbrook, *Shakespeare the Craftsman* (Cambridge: Cambridge University Press, 1969), 129.
6. Most recently Donald Foster, posting to Shakespeare Electronic Conference, vol. 6, no. 0533, 6 July, 1995. See below for further discussion of this posting.
7. The remark about his playing an old man is reported by Oldys and quoted by Steevens in Samuel Johnson's edition of Shakespeare's plays in 1778; Capell also tells the story in 1779. Both are cited in Samuel Schoenbaum, *William Shakespeare, A Documentary Lilfe* (New York: Oxford University Press, with the Scholar Press, 1975), 149. It was Nicholas Rowe who (in his edition of 1709) first recorded the tradition that "the top of his Performance was the Ghost in his own *Hamlet*." This is also cited in Schoenbaum, 148.
8. Introductory epistle to *Kind-Hartes Dreame* (1592), quoted in G. Blakemore Evans, ed., *The Riverside Shakespeare* (Boston, 1974), 1836; also in Schoenbaum, 117.
9. "To Our English Terence, Master Will Shakespeare," from *The Scourge of Folly* (1610), quoted in William Shakespeare, *The Complete Works,* eds. S. Wells et al. Oxford: Clarendon Press, 1986), xli; also in Schoenbaum, *Documentary,* 148.
10. *Brief Lives,* ed. Andrew Clark, 2 vols. (Oxford, 1898), 2:226.
11. [James Wright], *Historia Histrionica, an Historical Account of the Stage* (London, 1699), 4.
12. Caryl Brahms and S. J. Simon, *No Bed for Bacon* (Michael Joseph, 1941; reprint, New York: Penguin Books, 1948).
13. Marchette Chute, *The Wonderful Winter* (New York: Dutton, 1954), 150. He is also assigned the role of Henry VI (76).
14. Anthony Burgess, *Nothing Like the Sun, A Story of Shakespeare's Lovelife* (New York: Norton, 1964), 232.
15. John Arden, *Books of Bale, A Fiction of History* (London: Methuen, 1988; reprint, Minerva, 1989), 321.
16. Burgess, *Shakespeare* (New York: Knopf, 1970), 196. The emphasis on Shakespeare's poor memory is all the more ironic in that Burgess, taking his cue from Hamlet's complaints about clowns who ad-lib, has imagined that it was Shakespeare himself who was responsible for firing the improvising clown Will Kemp from the Lord Chamberlain's company, replacing him by the more docile Robert Armin, who could be counted on to be more faithful to the words of his script.

17. Schoenbaum, *Documentary Life,* 213.

18. See, for a more elaborate explanation, Foster's essay published on SHAKSPER, the electronic conference edited by Hardy B. Cook, vol. 6, no. 0533, 6 July 1995.

19. Meredith Skura, *Shakespeare the Actor and the Purposes of Playing* (Chicago: University of Chicago Press, 1993), 73.

20. Ibid. See also Alexander Leggatt, "Shakespeare and Bearbaiting," in *Shakespeare and Cultural Traditions,* eds. Tesuo Kishi, Roger Pringle, and Stanley Wells (Newark: University of Delaware Press, 1994), 43–53.

21. *An Apology for the Life of Colley Cibber,* ed. B. R. S. Fone (Ann Arbor: University of Michigan Press, 1968), 118.

22. Noel Coward, *Present Indicative* (London: Evergreen Books, 1940), 104.

23. Ibid., 137.

24. Kenneth Branagh, *Beginning* (London: Norton, 1989), 194–95.

25. *The Actor Speaks: Actors Discuss Their Experiences and Careers,* ed. Joan Jeffri (Westport, CT: Greenwood Press, 1994), 9. Susan Nussbaum, in another interview in this collection, also makes that point that, as actors can't always be in work, they ought to write both for the sake of creativity and because "you can always write for yourself" (119).

26. Richard Fawkes, *Dion Boucicault, A Biography* (London: Quartet Books, 1979), 14.

27. "Shakespeare and a Playwright of Today," in *Shakespeare, Man of the Theater* eds. K. Muir, J. L. Halio, and D. J. Palmer. (Newark: University of Delaware Press, 1983), 19.

28. Catherine Clive, *The Rehearsal: or, Bays in Petticoats* (London: R. Dodsley, 1753), act 2: 25.

29. *Coward the Playwright* (London: Methuen, 1982), 1–2.

30. Molière, *L'Impromptu de Versailles,* in *Théatre Complete,* ed. Robert Jouanny, 2 vols. (Paris, Garnier Frères, n.d.), 1: 519, 520.

31. Cibber, *Apology,* 23–24.

32. Branagh, *Beginning,* 194–195.

33. Fawkes, *Boucicault,* 22.

34. Cedric Hardwicke, *A Victorian in Orbit* (London: Methuen, 1961), 48. The actor-author rivalry is effectively dramatized in Henry Reed's radio play, *The Great Desire I Had.* Shakespeare is traveling in Italy, sees actresses onstage for the first time, and becomes excited about having them act his roles. He then discovers that these improvisational performers regard authors as part of a primitive stage in theatrical history, before actors were capable of inventing their own lines (Henry Reed, *The Streets of Pompeii and Other Plays for Radio* [London: BBC, 1970], 258).

35. Burgess *Nothing Like the Sun,* 211–13. Cf. Howard Brenton in *Hot Irons, Diaries, Essays, Journalism* (London: Nick Hern Books, 195): "Shakespeare fired his greatest clown, Will Kemp, for lewd improvisation" (80).

36. Quoted (from a BBC interview, 1965–66) in Peter Hay, ed., *Theatrical Anecdotes* (Oxford: Oxford University Press, 1987), 38.

37. Peter Holland, "Reading to the Company," in *Reading Plays, Interpretation and Reception,* eds. P. Holland and Hanna Scolnicov (Cambridge: Cambridge University Press, 1991), 8–29, esp. 27.

38. Interview with Michael MacOwan, in *Great Acting,* ed. Hal Burton (London: BBC and Bonanza Books, 1967), 168.

39. Rosenberg, *Masks of Hamlet,* 11.

40. Philip Edwards, *Shakespeare, A Writer's Progress* (London: Oxford University Press, 1986), 20–23.

41. Richard Dutton, "The Birth of the Author," in *Elizabethan Theater, Essays in Honor of S. Schoenbaum,* eds. R. B. Parker and S. P. Zitner (Newark: University of Delaware Press, 1996), 71–92; also, for a subtle and thoughtful argument against the protheatre approach, Harry Berger Jr., *Imaginary Audition, Shakespeare on Stage and Page* (Berkeley: University of California Press, 1989).

42. Eric Sams, *The Real Shakespeare: Retrieving the Early Years, 1564–1594* (New Haven: Yale University Press, 1995), 186.

43. Cibber, *Apology,* 57.

44. Dryden, "Defense of the Epilogue to the Second Part of *The Conquest of Granada,*" in *Of Dramatic Poesy and Other Critical Essays,* ed. George Watson, 2 vols. (London and New York, 1962), 1: 180.

"What Do I Do Now?" Directing *A Midsummer Night's Dream*

SIDNEY HOMANN

"WHAT do I do now?" my Hippolyta asked me, the first day of rehearsals for a production of *A Midsummer Night's Dream* I was directing for the Florida Theatre.[1] "After those first four lines, I've got nothing until act 4—and that's after intermission. So, do I just stand there like an idiot while Theseus talks to Hermia? Waiting around for my exit?" She was right about the lines—as far as the character of Hippolyta was concerned—for, like any actor, the moment she got her part and was handed the script she had highlighted Hippolyta's lines and knew that they were precious few Besides 1.1. and 4.1 (the conversation with Theseus about hunting dogs), there is Hippolyta's observation at the start of the last act ("'Tis strange, my Theseus, that these lovers speak of") that sends Theseus into a twenty-one-line harangue against poets, lovers, and madmen, after which she contends that, nevertheless, their stories "grow to great constancy," until the lovers' arrival halts the debate. Finally, during the performance of *Pyramus and Thisby* Hippolyta makes a few cynical observations about the actors before retiring to consummate the marriage.

Actually, my Hippolyta had more lines than this, for, like many other modern directors, I had doubled her part with Titania's—and, for good measure, doubled those of Theseus and Oberon, and old Egeus and Puck. This was part of a larger reading of the play, the "director's concept," that underscores the irony of Theseus, who has no sympathy for anything beyond the pale of his Athenian reason, having a doppelgänger in the King of the Fairies. Hippolyta's problems with the Duke echo on a cosmic scale the quarrel Titania has with Oberon. Like the doubling, that concept suggested that the play itself, our own imaginative collaboration with the playwright, whether as actor, director, or audience, unites the seeming opposites of its comic world: court / forest, left brain / right brain, reason / imagination, male / female, reality / illusion, *homo sapiens / homo ludens.* Peter Brook, to be sure, was just over my shoulder here.

So my Hippolyta was not confined to Hippolyta's lines, and her small part in that opening scene notwithstanding, she would appear moments later in 2.1, charging Oberon with unfound jealousies and swearing to forswear "his bed and company" (62). Still, my experience has been that actors, even when playing double roles, focus on the character at hand, on how to make him or her live and breathe, to *be* something each moment. Valuable to set and lighting designers and to the costumer, the director's concept—that larger reading of the play most resembling the sweeping, after-the-fact interpretations of Shakespeareans—may be a subject for conversation in some Brechtian discussion with the cast after rehearsals, but it is generally avoided by actors. As an actor-friend, who is also a fine Shakespearean scholar, once told me, "When I'm onstage, I'm just trying to make it to the next line. To win the moment both as a character, with a distinct view of the situation, and as an actor aware of the audience just offstage."

-I-

"What should you do?" I asked.

"Yeah, you've got me downstage-left with Theseus, the court upstage, and here comes five new characters, with a complaint that Theseus has to solve—and I've got nothing else to say."

"We'll find the motivation to move you in those opening lines."

I had, of course, my own reading of that ten-line interchange between Theseus and Hippolyta, yet I knew enough to wait for my Theseus and Hippolyta, to see what they would come up with. Now, I must admit at the first read-through with the cast to having colored their approach to some degree by a series of questions I had raised. Hippolyta has been a queen, leader of a band of warrior women in Brazil, bonding with her sisters and not needing the company of men. Theseus brings her back to Athens as his Duchess, but the decision was his, not hers: "Hippolyta, I wooed thee with my sword, / And won thy love, doing thee injuries" (1.1.16–17). How does she feel about this? For her, is going to Athens a step up—or down?

Hippolyta empathizes with the lovers, finding their story "strange" (as in "wondrous"). Theseus feels the need to correct her; his "strange" means "absurd" or "irrational." But after his harangue, she still finds the story "admirable," and while he dismisses the lovers' accounts of the night, all of which agree, despite the fantastic events of which they tell, she insists that the combined stories grow "to something of great constancy" (5.1.1–27). If she agrees with his sense of "strange," she quickly adds her own "admirable." The conversation—debate? would we want to hear more of it? could Theseus stand anymore?—is abruptly halted with the entry of the lovers. So, how harmonious is this couple? To what degree is Hippolyta arguing with, resisting Theseus and his view of what is real or rational? And, more important, if she is resisting, then why?

In act 4 she recalls hunting in the woods of Crete with Hercules and Cadmus, "with hounds of Sparta." Theseus has just proposed to go to the mountaintop and there listen to his own dogs barking in the valley below, their sound one of "musical confusion" (4.1.112–30). With the anticipated consummation on his mind—indeed, on his mind for four days now—Theseus sees the outing as a way to pass the time. But might it also be taken as self-congratulatory? He is proud of having picked his brace of dogs with care, their distinct barks forming a perfect chord on the scale, a chord to be amplified by the echoing hills. He may take Hippolyta's reference to Hercules and Cadmus as name-dropping, her pointed reference to Sparta—famous for its hounds—as competitive. Quick to assert that his hounds are also "bred out of the Spartan kind," he goes on to brag of how low to the ground they run, right on the scent, how they are powerfully built like Thessalian bulls, careful or dogged in pursuit ("slow"). He even expands on the quality of their barking: they are "matched in mouth like bells," and no cry "more tunable" has ever been heard "in Crete, in Sparta, or in Thessaly."

To make this passage something more than scene-painting, or references to hunting that will drive the editor into copious footnotes, to make the passage live onstage, actors will need to find the characters' objects here, their motivations. What are they after? Could it be that Theseus and Hippolyta have two very different objects? Perhaps she relishes her past, life before Theseus came to Brazil, that time when the dogs' barking seemed to link "the groves, / The skies, the fountains, every region near" (118–21) so that nature itself became "all one mutual cry," a moment when opposites were united: "So musical a discord, such sweet thunder."

In effect, here Hippolyta seems at one with the play itself, where dichotomy gives way to unity, where opposites dissolve. For a time the lowly Bottom becomes a fairy queen's lover; youthful, irrational lovers have a mystical experience denied more sober, rational adults like Theseus. And a potential *Romeo and Juliet* (Hermia = Juliet = Thisby; Lysander = Romeo = Pyramus; Old Egeus = Old Capulet) is at once saved by a comic ending in which three couples are married even as it dissolves into an unintentionally funny, poorly acted melodrama staged before the Duke. Theseus' object, again, may be that of asserting his status as a hunter, as a man, annoyed as he is when a woman he has conquered brings up her own days as a huntress. His dogs attest his status. How solid, therefore, is the union of Theseus and Hippolyta? To be sure, Hippolyta is on his turf; yet how cowed is she? As with the debate about the stories in the final scene, the conversation here is aborted when Theseus spies the sleeping Athenians.

How does Theseus view women? Hippolyta? Does he think she "owes" him something for the decision to marry, rather than execute her in Brazil? Does she have any reservations about being here, about giving up her former life?

-II-

Not so much armed with these questions as being willing to entertain them, the three of us (two actors and a director), after an hour or so of "table work" (or discussion before taking the stage), decided to *try*—for rehearsals are periods of experimentation, as signaled by the well-worn phrase "the rehearsal process"—the following objectives in the play's opening moment.

Theseus is dying to consummate the marriage; his first word "Now" rides a subtext something like: "I want you *now,* not four days from now. I deserve your body; you owe me that much for I could have left you dead in Brazil." He alternates between exposing his private desires and being socially discrete. So, one second the sexual act he yearns for is euphemized as a "nuptial hour," the next as a slow horse drawing on "apace." The moon—feminine, the goddess of chastity, Hippolyta's former symbol—bears the brunt of his anger born out of frustration: while four "happy days" will bring in the new moon of the marriage night, the fact is that tonight's moon wanes too slowly. The mutual "nuptial act" of the first line shrinks to "my desires," as if only Theseus' own sexual satisfaction were now at issue. Most telling is the clumsy metaphor with which he describes his condition. He is the young man, living with a maiden aunt, waiting for the old lady to die so he can collect his inheritance, yet she goes on living and living, and with each passing day uses up the money he thinks rightfully his for having endured life with a "stepdame, or a dowager."

A director-friend wryly observes, "Any actor can say lines. The real test is what to do onstage when you aren't speaking." As Theseus speaks, Hippolyta—at least in our construction of the moment, with the caveat that our option is just one of many—thinks to herself subtextually: "I gave up Brazil for this? This isn't that handsome would-be conqueror-turned-lover who swept me off my feet. Here's a self-centered MCP, concerned about *his* glands, his sexual satisfaction. As if I didn't exist! As if I, a woman, had no desires, no needs of my own! Well, I can't go back to Brazil. Here's a world where males have all the power. I'm a survivor. I'm stuck here. Let's see what I can do to soften this self-absorbed lover."

As we staged it, Hippolyta moved toward Theseus with "Four days will quickly steep themselves in night," saying, in effect: "It's only four days, not twelve, not twenty, and so the time will pass relatively quickly for *both* of us. Don't forget, it's four days for me as well." She gets no response from Theseus, even though she appeals to his accountant's mentality with "four days." Self-centered, Theseus has turned away from her on "young man's revenue." His visual, gestural subtext is a crude, petulant one: "If I have to wait too much longer, if these four days continue to pass so slowly, to draw on 'apace,' I'll become old with frustration, withered, impotent." The fact is that Hippolyta also looks forward to the consummation or—to be more accurate—*was* looking forward to it, yet her first concern here is Theseus. She ups the stakes, this time putting a consoling, almost maternal hand on his shoulder as she doubles her reassurance to him: "Four nights will quickly dream away the time." But Theseus is not to be consoled, and, somewhat irritated by him, in part giving up, she crosses downstage-right to find some space of her own, as she unleashes her own metaphor of the sexual act, as expansive, as beautiful, as "poetic" as Theseus' was constrictive, mundane, "un-poetic." For Hippolyta, the wished-for wedding night is not something owed, or her right, but, as she returns to her roots as a huntress, one where the male is the silver bow, bent and about to discharge, the consummation (their "solemnities") taking place under the moon's watchful eye.

Does he hear her own erotic hymn to the marriage night? Does she even care at this point? All that we know is that Theseus, rather than responding to her, barks out orders to Philostrate. My Theseus linked the moon and, by implication, Hippolyta's serene, cosmic picture with melancholy. He'll have none of this "pale companion," but wants, instead, a public celebration. Thinking Hippolyta is still at his side, not having noticed that she had left his presence after he rejected her attempts to console him, he turns around, expecting to find her on his right. She, instead, has now strolled to far downstage-right, with the results that his "I wooed thee . . . with reveling," spoken over a void, lacks intimacy. My Theseus added the following subtext to his paradox of war's turning to love, the initial plan to do "injuries" to a wedding "in another key": "I'm not sure just why you left my side. Is something bothering you? I can't imagine what. Surely, *I've* done nothing. If anything, you *owe* me your constant presence. I'll have to handle this later because here come Egeus and the lovers—I know he's going to insist that I support Demetrius for Hermia's hand."

Thus, by working with the two actors, by allowing them to establish this dark cloud in the relationship between Theseus and Hippolyta, one that would not dissolve until four days later when, Theseus' anxieties gone, they could enjoy a play together before going to bed, we had found the motivation for Hippolyta's cross, getting her out of the way in time for Egeus' angry entrance. She would have no more lines—that is true—but now, in her own "space" downstage-right, she could observe Theseus, assess him, sympathizing with her "sister" Hermia, as Theseus, supporting her crabbed father, delivers the ultimatum: either marry the man of your father's choice, or be sent to a nunnery or—worse yet—your death. Careful not to upstage the actors to her left, she could still "speak" with her face, her posture, a slight gesture or two. Her expressions implied: "So this is what Athens is like, this world where males have all the power? From what I see, Helena looks like a perfectly fine woman. (Hippolyta would even exchange glances with both Helena and Hermia.) Why would Demetrius reject her? Lysander and Demetrius look like generic, eligible young men, handsome, intelligent, equal in every way. Why can't Egeus be content with Lysander?"

With his frail body plagued by arthritis, unsteady on his feet, our Egeus brought onstage an enormous large black law book, so large that it dwarfed him and he had great difficult carrying it. On "And, my gracious Duke" (38), he managed to unload the volume on Theseus, who later, on "Either to die the death, or to abjure" (65), turned to the specific section where these harsh edicts were inscribed. I suggested that halfway through the conversation between the Duke and Hermia, Hippolyta cross to stage-left and, while the Duke was talking to Hermia on the left, take the volume from him, crossing back with it to her downstage-right position. She chose Theseus' "For disobedience to your father's will" (87) for that cross. Absorbed in his conversation with Hermia, Theseus could still feel her lift the book from his right arm, would catch her in the periphery of his eye and, distracted by Hippolyta, falter a bit on his next line. His subtext here was something like: "I'm not sure why you interrupted me the middle of my talk with Hermia. Why would you, a woman, want to look at a law book? Well, I can't deal with this now; we'll talk about it later—in private." As our stage manager suggested, Theseus has something of the E. F. Hutton mentality: when he speaks, everyone listens. Now back in her space downstage-right, Hippolyta could thumb through the law book, reading there a confirmation of her suspicions about Theseus' supposedly brave new world. Every once in awhile she would look up from her reading, sympathizing with her sisters, feeling for Lysander, looking contemptuously at Egeus and Demetrius, and—most certainly—showing increasing doubts about the man who, at the top of the scene, had reminded her of the consummation four days away.

One day in rehearsal Hippolyta accidentally slammed the law book shut on Theseus' "Or else the law of Athens yields you up" (119), making a sound that, given the size of the book, boomed across the stage. Startled, the actor playing Theseus looked in her direction, and I promptly suggested that he deliver the next line to Hippolyta (they were twenty-five feet apart): "Which by no means we may extenuate." With the line said to Hippolyta rather than Hermia, Theseus' subtext was: "Why did you slam that book, right in the middle of my speech? Why did you take it in the first place? Don't you understand that I'm just doing my job. I can't ignore or water down ('extenuate') the law. I'm the Duke. It's my job to enforce the laws in that book you're reading. What I personally think about the law is not relevant. We'll speak about this later."

He crossed stage-right to Hippolyta on "Come, my Hippolyta" (122); his line to her, "What cheer, my love?" had the modern sense of: "Why so glum? Why out of spirits?" After his final four lines, where he promises to confer with Egeus and Demetrius on "something nearly that concerns" them, Theseus, facing upstage with his profile to stage-right, offered his left arm to Hippolyta, his eyes saying: "It's time to go, and I need to discuss this strange behavior of yours as soon as we are in private quarters." Turning toward him, her profile to stage-left, Hippolyta, instead of linking her arm with his as he expected, put the law book in Theseus' left hand, the action speaking loudly: "Snuggle up with that tonight, honey." He glared at her, angry that she was embarrassing him in front of the courtiers, who were now whispering among themselves on stage-left. Then she glanced down at whatever women were in the front row's audience left—we added this Brechtian touch the second week of rehearsals—as if addressing them: "Sisters, this male will wait an eternity for me until I give him my right arm [Theseus had since passed the book to his right arm and was conspicuously holding his left arm open in invitation]. What do you think I should do? What would you do, if you were I?" Then, much to Theseus' relief but, by the delay, asserting her integrity and such power as a woman could have in this patriarchal world, she gave him her arm so they could exit.

-III-

Not coming out of a vacuum, still, my actress's "What do I do now?" had been the first in a chain of events, options, experiments that, taken together, pushed our *A Midsummer Night's Dream* toward a feminist concept, or statement (in critical terms). Here the women, especially Hippolyta and Titania, were at the play's imaginative center, able to entertain the idea of a world beginning with but expanding far beyond Athens, a world where dichotomies of the genders, of reason and imagination, reality and illusion, were dissolved. Earlier scholarship on the play had stressed the conflict between reason and passion. It saw the play as a debate, the rational Theseus as the center of value, Bottom with his ass's head representing the absurd depth to which man sinks when he abandons Athens.[2] In the 1960s Jan Kott would challenge that judgment: Athens and Theseus are the establishment, a constraint on our imagination; the trip into the forest, far from being a step down, as earlier readings would hold, is a step up. For Kott, Theseus' kingdom represents the "censorship of the day," the forest "the erotic madness liberated by night."[3] There, in the darkness, however fleeting on this summer solstice, men and women discover their true selves. Without negating either of these readings, our production offered another option—just another option and nothing more: a single, expansive world, embracing dichotomies, constructed of both reason and the imagination, merging them into a whole greater than the sum of its two parts.

But I stress, again, that word "option," for the theater as I see it, does not argue, let alone prove; it explores, tests out possibilities, stages and includes rather than argues against or excludes. Even as Shakespeare played on such sources as he had for *A Midsummer Night's Dream,* the director and actors play on Shakespeare, and their performance is in turn played out before an audience, who come to it with their own agendas, their own needs and idiosyncrasies.[4]

The option we had chosen shaped the rest of the production. That area downstage-right soon became a "woman's place," a retreat from the male world, an area of imagination or introspection occupied only by the women. With its own special lighting, no male in the cast was allowed to occupy it.

-IV-

Given the doubling, the tension between Theseus and Hippolyta, as we had staged it in the opening scene, returned in 2.1 as the quarrel over the changeling boy between Oberon and Titania (118–43). His three and a half lines demanding that she hand over the boy offer the actor, if not the scholar, a wonderful challenge. Oberon's strategy here changes from demanding the boy for no other reason than that women, in his view, do whatever men tell them to do ("Do you amend it, then; it lies in you"), to a rather childish question expressing his shock that a woman would behave so unwomanly ("Why should Titania cross her Oberon?"), to what must seem to Oberon a compromising of his demand with a justification: he isn't asking for the moon but only for "a little changeling boy." Like his other half, Theseus, Oberon speaks here with the posture of male superiority, but he cannot know how much, and why, Titania values the changeling boy. her "Set your heart at rest" had something of the blue-collar television character Archie Bunker's "Stifle it!" With "The fairy land buys not the child of me" our Titania rose and started to cross to that woman's spot downstage-right. As she did, we took the lights off Oberon center–stage, so that the ensuing speech became something of a soliloquy, an introspective moment Titania shared directly with the audience, especially any women on audience-left. She would not cross back to Oberon—nor would full stage lighting return—until the speech's coda: "And for her sake do I rear up her boy, / And for her sake I will not part with him." The equation she makes between a ship, its hold full of cargo, its sails puffed out by "the wanton wind" looking like a pregnant woman, with a pregnant woman who resembles a ship "rich with merchandise" was at one with that union of seeming dichotomies informing our production, from the doubling of roles to the questions raised in Theseus' character about the limits of reason and the significance of the imagination. Like that of Hippolyta in 4.1, Titania's vision is one of union, "all one mutual cry," as the inanimate ship is linked with the doubly animate pregnant woman. No less, Titania recalls an exquisite moment when two women bonded, one mortal and heavy with child, the other supernatural. The changeling boy is the sign of that bonding, and, Titania's explanation completed, Oberon's reply must be, for her, tawdry and grating: "How long within this wood intend you stay?" A businessman, like Theseus with his "young man's revenue," Oberon focuses only on schedules and time allotment! He has heard nothing she has said; little wonder that he cannot understand the boy's true value and meaning.

-V-

"A court scene at the start and the end, surrounding the main set in the forest"—this was the set designer's pithy assessment of his task. And he was right. In our production, the play began in a rigid, unimaginative male world, where cranky fathers, backed up by authority figures who, being lovers as well, ought to know better, control their daughters—a revisiting of *Romeo and Juliet,* which Shakespeare's company was possibly performing around the same time (1595). The intervening forest world, what Helen Gardner would call "a green world,"[5] is neither male nor female but one of dissolutions and mergings, fludity, rich confusion, a world that Bottom struggles to recall and in his failure recalls eloquently, however unintentionally: an indistinct place, a dream "past the wit of man to say what dream it was," where eyes can hear and ears see, a place profound "because it hath no bottom" (4.1.298–309). It is, above all, a world where opposites, antitheses, categories, hierarchies—all are abolished: the lowly, half-ass Bottom is loved by the Queen of the Fairies; the rejected Helena is for a time pursued by two men; compounds such as Peaseblossom and Mustardseed take animate form while humans in turn are reduced to a kind of arithmetic where "two of both kind makes up four" (3.2.438). It can be a magical world for men as well as for women, or rather for the man who, recognizing the "woman" in him, celebrates his own feelings and intuition, and even the irrational—a world for the male lover that Theseus himself is, when he isn't playing the patriarchal tyrant. Appropriately, Bottom, who gains entrance to this world, specializes, as he tells us, in playing both lovers and tyrants—though his preference is for the tyrant.

When the court world returns in the final act, it too is changed, transformed by our mutual journey—whether we be actor, character, or audience—through that intervening forest world. Our lighting designer signaled the change with a subdued, more suggestive atmosphere, as did the costume designer who replaced the sterile, Star Trek-like uniforms of the opening scene with multicolored, softer evening attire.

In 4.1 Egeus demands "The law, the law upon [Lysander's] head" for having robbed Demetrius of a bride and himself of the right to dispose of his daughter (4.1.157–62). But it is a gentler, kinder Theseus who now dismisses the old man, whose character has not changed, with a simple, "Egeus, I will overbear your will." Theseus, and Hippolyta no less, can be cynical and condescending about the actor's performance, yet the Duke has also mellowed somewhat, suggesting that "If we imagine no worse of them than they of themselves, they may pass for excellent men" (5.1.216–17). His anxieties of four days ago replaced by thoughts of the imminent consummation, concerns with his own needs or more serious matters now diverted by the amateur production, Theseus is—in a phrase—more human, less the tyrant who earlier could not extenuate the laws of Athens. Now he is just another lover, one among five lovers, watching a poorly staged play about tragic lovers that reminds us, if not its onstage aristocratic audience, of the *Romeo and Juliet* that *A Midsummer Night's Dream* would have become if it had not been for the forest. Theseus' other half, Oberon, has also reconciled with his Titania; the initial source of their contention, the changeling boy, is now his, without any explanation from playwright or character. In that final scene our Hippolyta had no problem with her lines or with her stage position. There would be no quarrelsome old men or frustrated lovers to rush on and upstage her. In her own words, "I like Theseus a little better in the final act."

I did give her one unvoiced "line" in the closing moments. Holding what well may be "Bottom's Dream," the epilogue, as told to Quince, he promised to deliver at Thisby's death "peradventure to make it the more gracious" (4.1.221–22), Bottom steps out of his role as Pyramus to ask the Duke if he would like "to see the epilogue" (again, as in 4.1, confusing eyes and ears). Eager to get to bed, joking with his fellow aristocrats about the wretched performance that is beyond excuse—though the thick-witted Bottom takes the barbs as compliments—Theseus has no time for an epilogue. Then, he suddenly reverses himself by taking Bottom's second choice, a Bergomask dance. Why, we asked, would he do this? After all, he is eager to consummate the marriage, has been eager for four days, and the dance will take at least as much time as an epilogue. The Duke, once again, is being selfish. In our production, Hippolyta, noticing how eager Bottom is to honor theatrical tradition by adding an epilogue or a dance, as a sort of aesthetic "chaser" to the performance, crossed to her husband. More sensitive to the feelings of others than the Duke, however mellow he may be at this point, Hippolyta whispered something in her husband's ear, to the effect: "Look at that poor man. He wants to add something. Be kind. If you don't want the epilogue, at least let him dance." Eager to please his wife, acknowledging this small display of her power or rights, he concedes, first asking for the Bergomask and then, saving face, adding "Let your epilogue alone."

Perhaps a hopeful sign that Hippolyta will continue to assert herself, is in scenes beyond what Shakespeare has given us? Still, it is unfortunate that Theseus declined the epilogue, because *if* it did chart Bottom's "translation" in the forest and *if*—a big "if" here—Theseus were attentive and willing to consider its message, then he would have heard—or, rather, "seen"—an account of that larger imaginative reality, dwarfing his own Athens, which would have radically altered his attitude toward everything from reason to the imagination. But this is to speak of a play we do not have. It is enough that Theseus, perhaps at his wife's urging (the option chosen in our production), is willing for a few minutes to forego his own pleasure, his desires that have been "lingered" since the opening scene, to watch a dance by actors—*fellow* actors, if he only knew the truth of his own imaginative reality.

-VI-

My actress's "What do I do now?" came back to haunt me in the staging of *Pyramus and Thisby.* This time I was the one delivering that line, and yet once again a seeming problem became a challenge that, in turn, both affected and was at one with the concept of the production. The producer had told us in no uncertain terms that he could afford only eight Equity actors for the production. "You'll have to double or eliminate parts, or do whatever you can—just keep it to eight." This was fine with me since I had wanted to show the rational Theseus' other, magical side in Oberon, as well as the irony of having a single actor play both the imaginative Puck and that legalist Egeus, who can think of no other reason for Hermia's choice than Lysander's having bewitched "her fantasy" with everything from "feigning voice" to "knacks, trifles, nosegays, sweetmeats, [and] messengers" (1.1.28–34).

Besides, doubling Hippolyta and Titania would give focus to the feminist motif of the production. In a larger sense, doubling would call attention to the play's insistent metadramatics that underscored multiple role-playing, the limits of realism and the virtues of imagination, and the presence of the stage (even if it be parodied in the Quince-Bottom production). In the final scene we watch Puck and Oberon watch Theseus and his court watch a wretched production of *Pyramus and Thisby.* Secure in his realism, condescending to attend a stage performance that for him serves only "to ease the anguish of a torturing hour" (5.1.37), Theseus cannot know that he himself owes his life to the theater.[6] Like Bottom's confusion of the five senses, the rustics' inability to separate stage and reality—they fear the ladies will confuse Snug with a real lion, and they bring on a character to designate moonshine as an aid to the audience's imagination—is also a virtue, when compared to Theseus' own rigid distinction between the two.

Only Bottom (Pyramus in the inner-play) could not effectively be doubled with any other character. However, besides the doubling of Theseus and Oberon, Hippolyta and Titania, Egeus would be Puck and Snug (Lion in the inner-play); Lysander, Flute (Thisby in the inner-play) and Cobweb; Hermia, Robin Starveling (Moonshine in the inner-play); Helena, Tom Snout (Wall in the inner-play) and Mustardseed; and Demetrius, Quince (Prologue in the inner-play). We deleted Moth and gave Philostrate's lines to Egeus in the final scene.[7] We could not afford the luxury of "Other Fairies attending their King and Queen" or "Attendants on Theseus and Hippolyta." To stress the multiple role playing, and the larger fact, as Bert O. States suggests,[8] that an audience responds both to the story and its enactment, both to theme and the actor's craft, we made little attempt to disguise characters. Indeed, when Theseus came onstage shortly after Oberon's exit in 4.1, Oberon simply froze in position, without leaving the stage, while a stagehand brought in the "Theseus robe," which was then, in full view of the audience, exchanged for the "Oberon robe."

In the final scene there were only Theseus and Hippolyta to constitute the onstage audience, since Hermia, Helena, Lysander, Demetrius, and Egeus would join Bottom in *Pyramus and Thisby.* Curiously, Hermia and Helena have no lines in this scene; I reassigned those of Lysander and Demetrius to that "audience" of two.

Egeus (or Philostrate) makes no commentary during the performance. To preserve some sense of illusion, we had planned to have Egeus (assuming Philostrate's lines) exit with Theseus' "Go, bring them in; and take your places, ladies" (84). He would not return; we deleted Philostrate's line on his re-entrance, "So please your Grace, the Prologue is addressed" (106), and changed Theseus' "Let him approach" to "I see the Prologue approaches." This, of course, allowed Egeus to go backstage and change into Snug's Lion costume. Demetrius stood close to the upstage-right exit and during Theseus' long speech before the Prologue enters ("The kinder we, to give them thanks for nothing" [106]), he would exit and change into Quince's Prologue costume. As he emerged from stage-left for his "If we offend, it is with our good will" (108), stage-right would be darkened, allowing Hermia, Helena, and Lysander to exit unseen, change into the costumes of Moonshine, Wall, and Thisby, and be ready, with time to spare, for their stage-left entrances. (I should add that since Snug, doubled with Puck, has no lines in the rehearsal scene, which Puck interrupts, I simply did not bring him onstage in 3.1.) At the end of *Pyramus and Thisby,* Theseus and Hippolyta could cross to the lit stage-left side for his "No epilogue, I pray you" (including her "whispered" line that he should at least let the actors do a Bergomask dance). His call to the other two couples ("Sweet friends, to bed" [307]) would only imply that Lysander, Hermia, Demetrius, and Helena were still on stage-right. Theseus and Hippolyta would exist stage-left, as did the actors after the Bergomask dance, with Snug's (formerly Egeus) having just enough time to change into his Puck costume to and re-emerge stage-right for "Now the hungry lion roars" (373). That speech would in turn allow Theseus and Hippolyta to be recostumed as Oberon and Titania, with Peaseblossom, Mustardseed, and Cobweb returning for the "song and dance" promised by the now united King and Queen of the fairies.

In a production eschewing illusion or, conversely, calling attention to the art of the theater through its obvious doubling, our one moment of illusion here in the final scene depended, therefore, on darkening stage-right to the degree that two actors would be able to represent an audience of seven. The darkened stage was also essential since, with the exception of the "hunting scene" (4.1), here within a single scene actors would need to make unseen exits as one character and visible entrances as another.

We had rehearsed for four weeks in a hall some blocks from the Florida Theatre; because of other productions, we would not be able to rehearse on its stage until three days before opening night.

The lighting director had been assured that the facilities were "top-notch," the board itself "*almost* state-of-the-art." The day we moved to the main stage, however, he told us the bad news. Mounted on the high ceiling above the house were five lights, relics of the theater's vaudeville days, that were essential for our basic stage lighting but which could not be adjusted during a production so that half the stage would be dark. Given the lights' primitive state, it was all or nothing with them. The real audience would therefore be able to see that our onstage audience excluded the four young lovers and Egeus; nor would darkness conceal their exits to reappear in *Pyramus and Thisby.* Our one attempt at full-blown illusion—"stage magic," to invoke the cliché—was doomed.

Having launched our voyage now rich with theatrical "discoveries"—a word dear to actors and directors, signaling that moment when some combination of thought, emotion, accident, and necessity suggests a new slant on a character or the delivery of a line—our Hippolyta came to the rescue. "You know, we haven't done much to pull the wool over their [the audience's] eyes; why worry now?" She was right. Not trying to use costumes as a disguise, rejoicing in multiple role-playing, celebrating that blurred line between onstage and off, allowing actors to address the audience directly in that special "woman's spot" downstage-right—hadn't we been doing everything possible to include the audience in the production, to make them collaborators in such illusion as our meager stage and small cast could afford? Why worry now? Why not ask the audience to make the ultimate in imaginative collaborations with the actor and director—to believe in an invisible audience (shades of Ionesco's *The Chairs*!), to "allow" five actors to change characters before their eyes?

Therefore, we would not darken stage-right—a conscious decision that usurped whatever necessity had forced on us. The actors would not go backstage to change into rustic actors; instead, they would cross to stage-left and change costumes in full view of the audience. After all, we had set a precedent in the onstage costume changes of Oberon/Theseus and Titania/Hippolyta in 4.1.

Denying the illusion of an aristocratic audience watching a production by their social inferiors would, paradoxically, only underscore the potency of the theater. What we know is an illusion, a fraud, is still significant, for the change from frustrated to requited love is a wished-for event in our own reality, where patriarchs, a rigid legal system, or conflicts between reason and the heart are all too common. Confessing the patent unreality of the stage, as we would be doing, only made of it an "honest woman" or "man."

The titles of Shakespeare's plays themselves beg us to dismiss them as of no or little consequence, a mere *Midsummer Night's Dream,* something *As You Like It* or *What You Will,* little more than a *Winter's Tale* told by the fire. For Genet, such theatrical honesty distinguishes the stage from life; for the latter, which is nothing but role playing, mistakenly assumes that it is real and thereby superior to the theater.[9] The confession of illusion is inseparable from the theater's celebration of its own significance, for the stage characters have been enacted by fellow humans, with their own life stories, needs, and desires. Taking place in space and time, the production is witnessed, ratified by fellow humans in the house, occupying precisely that same space and time. In this sense, the theater is the most real, the most tangible and literal of the arts. However impoverished, *Pyramus and Thisby* only reminds us of what would have been the lovers' fate—what is often our own fate—in a world without dreams, where there is no forest of transformation or potentiality. Theater itself is a two-way process, where the audience as well as the actor have a vital role. Or, as I tell my own actors, to be onstage speaking lines with no audience in the house is to be in rehearsal only, not in a production. Their presence validates ours; the ascription works both ways.

By design, by necessity, we had asked the audience to assist us in the production of *A Midsummer Night's Dream.* Onstage, humans had acknowledged the presence of fellow humans offstage. Now, with an audience in the house watching an audience onstage watch a performance, we were pushing that collaboration to the limits. I believe it worked. Or, as one audience member said to me, "Watching that actor who played Demetrius rush across that stage and become Quince . . . well, you know, you made me feel that we were all in it together. If you were willing to make believe, so were we." Another audience member put it more succinctly: "I felt that I was a part of the performance."

"What do I do now?" The actress's question, for me, describes the mutual role of actor and audience. For the actor portrays a character who, not knowing the story, must live and breathe line by line, can know only the "now" as he or she pushes his or her object through dialogue with fellow characters. Likewise, the audience, even if they know the story, know how the play turns out, nevertheless abandon such omniscience—at least, in a production that captures their interest—and respond beat by beat with that illusory character onstage who, a fraud, mere words, words, words, reminds them of and, in a more profound way, represents themselves. I have asked myself that same question—"What do I do now?"—in all of the plays, Shakespearean and otherwise, I have directed since *A Midsummer Night's Dream.*

Notes

1. *A Midsummer Night's Dream* was produced by the Fable Factory in Gainesville, Florida, in February 1985. By a lucky coincidence I also co-directed a production of *Romeo and Juliet* at the Hippodrome State Theatre the next month, and thus had the experience of being involved with two plays which, most likely, Shakespeare's own company had staged—perhaps back to back—in 1595. The text for *A Midsummer Night's Dream* is edited by Wolfgang Clemen in *The Complete Signet Classic Shakespeare,* gen. ed. Sylvan Barnet (New York: Harcourt, 1972).

2. For studies celebrating Theseus and his reason over the imaginative forest see Paul Olson, "*A Midsummer Night's Dream* and the Meaning of Court Marriage," *English Literary History* 24 (1957): 113; Peter F. Fisher, "The Argument of *A Midsummer Night's Dream,*" *Shakespeare Quarterly* 8 (1957): 307–10; and E. C. Pettet, *Shakespeare and the Romance Tradition* (London and New York: Staples Press, 1949), 234.

3. Jan Kott, *Shakespeare Our Contemporary* (Garden City, N.Y.: Doubleday, 234.

4. Marvin Rosenberg's books on Shakespeare's four great tragedies, besides proving invaluable to people working in the theater as each traces the play's onstage history, also remind us of a very basic distinction between actual theater practice and literary criticism of Shakespeare. Too much of dramatic criticism seems caught up in "search-and-destroy" syndrome, the assumption being that there is a single "mystery" at the heart of each play which, despite efforts of past critics, the present critic can best solve. Put another way, the assumption is that the world of the play, as reconstructed by a particular critical approach—an approach, I should add, that usually treats the play as literature rather than as something meant for enactment in a theater—is somehow more significant than worlds fashioned by other methods, especially those no longer in fashion. However, as Rosenberg records and comments on the numerous options that directors, over the centuries, have exercised in the staging of the plays, and the choices made by actors challenged with giving that illusory theatrical "life" to characters who are otherwise just words on the page, he shows us, instead, how theater practice is a collaborative art, one involving playwright, director, actor, and—ultimately—the audience. Here, rather than asserting a single meaning, or the superiority of a particular critical method, the focus is on options, choices, process, and discoveries, both in rehearsal and performance.

5. Helen Gardner, *"As You Like It,"* in *More Talking of Shakespeare,* ed John W. P. Garrett (London: Longmans, 1959), 17–32.

6. I think the best discussion of the play's theatrical commentary and of the division between reason and imagination remain David Young's *Something of Great Constancy: The Art of "A Midsummer Night's Dream"* (New Haven: Yale University Press, 1966); and James Calderwood's *Shakespearean Metadrama: The Argument of the Play in "Titus Andronicus," "Love's Labour's Lost," "Romeo and Juliet," "A Midsummer Night's Dream," and "Richard II"* (Minneapolis: University of Minnesota Press, 1971).

7. See Philip McGuire's discussion of Egeus' presence in the play, particularly in the final act, in "Intentions, Options, and Greatness: An Example from *A Midsummer Night's Dream*," in *Shakespeare and the Triple Play: From Study to Stage to Classroom*, ed. Sidney Homan (Lewisburg: Bucknell University Press, 1988), 177–89.

8. Bert O. States, *Great Reckonings in Little Rooms: On the Phenomenology of Theater* (Berkeley: University of California Press, 1985).

9. Jean Genet, *Reflections on the Theater, and Other Writings*, trans. Richard Sever (London: Faber and Faber, 1972), 79.

Statues: Mary Anderson, Shakespeare, and Statuesque Acting

CARY M. MAZER

"Mary Anderson was no actress."

THUS wrote Bernard Shaw, twice, in reviewing Anderson's 1896 autobiography, *A Few Memories,* in his theater column in *The Saturday Review* (2.85,86). And there is abundant contemporary critical opinion—from the reactions to her London debut in 1883 through retrospective analyses of her acting years after her retirement in 1889—to support Shaw's conclusion (which one should otherwise never take at face value, given the agendas, hidden and otherwise, at work in Shaw's theatrical criticism).

Notwithstanding such devastating criticism, "Our Mary" had an immensely successful career in the theater, drawing a wide circle of admirers along with thousands of paying spectators into the theater. She certainly drew spectators into the theater for her production of *The Winter's Tale,* the third and last of her Shakespearean productions, which opened on 11 September 1887 at the Lyceum Theatre in London, and which ran an entire season of 164 performances (and, she claims in her autobiography, could have run for another 100 had Henry Irving not wanted to reoccupy his theater).

Anderson's performance as Hermione was the capstone of her brief career: her last production, her last new role, her last London appearance. And, as we shall see, after she went on tour with a repertory of her roles the following year, Hermione unexpectedly proved to be the last role in which she appeared onstage.

Hermione serves as a reverberant role through which to examine the art of Mary Anderson, and to examine the ways that her performance and her career served as a nexus of High Victorian critical and theoretical opinion about the art of acting in general, and the art of the *actress*—the much-debated *nature d'actrice*—in particular. For *The Winter's Tale* itself—and the ways that women are represented in the play—comments directly on the nature of woman as person, as performance, and as artistic object. In the final scene, life, death, forgiveness, redemption, and grace are all mediated by a physical body onstage—the statue of Hermione—which, when we and Leontes first gaze upon it, may or may not be Hermione herself. The statue may be either an artistic representation of Hermione—a statue—or else Hermione posing as a statue—a person performing her own body, occupying, like the actress who plays her onstage, a liminal performative space between art and life. And the other principal female character in the play, Perdita—a role also played by Anderson in 1887, doubling the roles of Hermione and Perdita for the first time—participates directly in a lively debate with Polixenes about the relationship between art and nature. Like the circumstances of Mary Anderson's personal life and professional career, *The Winter's Tale* occupies the boundaries between life and art and between emotion and representation, and explores the dangers and moral ambiguities of love and marriage.

There is a further appropriateness to Anderson's farewell role of Hermione and the way that it mirrors the issues raised by her art and career. For Anderson's appearance as a statue at the very end of her short career brackets a similar role that she played at the beginning of it. Stagestruck at a young age, Anderson resolved to enter the theater profession, not as an apprentice but as a star; and she succeeded in this goal through skillful personal management, carefully cultivated connections, and coaching from mentors in the profession. She had been on the professional stage for only six years in her native America when she rented the Lyceum for her first London season, playing roles that were already old-fashioned in 1883: Parthenia in *Ingomar;* Pauline in *The Lady of Lyons,* and, most significantly, Galatea in W. S. Gilbert's 1871 comedy, *Pygmalion and Galatea*—yet another statue that comes to life.

There is an odd appropriateness to Anderson's fame in playing two statues, for the contemporary theatergoers who wrote about her, pro and con, frequently discuss her acting in terms of statuary. The actress, they write, is strikingly beautiful, tall, slightly remote, oddly cold, marmoreal, emotionally inept, inexpressive, or perhaps even insincere. Even her supporters used the imagery of statues. Lord Lytton ("Owen Meredith"), writing in *The Nineteenth Century* in a lengthy defense of her 1884 Juliet, praised her expressiveness ("a play of countenance which, without the aid of voice or gesture, expresses in rapid alternation, tenderness, scorn, sorrow, terror, and dream reverie"); but he reserved special praise for her statuesque stillness: most actors, he writes, "seem incapable of expressing emotion without movement, and whenever they are not in movement they are awkward. Miss Anderson is able to express strong feeling without moving a limb" (quoted in Shattuck, 106).

The statuary imagery associated with Mary Anderson's acting is in part a document of what Michael Booth, Nina Auerbach, and others have described as "pictorial acting," the organization of histrionic effects around discrete poses, pictorial compositions, and iconographic allusions to contemporary visual arts. And there is certainly substantial evidence, in Anderson's Shakespearean performances, of her organizing her performances around effective pictorial moments, either static or mobile, which replace both verbal delivery (though Anderson was said to have a lovely, powerful yet "feminine," rich contralto voice) and dramatic interaction with other characters. Lytton catalogues several such moments from Anderson's 1884 Juliet: Juliet's first entrance, pulling aside a curtain revealing herself standing on a stair framed by an arched doorway; her leaning over the balcony "in an attitude of passionate and tender yearning, her hair falling loose over her neck, and her arms folded as already clasping the deer prize of her bosom" (quoted in Shattuck, 106); a macabre moment after Juliet stabs herself, in which she snuggles tenderly in the arms of her dead husband; and her famous fall, at the end of the potion speech, with her head hanging upside down, eyes open, over the downstage edge of the bed. Similarly, more column inches seem to have been spent in describing Anderson's costumes as Rosalind and Ganymede in *As You Like It* (Stratford and on tour, 1885) than in describing her performance (see Derrick).

Anderson's performances in *The Winter's Tale* seem to have been organized around grandly pictorial moments: the game of feigned terror that Hermione plays with Mamilius as he tries to tell her a ghost story; and another equally famous fall when, on hearing the news of Mamilius' death, Hermione suddenly wraps her veil around her head and falls lifeless to the floor, bringing down the curtain with her (Leontes' reaction to the news and his subsequent recantation were cut, and the act ended with Hermione's fall).[1] Anderson made her entrance as Perdita dancing with the other shepherds and shepherdesses. And in the statue scene, Hermione's statue was concealed behind a red curtain at the top of a flight of marble stairs (in the scenery designed by Anderson's friend and admirer, Alma Tadema); when the curtain opened, the audience could now see that the stairs continued upward into the distance behind her, as the statue slowly descended toward the prostrate Leontes, the stand-in with her back to the audience now filling in for Perdita, and the expectant audience.[2] The pictorial effect of these moments was evidently considerable. G. C. D. Odell called Perdita's entrance "one of the imperishable memories of all who saw it" (*Shakespeare,* 2:383). And he wrote about the descent of the statue twice: in *Annals of the New York Stage* he noted rhapsodically that "Mary Anderson's descent of those steps, arrayed as she was in inconceivable beauty of feature, form, and costume, was a sight to be experienced but rarely in this life. I have, in fact, never seen anything like it, before or since" (14:18–19). In *Shakespeare from Betterton to Irving,* he gushed: "And what a statue! Mary Anderson in the prime of her classic beauty, posed as only she could pose! As she slowly came down those steps, she presented a picture given to any generation to behold hardly more than once" (2:437–48).

The pictorial vocabulary of Anderson's acting style was by no means unique to her. But it is, I think, significant how Anderson incorporated this vocabulary into a "statuary" aesthetic of generalized—and generically *feminine*—mood, tone, and character. Critics who faulted her emotional connectedness and expressiveness were tacitly recognizing that the representationally and iconographically generic was being made to substitute for the psychologically specific. Juliet's innocence, her devoted (and, needless to say, chaste) love for Romeo, Rosalind's girlishness, Rosalind's boyishness, Hermione's wronged innocence (not a "tragic queen," one critic observed, but "a gentle loving woman" [quoted in Shattuck, 109]), Perdita's virginal innocence, were so many stages of being to be represented (rather than "personated," to use a Victorian pre-Stanislavskian word for emotional and psychological embodiment) through a wash of general demeanor and pictorial attitude.

The first of the two statues in Anderson's repertoire is illustrative of this emotional-waxworks histrionic technique. The comedy of Gilbert's play depends upon the contrast between the worldly banter of Pygmalion, his wife, and his patrons on the one hand, and on the other hand Galatea, the statue come to life, who participates in the events of this world with no innate knowledge of it. In her autobiography, Anderson reports that she and Gilbert could not agree about how Galatea should be played. The playwright, Anderson reports, felt that his play was merely "a nineteenth-century comedy dressed in Greek costume," and insisted "that Galatea should speak certain comic speeches with a visible consciousness of their meaning." Anderson, who "had undertaken the part on condition that I should act it according to my own ideas," felt, by contrast, that Galatea, "a statue come to life, could not, it seemed to me, think, look, stand, or speak like an earthly-born maiden; some remnant of the inanimate marble would inevitably linger about her, giving her movements a plastic grace, and to her thoughts and their expression a touch of the ethereal." She writes, "painful and embarrassing as it was for me not to be versatile enough to carry out the brilliant author's wish . . . I felt convinced that my only hope of success was to stamp every word, look, tone, and movement with that ingenuousness which seemed to me the key-note of her nature" (147–48). Note how Anderson distills the "keynote" of the character's "nature" into a physical grace and beauty (appropriately) like that of a statue.

Such is her method with the other characters she plays—even those who, unlike Galatea and Hermione, are not actually statues. In the case of Galatea, the character's otherworldly, statuesque ingenuousness is not only the distilled essence of the role, it is the character's action: at the end of the play, on seeing how her presence in Pygmalion's life has threatened his marriage with his wife Cynisca, Galatea renounces love and life and becomes a statue once more. Similarly, Anderson's statuary distillation of her other characters' essences is transfigured in the plays in which they each appear: Juliet's pure love is enshrined in the immobility of death; Rosalind appears, now virtually silent, as Orlando's bride in the masque of Hymen at the end of *As You Like It;* Hermione dies (or appears to) in the swoon that brings down the curtain in Anderson's truncated version of the trial scene in *The Winter's Tale,* an erect statue of wronged motherly affection toppled by grief; and though at the end of the play the immobile statue of Hermione returns to life and descends Alma Tadema's marble staircase, in Anderson's performance Hermione's descent is more an ascent and transfiguration, the immobile statue becoming an even more rarefied distillation of redemptive wifeliness and motherhood, ascending into transcendent, statuesque life.

Anderson's decision to double the roles of Hermione and Perdita is consistent with the actress's attempt to distill an essence of the character that can be generically and statuesquely represented. In her autobiography Anderson defends the doubling, claiming that the play's relative lack of success in previous productions had been due "to the undue prominence given to several less important characters, and the comparatively short and interrupted appearance of the two heroines, which breaks the continued interest of the spectator. The first difficulty was to cut these secondary parts without marring the beauty and meaning of the text; and the next, to keep alive the sympathies of the audience with both Hermione and Perdita from beginning to end" (244). The sympathies of the audience, then, would be invested in two complementary aspects of a single persona, two manifestations of a feminine principle of honesty, love, and sacrifice, one maternal and wifely, and the other virginal and romantic. Moreover, because the trial scene ended with Hermione's presumably-fatal swoon, and the next act began with Perdita's dancing entrance (Time was cut, and the Autolycus scenes and the exchanges of the Old Shepherd and the Clown were either cut or shifted), Hermione was, in the imagination of the audience, reborn in the person of her own daughter Perdita, embodied by the same actress.

Anderson's aesthetic of doubling is, in this, significantly different from other instances of star-actor doubling on the Victorian stage. In other cases, the star-actor (almost exclusively male) plays radically contrasting roles—the murderer Dubosc and the innocent bourgeois Lesurques in *The Courier of Lyons (The Lyons Mail),* as played by Charles Kean and then by Henry Irving; or Dr. Jekyll and Mr. Hyde, as played by Richard Mansfield and much later by H. B. Irving. In such virtuoso double-performances, the actor asserts that his body and soul contain two radically distinct personalities, just as the respectable Alsatian burgomaster Matthias in *The Bells* contains a second, secret self within capable of murdering and robbing an itinerant Polish Jew. Mary Anderson's body and soul contain no such secret corners or conflicting personae. Her two roles in *The Winter's Tale* are two versions of a single dramatic principle in the form of two dramatic characters, a single statue viewed from two different angles.

Mary Anderson's aesthetic of statuesque representation, and her reputed failure in "personating" the characters she played, came to London at precisely the time that the art of the actor was being articulated and debated, and an ideal of "emotionalist" acting was first being articulated: an English translation of Diderot's anti-emotionalist *Paradox of Acting* appeared in 1883, with a hostile introduction by Henry Irving; in 1887, Coquelin published a pro-Diderot essay in *Harper's Monthly,* initiating a series of responses and counterresponses in various publications by Henry Irving and Dion Boucicault; and William Archer's pro-emotionalist historical and contemporary survey of actors, *Masks or Faces?* appeared in 1888.

Anderson took center stage in these debates, in part due to the role in which she was cast in two polemical works of fiction. In winter 1884, Anderson attended a reception in the house of Mrs. Humphrey Ward, where she met Henry James. In the fall of 1884, Mrs. Humphrey Ward's first novel *Miss Bretherton* appeared, an account of the artistic education and personal development of a beautiful and wildly successful actress, who otherwise lacked the technique, both physical and emotional, to give genuinely soulful performances. Ward had told her friend, Henry James, about the scheme of *Miss Bretherton* when she first conceived it, and James wrote her with his reactions to it when it was first published. *Miss Bretherton* and the issues about acting and the aesthetic and social identity of the actress subsequently served as the jumping-off point for James's own novel about the *nature d'actrice, The Tragic Muse.*

Of these two novels, *Miss Bretherton* is much closer to the issues raised by the paradoxes of Mary Anderson's acting and popularity, and the actress was instantly identified in the press as the model for its title character. The novel narrates the artistic development of a popular young actress, Isabel Bretherton, through the eyes of an intellectual theatergoer, Eustace Kendal. The story begins when Miss Bretherton is already the talk of the town due to her charming personality, her physical grace (which Kendal considers mere "posing" and "attitudinising"), and her great personal beauty. Kendal recognizes in Miss Bretherton a unique temperament that runs much deeper than the actress's superficial onstage personality and a potential for strong emotion (no more so than when she berates him after he tells her honestly what he thinks of her meager acting abilities); but he also sees that the actress is shallow and vulgar, has no technique, and is incapable of channeling her emotions or her real "self" through the roles she is playing onstage. He concludes: "an actress must have one of the two kinds of knowledge: she must have either the knowledge which comes from fine training—in itself the outcome of a long tradition—or she must have the knowledge which comes from mere living, from the accumulation of personal thought and experience. Miss Bretherton had neither" (58).

The central section of the novel focuses on Miss Bretherton's acquisition of these two types of knowledge. The actress moves to the continent—free from the English temperament and from the English public's obsession with personality and charm—and studies under the tutelage of Kendal's sister and her French husband, Paul, a devotee of Diderot. From her sojourn on the continent Miss Bretherton acquires culture and refinement. From Paul she learns technique; and once she learns to use that technique to channel her own emotions into her acting, she is equipped to reject Paul's anti-emotionalist theories (playing Juliet's potion speech effectively for the first time, she shouts "Diderot is wrong, wrong, wrong!" [202]). Finally, from Kendal's sister—particularly, toward the end of the novel, when the sister dies—she learns to have genuine, womanly emotions to channel into her art. Seeing Miss Bretherton's superior acting on her return to the London stage, Kendal is inspired by the actress's emotional expressiveness to get in touch with his own emotions and discovers that he is in love. Miss Bretherton's acting is now so in tune with her emotions that it begins to take its toll on her physical stamina, and she faints in the middle of a performance. Kendal and Miss Bretherton come together at the end of the novel, sharing their grief for the dead sister. Now that they are each in touch with the passions that the actress's emotionalist acting has taught them both to express, they resolve to marry, and Miss Bretherton resolves to leave the stage.

Midway through Miss Bretherton's training, Kendal's sister writes to him about her progress: "Personally, there seems to be the stuff in her on which an actress is made; will she someday stumble upon the discovery of how to bring her own individual flame and force to bear upon her art?" (182). *Miss Bretherton* seems to be asking the same question about Mary Anderson. The title character of the novel makes the necessary discovery before she leaves the stage; indeed, her discovery is what leads her to decide to leave the stage: to be a real actor, and to be a woman, is so physically and emotionally taxing that one must cease doing it. Anderson, evidently, never did, retiring from the stage before she ever stumbled upon the discovery.

The stories of Isabel Bretherton and Mary Anderson appear to diverge on this point. But, according to Henry James at least, they are nonetheless following very similar paths. In Mrs. Humphrey Ward's novel, Miss Bretherton learns to act and learns to love at the same time; her decision to leave the stage for marriage is not a rejection of her art but its triumph, for once she has opened herself to genuine emotions, she is equipped to choose a more fulfilling, less debilitating, and less public arena for their expression. But for James, the ending ruined his ability to believe in Miss Bretherton as an actress; he wrote to Mrs. Humphrey Ward on 19 December 1884, after he finished reading *Miss Bretherton:*

> Isabel, the Isabel you describe, has too much to spare for Kendal—Kendal being what he is; and one doesn't feel her, see her, enough, as

> the pushing actress, the *cabotine.* She lapses toward him as if she were a failure, whereas you make her out a great success. No, she wouldn't have thought so much of him, at such a time as that,—though very possibly she would have come back to him later. You have endeavoured to make us feel her "respectability" at the same time as her talent, her artistic nature, but in taking care to preserve the former, you have rather sacrificed the latter. (Quoted in Gordon and Stokes, 120)

The key here is "respectability." Early on in the novel, Miss Bretherton refuses to be introduced to a famous French actress because of her infamous immorality:

> I can't separate her acting from what she is herself. It is women like that who bring discredit on the whole profession—it is women like that who make people think that no good woman can be an actress. I resent it, and I mean to take the other line. I want to prove, if I can, that a woman may be an actress and still be a lady, still be treated just as you treat the women you know and respect! I mean to prove that there need never be a word breathed against her, that she is anybody's equal, and that her private life is her own, and not the public's. (89)

Kendal sees Miss Bretherton's moral tone as prudery, and the latter's subsequent theatrical education convinces her to transcend the tidy divisions she had previously drawn between one's private life and the public display of one's talents. But neither the characters in the novel nor the novel itself transcend Miss Bretherton's sense of moral indignity; no sooner does the actress acquire real emotions and learn to channel her emotions into her art effectively, than she chooses to leave the stage, to express her emotions in the sublime privacy of marriage, rather than consuming herself and her energies by expressing them before the public gaze.

Henry James would have none of this. At the height of the public debates about Mary Anderson's acting, he wrote Mrs. Humphrey Ward from Paris, "I have seen plays and performers that have dropped as a curtain over that last aberration of the misguided Mary. . . . The distance from Paris to London is surely not hundreds, but hundreds of thousands of miles" (21 February 1884, quoted in Gordon and Stokes, 139). And he soon set about conceiving a theatrical novel of his own, about an actress whose public personae and private emotions are unknowable to others, whose private emotions are neither neatly compartmentalized nor displayed untranslated on the stage, and who doesn't leave the stage for marriage at the end of the novel. That novel, *The Tragic Muse,* is not so much James's answer to *Miss Bretherton,* then, as it is a complete rejection of the terms of the debate that *Miss Bretherton* frames and that Mary Anderson's life and acting exemplify.

Bernard Shaw retrospectively viewed Anderson's retirement from the stage in very similar terms to the ones James used in reaction to the ending of Mrs. Humphrey Ward's novel. In his review of *A Few Memories,* he writes:

> In no pages of these memoirs can you find any trace of the actress's temperament. Mary Anderson is essentially a woman of principle, which the actress essentially is not: the notion that all bravery, loyalty, and self-respect depend on a lawless and fearless following of affectionate impulses—which is the characteristic morality of the artist, especially the woman artist of the stage—is, to her, simply immorality. The actress lives only to give herself away so that she may gain the love of the whole world: Mary Anderson, asking what it shall profit to gain the whole world if she loses her own soul, retires or rather recoils from the stage before her apprenticeship is over, because she cannot gratify her love of Shakespear and rhetoric without giving herself away to the public nightly to be stared at. (2:86).

Anderson's autobiography is filled with such language. As early as her voyage to England, on the eve of her debut in London, she recalls having second thoughts about her career. Envying poets, composers, writers, and painters, who "could express their innermost thoughts and inspirations through the impersonal mediums of canvas, music, literature, and still be protected by that privacy which is so dear to most women," Anderson concludes that "the disappointments connected with the art itself—the painting of one's picture with one's own person, in the full gaze of the public . . .—made me, young as I was, long to leave the stage for the peace and privacy of a domestic life" (128).

A little more than half a decade later, overwrought with "the strain of living so many lives in one" (255), Anderson finally did leave the stage. On tour in Washington, D.C., in 1889, during the week of the inauguration of Benjamin Harrison, she was performing in *The Winter's Tale.* She describes her last night on the stage in the last chapter of her autobiography:

> The theatre was crowded. Perdita danced apparently as gayly as ever, but after the exertion fell fainting from exhaustion, and was carried off the stage. I was taken into the dressing-room, which in a few moments was filled with people from the boxes. Recovering consciousness quickly, I begged them to clear the room. Realizing then that I would probably not be able to act any more that season, though there were

> many weeks yet unfinished, I resolved at any cost to complete that night's work. Hurriedly putting on some color, I passed the groups of people discussing the incident, and before the doctor or my brother were aware of my purpose, ordered the curtain to be rung up and walked upon the stage. As I did so I heard a loud hum, which I was afterwards told was a great burst of applause from the audience. The pastoral scene came to an end. There was only one more act to go through. Donning the statue-like draperies of Hermione, I mounted the pedestal. My physician, formerly an officer in the army, said that he had never, even in the midst of battle, felt so nervous as when he saw the figure of Hermione swaying on her pedestal up that long flight of stairs. Every moment there was an hour of torture to me, for I felt myself growing fainter and fainter. All my remaining strength was put into that last effort. I descended from the pedestal, and was able to speak all but the final line. This remained unuttered, and the curtain rang down on my last appearance on the stage. (256–57)

The next paragraph (which is the final paragraph of the autobiography) begins: "The following November (1889) I became engaged to Antonio F. de Navarro, whom I had known for many years, and in June of 1890, at the little Catholic church at Hampstead, London, we were married" (257).

In 1884, as Galatea, the first statue that she played, Mary Anderson renounced love and stepped back onto her pedestal. Like most actresses (and their spiritual cousin, the sympathetic courtesan) in the Victorian drama (such as Peg Woffington in Reade and Taylor's *Masks and Faces* and Marguerite Gautier in Dumas fils's *The Lady of the Camelias*), the woman brought to life by love must use her talents as an artist to renounce the very love that she has discovered, sacrificing her own happiness for the happiness of other, more domestic and domesticated, creatures. These women renounce love and become, or remain, artists; Galatea renounces love and becomes a work of art.

Half a decade later, playing another statue, Anderson as Hermione stepped down from her pedestal, down the flight of stairs of Alma Tadema's set, and walked silently off the stage into matrimony. Reenacting the fable of Miss Bretherton, Anderson breathed life into the cold marble of her art only by leaving her art and becoming a wife.

Notes

1. According to the promptbook (Folger Library PROMPT *Wint. T.* 3), the full effect of this act-ending was created relatively late in the rehearsal process. The

promptbook is based on a printed script for the production, which initially ends the act after Paulina's reentrance with the news of Hermione's death; Paulina's "The sweetest creature's dead; and vengeance for't / Not dropped down yet!" is followed immediately by the printed stage direction *"exeunt,"* cutting all of Leontes' reaction and Paulina's castigation of him. After the script was printed, the scene became even more streamlined and pictorial, judging by the alterations in pencil: Leontes' response to the news of Mamilius' death ("How? Gone?") is reassigned to Hermione, so that she has a line to speak immediately before collapsing. Paulina's exit, as Hermione is carried out by her ladies, is cut, as well as all of Leontes' remaining lines in the scene. The lifeless Hermione, therefore, remains onstage; Paulina sees that she is dead as she says, "The news is mortal to the Queen—look down / And see what death is doing"; the general *"exeunt"* cue is excised; and a new direction is added in pencil: *"moan till curtain."* Thus the scene and the act end with Hermione's fall, a few lines of reaction (by Paulina, but not by Leontes), and a tableau.

2. Hermione's speech to her daughter ("You gods look down . . .") ends the play, with the addition of a couplet at the end of the speech:

> All yet seems well if it ends so meet,
> The bitter past, more welcome is the sweet.

References

Anderson, Mary (Mme. de Navarro). 1896. *A Few Memories.* New York: Harper.

Bartholomeusz, Dennis. 1982. *The Winter's Tale in Performance in England and America, 1611–1976.* Cambridge: Cambridge University Press.

Booth, Michael R. 1986. "Pictorial Acting and Ellen Terry." In *Shakespeare and the Victorian Stage,* edited by Richard Foulkes. Cambridge: Cambridge University Press.

Derrick, Patty S. 1985. "Rosalind and the Nineteenth-Century Woman: Four Stage Interpretations," *Theatre Survey* 24:143–62.

Era, The. 1 October 1883, 207–8; 1 October 1892, 186–88.

Gordon, D. J., and John Stokes. 1972. "The Reference of *The Tragic Muse.*" In *The Air of Reality: New Essays on Henry James,* edited by John Goode. London: Methuen.

James, Henry. 1957. *The Scenic Art.* New York: Hill and Wang.

Lord Lytton. 1884. "Miss Anderson's Juliet." *Nineteenth Century* 16:879–900.

Mullin, Donald, ed. 1983. *Victorian Actors and Actresses in Review.* Westport, CT: Greenwood.

Odell, George C. D. 1927–49. *Annals of the New York Stage.* 15 vols. New York: Columbia University Press.

———. 1920. *Shakespeare from Bretherton to Irving.* 2 vols. New York: Scribner.

Shattuck, Charles H. 1987. *Shakespeare on the American Stage from Booth and Barrett to Sothern and Marlowe.* Washington, D.C.: Folger Books.

Shaw, G. Bernard. 1932. *Our Theatres in the Nineties.* 3 vols. London: Constable.

Ward, Mrs. Humphrey. 1884. *Miss Bretherton.* 2d ed. London: Macmillan.

Winter, William. 1915. *Shakespeare on the Stage,* 2d ser. New York: Moffat, Yard.

———. 1913. *The Wallet of Time.* New York: Moffat, Yard.

"My learned and well-beloved servant Cranmer": Guthrie's *Henry VIII*

Ralph Berry

Romance or history? The main generic alternatives always float before the director of *Henry VIII.* In the past the choice was virtually preempted by tradition. When the Old Vic put on *Henry VIII* in the coronation year of 1953, J. C. Trewin saw it as "an almost regulation choice for the ceremonial event."[1] The great events of the play were subsumed into G. Wilson Knight's formulation: "Ritual is our true protagonist."[2] For directors and audiences alike, *Henry VIII* was a patriotic pageant or costume spectacular.

Of recent years, the generic alternative has made some headway. On this view, *Henry VIII* is a history in the way that *Henry V* is a history. It is a close examination of the mechanisms, the working parts of power. The most thoroughgoing advocacy of this approach was Brian Rintoul's production at Stratford, Ontario (1986). It was much strengthened by the play's being in repertory with Robert Bolt's *A Man for All Seasons,* a pairing that suggested that the same political situation was being analyzed from differing but not incompatible viewpoints.[3] There was also Howard Davies' gesturally Brechtian production for the RSC (1983). But this was widely seen as a failure, and Nicholas Shrimpton's judgment that the reading was "consistently ironic and unillusioned"[4] doesn't stand up. The benign persona of Richard Griffiths as Henry worked against the impression of history in the raw; and the cut-out flats and Weill-type music were limply fashionable. The RSC and RNT have so far failed to offer a large-scale exposition of *Henry VIII* as Tudor *Realpolitik;* but the generic choice is on file, waiting to be activated. If any one person opened the file it was Tyrone Guthrie.

* * *

Unlike most modern directors, Guthrie liked to return to a play again and again. He specialized, for example, in the Problem Plays, putting on *Measure for Measure* four times, *All's Well That Ends*

Well three times, and *Troilus and Cressida* twice. He directed *Henry VIII* on four occasions from 1933 to 1953. The core of his thought is in the major production he directed at Stratford-upon-Avon in 1949, with recast versions in 1950 and 1953. Robert Hardy, who played in all three versions, gave his verdict on Guthrie's approach to the text:

> And Guthrie made it a thoroughly political piece. He had an extraordinary comprehension of power politics, in any country. He was fascinated by the politicking, chasing power, the weaknesses and strengths of people. He made all the political scenes, which read dully on the page, absolutely electric. He worked and worked with the actors in those scenes, until they became politicians.[5]

How was this done? A couple of primary decisions point the way. First, the casting of Henry. The essential is to have an unsentimentalized, hard-man persona. Guthrie chose Anthony Quayle in 1949–50, a man with an excellent war record whose masculinity dominated the stage. Paul Rogers (Old Vic, 1953) was "the autocrat battering bluntly at circumstance."[6] A Holbein costume is more or less obligatory for Henry—this play really cannot be taken out of its Tudor frame—but the bluff King Hal should not be overstated or glamorized. The text rests on the unstated premise that the King is an old brute, whose pattern is to destroy all who fail to yield to him. The director must decide how far to realize this conception. The ingratiating Henrys of Richard Griffiths (RSC, 1983) and John Stride (BBC-TV, 1979) were a mistake; much better the menacing and violent Henry of Leon Pownall (Stratford, Ontario, 1986), or for that matter the non-Shakespearean Henrys of Keith Michell, in *The Six Wives of Henry VIII* (BBC-TV, 1970) and Robert Shaw in the film of *A Man for All Seasons* (1966). Take Henry at his own valuation, and the play is lost or degenerates into sycophancy.

The second point is the casting of the Prologue/Chorus. Chorus is the soul of the play, and *Henry VIII* has offered some interesting variations in performance. At Stratford, Ontario, Brian Rintoul assigned the lines to three courtiers fearful lest their words miscarry to Henry. That watchful tyrant was shown as paying close attention to the words of his subjects. That was objective history; but Howard Davies, in assigning the Prologue to Henry himself, acquiesced in Henry's view of himself. It might be argued that the casting showed the King in command of the media, but this was toothless cynicism. It came over as a move toward historical romance. Guthrie's thought varied, as we shall see.

In 1949 he was much acclaimed for an original stroke of casting.

> The Prologue was spoken by the Old Lady, Anne Bullen's friend (Wynne Clark)—a sound device to associate its serious and pertinent comment with the theme of the Tudor succession which is responsible for the structure of the whole play. Miss Clark was a perfect Holbein portrait to look at, and she seized her twofold opportunity firmly: the quality of life in her, the persuasive zest of her way of speaking and the authenticity of her appearance, all struck the dominant role of the entire production. The emphasis laid on the "truth" of the play, "our chosen truth," came over with full force as she drew us straight into a novel intimacy, speaking from the extreme front of the forestage (left). When she adjured us
>
> think ye see
> The very persons of our noble story
> As they were living,
>
> upstage, right, the Dukes of Norfolk and Suffolk with three other nobles were seen for a moment in converse—a moment of breath-taking reality upon which the mind dwells with delight. . . . Then, as she began to speak her last line, what had held us at the timeless instant dissolved; and the play itself swept into action with the entry, right, of the Duke of Buckingham (Leon Quartermaine).[7]

This looks, and was, a first-class director's aperçu. It was repeated in 1950 with a different actress. But by 1953 Guthrie had moved on, as Robert Hardy tells us:

> Tony gave me the Lord Chamberlain, lots of comedy, another old man, a controlling role in the mechanics of the play. In an early rehearsal, Tony said to me, "Going to change what we did before. Going to give you the Prologue and the Epilogue." They had been done at Stratford by a very good elderly actress who was also "inside" the play. And she came again to the Vic. He said, "It would be much better if the Chamberlain had all that, and controlled the whole entertainment 'inside' and 'outside' the play at the same time. Can't think why I didn't do it before."[8]

There were difficulties with the actress, and Guthrie decided to abandon the change of casting. Still, the conception of a controlling Lord Chamberlain, inside and outside the frame, is notable. It concedes nothing of the "political" view of the play. And the Stratford, Ontario, connection with Guthrie kept the casting alive. George McCowan had his Lord Chamberlain speak the Prologue there in 1961.

Guthrie played up the actuality of Tudor life. He extracted more fun from courtiers stepping into dog-dirt, though Gielgud for one felt that such devices "destroyed the dignity of the rest of the play."[9] Always Guthrie sought to bring out the realities of the text. Michael Langham recalled a telling moment in the scene when Katherine pleads her case to the King:

> By Henry's choice this was made into a public, not a private scene, although she strove to keep it private between husband and wife. In the middle of her long speech, Henry started tapping a ruler on a table . . . rap . . . rap . . . rap. Quietly and slowly at first, while he beamed with an ever-so-winning expression of long-suffering boredom to his sycophantic court; then louder and more insistent, as she continued (in the face of ribald laughter) with a parallel growth of desperation. This "rap-rap" not only served to make her speak louder and therefore unwittingly publicly; it also served to show the world that he, Henry, regarded her remarks as unworthy even of attention and that the world, including the Pope, had better take note. A seductive, private plea was ruthlessly made public, laughable and, in the end, painfully touching.[10]

Another incident in the same scene (2.4) comes into view through Guthrie's biographer, James Forsyth. This is the Katherine of Diana Wynyard in 1949:

> She was in the middle of that great inquisitorial scene, fighting for her life and dignity as Katherine, the several clerical recorders of the court's proceedings bent over their manuscripts. But with their quill pens—under direct encouragement from the director—they were noisily scratching away to her total distraction. She thought this was surely a mistake. "No," Tony said. "Wanted it—still want it." "And am I really to play over that frightful noise?" "Yaas," was the reply. He might be wrong. He was seldom uncertain. And he knew when, and exactly when, he wanted the noise to stop, and the intense and total focus to fall on Katherine.[11]

That bureaucratic undermining of Katherine—today we should call it "dirty tricks"—is part of the political reality, being of course sanctioned by the King. It set up a stage coup, the moment when the pens ceased their noise. But that scene ended with the clearest demonstration of Guthrie's insight into the political process.

* * *

> *King Henry.* I may perceive
> These cardinals trifle with me: I abhor

> This dilatory sloth and tricks of Rome.
> My learned and well-beloved servant Cranmer,
> Prithee return; with thy approach, I know
> My comfort comes along.—Break up the court;
> I say set on.
>
> (2.4.233–39)

Every editor I have consulted marks this passage with *Aside,* the force of which governs the delivery until the final "Break up the court." R. A. Foakes in his New Arden edition (1966) explains the reasoning: ". . . as the next scene makes clear, cf. III.ii.63, 400, Cranmer cannot be present here, and his dramatic function is to reveal the king's power and mercy in the last act, not to replace Wolsey" (88).

Perfectly logical, but not the way Guthrie saw it. For a start, he was far from being under the spell of Wolsey. Andrew Cruickshank, who played the part in 1950, is revealing on Guthrie's sense of Wolsey:

> As far as the character of Wolsey was concerned he was a great churchman. And Tony didn't like that at all. I think one day he said, "Can you play it with a stick or something, as though you had gout?" Well, of course, this was all against the view of Wolsey as a great cleric, whom people regard as much in the way of his last line, "Had I but served my God with half the zeal with which I serve my King he would not in mine age have left me naked to mine enemies." This redeems the whole character. Not for Guthrie. He saw the *awful* politics and chicanery behind the Catholic Church, and everything like that.[12]

Guthrie, one should add, was an Ulsterman.

Then comes Guthrie's handling of Henry's "aside." Cruickshank brings this out in a way no other commentator does:

> There's a line when Henry comes on, and things are very difficult between himself and Wolsey, and between himself and the Catholic Church. And he can't get away from Katherine, and he comes on the stage and says, simply, these words, "My learned and well-beloved servant, Cranmer" and takes Cranmer off with him. Now as Guthrie produced this on the stage—there is a court in high session with Wolsey in his chair, and Tony Quayle as Henry comes on absolutely full of gout. He stands and looks and says, "My learned and well-beloved servant. . . ." And Wolsey rises to come forward to him, and takes a couple of steps. ". . . Cranmer." And there's a great bank of English priests there. At the very back this little figure of Cranmer winds his way through all the priests, and then Henry takes him in his arms and

> leads him off for some sort of conference. In this one moment on the stage there is the Reformation. Everything is concentrated into this—there's the difference between the Catholic Church, the English Church, and Henry. "My well-beloved servant. . . Cranmer."[13]

That is very remarkable stagecraft, especially for its time. Guthrie chooses to go against the intellectual logic of the text, and instead to realize its historical—and emotional—content with a full-throttle theatricalization. He converts the inner yearning for Wolsey's return into a public-relations embracing of Cranmer as the King's chief adviser. Today this staging would scarcely seem revolutionary. The Cheek by Jowl company would not spend five minutes over the crux. Declan Donnellan routinely peoples his stage with characters from scenes to come (or past). Shadowy mental presences can be filled out with advantage on the stage. It is merely a matter of telescoping time, and making theatrically overt the truth of a transaction.

* * *

The trajectory of Guthrie's thought continued in his audacious handing of the great procession:

> . . . a silent scene was substituted for the coronation show. Anne herself came dancing on to the stage, and went proudly up the central steps and off as the bells began to ring out. It seems to me a legitimate and imaginative touch, if we grant that Guthrie does well to cut the coronation procession which otherwise gives us our last glimpse of Anne Bullen. I was more moved by Miss Michael's brief moment, the gaiety and then the proud carriage of the slight figure and that thrown-back head, than I have ever been by the famous "show." It was more real, and therefore more congruous in this play, than the splendours of spectacle.[14]

Think of it, the longest stage direction in Shakespeare, the most open and irresistible invitation to costume spectacular, cut! And the staging highlighted the tragedy of Anne Bullen. Guthrie meant his audience to know what was to come.

The plan now becomes a drama-documentary, *All Is True*. The coronation is seen through the eyes of the crowd, represented by the First Gentleman and Sands and joined by the Lord Chamberlain. They are the ancestors of the media commentators who transmit the interior of Westminster Abbey to the world. Little is needed to adjust their commentary to the idiom of the twentieth century. Reinforced by the Lord Chamberlain—who has obviously found the pressures of the crowd in the Abbey too much for him, and now joins his colleagues in the outside broadcasting unit—Guthrie's choric team brings together a balanced picture of a great occasion. The whole passage, said Byrne, is "the grandmother and grandfather of all running commentaries."[15]

The final scene, much praised by the reviewers, was an explosion of rejoicing in Tanya Moiseiwitsch's gold and white. The tiny baby was the visual focus: Elizabeth, hope of the land and promise of the future. Byrne regretted the cut passage about James I (40–56), but that was a formal genuflection by the Shakespeare-Fletcher team to the reigning monarch, not a theatrical necessity. After all the rigorous analysis of history and politics, Guthrie switched the play to its final track, the theme of hope and glory, the commedia of the nation.

All this is the proof of a master director, a man in whose hands the materials of his work are understood yet malleable, there to be shaped to his will. The conclusion is plain. For the prototype model of the political-historical *Henry VIII,* one turns to the three mature productions of Tyrone Guthrie.

Notes

1. J. C. Trewin, *Shakespeare on the English Stage, 1900–1964* (London: Barrie & Rockliff, 1964), 224.
2. G. Wilson Knight, *The Crown of Life* (London: Methuen, 1948), 326.
3. See my review, "Resurgence at Stratford," *Queen's Quarterly* (winter 1986):750–59.
4. Nicholas Shrimpton, "Shakespeare Performances in Stratford-upon-Avon and London," *Shakespeare Survey* 37 (1984):163–73, esp. 170.
5. Alfred Rossi, *Astonish Us In the Morning: Tyrone Guthrie Remembered* (Detroit: Wayne State University Press, 1980), 138.
6. T. C. Kemp, "Acting Shakespeare: Modern Tendencies in Playing and Production," *Shakespeare Survey* 7 (1954):121–27, esp. 124.
7. Muriel St. Clare Byrne, "A Stratford Production: *Henry VIII,*" *Shakespeare Survey* 3 (1950):120–29, esp. 121–22.
8. Rossi, *Astonish Us In the Morning,* 141.
9. Ibid., 73.
10. Ibid., 284.
11. James Forsyth, *Tyrone Guthrie* (London: Hamish Hamilton, 1976), 210.
12. Rossi, *Astonish Us In the Morning,* 119.
13. Ibid., pp. 119–20. The promptbooks for the 1949 and 1950 productions, lodged at the Shakespeare Birthplace Trust Library, show that Guthrie retained the text of Henry's speech with a minor alteration: "Prithee return" was changed to "Prithee, come here." The 1950 promptbook is clear on the staging and confirms

Cruickshank's recollection. The verso has (at "here") "Wolsey x to HENRY (followed by J. Wright)—thinking he is wanted." And at "Cranmer," "General reaction of surprise."

14. Byrne, "Stratford Production," 127.

15. Ibid., 128.

Techniques of Restoration: The Case of *The Duchess of Malfi*

JOHN RUSSELL BROWN

> In country after country, people have told us how clever we were to choose such a timely play. But that's because a very rich stew builds up. It's about the supernatural. It's about sex. It's about politics. It's about redemption. It's about spirituality. Webster's characters are everywhere.[1]

THIS is the report that Declan Donnellan and Nick Ormerod, director and designer, respectively, of Cheek by Jowl's production of John Webster's *Duchess of Malfi,* gave to the press, just before this touring theater company's production reached the West End of London at Wyndhams Theatre early in 1996. They had taken the show to towns around England, to Blackpool, Cheltenham, Coventry, Oxford, and around the world, to Rome, Melbourne, Dublin, New York (at the Brooklyn Academy of Music); and everywhere the production had been acclaimed. After a month in London, it would go Valletta, Budapest, Ljubljana, Vienna, Hong Kong, Mexico City, and Bogota. Never has Webster's work had such an airing; never have so many and so diverse people had opportunity to judge the worth of his duchess "lively body'd" on the stage, as the actor-dramatist William Rowley wrote of his experience at an early performance.[2] Moreover, it was coming to a theater that in the same season had been home to another production of *The Duchess* that had originated at the Greenwich Theatre on the outskirts of London and had, similarly, reached town after a provincial tour. This earlier production had had nowhere else to go but stayed in the West End well beyond a hundred performances, until its leading actors were contracted elsewhere.

It might seem that the time had come for Webster's tragedy to reach a newly receptive audience. Seldom is a play by Shakespeare available in two productions so close in time to each other in a single city; still less frequently does the work of one of his contemporaries enjoy such popularity. Welcoming the production, John Peter wrote in *The Sunday Times* (London, 7 January 1996) as if *The Duchess of Malfi* had achieved top-of-the-line status:

> There are few things in the English classical theatre to equal the scene in which the proud duchess woos her steward, or the portrayal of Bosola the mercenary whose soul is torn apart by respect and pity for his victim.

But other critics were not so sure of the play's virtues: most held that the triumph belonged to the director and actors, and they took Webster to task for the most obvious faults of stagecraft, as he has been ever since the start of the eighteenth century. The success of the two productions in 1995–96 does not prove that this Jacobean tragedy is once more safe material for commercial producers: the general opinion is that it needs a very special restoration job before it is playable. Only a couple of years earlier, John Peter had found that a strongly cast *Duchess* at the Bristol Old Vic was "impressively presented but doggedly under-acted":

> This is an efficient production, which is obviously better than a bad one; it is only that with this majestically poetic text, the gap between efficiency and greatness happens to be unusually wide.[3]

When Richard Allen Cave chose two productions to feature in his book on Webster in the series *Text and Performance* (1988), neither one had enjoyed a generally acknowledged success. This scholar rated Peter Gill's direction at the Royal Court in 1971 to be more successful than many journalist critics had done, but his praise of the acting was reserved for the Duchess and Antonio: only they had established "the psychological dimensions of Webster's tragedy." The intimate focus that the director brought to the play had made his actors "particularly vulnerable and not all [the] cast could stand up to such rigorous scrutiny of their technique" (63). Of his other exemplary production, which Philip Prowse had directed for the National Theatre in 1985, Cave wrote that

> By trying visually to realise the atmosphere of the play [the director had] drastically simplified or undermined Webster's meaning . . . and robbed the action of Webster's compassionate concern with the intricate, enigmatic impulses that shape his characters' moral natures. (69)

Although Webster's art had not been entirely vindicated, the success and longevity of the two touring productions of 1995–96 have given an opportunity to inquire how this "poetic text" can be "restored" to find favor with a modern audiences and provide, perhaps, such a deeply moving experience as Thomas Middleton recalled in 1623:

> For who e'er saw this duchess live, and die,
> That could get off under a bleeding eye?[4]

They may also illuminate more than Webster's art. As modern directors, designers, and actors stage this text, with its history of misdirection and disappointment, they are tested more stringently than when working on the more familiar territory of a play by Shakespeare; they are likely to reveal more of their working methods and interpretative predilections than when they feel reassuringly at home. An observer may therefore learn something about the ways in which Shakespeare's plays are turned to modern advantage and a clearer view of what may be the costs of this treatment. Webster and Shakespeare have enough in common for success with the less accessible author to suggest ways in which the more congenial might be brought to fuller life on the modern stage.

* * *

Wyndhams is a small theater with a small proscenium stage; the Greenwich Theatre has no proscenium but a still more intimate auditorium. Not surprisingly, therefore, Duncan C. Weldon's Triumph Proscenium Productions, Ltd., in association with the subsidized Greenwich Theatre, had kept everything small in scale. The set was a wall of doors and panels, capable of variations to suggest a change of location rather than differences of wealth, power, or intimacy. The actors numbered only twelve, together with one young boy. The show was not to be sold on its spectacle or on the strength of its company, but on the presence in its cast of Juliet Stevenson and Simon Russell Beale; the former had won many awards on stage and in film, and the latter had recently been made an associate artist of the Royal Shakespeare Company after four seasons in which his roles had become progressively more challenging and more successful. The producers had made sure that the Duchess and Ferdinand, her twin brother, were in hands as safe as any to be found in British theater. Philip Franks, actor turned director, was comparatively inexperienced, although among his credits was a performance as Hamlet with the RSC; he also had recently edited an anthology with his leading lady, *Shall I See You Again?* for Pavillion Books.

From its two star actors, handled with care and respect rather than with interpretative or technical authority, the production took life. Among the consequences of this strategy were extensive cuts and rearrangements that brought the play within the grasp of the small company and reduced its playing-time to what was comfortable for its audiences. Out went the scene at the shrine of Our Lady of Loretto (3.4), Julia's wooing of Bosola in 5.2, and much else besides. These cuts inevitably damaged the context in which Webster had placed his leading characters so that their story was told as if they were persons who lived only in private. Individual courtiers were doubled or merged together, with the result that Castruchio, Silvio, and Delio were the only ones to remain in the list of characters. Ferdinand offers Malateste to the Duchess for a husband, but he is never seen on stage. As the program has it, "Courtiers / Armed Men / Madmen / Executioners [are] played by members of the Company." Actors and actresses did what they could with the pomp and circumstance of the formal scenes and with the activity and turbulence needed for the emergencies at court in the wake of the birth of the Duchess's first child and Ferdinand's visit to her bedchamber (3.2); almost inevitably, however, with few actors on a small stage, these scenes were too awkward and ineffectual to suggest the tensions that go with the exercise of power or realization of danger. Little attempt was made to stage the interlude of the madmen in 4.2: it was played behind a grill with only hands and faces visible; its text was greatly cut and replaced with rhythmically repeated words, as in a students' acting improvisation.

Many incidental similes, illustrations, and elaborations were also cut. The naturalistic pulse of Webster's dialogue, which gives an impression of thoughts developing as if of their own accord, is the very characteristic that makes incidental verbal cuts easy to accomplish; it is like removing a few heartbeats from among many. Not surprisingly, Bosola suffered most. His trenchant irony and seemingly inexhaustible curiosity, and the energy driving his restless mind, had little chance of making the mark that the stage-history of this play shows to be one of its most constant attractions in the theater as well as on the page. His inward journey from cynicism and candor, through amazement and, perhaps, terror, and certainly through apprehension and pity, toward something like devotion and nobility (though cut through with despair and a still powerful cynicism) takes more time and many more words to be expressed than were allowable in this production.

How then did the play hold its audience? One answer was obvious: however much the text had been cut, time was taken to realize both the physical and the mental changes that lie behind the words that are spoken. The principal actors were given their heads so that they could think through everything they had to say, instead of allowing the words to take their own course. The actors set themselves to work so that, whether in pauses and silences or in collusion of thought and action, every antecedent and consequence of their words would be palpably present on stage in bodily and mental enactment. The Duchess was, indeed, "lively body'd" in the performance—that this phrase was William Rowley's for describing early performances suggests that something similar to this technique was practiced among the play's original actors.[5]

Following the advice of Stanislavski and many others, modern actors often believe that they must use their own emotional memories to bring reality to what they act and that they must discover and subsequently enact an appropriate "physical action" to create and release emotion. By these two processes they are to make their performances both "true" and "alive."[6] Instructions such as these stem from Chekhovian and later naturalism, but they offer such assurance to actors that they and their mentors and directors are apt to apply the same methods to any text that needs special care in production. Here it brought the thrill of actuality to many moments in Webster's tragedy: and the strangeness of the dramatic situation was able to make that immediacy grip attention, while the sensitivity of the dialogue made it revelatory of inmost experience. However, all was not always to the advantage of the play. Often the text suffered and the play's characters with it: physicality can be a heavy or dull virtue, and the mental processes of making a part one's own can hold back dramatic drive and interfere with the speaking of dialogue.

Phrasing, rhythm, and meter all suffered, and that sense of inspired and intuitive feeling that a silent reading of the play will often bring was too often missing. So the Cardinal speaks of seeing "a thing, arm'd with a rake" in his fish-ponds and then stops, as if still not fully realizing what he is seeing; after a pause he adds: "That seems to strike at me" (5.5.6–7). He has moved slowly and stubbornly toward apprehension, whereas the text seems to demand a union of thought and feeling, a flash of recognition that flows through two and half lines of verse with no hindrance—as appropriate for a man who is said to fall faster of himself than calamity can drive him (5.5.42–44). Speaking during her last minutes to Cariola, the Duchess says "Give my little boy . . ." and then pauses before adding "Some syrup for his cold" (4.2.203–4), as if she, or the actress, needed time to think about what is the correct medicine or what might be available in a prison; or as if she needed time to invent something to say, or found herself wanting to say something dangerous or rebellious, and then deciding not to at the last moment. Something within the actress's mind had broken the phrasing of the text. Perhaps the line-ending after "boy" had seemed to invite some change of thought and this took over from the duty of saying only what Webster had written.

These moments, and many like them, showed the actors taking time to re-create the thought processes implied by the words they had to speak, rather than speeding up or deepening their thoughts and feelings to keep pace with the aroused and exceptional mental activity that the play's action provokes in its characters. A broken and slow delivery changed the effect of Bosola's last lines:

> Let worthy minds ne'er stagger in distrust
> To suffer death, or shame for what is just—
> Mine is another voyage.
>
> (5.5.103–5)

To say "Mine [*long pause*] is another [*short pause*] voyage" is to make the process of his death into something quite different, emotionally and, perhaps, intellectually. These actors seemed ready to assume that the sound and syntax of their text, the shape and weight of each sentence, were not an intrinsic part of the play's message—of what it does for an audience in performance.

Ferdinand's treatment of one famous line shows how willfully this liberty was sometimes taken when stage business was added to explicate the verbal facts of speech. "Cover her face, my eyes dazzle"(5.2.264) is spoken as one phrase, as though Ferdinand is giving Bosola a single order; here the actor had decided to manage these words by running the two thoughts together, instead of negotiating and giving reality to the syntactical break. Then Ferdinand goes closer to his sister, bending down to her very face and scrutinizing it minutely; and then speaks only as he is rising, adding: "she died young." The actor's determination to be sure of what he was doing in a way that "worked" in his own mind had caused this Ferdinand to sound like a doctor replacing an expected diagnosis with an irrelevant observation.

But the play as a whole worked for its audience and won over the critics, and by using these very same means. Not only could moments become thrillingly alive, when thought, feeling, speech, and action fused all into one impression, but some whole episodes were played in this way so that the audience sensed a deep and subtle involvement, in happiness, terror, joy, wonder, suffering, sexual desire, and guilt. The characters' fully realized responses to the more personal issues proved sufficient to carry the audience with them and restore the play to enthusiastic acceptance. Most remarkable were the opening sequences of 2.2 for which the Duchess and Antonio lay at ease on cushions, right downstage and close to the audience. He is almost naked, ready to take her to bed; she takes delight in provocation and delay. The jokes about naked goddesses and ugly faces, about labor and keeping an eye on the time, were accompanied by physical contact and playfulness. Cariola is drawn into their game because all barriers seem to be down between these lovers who are used to intimacy and satisfaction. The center of this scene is secure and calm—until the mood is wrenched aside by Ferdinand's entry, and violence and shouting take over.

Juliet Stevenson gave to the Duchess a cool, thoughtful sexual awareness, both yielding to desire and remaining in command of herself and others. When control slips, the underlying passion is seen, hard and narrow with frustration. In act 1, when she woos her steward, the mood is more mercurial, excited and nervous:

> and if you please,
> Like the old tale, in 'Alexander and Lodowick',
> Lay a naked sword between us, keep us chaste:—
> (499–501)

is said in jest, mocking her own eagerness and taunting him for silence. The next two lines, her last in the scene, acknowledge deeper necessity and vulnerability:

> O, let me shroud my blushes in your bosom,
> Since 'tis the treasury of all my secrets—

There is no more text and thereby Webster has insisted that physical performance should take over in a silent exit, an opportunity that these two actors were very able to take. The presence of the Duchess was often most impressive in silence, as the text often requires and notably in act 4:

> She will muse four hours together, and her silence,
> Methinks, expresseth more than if she spoke.
>
> (4.1.9–10)

Although she knows that "reason / And silence make me stark mad" (4.2.6–7), she accepts this risk:

> —What think you of, madam?
> — Of nothing:
> When I muse thus, I sleep. . . .
>
> (4.2.15–16)

In this production, the actress could take the audience into that almost desperate musing, her performance even more subtle and commanding than in speech. When Bosola, as the Common Bellman, tells her to "don clean linen, bathe your feet," she does just this, preparing her body solemnly and gently for death. This scene was often played very quietly but this was sufficient in the intimate theater to hold the focus of attention.

With Simon Russell Beale's Ferdinand the production's determination to provide physical realization of inward experience magnified the hints in the text of an incestuous obsession with his sister. He paws her longingly in the very first scene. In 2.4, when he imagines himself digging up a mandrake, he sweats visibly; as he visualizes the "strong thigh'd bargeman" who enjoys his sister, he shudders with frustrated desire. By act 3, he is torn with pain and rendered physically incapable of confronting Antonio or even looking at his sister. In act 4, when she is dead, he presses against her and attempts to slake his passion; he grasps her discarded clothes against his groin and smells them ravenously. In act 5, no doctor attends this Ferdinand, so he chastizes himself; the gown to which he refers is his sister's, which he carries wherever he goes.

Repeatedly this production staged the physical actualities implied by "this majestically poetic text" and often went beyond its suggestions. The Cardinal takes Julia onto the floor and assaults her from behind. Not only does the Duchess return to the stage for the echo scene (5.3), but she is also there is the last scene: as Delio says his concluding lines, cradling his friend Antonio, the Duchess enters and joins her husband. Toward the end of the play, as death, cunning, and complication begin to dominate its action, this practice accentuated what was fortuitous and grotesque. The audience might well have greeted the strange antics and inadequate speech with incredulous laughter, assuming that something had gone absurdly wrong, or that the author had set all at odds, destroying the subtlety previously present and making a mockery of whatever any character could achieve. At first the actors and their director must have been troubled by such a response and, not surprisingly, they tried to preempt the audience's laughter by giving their characters outbursts of cynical and hopeless laughter that showed they recognized the shift into desperate or futile expediences.[7] By doing so they had, perhaps, discovered a way of responding to another strand of the text: the characters' instinct to withdraw from brutality and from both "reason and silence" into recognition of their helplessness or the onset of madness. Consequently the tragedy could awaken wider issues at its close by emphasizing the debasement that is the consequence of a pursuit of "ambition, blood, and lust" (5.5.72). That laughter which denies good sense and silence had become a necessity at a time when tears and sensitivity were no longer possible.

Webster has often been criticized for writing a muddled and ineffectual last act, for keeping the play going long after the death of the Duchess who alone could hold all together. Perhaps that is because critics have failed to acknowledge a crucial change in how the play is meant to work in performance. Experimentally these actors, who had insisted on realizing the text's suggestion of inner tensions and physical activity, found that to retain control over the audience during the last scenes they had to resort to strained or compulsive laughter. If the author had foreseen this, he might have been working against the audience's earlier empathy with his characters and establishing a new distance from them. In this way the tragedy would provoke questions about the worth of men and women who spend their lives aspiring to "greatness." The characters sometimes express this view of their author's purpose, as in Delio's concluding speech:

> These wretched eminent things
> Leave no more fame behind 'em than should one
> Fall in a frost, and leave his print in snow;
> As soon as the sun shines, it ever melts,
> Both form, and matter.
>
> (5.5.113–17)

Earlier, Antonio's dying words had expressed the same idea, making ambition sound still more ridiculous and defeatist:

> In all our quest of greatness,
> Like wanton boys whose pastime is their care,
> We follow after bubbles, blown in th'air.
>
> (5.4.64–66)

Still earlier, in a moment of stillness after he has confronted his sister in the bedchamber, Ferdinand had conjured up an image of the peaceful and loving life that is possible without ambition:

> Love gives them counsel
> To inquire for him 'mongst unambitious shepherds,
> Where dowries were not talk'd of, and sometimes
> 'Mongst quiet kindred that had nothing left
> By their dead parents.
>
> (3.1.126–30)

While bitter and self-generated laughter can make the audience remain attentive to the desperate happenings at the conclusion of this tragedy, it may also help to shape the kind of response that its author envisaged. In his earlier *White Devil,* Flamineo's false death and his puns and mockery up to the very last moments are unmistakable clues that Webster saw the value of this kind of laughter and worked to arouse it.

* * *

The Greenwich production of *The Duchess of Malfi* showed that when staging Elizabethan and Jacobean plays actors can find good use for those techniques that have helped them realize the subtextual life of modern plays that deal more obviously with reflections of actual lived experience. Sometimes this leads to the adoption of strange stage business and idiosyncratic interpretation or phrasing of the text but, equally and more importantly, it can hold attention and carry the action forward strongly; it may also discover qualities in the play that would not have been recognized in other ways.

Similar reflections arise from Declan Donnellan's modern dress production for the Cheek by Jowl Theatre Company, only here a further modern acting technique was given greater scope: the use of improvisation as a means of involving the actors' own instinctive reactions in performances and making their own individualities more adventurously and strongly present.[8] Journals and newspapers hardly knew what to make of the result, variously calling the production "startling, revelatory, jolting, arresting, dynamic, tough, rich, smart," and "ponderous";[9] spurred on by these comments, audiences had filled the London theater daily. This company had forced a new appraisal of the text and, in keeping with its usual way of working, the production changed during its tour, from day-to-day reflecting the concerns of both actors and audiences, finding still further nuances and excitements. Performances were altogether more bold, outgoing, outrageous, and playful than those of the Greenwich *Duchess*. This production was often like the other in calling for close and quiet attention, and yet it also had a stronger and more obvious energy running throughout. A sense of committal and competition between the actors brought it closer to a style that might have been appropriate to the outdoor conditions of the original performances at the Globe Theatre and to the improvisation required by the large and daily-changing repertoire of the King's Men, whether at the Globe or at the more intimate Blackfriars.

The strength of the acting was in the company, rather than in two star actors, and in its way of rehearsing and playing. Still more of the minor characters had disappeared, to be replaced by a group of actors who took on a number of functions, as nameless courtiers, soldiers, acolytes, madmen, executioners, and doctors. They were given some of the functions of a Chorus in that their positions on stage around the protagonists acted as a kind of set, restricting space or opening it out, and defining the occasion. They gather tightly around the Duchess as she is slowly strangled, only her hands visible to express the agony. They line up as acolytes to take communion at Mass, so providing the ordered submission of a religious setting in which the Duchess and her husband are refused the sacrament. They follow the mad Ferdinand as doctors, multiplying the confident impertinence of the single one named in the text. In the mad scene, instead of using Webster's dialogue, they invent and play a childish game with a crown and an infant at the moment of birth. They are also used with the named characters to stand stone-still and unresponsive at the beginning of the play as dialogue between one or two characters sets the action going. At the end of the play the whole cast again assembles still and silent on stage, the principals posed in a group as if for a family photograph. The effect of all this was to place the tragedy in a simplified and well-drilled world. The stage set was nothing more than tall, dark green curtains along the back and a few scattered chairs, so that little besides this variable human context for action was there to distract attention from the performances of the principal actors. Yet the handling of these supernumerary actors was so incessantly inventive that it drew attention to the theatricality of the production, giving the audience a sense that all was being put on stage with the help of a mastermind that did not hesitate to act on its own account without any text in support.

The production as a whole was a demonstration of how actors can "play" with a text. Those who took the main roles had discovered in improvisational rehearsals a wealth of business that could subvert meaning or thrust a new interpretation into sudden prominence, or force a readjustment between one character and another, or contrive shock or absurdity in a moment. Over the years, actors in Cheek by Jowl have described how Declan Donnellan achieves this kind of performance in rehearsal:

> *Peter Needham:* He creates an environment where all sorts of things can and mostly do happen, and then we go in that direction collectively. . . . one of Declan's great strengths is that he can respond to the individual actor. What Peter Needham wants is what Peter Needham wants; my needs are my needs; somehow Declan is intuitive enough to realise those needs in each of his individual actors.
> *Anne White:* Declan allows the actor to bring what they have to a part. . . . He brings things out of you that you didn't know you had. He has a favourite phrase which is "Turning on a sixpence." In other words, the quickfire of emotions rather than getting stuck into one.
> *Duncan Bell:* He doesn't insist on analysing the text. It's very much an on-your-feet experience.[10]

Nothing is permanently fixed; the director and designer accompany the actors on their extensive tours giving fresh notes and calling more rehearsals as they went. "Performances would grow and change, and then grow and change more because of their constant input."[11]

The costumes gave the actors freedom for large movements, being almost as simple as the physical setting. In place of elaborate Renaissance dress were items of modern clothing, many of them in the styles of the first decades of the twentieth century. The bodies of the actors were more visible than they would have been if conforming to the outlines of broad gowns, corsets, and doublets, or if hidden by the many layers that were then in use. They were also unencumbered by period manners. The production was free to take on the appearance of a parade of uniform figures, or a high-strung dance of wooing, taunting, or intimidation, or of variable oppositions in contest, or of persons locked in close physical contact. Although its visual means were spare with mostly muted colors, the action had flamboyance, daring, and sustained energy; and kept providing a sequence of arresting images dominated by the presence of the principal characters.

The physicality of this production was often realistically conveyed, as in the Greenwich production—for example, Bosola actually measures the Duchess for her coffin with a pocket tape measure, and Cariola has a portable crucifix so that she can kneel and pray even in public—but it often surpassed realism with exaggeration, sudden surprise, and lack of restraint. The Duchess of Anastasia Hille is restless, easily aggressive or dismissive, laughing harshly or nervously, switching suddenly to simple and sustained silence, or simple speaking a few affecting words. The Ferdinand of Scott Handy is a badly behaved doglike boy-man, given to fighting or hugging his sister. The Cardinal of Paul Brennen employs a slow and sardonic delivery and has a brutal relationship with Julia, who has to take the sexual initiative. George Anton's Bosola (as at Greenwich, losing about half his lines) has assumed a dour Scottish accent and plays against the dominant style of the production by standing coldly apart and seeming to lack a personal instinct toward action. The play became a doomed entanglement, a game-playing in which each character strives by all means to out-do the others. So absorbed are the actors that each character seems impelled to do what he does: when Ferdinand says his sister's "guilt treads on / Hot-burning coulters" (3.1.56–57), or when she declares herself to be "full of daggers" (4.1.90), they seem to speak no less than truth. Moreover, as the narrative unfolds from one crisis to another, a shared energy and restless invention drive the action forward more strongly than a more sober and well-mannered production could ever manage.

The more extravagant inventions of the actors and their director forced the audience to be aware of impulses that go beyond any obvious meaning of the words their characters speak. When early in the play Ferdinand says "You are my sister" (1.1.330), she has been lighting a cigarette but now turns suddenly and gives him a slap across the face. When on parting he calls her "lusty widow" (1.1.340), he lunges toward her and she laughs harshly. When in 3.2 she confesses, "I pray sir, hear me: I am married" (82), she takes him off guard, brings him to the floor, gets astride him, and brandishes the dagger at him. During his subsequent rant, she goes on drinking whiskey. When he touches a deeper note of pain:

> For thou has ta'en that massy sheet of lead
> That hid thy husband's bones, and folded it
> About my heart,

she replies loudly and sarcastically, "Mine bleeds for it" (3.2.112–14), and breaks off into coarse laughter. By the time Ferdinand starts to tell the story of "Reputation, Love, and Death" (119–35), both are near exhaustion and are sitting side by side on the floor, like children after too rough a game. He then gathers his strength again and, crying out "I will never see you more," clasps his hands over his eyes, rushes from the stage, and trips over a chair as he exits.

Above all, it would seem, the director had encouraged his actors to be as dynamic and as varied as possible. At the beginning of 4.1, in the prison, Ferdinand and the Duchess are again fighting each other on floor, but they also embrace and feverishly exchange greetings. In contrast, the business of the dead man's hand is taken slowly: she is blindfolded and Bosola has plenty of time to bring the hand onstage and deliver it to Ferdinand. The audience sees the whole deception as it is being arranged, not with the sudden surprise of the Duchess as she experiences its effect, but in deliberate slow-motion in the half-light. Her scream on realizing the trick is horrible, as the text demands, but soon the tempo and pitch of performance drop again. "There is not between heaven and earth one wish / I stay for after this" (61–62) is one of the Duchess's most quiet and simple moments—only to be back at high power to express anger and frustration. More fully aware of her situation, she rejects the wish for a long life and vows "I'li go pray" (95), as if preparing herself for death, and then she stops; this is not the end of a verse line, but from this point a very long silence is maintained during which the audience and the Duchess have time to notice that Cariola is kneeling apart and already praying. Eventually this near silence and stillness are shattered by a dangerously angry, "No, / I'll go curse," shortly to be followed by "and say I long to bleed," at which point, "turning on a sixpence," she suddenly breaks down in terror and gives way to loud weeping.

Sometimes it seemed as if these actors could never be satisfied with what they had discovered to do with any line of text and had gone on adding to it. When death is very close and Bosola has announced that he is her tombmaker, "I am Duchess of Malfi still" (4.2.142) is said as if the Duchess is tired of the very thought; and then, wearing a toy crown left by the madmen, she gives a dismissive and harsh laugh. After "What death?" (206), which is as controlled as its sparse language, she adds another reaction by taking a long drag on her cigarette. When the text calls for violent reactions, the actors would often take the instruction to extreme lengths. When the eating of apricots causes the pregnant Duchess to go into labor, she has to be carried offstage struggling and screaming with pain. When Ferdinand enters in the grip of Lycanthropia, he does so nearly naked, crawling along the floor, howling and slobbering like the wolf he thinks he is. In the first act, when offering herself to Antonio as his wife, the Duchess slips off her dress to bare her breasts; coming as this does in a scene where contact between mistress and servant is hedged around with protocol and danger, the gesture forces the scene forward, grabs attention, and provides a coup de thèâtre, which *The Daily Telegraph* called "the most erotic on the London stage" (4 January 1996).

A degree of wilfulness in all this elaboration was plain to see, but it served the play better than might have been expected. While the production was chiefly memorable for its many moments of shock, disrespect, harsh feeling, physical brutishness, and sexual activity, and for its contrasting moments of hushed simplicity and softer feeling (often seeming too contrived to carry full conviction), that was not all: the play as a whole also had an undeniable narrative power because the director had heeded Webster's use of varied stage images to alert the audience to narrative development. A silent reading of its text can give little idea of the succession of events that are called into being. As these follow each other, a slowly maturing sense is given that these characters are striving restlessly to reach an end that was predicated long before they could have foreseen it. However strongly the elaboration of certain episodes threatens to confuse the narrative line, the main story of the Duchess, her brothers, her husband, and Bosola continually reasserts its pole position. The imposed and silent groupings used by the director in setting the first and last scenes enhanced the sense of a foreseen conclusion that is latent in the text itself in its repeated setting of key scenes in a "presence chamber." The large demands made on the actors' physical resources also contributed to the sense of a story moving to completion, the action becoming like a game played ruthlessly—the actors seldom made it easy for each other—until everyone is played out. Perhaps Webster planned something like this, because the ordered groupings, sustained encounters, and deliberate watchfulness required in performance of the earlier acts are followed by slow and painful concentration in the prison scenes of act 4 and then by the dispersed and individual movements, extreme attitudes, stubborn but failing energies, and accelerating and rending dissolutions that make up the last act. Exhausted and now only briefly assertive, the actors present their characters stumbling toward disintegration and the audience watches spellbound, even by the mere spectacle.

For experienced playgoers, the Cheek by Jowl production also held attention through a tension between what was expected and what was provided. The character of the Duchess was at the center of this interest, for Antonio's description of her "sweet countenance," "continence," and "noble virtue" (1.1.187–205) was clearly contradicted by a nervous, taut, and potentially violent woman. An ability to inspire Bosola with a vision of heaven and hope of mercy (4.2.347–49) was a most unlikely attribute for such a protagonist. The new interpretation would have found little justification in a reading of the text—as if the director had not bothered to analyze it for meanings and instructions—yet at certain times the text itself emerged with entirely new force and conviction, as if responding to the mistreatment, as if the wrenching of meaning and sudden shifts of attention and mood were appropriate to Webster's way of writing for performance. Improvisation, boldness, and violence appeared as more suitable than sober calculation as a way of reacting to the often confusing messages of the play's dialogue.

* * *

Both productions were driven by their actors' invention and realization of individual character. Both were performed in a theater whose overall dimensions are not much larger than those of the Globe Theatre and allow a similarly close focus. The play had immediacy and seemed both timely and vital. It was nervously, sensuously, and sexually alive in ways that caught the audience's attention for its strange and dated fictions. Duchess, Duke, Cardinal, and Steward could not be confused with persons in contemporary society, but nevertheless they seemed to belong there: as Declan Donnellan said, "Webster's characters are everywhere"—if given the chance, it may be added, to leap out of the past into present consciousness and actuality. However, both productions were stronger in private moments than in sustained and public scenes; and in both Bosola failed to make a strong impression.

One reason for these shared characteristics and shared success was the small scale of each enterprise. Elaborate stage effects did not detract attention from the actors or slow up the play's progress while elaborate stage images were assembled. This suggests that the expensive and eye-catching set designs and stage management preferred by more established theater companies across the world are not necessarily advantages when staging English Renaissance plays: a close focus and actors actively and freshly engaged are to be valued more highly.

However, the limited budgets did have disadvantages. Had they wished to show the allure of great wealth and self-esteem, these productions did not have the funds to do so. Nor did they have the manpower to stage a full court in which the power-game is played with quiet watchfulness and where public ceremony is the occasion for careful manipulation and covert exchanges. Neither of them succeeded in showing how the "consort of madmen" could terrify the Duchess by expressing repetitive and destructive sexual fantasies. Neither could show the confinement caused by the exercise of power contrasted with the precarious freedom of escape and isolation. These are all qualities in English Renaissance plays that are expensive to stage in modern conditions because of the number of actors required. (In time, perhaps, new technology will find a quick and reasonably priced way to give these scenes a virtual reality in the theater.)

Another reason for underplaying the political implications of Webster's text and others from the same period is the prevalent emphasis on *moments* of truth in both rehearsal and actor-training: actors do not give the same level of attention to the development of an argument or a consistent point of view. This failing is encouraged by Webster's dialogue that is particularly concerned to represent fragmented thought and thus can be cut easily; in doing so, however, a director can lose the shaping power of the writing, its often concealed but tenacious hold over the development of ideas, through all its repetitions, hesitations, and digressions. With his speeches pruned of any farfetched or not strictly necessary detail, and with some speeches removed altogether, Bosola did not stand a chance of offsetting the play's extraordinary events with an inward-tuned consciousness, nor could he present clearly his change from malcontent to revenger, cynic to moralist, hired intelligencer to surrogate protagonist. None of this can be made apparent to the audience with a series of isolated moments of "truth," however delicately real or blatantly theatrical their enactment. In a foreword to a celebratory book about the company, Michael Racliffe noted that Cheek by Jowl's *Hamlet* was one of the two productions in their first ten years that had disappointed him when he followed their work as a critic: its "intended simplicity," he wrote, "seemed, most uncharacteristically, to give the play no firm direction or narrative shape."[12] The sustained and tormented inward life of Hamlet can be given its central place in the tragedy only by the same means as those needed to bring Bosola to full life on the stage; directed to achieve only moments of truth, both *Hamlet* and *The Duchess of Malfi* will lose coherence and these two characters their prominence.

A third reason why the political and philosophical aspects of the tragedy were undervalued is that both productions concentrated attention on the sexual relationships of Duchess to Ferdinand and Antonio, although only one of them had given star-treatment to the actors playing them. Both also emphasized the Cardinal's sexual proclivities rather than his power over others that derives from his intellect and his position in the church. When actors are encouraged to work from their own sense of their characters' situations, a Renaissance play is very likely to be reduced to the measure of those aspects of modern life that are most readily related to the dramatic text, and not those deriving from political realities that are outside the experience of ordinary citizens or from ideas that are far from easy to understand and define. Putting on such plays as *The Duchess of Malfi* should involve more than the actors and director finding what "works" for them and how "life" can most readily be breathed into the text. The incessant exploration of Cheek by Jowl productions and the self-imposed critical sense of the experienced actors in the Greenwich production will always help to reach beyond what is merely conventional or easily successful, but a more rigorous intellectual inquiry and a greater concern for historical processes are also required if texts such as this one are to yield further secrets and productions realize their less accessible possibilities.

No one who cares for the plays of the English Renaissance can be other than grateful and glad that these two companies brought so much finesse and energy and such open-ended and committed exploration to their productions of *The Duchess;* these are techniques needed to restore plays like this to favor in our theater, and these companies have shown others the way to follow. Their success has also demonstrated that large theaters and expensive stage settings are not important but rather militate against suitable performance and reception. Better finance should rather be used to pay four or five more actors and to allow longer initial rehearsals; with these advantages, both productions would have been better able to tackle the play's political and intellectual issues.

Notes

1. "Dramatic restorers at work," Declan Donnellan and Nick Ormerod interviewed by Benedict Nightingale, *The Times* (London, 29 December 1995).

2. From verses prefixed to the first edition of the play, 1623; quoted, as all passages from *The Duchess of Malfi,* from the Revels Plays edition, ed. John Russell Brown (London: Methuen, 1964).

3. *The Sunday Times* (London, 13 February 1994).

4. From verses prefixed to the first edition of the play, 1623.

5. The performance described in this article was given on 15 May 1995, shortly before the production's hundredth performance in London; some details were checked in subsequent discussion immediately afterward with Robert Demeger, who played the Cardinal.

6. John Harrop's *Acting* (London: Routledge, 1992) offers a clear compendium of such advice: on sense-memory see esp. 39–42; on physical action, 54–55.

7. According to Robert Demeger (see note 5), the characters' laughs had been added during the pre-London tour as the actors and director learned what was needed to retain their audiences' attention and belief, and to stop them from laughing at their performances.

8. The performance that is the source for most of the following observations was on 4 January 1996.

9. These comments are from the following sources, named in the order in which they have been quoted: *The Guardian, The Independent, The Evening Standard, The Financial Times, The Observer, The Sunday Telegraph, The Spectator, The Independent on Sunday, The Daily Express.*

10. Simon Reade, *Cheek by Jowl, Ten Years of Celebration* (Bath: Absolute Classics, 1991), 107, 101, 102.

11. Amanda Harris in ibid., 101.

12. Reade, 7.

Women Play Women in the Liturgical Drama of the Middle Ages

DUNBAR H. OGDEN

FROM the tenth through the sixteenth century the *Visitatio Sepulchri (The Visit to the Sepulcher)* was staged all over Europe, performed steadily for seven hundred years. It was the dramatization of the three Marys coming to the sepulcher of Jesus, sung as part of the church liturgy on Easter Sunday morning. Today about 1,000 manuscripts still survive, many with musical notations, from nearly 700 monastic and municipal churches. All of the roles were sung by male clergy, including the Marys, as well as the roles of Angels (with a few boys as Angels), the Risen Christ, and the disciples Peter and John when their scene was included in the *Visitatio,* with one striking exception: performance in the nunnery. In every extant text of the *Visitatio* from a nunnery or from a chapter of cathedral canonesses (and we possess twenty-one) the roles of the women were taken by women. No other liturgical dramas were performed in nunneries. The roles of the three Marys provided the first, the oldest, and the longest performance practice for women in the drama of the Western world.[1]

One could argue that these twenty-one music-dramas performed by women comprise a precious, isolated phenomenon, born in the twelfth century and dying out around 1600. Certainly one does not trace direct theatrical lines from these nuns to the professional actresses on the stages of sixteenth-century Spain and Italy. Nor does the liturgical drama bear direct import upon the flourishing of Renaissance drama. Yet with their cult of Mary Magdalen and with their practices over seven centuries in music, language, and movement, the dramas feed and were fed by the wellsprings of medieval culture. They answer a need for dramatic expression by women and for the education of women.

What, if anything, distinguished the twenty-one performance traditions with women from the usual, all-male performances? What happened when women instead of men played the Marys at the

Easter Sepulcher? And when a woman took the part of Mary Magdalen? Are there any traces left, however faint? Did the sound of female voices, the appearance of female body language, the very presence of women make any impression on the remaining texts, our only sources, with their words and music and their stage directions? Who composed them? Or compiled them?

The original *Visitatio Sepulchri* emerging in the tenth century is a compilation of traditional antiphons and tropes such as "Quem quaeritis," borrowed from the liturgy and patched together to tell the story of the Marys and the Angel(s) at the Easter Sepulcher. As the play spread throughout Europe, variations were made in the text and music. A number of the women's dramas seem to reveal new work by a single hand, some individual who has meticulously crafted the coalescing of traditional antiphons with new composition. That person may have been the Abbess.

The Abbess

Chief among the women of a convent stood the Abbess. She was the head of the house: usually a woman of some social rank and education and frequently authoritarian in her rule. It was she who would take in hand any cloistral performance. Rarely in the Middle Ages could a woman exert independence and exercise leadership, but as an Abbess a woman might reach beyond the confines of quotidian routine toward power and invention. When we come upon an unusual rendering of the *Visitatio Sepulchri* from a women's convent, it is quite likely that an Abbess was the one who made it for her nuns to perform, annealing existing music and texts with fresh compositions, perhaps even her own.

Two of the twenty-one surviving women's manuscripts actually name an Abbess. At Barking, it was Katherine of Sutton (Abbess, 1363–76) who, according to the manuscript, promoted the *Visitatio* with its singular Harrowing of Hell ceremony. She encouraged this dramatization to counteract what she perceived as "stultified devotion" and local "indifference" toward Easter celebration. At Origny, one manuscript of the *Visitatio* records the name of Isabelle d'Ascy (1286–1324) as the Abbess who had had the older text copied; she was probably also responsible for its stage directions in French; whether she augmented the text and music in any way, we do not know. These pioneers belong to the ranks of other powerful, often autocratic Abbesses who emerged in the Middle Ages, such as Hildegard von Bingen (1089–1179) with her original music compositions, her writings on natural science, and her wide-ranging correspondence. Some Abbesses were known for their homilies. The daughters of the Lüneberg nobility and the House of Braunschweig were educated at the convent of Medingen, where Abbesses enjoyed a considerable reputation as preachers and where in the *Visitatio* women played the Mary-roles.

One piece of evidence comes from Essen in the Ruhr area in Germany. It is very probable that a woman, perhaps the Abbess, created the fourteenth-century *Visitatio* for the Collegiate Church of Canons and Canonesses at Essen. From the St. George nunnery in Prague comes a unique thirteenth-century *Visitatio* that reveals, as Susan Rankin, the leading authority on this music, points out, "its own newly composed melodies." There as elsewhere, the figure of Mary Magdalen began to emerge. Rankin goes on with her musical analysis: new composition in the Mary Magdalen scene with the Risen Christ made it possible to realize modal and stylistic unity with the surrounding texts and melodies. In fact, because its set of texts and melodies was transmitted en bloc, the Mary Magdalen scene may have been composed "by one person at one time."[2]

Manuscripts from nunneries reflect a sense of the Abbess and her women. In fact, from beginning to end the Abbess presided. Nuns in a convent normally observed the hours unto themselves, including matins. However, Easter matins was a special event, and it seems that even in a convent members of the male clergy participated in it with the nuns. When Easter matins included the little drama and the time came for its performance, the male celebrant might lead off a procession; and when the play was finished he or his Cantor usually intoned the music that concluded matins, the *Te Deum*.

But when the drama was sung by nuns or canonesses, one felt everywhere the presence of the Abbess. It was she who processed from the nuns' or canonesses' choir loft with the women's chorus (the *conventus*) out into the nave of the church for the *Visitatio*. At Prague she led off a great procession into mid-church as a prelude to the performance; at Troyes, with a light, a book, and the Marys, she marched at the climax of a huge procession of male clergy. At Poitiers she took up a central position in the east choir as the drama commenced, with the Angel, two servant-nuns, and her sacristan distributing lights to the participants. It was she who at Nottuln signaled her *Cantrix* to conclude the *Visitatio* with the singing of the *Te Deum*.

From beginning to end the Abbess presided. At Gandersheim only the Abbess entered the Sepulcher during the *Depositio* (the Good Friday burial ceremony of the cross)—in the presence of novices as well as townspeople. During the *Depositio* at Essen she led her convent out into the nuns' cemetery, where she then stood on one dish of a giant scale, a ham and a lamb on the other dish, symbolizing Christ's sacrifice as righting the balance over against the weight of man's sin. During the *Visitatio* at the convent of Gernrode the three Marys emerged from the Sepulcher (a stone replica of the Holy Sepulcher in Jerusalem) to move through the church to the Abbess, singing of their discovery, "Surrexit cominus," directly to her. They also paused in mid-church to sing an antiphon at the tomb of Hathui, the much-revered founding Abbess. This gesture linked Hathui with Christ's Resurrection, bestowing a special blessing upon Hathui. At the same time, the gesture drew from Hathui's tomb an assurance to the Gernrode nuns of their own eventual resurrection. At the end of matins as the nuns of Gernrode ascended again back into their choir loft, the manuscript says that the Abbess collected from them the candles she had distributed at the outset of the *Visitatio*.

The Marys or, if included in the play, Peter and John (always played by male clergy), finished every version of the *Visitatio* by taking the sacred gravecloth from the Sepulcher and holding it up for all to see, tangible evidence of the Resurrection. In the early performance at the St. George convent of Prague (from the twelfth century), Peter and John concluded the drama with that public gesture. But the nunnery at Prague added a unique touch. There the Abbess initiated a little ceremony by going over and kissing the gravecloth—followed by the nuns *(sorores)* and then by the townspeople standing nearby *(populus circumstans)*.[3]

The Rite of Purification: The Abbess and the Three Marys

At Origny the nuns who were to play the Mary-roles first went through a rite of purification. This little ritual is documented in manuscripts for four convents in the following years: Barking (1363–76); Origny (c.1286, and fourteenth century); Troyes (thirteenth century); and the Abbey of St. Edith's at Wilton (1250–1320). Such a ritual of cleansing does not occur in a single one of about 680 churches where men played the roles of the Marys, in either secular or monastic churches.

The manuscript rubrics from the French convent of Origny read as follows (in French-Picardy dialect):

> . . . they [the three to play the roles of the Marys] should confess and go to my lady during the canticles of Matins, and each one should give (donate) some possession [*propriété*] on her own and place [there] whatever they have of their own will, and they should say the "Confiteor," and my Lady should say the "Misereatur" and the "Indulgentiam." Afterward, the Marys should go and get dressed [in their white tunics (shifts) and in their cloaks (mantles) and in white underveils (couvre-chefs) without a veil *(dens leur blans chainses et leurs mantiaus et en blans cueurechies sans voil)*] and come before the altar of Magdalen, and they should be at prayer until the time set for going to the Sepulchre.

Since the ninth century this "Confiteor" or confession, a formulaic prayer, was said by the celebrant during two of the canonical hours, Prime and Compline. With the "Confiteor" he was acknowledging his sinfulness and begging the mediation of those who assisted him in the service. They immediately give him this mediation, saying the "Misereatur," and, in turn, saying the "Confiteor." The priest-celebrant responded with the "Misereatur" and went on to give them Absolution, saying the "Indulgentiam." By the early eleventh century this observance had also been inserted into the Mass. In each instance it was performed at the high altar. It is a liturgical confession, a formal act using established formulaic wording just like the rest of the liturgy.

A second type of confession marked monastic as well as secular life of the Middle Ages: sacramental Confession. A monk said confession weekly to a spiritual director selected from the monastic community. In like manner it was often the case in the monastery that the celebrant-priest, before going out to say Mass, said a private confession to his spiritual father. And at the farther range, each Christian believer was required to make confession at least once a year, normally preparatory to Easter. In every instance, the basic formula for this private, or sacramental confession was the same as for the public, liturgical confession. The confessing individual said the "Confiteor," and the spiritual father responded with the "Misereatur" and granted him absolution with the "Indulgentiam." This sacramental confession was part of personal purification, whereas liturgical confession was part of public ceremony.

In the convent at Origny, the rite between the Abbess and the Mary-role players partakes of both liturgical confession and sacramental confession. In the spirit of liturgical confession, the Marys make confession to the Abbess just as those assisting in the canonical hours and at Mass make confession to the priest-celebrant. Thereupon the Marys receive absolution from the Abbess just as those assisting in the hours and at Mass receive absolution from the priest-celebrant. In that sense, the Abbess is taking on special powers reserved for the male priesthood. And just as in the liturgical confession, so the Mary-role players will kneel at prayer at an altar at Origny, here the apposite altar of Mary Magdalen.

In addition, this rite just before the *Visitatio Sepulchri* at Origny is also like the second kind of confession, sacramental confession. In that sense, removed from the ongoing service of matins the Marys say the private "Confiteor" to the Abbess as their spiritual director, just as each of them in her life as a nun used the formula "Confiteor" in her weekly confession to her spiritual director. This individual cleansing is reinforced at Origny with the giving of a personal gift, each presented by the nun expressly of her own free will.

Moreover, in this private, sacramental sense, the confession of the Mary-role players parallels the private, sacramental confession of the priest-celebrant in a monastery before he goes out into the main church to say Mass. Upon receiving personal absolution from the Abbess, each of the nuns will dress in white, pray at the altar of Mary Magdalen, and then go out into the main church to carry a sacred reliquary—a blessed cloth between her hands and the reliquary—to the Easter Sepulcher. In that moment they are the *celebrants.*

This rite embodies some remarkable phenomena. Here the Abbess takes unto herself sacred powers reserved for the male clergy. Moreover, the women undergo a rite of purification before they can perform the roles of the Marys. It is both public-liturgical and private-sacramental. It is a rite that not a single member of the male clergy underwent before playing in a liturgical drama—a rite that links to numerous religious acts where women must be cleansed in some special way before participating in a sacred observance.[4]

The order of events in this confessional act signals symbolic steps in preparing the nuns to perform their roles. At Origny they first confessed at the Magdalen altar, then dressed in white; then they prayed at the Magdalen altar; finally they rose and each received a reliquary on a blessed cloth; and then they went out into the church and moved to the Sepulcher. At St. Edith's nunnery at Wilton the order is also the same: first they are cleansed, then they change clothing. The three *cantrices* get up from the choir, wash their hands, take off their veils ("absconso velamine"), and put white underveils on their heads "candidum velum . . . in similitudine mulierum." Then they take up phylacteries, candlesticks, and thuribles and go out searching for the Sepulcher. There is this literal washing, but no "Confiteor." Wilton had strong ties with Origny.

The positioning of the confessional rite in the observance also imbued it with special power. At Origny, to say confession prepared the nuns to wear white (and to handle sacred relics). Whereas at Barking to wear white prepared the nuns to say confession. In the English nunnery of Barking the Abbess herself dressed the Marys, and *after* that—rather than *before*—she heard their confession. Following a Harrowing of Hell ceremony, the Abbess and the three nuns chosen to play the Marys entered into the Chapel of St. Mary Magdalen. There the nuns exchanged their black vestments for white surplices, and the Abbess put a snow-white veil on each of them (*nigris vestibus . . . exute, nitidissimis superpellicijs induantur, niveis velis a Domina Abbatissa capitibus earum superpositis*—note the emphasis on *nitidissimis,* the brightest, finest). Then each took up a silver vessel. Thereupon they said confession to the Abbess (the "Confiteor") and she gave them absolution. And then they stood with candles, and Mary Magdalen began to sing.

As at Barking, so in the Notre Dame Convent of Troyes there was first the costume change, then the confession. At Troyes the three Marys dressed in their habits, together with two children in white as the Angels *(iij. Dames en lor habiz et li Enfant si sont toutes blanches et crevechie blanc sor lor testes).* Then the Marys came before the high altar, knelt down, and said confession (the "Confiteor"); then each Mary received a candle, a cloth, and a vessel; whereupon a great procession led them out into the church and to the western extreme of the nave for the *Visitatio.*

However, at Troyes the Mary-role players said their confession not to their Abbess but to the celebrant-priest. It was he who, in turn, said the "Misereatur" and gave them absolution—and then presented each with a candle, cloth, and vessel. There at Troyes the Marys performed a much more public act of confession than at Origny and Barking, and in kneeling at the high altar they were undertaking the same age-old confession as did a celebrant-priest before he said Mass.

Nowhere is such a practice of purification recorded when the *Visitatio Sepulchri* was performed by the male clergy. The little confessional rite is an act of inner purification. It retains the sense that women must be cleansed, a folk-practice reaching back into the mists of prehistory as it reaches forward into our own day.

Furthermore, in presiding over the solemnity of confession the Abbess at Origny and Barking appropriated to herself a religious power normally reserved solely for men, for priests. Thus not only does this ceremonial appear to carry age-old practice of cleansing women, but it also reveals a singular, sacred act by the Abbess.

Fresh Composition and Human Feeling—at Origny and at Barking

ORIGNY, STE. BENOITE

Examinations of the four texts from the French nunnery of Origny and then, comparatively, of the ceremony and play from the English nunnery of Barking reveal patterns of fresh creation, work possibly even composed in these women's religious institutions by the women themselves.

Let us first consider the exchange between Mary Magdalen and Jesus in the dramatic *Visitatio* from Origny to perceive exactly what distinguishes this moment from its counterparts in versions performed by men and from its counterparts in other versions where the Marys were played by women.

According to thirteenth-and fourteenth-century *Visitatio* texts from Origny, L303 and L303a, toward the end of Easter matins the three nuns who are to play the three Marys are prepared before the Altar of the Blessed Mary Magdalen, offstage as it were. Each says confession and is given absolution by the Abbess. Thereupon they dress in white—albs, copes, and headdresses without veils—and pray at the Magdalen altar until it is time to go to the Sepulcher for the drama. A ceremonial occurs at the Sepulcher, an exchange that one can just barely call a drama.

But a third manuscript (with music) from Origny (c. 1220, copied 1315–17, L825) contains a remarkably ample dramatic composition. From here we follow L825. A priest with a censer then leads a procession. Each of the Marys has a lighted candle; Mary Magdalen also carries a (spice) box. Then comes the chorus, each of the women with a lighted candle. The antiphon here, "Quis revolvet ergo nobis ab hostio lapidem" ("Who will roll the stone away from the entrance for us"), is a new composition.[5]

They meet the merchant *(li Marchans),* this and all other roles—except the Marys—played by male clergy. Mary Magdalen pauses, alone in pain, while the other two Marys bargain for spices. Nowhere else do we find such a moment, with Magdalen grieving as her two companions deal with a Spice-Seller. There follow ten stanzas of dialogue sung in French that are unique to this drama; they are original, not translations of Latin. The merchant is young and caring, eager to honor "tres grant Signeur."

The two Marys return to Magdalen, and the three continue their journey. Two Angels await them—one at the head of the Sepulcher, one at the foot. The Angels open the Sepulcher "un peu" and point with their fingers, singing "Non iacet hic." Then the Angels open up the Sepulcher completely, the three Marys approach it and kiss it, and the Angels close it. This is the only such gestural sequence that I know. The Marys' kissing the Sepulcher also occurs at Barking convent and at the Cathedral of Rouen, while only here do we find this partial opening, full opening, and then closing.[6] The Marys' ensuing lament, "Heu, infelices"—they are left unsatisfied by the sight of the empty grave—is unique. It extends and underscores their grief. The two Marys leave and Mary Magdalen remains by herself. Continuing the newly composed lament, "Infelix ego misera," she carries forth her exchange with the Angels, and then Jesus appears, singing the familiar text "Mulier, quid ploras? Quem queris?" but to a new melody. Magdalen bows to him (thinking him the gardener), asking "Domine, si tu sustulisti eum" ("Sir, if you have taken him [the body]"). Immediately the recognition takes place. Mary Magdalen sings "Raboni!" at Jesus' feet and then "throws herself" on the ground as Jesus sings "Noli me tangere."

This act of prostration occurs in two other Mary Magdalen scenes when played by a woman, at Barking and at Wilton, but in eight or nine such scenes where men play Mary Magdalen. Could this body language suggest a different concept of character, perhaps a more abject, self-abnegating Magdalen when performed by male clergy?

The text through here belongs to a French tradition, but the melodies are unique. Mary Magdalen thereupon gets up and remains alone in front of the Sepulcher while Jesus goes over to the other two Marys. Barking Convent and the Cathedral of Rouen provide the only other texts in which the Risen Christ appears first to Mary Magdalen and then proceeds to the other two Marys. They also throw themselves at his feet—again, an act singular to Origny, Barking, and Rouen. The two Marys then rise before him as he sings to them, "Ite nuntiate fratribus meis."[7]

In the Origny manuscript Jesus exits and the three sing "Eya nobis internas mentes," a unique adaptation of "Heu nobis internas mentes." The composer has taken a stanza that belongs to the opening lament of the three Marys (just prior to "Iam percusso"), moved it to this position, and turned it into a triumphal song. Rarely does one discover such sophisticated little alterations of the original material toward the creation of a new version of the *Visitatio*.

The Marys sing of their discovery, as usual, and the chorus of nuns responds "Deo gratias." Thereupon two apostles (Peter and John) come to the Marys. A unique gestural sequence follows: "taking Magdalen a little aside by the sleeve" *(prendent le manche le Magdelainne un peu de lons),* the apostles ask the standard question about what she has seen, "Dic nobis, Maria . . . ?" ("Tell us, Mary . . . ?"). They then let go of her sleeve *(laissent le manche le Magdelainne),* and she points with her finger to the Sepulcher (*demonstre au doit le Sepuchre* [*sic*]), singing forcefully *(en haut)* "Sepulcrum Cristi." When the two Marys come over, Magdalen again points with her finger to the Sepulcher. Finally she lays her hand on her breast *(met se main a sen pis),* singing "Spes nostra" ("Our hope") instead of the usual "Spes mea" (My hope"). She thereupon turns to point with her finger in another direction *(trestourne sen doit dautre part),* to sing "Precedet vos in Galileam." Other characters in a few other texts do point sometimes, but not Mary Magdalen. This pointing or gesturing in a direction seems to be a French tradition. I find four similar examples, but none—except at Barking—matched in this way to this particular exchange where she stands unaccompanied by the other women and, while singing, points with her finger.[8]

As the two disciples go to the Sepulcher, the normal antiphon at this point, "Currebant duo simul," has been turned into an exchange between disciples and chorus. This is the only such instance in the *Visitatio* drama. The disciples emerge with the sudary, the three Marys kneel and kiss it, and the disciples then carry it away from the Sepulcher. This act may have to do with one of the many relics at the cloister.[9] In the convents at Barking, Prague, and Wilton we find similar gestural patterns. At Barking, at "Dic nobis Maria," Mary Magdalen points with her finger to the Angel at the Sepulcher and then offers the sudary to be kissed by the clergy. At Prague, Peter and John hold the sudary while the Abbess, the nuns, and then the people standing nearby kiss it. At Wilton the Marys first venerate a sacred book *(textum),* and then the nuns and the populace may kiss it. The Origny manuscript breaks off at this point.

No men's religious order had the *Visitatio* so publicly led by an abbot or bishop as the Convent of Origny was led by its Abbess;

and none had the role-players say confession. No other men's or women's religious order had Mary Magdalen sing this amount of freshly composed music, engage with the other Marys in kissing the sudary, point with her finger to the Sepulcher and to Galilee, or be pulled aside by the sleeve.

Barking

In the fourteenth century, abbesses from both Origny and Barking seem to have augmented thirteenth-century *Visitatio* texts from their respective abbeys. The Barking text is also sui generis, a whole composition unified in its conception, where likewise the composer-author has woven together threads from both the Anglo-Norman and the French practice, intertwined with new, unique composition. Would that the music from Barking had survived, as it has from Origny.

Here too, at Barking, one feels the controlling presence of the Abbess. The *Elevatio* of the surviving text actually names Abbess Katherine of Sutton (Abbess of Barking, 1363–76). She promoted and may have elaborated the much older Easter ceremony and drama, because, according to the rubrics, she was concerned about "rooting out indifference" in the gathering of the people *(populorum concursus),* "and in order to stimulate the most ardent celebration." Here too a general populace was present.

A unique *Elevatio* served as antecedent to the *Visitatio,* both performed just before the end of matins. A procession led by the Abbess, with the entire convent together with some priests and clerks, each priest and clerk with a palm and an unlighted candle, entered the Chapel of St. Mary Magdalen, apparently within the main church. Then they closed the chapel door. A Harrowing of Hell ceremony followed, where from outside a priest beat on the door three times—Christ knocking on the gates of hell—whereupon "the gates should fly open," and the priest led the group out "like the patriarchs," through the middle of the choir, and over to the Sepulcher. What the Sepulcher looked like, we do not know. The priest entered the Sepulcher, removed the Host, and took it to the high altar. The procession moved on to the Holy Trinity Altar, "in the manner in which Christ proceeded to Galilee after the Resurrection, with His disciples following."

This is the only such Harrowing of Hell sequence in a women's institution, and, together with the *Ludus Paschalis* from Klosterneuburg, the only one performed within matins (not before) and located within a church chapel. Otherwise, wherever the rare Harrowing of Hell is presented, a procession winds around the outside of the church prior to Easter matins, and the knocking, with singing from within, occurs at an exterior door.

At Barking thereupon three sisters *(Tres Sorores)* selected by the Abbess, together with the Abbess herself, return to the Chapel of St. Mary Magdalen. They like the entire convent were dressed in black. The Abbess then dresses the Marys in the purest white surplices with while veils on their heads. Thus prepared, and each holding a silver vessel, they make confession (they say the "Confiteor") to the Abbess and she gives them absolution ("et ab ea absolute"). They then sing three passages unique to Barking. As previously noted, the convents of Barking, Origny, and Wilton contain the only documentation of such a costume change done at this point and in this manner, and at Barking, Origny, and Troyes the only saying of confession by the role-players (at Troyes, not to the Abbess but to a priest).[10]

After the exchange with one of the two Angels, played by a clerk *(clericus),* the women enter and kiss the sepulcher, a gesture also found only at Origny and Rouen Cathedral. Magdalen picks up the sudary. During the subsequent exchange the Angels say or sing (we have no music from Barking) "Quid queritis viventem cum mortuis?" ("Why do you seek the living among the dead?"), a direct quote from Luke 24:5.[11] It is followed by a unique rubric, "Then they still doubting the Resurrection of the Lord shall say mourning to each other: 'Heu dolor . . .'" (*Tunc Ille de Resurrexione Domini adhuc dubitantes plagendo dicant ad invicem:* "Heu dolor"). Only at Barking does a stage direction convey this doubt as to the Resurrection. Mary Magdalen sighs *(suspirando),* singing "Te suspiro . . ."; only in the text from Coutances Cathedral do we hear again this particular expression of vocal mourning.

Jesus appears, at the left side of the altar—whether now the high altar, we do not know—and eventually Mary Magdalen prostrates herself at his feet singing "Raboni!" Jesus, singing "Noli me tangere," draws back and then goes away. Thereupon follows a moment unique to this drama—

> . . . Maria gaudium suum consociabus communicet voce letabunda hos concinendo Versus:
>
> Gratulari et letari. . . .

> Mary joyfully imparts to her companions, singing in a glad voice this verse:

Give thanks and rejoice. . . .

As at Origny, Jesus reappears—to the right of the altar—now to the three Marys together. And they, prostrate on the ground, hold and kiss his feet. This prostration also occurs at Origny, but not the holding and kissing.[12] Again, something original follows here from the composer-author. Not only is the ensuing piece, "Ihesus ille Nazarenus," newly composed and unique to Barking, but, the prostration finished, each of the three women is instructed to sing a different stanza, each to a different melody.

The next piece is also unique to Barking: "Alleluia. Surrexit Dominus." In singing it the three Marys stand on the step in front of the altar and turn toward the populace. The nuns' chorus responds in repeating the "Alleluia."

Another newly composed piece introduces a turn in the scene as priests and clerks in the role of disciples come forward to sing "O gens dira."

The "Dic nobis Maria" is very similar to that from the convents of Origny and Troyes. As at Origny, Mary Magdalen points with her finger to the Sepulcher—"where the Angel was sitting," the Barking text adds.

But quite different from the Magdalen at Origny, at Barking she holds the sudarium and offers it to the clergy *(sacerdotes et clerici)* to be kissed. Only at Origny, otherwise, do participants kiss the sudary—there the Marys—and at Prague, where the abbess, convent *(sorores),* and populace kiss the gravecloth (held by Peter and John). It is a liturgical kiss that parallels the kissing of the Sepulcher by the women at Origny.

Men and women sing together the "Credendum est" and the "Scimus Christum," whereupon Magdalen begins "Christus resurgens" and both the clergy and the women's chorus pick it up. We also find men and women explicitly singing together at Origny.

During the singing of the *Te Deum,* the priests who had been the disciples (now in their usual vestments) reenter from "the chapel," probably the Magdalen chapel, and with candles they cross through the choir to the Sepulcher, pray, return, and pause—here a unique, mimed reminder of the race to the tomb by Peter and John. The Abbess then gives them the signal to exit. And Lauds commences.

Special Features of Men's Texts

It is also in the *Visitatio* texts that the scene between the Marys and the Spice-Seller first emerges—at Vich in Spain (eleventh to twelfth-century manuscript). The Spice-Seller's second oldest appearance occurs in a women's text, from the St. George nunnery in Prague. The Marys purchase their funeral ointments from him. And thereafter he appears in men's texts: for example, a single Spice-Seller at Klosterneuburg, and together with a younger merchant at Egmond *(Specionarius, mercator juvenis).* In the Tours manuscript (from a nunnery?) the cast also includes a *Mercator* and a *mercator juvenis,* while at Benediktbeuern *Apothecarius* even has a wife *(Uxor Apothecarii).*

Many of the twenty-one extant men's plays with the character of Mary Magdalen also manifest other inventive variations; but *all* of the twenty-one women's plays contain fresh material (fourteen that single out Magdalen among the Marys; and seven that do not single her out).[13]

Women Identify with the Marys

In addition to the role of the Abbess and the purification rites, what is particular about the drama texts from women's orders with women singing the Mary roles? One is struck, first of all, by the emerging presence of Mary Magdalen in them. While she appears in liturgical plays from a total of thirty-five different monastic and secular churches, counting both men's and women's institutions, her role is emphasized in 70 percent of the texts originating from women's orders (14 out of 21), and in only 3 percent of the texts deriving from men's orders and from secular churches (21 out of about 680). Some of the dramatic texts actually make use of a Mary Magdalen chapel (plays from the nunneries of Barking and Marienberg; a Mary Magdalen altar at Origny). These chapels and altars are a sign of the cult of Mary Magdalen that arose in the twelfth and thirteenth centuries.[14] Nuns and canonesses could identify as women with the Marys and especially with Mary Magdalen. According to the biblical narratives it was to the women that the news of the Resurrection was first given. It was to Mary Magdalen that the Risen Christ first appeared—she a "fallen woman," a sinner given special blessing, one with a unique relationship to Jesus. Nuns, from the beginning of female monasticism, could see themselves reflected in these biblical women. Then as now they were "the brides of Christ," in their devotions and liturgies. To make the next move from singing antiphons and other ecclesiastical music in the Divine Office to singing antiphons and other verses in the *Visitatio Sepulchri* demanded but a small step.

The liturgical drama emerged from ceremony with the creation of mimetic action and character. Mary Magdalen was central to that process because she was featured in the first truly dramatic Easter scene where at the Sepulcher she weeps over Jesus' death, Jesus appears to her, she mistakes him for the gardener, and then in the most famous recognition scene in Western literature he sings only her name, "Maria" in the liturgical drama, and she, recognizing him, sings "Rabboni" ("teacher"), falling at his feet, as he backs away, singing, "Do not touch me."

This little scene gave impetus to new poetic and musical creation. Whereas the earliest texts of the *Visitatio* itself date to the tenth century, the earliest texts with Mary Magdalen as a character date to the twelfth century. In these plays and in almost every one of the subsequent Easter plays with Mary Magdalen as a character, something unusual occurs, whether played by a man or a woman: fresh musical composition, a new ceremonial moment, a unique gestural pattern.[15]

The following manuscripts of the *Visitatio* from convents are unique in another respect: those from Gernrode, Münster (Liebfrauen), Origny, Regensberg, and Troyes contain descriptive rubrics that are not in Latin, as is the case with all other extant manuscripts of liturgical drama. From Gernrode, Münster, and Regensburg, rubrics are in German; from Origny and Troyes, rubrics are in French. Why the vernacular in manuscripts from five out of 700 localities? Perhaps they acknowledge the rarity of women trained in Latin. It is only from women's orders that liturgical drama texts exhibit this vernacular phenomenon. The Origny play even includes some newly composed passages to be sung in French.

A different kind of rubric also suggests fresh composition rather than a copy of a *Visitatio* text and music borrowed from another church. Four of the dramas with women as the Marys call for the use of special prompt scripts during performance—and at Origny, a prompter. There in a pair of the Origny manuscripts (L303, 303a), when the Marys come to the door of the Sepulcher, "the cantor [masculine] should be with them, who should teach them what they should say." At Poitiers the *capiceria* (sacristan) gave various participants—including the Abbess—each "a taper or candle to illuminate what they say [sing]." At Regensburg-Obermünster each of the three Marys took a "Zetl" with her, presumably a slip of paper with the role written out. At Essen the Angels seated in the tent used as the Sepulcher "have a book which contains the songs they are to sing if they do not know them by heart, and candles in order to see." This direction also suggests a special lighting effect because the candles provided the only illumination within the Sepulcher. At Troyes the Marys were guided by a nun processing along beside them with a torch "to light them and bringing the book into which they look." There too a special lighting effect was achieved. At the proper dramatic moment two candelabra-bearers entered the Sepulcher with the Marys and the door was then shut. Whether or not the rest of the congregants at Troyes could see flickering firelight through openings in the Sepulcher walls, we do not know. But after a ceremony at the altar inside the Sepulcher, the Marys emerged with the gravecloth to move to the convent-choir and sing the good news to them: "Surrexit Dominus de sepulcro."

If any one characteristic of these innovative details makes the performances by women as Mary Magdalen and the other Marys distinctive, it seems to exist in the expression of human feeling. Something from inside the characters is revealed a little more frequently and a little more insistently than in the men's texts. To single out one graphic example let us recall the previously discussed emotional moment where, after Mary Magdalen has met the Risen Christ in the *Visitatio* at the nunnery of Origny, the apostles come and ask what she has seen, singing the traditional "Dic nobis, Maria" ("Tell us, Mary"). At Origny the stage direction reads: "And the two apostles [Peter and John] come before the Marys, and, taking Magdalen a little aside by the sleeve, they say [sing], 'Dic nobis, Maria'."

Nowhere else in the entire canon of the liturgical drama does that tiny gesture occur. It is a moment of intimacy, an expression of urgency, perhaps a tug to one side for secrecy, possibly driven by fear—or excitement. It is a fleeting glimpse of intense human feeling.

Three Types of *Visitatio* Performances by Women

The twenty-one texts where women played women fall into three groups, all performances with the exception of Brescia, in the context of Easter matins. Examples of the first kind of drama come from Origny (L825) and Barking, and from Wilton. As already discussed, each comprises several scenes with extended sung dialogue.

A second type of women's *Visitatio* comprises a briefer drama than the first and seems to play out with less appended ceremony. Yet each of this second group is also marked by some unique feature: for instance, the Abbess alone entering the Sepulcher in the *Depositio* at Gandersheim; or a pair of alternative melodies provided for the "Surrexit Dominus" in a manuscript from Andernach.

Most examples of the women's *Visitatio* belong to a third type. Here the drama is also a simple little play, but it is embedded within the framework of an elaborate processional celebration: at Essen, Gernrode, Nottuln, Poitiers, Prague, Regensburg, Troyes, and two texts from Origny (L303, 303a). Each of this third kind of women's text exhibits unique features. For instance, as just noted, a light and a book for prompting were carried in the processionals at Essen, Poitiers, Regensburg, and Troyes. At Gernrode the three Marys wore special nuns' habits, including white wimples with red crosses on them. Likewise at Regensburg each of the Marys donned a special vestment, probably a surplice with its wide sleeves ("weit Ermel"). At Nottuln, Christ appeared barefoot, carrying a spade and wearing a wool cap; after Mary twice genuflected and then prostrated herself, Christ bent down and raised her up. Extensive processions occurred at Poitiers (into the westwork, a major architectural structure at the western extreme of the nave, with a singular scene between Mary Magdalen and an Angel), at Troyes (where the Marys said confession to a priest at the high altar), and at Prague, with its character of the Spice-Seller and its major juxtapositions and fusions of men's and women's voices.

Voices

In addition to the striking visual impact often specified in these women's texts, the sound of their music was different. One did on occasion hear a coalescing of men's and boys' voices in the drama, as in the liturgy, in monastic and nonmonastic churches. Once in awhile the roles of the Angels were sung by boys; more frequently, the schola of boys joined with the clergy to form the chorus. But in the nunneries one always heard the conjoining and alternating of male and female pitch, timbre, and resonance. There the male roles—Jesus, the Angel(s), and, in some dramas, the disciples Peter and John—were always taken by men. Thus one heard a singular mixture of male and female voices in the exchanges between the Marys and the Angel(s), between Mary Magdalen and Jesus, and, when the scene was included, between the women and the disciples. In the latter scene an almost operatic effect must have been achieved at Wilton. After her visit to the Sepulcher, Mary Magdalen is questioned by five monks, "Dic nobis, Maria." She displays the gravecloth, sings "Angelicos testes" ("Angelic witnesses"), and then sings "Credendum est magis" ("The single, truthful Mary") together with the five monks.

In a convent the nuns alone without a priest could and did celebrate the canonical hours that divided each of their days. At Mass and other special services they always formed the house choir. Thus at their matins on Easter morning (the first service of the day) they became the chorus for the drama. Often the manuscript rubrics direct the women to leave their own reserved choir area and move into the nave of the church to sing the *Visitatio*. An ordained priest always celebrated the Mass with its sacrament of the Eucharist—in all churches, including women's convents. Interestingly enough, in each of the women's *Visitatio Sepulchri* texts from the twenty-one different localities, not only did male clergy sing the male roles (including the Angels) but one or more members of the male clergy also participated in the matins service.[16]

Even more striking must have been those performances where male and female choruses sang the chant together, for instance, in a convent directly linked to a monastery such as at Gernrode, Münster, and Marienberg bei Helmstadt, or in a cathedral with a chapter of canonesses as well as canons, as at Essen. There at Essen three canonesses sang the roles of the Marys. During the performance the chorus of canonesses, descending from their own choir loft, joined the chorus of canons and the boys' schola on the main floor of the cathedral in front of the east choir. When the time came, the women sang the antiphon "Maria Magdalena" while up above the Marys passed along the second-story, south gallery toward the Sepulcher in the westwork. At a later point in the drama the men sang "Currebant duo simul" ("Two ran together") while Peter and John in like fashion passed along the second-story, north gallery to the Sepulcher. The Sepulcher, a coffer *(archa)* within a tent, stood in the second gallery of the westwork. The three Marys (played by canonesses) bent over and peered into the tent and said, "'Ubi est Jhesus?' vel similia verba" ("'Where is Jesus?' or similar words"). But they did not go in. Only the men, Peter and John (played by canons), were allowed to enter; not the women. Toward the end, when one of the disciples sang out the announcement of the Resurrection from the third story of the westwork, the canonesses' chorus down below responded with "Deo gratias." At the drama's finish, it was their *Cantrix* (choir leader) who led off the concluding music of the service, the singing of the *Te Deum lauda-*

mus, whereupon everyone joined in—women, men, boys, and the townspeople of Essen and vicinity.

Women Play Women

Did the presence of women in the liturgical drama effect any substantive difference? Taken together the innovations in medieval texts with women as role-players begin to point toward a more general pattern in societal change. From this perspective perhaps the *Visitatio* in the convent can be looked upon as a kind of paradigm. The convent as a community of women had existed for an extensive period of time. Then along came a pioneer, a literate individual and an explorer in many different areas. In the liturgical drama the innovator was most likely a woman, an Abbess. She functioned not *de novo* but as someone who galvanized what had been in existence for centuries: in this instance, bringing together the nuns and the already widespread and thriving *Visitatio.* As head of the convent she worked with the establishment, with the men of the Church of Rome. Much of the Abbess's leadership consisted in collaboration: in this example, men and women performing the *Visitatio* together. As a result of the sudden coalescence in the long-established community of women, many often surprising innovations burst from a single, central invention.

When one thinks of women and the drama of the Middle Ages, perhaps one thinks first of Hrotswitha from Gandersheim (c.935–973), with her six Latin one-act plays composed as Christian imitations of Terence. But these little dialogues with their sometimes elaborate, discursive stage directions must be considered as moral disquisitions, to be read aloud—there was no silent reading in this era—along with other didactic and devotional literature such as sacred history and saints' lives. Hrotswitha herself was not a nun but a noblewoman living voluntarily within a women's religious order, writing her histories and other poetic works in the brilliant cultural matrix of Gandersheim convent together with Hildesheim, its monastic counterpart. So far as we know, she had nothing to do with the liturgical drama or with any other plays that might have been acted.

For dramatic performance in the women's cloister one must look not to a Hrotswitha but to the person of the Abbess and to the *Visitatio Sepulchri.*

Convents for women had flourished under the aegis of the Church of Rome almost from its inception. When the women of the convent began to play the Marys, other distinctive phenomena also sprang up. Mary Magdalen emerged as a character, unusual acting instructions appeared, details of emotional expression evolved, new phrases and whole pieces of music were composed, original poetry was written, costumes were changed from black to white at the miraculous moment, and in some convents the female role-players first underwent a purification rite.

The longer *Visitatio* from Origny best exhibits this pattern of innovation. It also manifests another important inception principle, a combining of elements from two major traditions of the *Visitatio*: one belonging to the Anglo-Norman area, the other French. The composer of this particular drama fused elements from the two traditions together with her (or his?) own original compositions, textual and musical, fashioning finally not a collage but a complete and new artistic entity. Each detail has been shaped or carefully reshaped to fit an artistic unit. Taken as a whole, the plethora of minute elements that we can single out as musically and dramatically unique—from rearranged stanzas to fresh dialogue to singular gesture and body language—all yield a movement toward greater emotive expressiveness on the part of the characters, in particular on the part of Mary Magdalen.

Most likely the composer was an abbess. It is she who may even have freshly compiled, composed, and written a distinctive version of the *Visitatio* for her convent. Indeed she seems to have taken the *Visitatio* into her own hands just at the time when, toward 1200, medieval Europe was on the verge of a momentous period in the history of music and the development of the liturgical drama. With the *Visitatio* the Abbess made manifest the female religious experience: in the act of cleansing, in emotional expression, and in identification with the figure of Mary Magdalen.

TEXTS OF THE *VISITATIO SEPULCHRI*

—From the Lipphardt Edition, with Lipphardt text number and manuscript date. (The respective play itself often dates to a period earlier than the extant manuscript.) Walther Lipphardt, *Lateinische Osterfeiern und Osterspiele,* 9 vols. (Berlin: Walter de Gruyter, 1975–90).

"Visitatio" Texts from Churches, Nunneries with Women as the Marys

Andernach, St. Thomas, L355a (14th century)
Asbeck, L182–84 (1518, 16th century, 1524)
Barking, L770 (1363–76, 15th-century copy, text from 13th century or earlier)
Brescia, St. Julia, L8 (1438)
Essen, Cathedral, L564 (14th century)
Gandersheim, L785 (1438, 16th-century copy)
Gernrode, L786 (c. 1500)
Gerresheim, L213 (15th century), L214 and L574 (1692–95)
Havelberg, L787 (15th century)
Lichtenthal bei Baden-Baden, L832 (13th century)
Marienberg bei Helmstedt, L791 (13th century)
Medingen bei Lüneburg, L792 (c. 1320)
Münster, Liebfrauen, L793 (c. 1600)
Nottuln, L794 (c. 1420); L795 (pre-1493)
Origny, Ste. Benoîte, L303 (pre-1214, copied 1286); L303a, L304, and L825 (1315–17, text and music from c. 1220 or earlier)
Poitiers, Holy Cross Nunnery, L151–53 (13th to 14th century)
Prague, St. George Nunnery, L798–806 (12th to 14th century), L387 (15th century)
Regensburg-Obermünster, L796 (1567–87)
Salzburg Nonnberg, L718 (15th century)
Troyes, Notre Dame, L170 (13th century)
Wilton, St. Edith's (Rankin, "A New English Source") (1250–1320)

"Visitatio" Texts from Churches, Monasteries with Male Clergy as the Marys

Besançon, L94 (13th century)
Braunschweig, Cathedral, L780 (14th century) [canonesses as Marys?]
Coutances, Cathedral, L771 (c. 1400) [canonesses as Marys?]
Dublin, L772 (14th century)
Egmond, L827 (15th century) [Rijnsberg Nunnery performance?]
Joachimsthal (former Czechoslovakia), L789 (1520–23)
Klosterneuburg, L829 (13th century)
Le Mans, L113–14 (after 1482, 15th century)

Maastricht, L826 (c. 1200) [canonesses as Marys?]
Mont St. Michel, L773 (14th century)
Narbonne, L116 (n.d.)
Padua, L427 (13th century); L428 (14th to 15th century)
Paris, Ste. Chapelle, L148 (14th century); L149 (15th century)
Parisian texts, L123–49 (13th to 14th century)
Rheinau, L316 (c. 1600); L797 (13th century)
Rouen, L775–78 (12th to 14th century)
[Rouen, L812, *Officium Perigrinorum* (13th century)]
St. Gall, L331 (1582)
Vich, L823 (11th to 12th century)

"Visitatio" Texts with Unknown Ecclesiastical Origins

Tours, L824 (13th century)

Notes

1. A somewhat different version of this article on "Women Play Women," was published in *On-Stage Studies* 19 (1996):1–33.

I wish to thank Professor Georgia Wright for her help with material on women's religious institutions in the Middle Ages, and Professor Desirée Koslin for her guidance in work on the clothing worn by members of medieval women's orders.

2. Susan Rankin, "The Mary Madgalene Scene in the 'Visitatio Sepulchri' Ceremonies," in *Music in Medieval and Early Modern Europe,* ed. Iain Fenlon (Cambridge: Cambridge University Press, 1981):241, 250.

Another indication that nuns were creating their own individual versions of the *Visitatio Sepulchri* comes from the St. Thomas convent in Andernach. There a fourteenth-century manuscript includes two alternative melodies to the "Surrexit Dominus," the joyous antiphon that climaxes the *Visitatio.* To the best of my knowledge, it is the only such musical choice among the manuscripts of the liturgical drama. In addition, the superscript over this drama is unique: "Ordo Ad Sepulcrum Angelorum."

3. At Origny the three Marys kneel and kiss the gravecloth held by Peter and John, a gesture no doubt linked with a relic in the treasury of the nunnery (L825). Two other texts from Origny say that at the conclusion of the *Visitatio* the townspeople *(les bonnes gens)* are to be allowed to kiss the reliquaries (L303, L303a).

At Wilton, a *Visitatio* with many strong textual and musical links to Origny, the three Marys venerate ("adorent") a book extended to them by a subdeacon, and then the nuns and the townspeople kiss it ("omnis et populus"). Susan Rankin, "A New English Source of the *Visitatio Sepulchri,*" *Journal of the Plainsong and Mediaeval Music Society* 4 (1981):1–11.

4. For information about the "Confiteor," the "Misereatur," and the "Indulgentiam" throughout this period, see Joseph Jungmann, *The Mass of the Roman Rite,* 2 vols. (1951–55; reprint, Westminster, MD.: Christian Classics, 1992).

I wish to thank Prof. Joseph Duggan for his help in translating the medieval French and Richard D. McCall for his discussions of Jungmann et al. Any errors in the analysis of this purification rite are mine, not theirs.

5. Particular costumes of other Marys played by women: At Regensburg-Obermünster the Marys dress in the overgarments also used for the Maundy observances (washing of feet, feeding of the poor), possibly white surplices with their wide sleeves ("weit Ermel"). At Gernrode they dress in special nuns' habits with red crosses on their wimples.

For men's performances, the only Marys specified in the rubrics as wearing white are at Dublin, with surplices, and Mont St. Michel, with boys as the women *(iuveni)* in white dalmatics with the hoods pulled up "in the manner of matrons [women]" *(dalmaticis albis, habentes amicta super capita ad modum MATRONARUM).*

At Marienberg as well as at Barking the women prepare to perform the Mary-roles in the Mary Magdalen chapel.

6. At Rouen Cathedral an Angel points with his finger to the Sepulcher (L776).

The *Visitatio Sepulchri* at Winchester and at Rouen served as models for Barking. Barking, in turn, served as a model for Dublin. Rouen also served as a model for Origny. See, for example, Diane Dolan, *Le drama liturgique de Pâques en Normandie et en Angleterre au moyen-age* (Paris: Presses universitaires de France, 1975), 137ff.

7. Mary Magdalen also prostrates herself before the Risen Christ at the nunnery of Nottuln, but this is part of a little four-phase ceremony where she sings three pieces, genuflecting to Jesus at each of the first two and prostrating herself at the third, whereupon Jesus bends down and raises her up and blesses her. There is no "Noli me tangere" moment.

Rouen provided one of the models or sources for the author-composer of the Origny *Visitatio.* However, Mary Magdalen is not further singled out there save as *medius mulierum.*

At Wilton the three Marys approach the Sepulcher and prostrate themselves "one by one" when the Angel invites them, "Venite et videte."

8. Mary Magdalen at Barking points with her finger to the place "where the Angel was sitting" *(ubi Angelus sedebat),* the only overt indication of an exit by the Angel(s).

At Ste. Chapelle, Paris, the first two Marys point with their fingers to the Sepulcher and to the Angels respectively. In the *Visitatio* at Rouen, it is the Angel who points with his finger—singing "Non est hic" and indicating the Sepulcher to the Marys. At Narbonne, Magdalen points with her finger to the Angels. At Rheinau (a very ceremonial, late text, c. 1600) a priest points with his finger to the Angels.

Gesturing toward the Sepulcher, the Angels, and the gravecloth(s) occurs somewhat more frequently. At Dublin two of the three Marys respond *quasi monstrando* to "Dic nobis, Maria?" In the Tours manuscript, Mary Magdalen indicates four times with a gesture (e.g., *Maria ostendat eis Sepulchrum*)—toward the Sepulcher, the Angel, the sudary, and the cross—and two or three times at Maastricht. At Besançon, the second Mary shows or points to the gravecloths and the Angels *(ostendens sudarium et vestes et Angelos).* At Padua, Magdalen gestures toward the Angels and the gravecloth; in a later text, toward the Sepulcher and then the Angels. And in a late (1582), very ceremonial text from St. Gall, four boys as Angels gesture with their hands toward the Sepulcher.

The Magdalen character in the Cathedral of Rouen displays and unfolds the gravecloth(s) during the Easter play of *The Wayfarer,* the *Officium Peregrinorum (ostendat et explicet unum syndonem ex una parte loco sudarii, et alium ex altera parte loco vestium).*

The rare "Spes nostra" (Our hope) instead of "Spes mea" (My hope) in the Origny text also occurs at Barking; and at Le Mans, and in a body of Parisian texts.

9. A thirteenth-and a fourteenth-century text from Origny (L303, 303a) have "les bonnes gens" permitted to kiss reliquaries at the Sepulcher following the performance.

During the *Depositio* at Essen, an ivory-bound missal from the eleventh century, one of the treasures of the cathedral, was carried in procession and placed in the Sepulcher.

Rubrics from the following manuscripts call for the use of a Gospel Book as sacred object in the performance of the *Visitatio Sepulchri:* Fruttuaria, Monz, Fleury, Gerona, Vien (it is gold), St. Lambrecht, and in the Fleury Playbook (L9, 25, 49, 50, 74, 728, 779).

10. Note the useful English translation of the *Depositio, Elevatio* (with the Harrowing of Hell), and *Visitatio* from Barking in *The Staging of Religious Drama in the Later Middle Ages,* eds. Peter Meredith and John E. Tailby, Early Drama, Art, and Music, monograph ser. 4 (Kalamazoo, Mich.: Medieval Institute Publications, 1983), 226–29.

11. The quotation from the Gospel of Luke appears in but one other liturgical drama: in the Mont St. Michel text. It is not an antiphon.

12. Jesus' reappearance to the three Marys together and their prostration—but not the holding and kissing—also occurs in the older Rouen text, a major source for Barking and Origny.

Anke Roeder, *Die Gebärde im Drama des Mittelalters. Osterfeiern. Osterspiele* (Munich, 1974). *Münchener Texte und Untersuchungen zur dt. Lit. des Mittelalters,* 49:60–61: "In dieser Feier erscheinen drei Formen des Kusses: Altarkuss [richtiger: der Kuss der Stelle im Hl. Grab, wo der Herr gelegen hat—W.L.], Fusskuss und Kuss der Leintücher. Es sind liturgische Gebärden, die in dieser Feier an theatralische-wirkungsvoller Stelle in den Darstellungszusammenhang eingegleidert sind." ("Three Forms of the kiss occur in this ceremony: kissing the altar [more correctly: kissing the place in the Sepulcher where the Lord's body had lain—W. L. (inserted note by Walther Lipphardt)], kissing the feet, and kissing the gravecloths. In this ceremony these are liturgical gestures inserted into the framework of performance and positioned for theatrical effect.")

Also as at Origny (and at Le Mans, and in a group of Parisian texts), the Magdalen of Barking sings "Spes nostra" instead of the usual "Spes mea."

13. In regard to whether men or women played the Marys, four *Visitatio* texts remain especially puzzling and tantalizing. Each contains a major Mary-Magdalen role as well as elaborate and detailed stage directions for acting, particularly for the expression of emotion: manuscripts from the Cathedrals of Braunschweig and Coutances, respectively; a manuscript from the monastery of Egmond; and from the Municipal Library of Tours a manuscript whose ecclesiastical home we do not know. It is possible that nuns or canonesses took the roles of the Marys in all four? However, I have counted these four among the twenty-one men's texts with a Mary Magdalen.

14. See, e.g., Susan Haskins, *Mary Magdalen, Myth and Metaphor* (New York: Harcourt, 1994).

15. A group of women's plays from Benedictine convents share a recomposition of the *Quem quaeritis* text and music: Origny, Poitiers, Troyes, and Wilton. For a transcription of the music see Susan Rankin, "Liturgical Drama," in *The New Oxford History of Music,* vol. 2, *The Early Middle Ages to 1300,* eds. Richard Crocker and David Hiley (Oxford: Oxford University, 1990), 335, EX. 103.

The earliest *Visitatio* texts with Mary Magdalen as a character: from Vich in Spain (possibly eleventh century), and St. George nunnery in Prague (twelfth century).

16. A singular situation is recorded by the 1438 *Visitatio* text from the St. Julia Convent in Brescia. It is one of the rare Italian documents linked with this drama. There two nuns as Angels were led by the "Cantoria" *(Cantoria accipiant Duas Dominas)*—"Cantoria" presumably the lead singers (male or female?)—to the high altar, and then three nuns ("Tres Dominas") as the Marys were led to the middle of the (east) choir. Thereupon they sang the "Quem quaeritis" exchange across the high altar. No male clergy seems to be involved. This little ceremonial observance is also singular in that it segues seamlessly into the Introit of the mass. It does not occur at the close of matins, just before the concluding *Te Deum*. And as a prelude to mass, one or more priest-celebrants had to be present. Although the manuscript itself comes from a late date, it records an ancient practice, perhaps even predating our earliest secure evidence for the *Visitatio* played by women. In addition, the Brescia text documents the only *Visitatio* where women sang the roles of Angels.

List of Contributors

JOHN F. ANDREWS, formerly editor of *Shakespeare Quarterly* and chairman of the Folger Institute of Renaissance and Eighteenth-Century Studies, is president of the Shakespeare Guild and editor of *The Everyman Shakespeare.* He has also edited the three-volume collection of essays on *William Shakespeare: The Man, His Work, and His World.*

STEPHEN BOOTH is professor of English at the University of California, Berkeley. A frequent contributor to scholarly journals on Shakespeare, he is also the author of *"King Lear," "Macbeth," Indefinition, and Tragedy,* and a highly regarded edition of Shakespeare's sonnets.

RALPH BERRY has taught Shakespeare and other drama in universities throughout the world. Among his many books are *Shakespeare in Performance: Castings and Metamorphoses, Changing Styles in Shakespeare,* and *Shakespeare's Comedies: Explorations in Form.*

JOHN RUSSELL BROWN is the author of many books, including *Shakespeare's Plays in Performance, Free Shakespeare, Shakespeare and His Comedies,* and most recently *William Shakespeare: Writing for Performance.* He has edited Webster's *The Duchess of Malfi* as well as Shakespeare's *Merchant of Venice* and other plays.

MAURICE CHARNEY is Distinguished Professor of English at Rutgers University. Among his many publications are *All of Shakespeare, Hamlet's Fictions, Comedy High and Low, Style in "Hamlet," Sexual Fiction,* and *Shakespeare's Roman Plays.* He has served as president of the Shakespeare Association of America and is a recipient of the Medal of the City of Tours.

THOMAS CLAYTON is professor of English and director of the program in Classical Civilization at the University of Minnesota. Author of many essays on Shakespeare, he has also edited the poetry of Sir John Suckling, the Cavalier Poets, and an important collection of essays, *The "Hamlet" First Published.*

MICHAEL GOLDMAN, professor of English at Princeton University, is the author of *Shakespeare and the Energies of Drama, Actors and Acting in Shakespearean Tragedy,* and several collections of his own poems.

JAY L. HALIO, professor of English at the University of Delaware, has edited *King Lear* three times in three different ways: a conflated edition in old spelling, a folio-based edition, and an edition of the first quarto. He is the author of *Understanding Shakespeare's Plays in Performance* as well as other works on Shakespeare and modern literature.

BARBARA HODGDON, Ellis and Nelle Levitt Professor of English at Drake University, is the author of *The End Crowns All: Closure and Contradiction in Shakespeare's Histories* and, for the *Shakespeare in Performance* series, *Henry IV, Part Two.* Her recent work is called *Restaging Shakespeare's Cultural Capital,* and she is the Arden III editor for *The Taming of the Shrew.*

SIDNEY HOMANN, an actor and director in professional and university theaters, is professor of English at the University of Florida. He is the author of nine books on Shakespeare and modern playwrights, including *Audience as Actor and Character, Shakespeare's Theater of Presence, Shakespeare's More Than Words Can Witness,* and *Shakespeare and the Triple Play.*

BERNICE KLIMAN is professor of English at Nassau Community College, State University of New York. Among her books is *Shakespeare in Performance: Macbeth.* She is coeditor of the parallel texts of *Hamlet* and currently editing the New Variorum edition of that play. For sixteen years she was coeditor (with Kenneth Rothwell) of *The Shakespeare on Film Newsletter.*

JAMES LUSARDI, Francis A. March Professor of English at Lafayette College, is coeditor with June Schlueter of *Shakespeare Bulletin.* He is also coauthor (with Schlueter) of *Reading Shakespeare in Performance: "King Lear"* and coeditor of *The Complete Works of St. Thomas More.*

CARY M. MAZER is associate professor of English and chair of the Theatre Arts Program at the University of Pennsylvania. He is the author of *Shakespeare Refashioned: Elizabethan Plays on Edwardian Stages* and of essays on Shakespeare in performance and on Victorian and Edwardian theater.

PHILIP C. MCGUIRE, professor of English at Michigan State University, is the author of *Shakespeare: The Jacobean Plays* and *Speechless Dialect: Shakespeare's Open Silences* as well as coeditor of *Shakespeare: The Theatrical Dimension.* He is a frequent participant in NEH summer seminars "Shakespeare in Ashland: Teaching from Performance."

ELLEN O'BRIEN is professor of theater studies and English at Guilford College. As an associate director, dramaturge, and coach she has assisted in many Shakespeare productions throughout the United States, while at Guilford she has directed Shakespeare's *Measure for Measure* and *Henry V.* Her essays appear in *Shakespeare Quarterly, Shakespeare Survey,* and *Shakespeare and Cultural Traditions,* the Proceedings of the 1996 World Shakespeare Congress in Tokyo.

DUNBAR H. OGDEN, professor of dramatic art at the University of California, Berkeley, is the author of *The Italian Baroque Stage, Actor Training and Audience Response,* and *Performance Dynamics and the Amsterdam Werkteater,* as well as the editor of several volumes, including *The Play of Daniel,* which he staged in 1994 in New York and at the International Congress on Medieval Studies, and in 1996 at the Musica Sacra Festival, Maastricht.

LOIS POTTER, Ned B. Allen Professor of English at the University of Delaware, is an inveterate theatergoer and the author of many essays and reviews on Shakespeare in performance. Editor of the new Arden edition of *The Two Noble Kinsmen,* she is currently preparing a book on *Othello* for the *Shakespeare in Performance* series.

HUGH RICHMOND is professor emeritus of English at the University of California, Berkeley. His Shakespeare Program there has produced the video-documentary, *Shakespeare and the Globe,* and has staged *Much Ado about Nothing* at London's newly recreated Globe Theatre. Among his books are those on *Henry VIII* and *Richard III* for the series *Shakespeare in Performance,* and *Shakespeare's Political Plays.*

JUNE SCHLUETER, Charles A. Dana Professor of English and Provost at Lafayette College, is the author of *Dramatic Closure: Reading the End* and many other books on British and American literature, including *The Plays and Novels of Peter Handke* and *Feminist Readings of Modern American Drama*. She is also coeditor (with James Lusardi) of the *Shakespeare Bulletin.*

G. B. SHAND is professor of English and drama studies at York University's Glendon College (Toronto), author of numerous articles on early drama, and editor of several texts for the Oxford *Middleton.* In the professional theater he serves frequently as a text consultant and coach.

ZDENEK STRIBRNY is Emeritus Professor of English and American Literature at the Charles University, Prague. Among his many publications are *Shakespeare's History Plays, Shakespeare's Predecessors,* and *A History of English Literature.* He is preparing a study of Shakespeare and Eastern Europe.

GÜNTER WALCH holds the Chair of English Literature at Humboldt-Universität in Berlin. He has published widely on English narrative art, the functions of literature, and genre theory. He has also written on a whole range of authors, including Bunyan, Kipling, Wilde, Conrad, E. M. Forster, and Richard Aldington, and edited several works by these authors as well as Shakespeare's *The Tempest* and *The Sonnets.*

Index